D0880854

Expositions of the Psalms

Augustinian Heritage Institute, Inc.

THE WORKS OF SAINT AUGUSTINE
A Translation for the 21st Century

Part III – Books
Volume 15:
Expositions of the Psalms
1-32

THE WORKS OF SAINT AUGUSTINE
A Translation for the 21st Century

Expositions of the Psalms
1-32

III/15

introduction by
Michael Fiedrowicz

translation and notes by
Maria Boulding, O.S.B.

editor
John E. Rotelle, O.S.A.

New City Press
Hyde Park, New York

Published in the United States by New City Press
202 Cardinal Rd., Hyde Park, New York 12538
©2000 Augustinian Heritage Institute

Cover picture: Christ appears to Saint Augustine while writing his commentary
on the psalms. From Vat. Lat. 451 (II part), fol. 1r – 15th century.

Library of Congress Cataloging-in-Publication Data:

Augustine, Saint, Bishop of Hippo.
    The works of Saint Augustine.

    "Augustinian Heritage Institute"
    Includes bibliographical references and indexes.
    Contents: — pt. 3, v .14. Expositions of the Psalms, 1-32
—pt. 3, v. 1. Sermons on the Old Testament, 1-19.
— pt. 3, v. 2. Sermons on the Old Testament, 20-50 — [et al.] — pt. 3,
v. 10 Sermons on various subjects, 341-400.
    1. Theology — Early church, ca. 30-600.   I. Hill,
Edmund.   II. Rotelle, John E.   III. Augustinian
Heritage Institute.   IV. Title.
BR65.A5E53   1990   270.2   89-28878
ISBN 1-56548-055-4 (series)
ISBN 1-56548-126-7 (pt. 3, v. 15)
ISBN 1-56548-140-2 (pt. 3, v. 15: pbk.)

Nihil Obstat: John E. Rotelle, O.S.A., S.T.L., Censor Deputatus
Imprimatur: + Patrick Sheridan, D.D., Vicar General
                Archdiocese of New York, July 22, 1999

The Nihil Obstat and Imprimatur are official declarations that a book or pamphlet is free of doctrinal
or moral error. No implication is contained therein that those who have granted the Nihil Obstat and
Imprimatur agree with the contents, opinions or statements expressed.

Printed in the United States of America

Contents

General Introduction

1. The Place of the Psalms in Augustine's Life

The book called *Expositions of the Psalms* is the most comprehensive of all the works by the Bishop of Hippo.[1] In terms of its monumental size alone it surpasses all other patristic commentaries on the psalms put together. We have an indication of the importance he attached to this book of the Bible in the fact that he seems to have labored at the task for nearly thirty years. The completion of other important writings, such as his book on the Trinity, often had to be deferred in favor of his explanation of the psalms, which was expected to be of greater profit to the general public.[2]

In addition to the *Expositions of the Psalms*, thirty-one sermons on psalms or verses of psalms has been preserved among Augustine's sermons on the Old Testament.[3] His *Confessions* has been described as an "amplified psalter"[4] because of the powerful impact of the psalms on its idiom. Furthermore, in Augustine's whole output more than ten thousand citations of the psalms can be detected, making his work seem like one vast exposition of the psalms.[5]

All this can be understood only in the light of a particular affinity and connatural relationship to the psalms on Augustine's part.[6] He himself testifies to the overwhelming impression the discovery of them made upon him during

1. For a comprehensive study of the work, see M. Fiedrowicz: *Psalmus vox totius Christi. Studien zu Augustins Enarrationes in Psalmos* (Freiburg, 1997).
2. See Letter 169,1 (CSEL 44,612).
3. CCL 41. For the English translation see *The Works of Saint Augustine, A Translation for the 21st Century*, Part III, Volume 1, 331-337 and Volume 2, 15-136. 154-165.
4. H. Lausberg: "Rezension zu G.N. Knauer: Psalmenzitate," *Theologische Rundschau* 53 (1957) 16f. Compare G.N. Knauer: *Psalmenzitate in Augustins Konfessiones* (Göttingen, 1955); S. Poque: Les Psaumes dans les Confessions, in A.-M. La Bonnardière (ed.): *Saint Augustin et la Bible* (Bible de tous les temps 3; Paris, 1986) 155-161; J.A. Silvester Johnson: *The Psalms in the "Confessions" of Augustine* (Dissertation, The Southern Baptist Theological Seminary, Louisville, KY, 1981).
5. See E. Bouvy: "Saint Augustin. Les Énarrations sur les psaumes," *Revue Augustinienne* 3 (1903) 418-436, esp. 419.
6. See G. Bardy: *Saint Augustin. L'homme et l'oeuvre* (Paris,³ 1940) 350.

the days he spent at Cassiciacum in September 386.[7] Their incomparable significance only becomes apparent, however, in Possidius' account. According to the
testimony of his biographer, the Bishop of Hippo when on his deathbed wished
to end his days alone with the penitential psalms.[8] Anyone who has a mind to
discover the most personal expression of Augustine's spirituality will scarcely
find a better approach than through his explanations of the psalms.

2. *Origin and Literary Form of the Expositions of the Psalms*

On one occasion Augustine formulated the underlying principle of his
preaching as follows: "I nourish you with what nourishes me; I offer to you what
I live on myself."[9] Augustine's explanation of the psalms is the reflection of his
own spirituality, inspired by them. Already at Cassiciacum, soon after his
conversion, he was animated by the desire to give to that "joy of our spirit"
(*deliciae spiritus nostri*)[10] a universal expression:

> "How loudly I cried out to you, my God, as I read the psalms of David,
> songs full of faith, outbursts of devotion with no room in them for the
> breath of pride! . . . How loudly I began to cry out to you in those psalms,
> how I was inflamed by them with love for you and fired to recite them to
> the whole world, were I able, as a remedy against human pride!"[11]

Shortly after his ordination to the priesthood in the year 391, possibly during
the time he had begged his bishop, Valerius, to grant him for studying the scriptures,[12] Augustine began to put his great plan into effect. The exegesis of the first
thirty-two psalms initially took the form of concise notes and explanatory para-
phrases of the biblical text, but these were soon succeeded by numerous longer
expositions, which originated in the context of his liturgical preaching. This
meant that several psalms on which he had commented in the first written series
were revisited. According to the testimony of a letter written in 415,[13] the Bishop
of Hippo then began to complete the collection that had grown up in the mean-

---

7. See H.J. Sieben: "Der Psalter und die Bekehrung der VOCES und AFFECTUS. Zu
   Augustinus, Conf. IX,4,6 und X,33," *Theologie und Philosophie* 52 (1977) 481-497; S.
   Poque: "La prière du catéchumène Augustin en Septembre 386 (conf. 11,4,8-11)," in
   Congresso internazionale su S. Agostino nel XVI centenario della Conversione, Roma
   15-20 settembre 1986, Vol. II (Studia Ephemeridis Augustinianum 25; Rom, 1987) 79-84;
   H. Sundén: "Saint Augustine and the Psalter in the light of Role-Psychology," *Journal for
   the Scientific Study of Religion* 26 (1987) 375-382.
8. Possidius: *Life of Augustine* 31, 2.
9. Sermon 339, 4.
10. Exp. Ps 145,1.
11. *Confessions* IX,4,8 (CCL 27,137). See M. Vincent: *St. Augustin, maître de prière d'après
    les Enarrationes in Psalmos* (Paris, 1990) 449-453.
12. See Letter 21 (CSEL 34/1,49-54).
13. See Letter 169,1 (CSEL 44,612).

time with more extensive commentaries. As the prologue to his Exposition of Psalm 118 recounts, and as the exegesis of the dictated expositions also reveals, it was the manifold difficulties raised by those psalms that led Augustine repeatedly to postpone his commentaries on them, and eventually to undertake them in written form only.

Those expositions of the psalms printed under the title *Enarrationes* (a title coined by Erasmus and canonized by the Maurists)[14] and undoubtedly compiled by Augustine himself, therefore comprise very different literary forms. In the manuscripts these forms were largely undifferentiated and described as *expositio, sermo, tractatus, commentum,* or *explanatio.*[15] Brief exegetical notes rub shoulders with well-formed rhetorical homilies taken down by secretaries[16] and to some extent checked afterward by Augustine. In quantitative terms these homilies are the heart of the work. More detailed commentaries, dictated with future readers in mind, alternate with written outlines of sermons prepared for his own use, and alongside these are specimen homilies designed as preaching aids for other clerics.

3. Determination of Date and Place

Apart from the collections of Sermons and of Letters, no work of Augustine's occupied as long a stretch of his life as did his explanations of the psalms. The task of commenting on all of them, begun shortly after his priestly ordination, demanded three decades before he concluded it with an interpretation of Psalm 118(119)[17] in the year 421 or 422. With the exception of Psalms 1-32, 110-117, and 119-133, the expositions did not keep to the numerical order of the psalter, but were only put in order by Augustine afterward. Furthermore the *Expositions*, like the Sermons, were not mentioned in his *Revisions*. From these facts it is obvious that the assignment of individual *Expositions* to definite dates is fraught with difficulties.

In addition to scattered hints in Augustine's letters,[18] internal indications are our principal resource. These point either to relative dates, as in the cases of

---

14. See the title of the Erasmus edition: S. Aurelii Augustini Hipp. Episc. Opus, continens Enarrationes in Psalmos, Basilea 1529.

15. See A. Wilmart: "La tradition des grands ouvrages de Saint Augustin," in *Miscellanea Augustiniana* II, 257-315, especially 295, 2; F.J. Tovar Paz: "Aproximación a los genéros literarios de las 'Enarrationes in Psalmos' de Agustin de Hippona," *Cuadernos de filologia clásica* N.S. 6 (1994) 147-156.

16. See Exp. Ps 51,1. Compare B. Altaner: "Zur Kenntnis des schriftstellerischen Schaffens Augustins," in B. Altaner, *Kleine patristische Schriften* (Texte und Untersuchungen zur Geschichte der altchristlichen Literatur 83) ed. G. Glockmann (Berlin, 1967) 3-56, esp. 43.

17. The numbering follows the Vulgate. Modern numbering is given in parentheses.

18. See Letter 140,13 (CSEL 44,165); Letter 149,5 (CSEL 44,352); Letter 169,1 (CSEL 44,612).

self-quotation, internal parallels, or grouping of psalms, or to absolute dates, as in the case of references to liturgical occasions, or anti-Donatist or anti-Pelagian controversy. Another procedure which often makes chronological precision possible is the comparison of Augustine's use and interpretation of other scriptural texts with the use he makes of them in other works, where the date of origin is certain.

Nonetheless it is only for a modest part of the *Expositions* that a consensus on dating has been reached among researchers. Many attempts are largely hypothetical.

With regard to questions of topography, indications in the manuscripts, which in some cases go back to Augustine himself, can be combined with internal clues,[19] and the place where a sermon was preached can therefore be identified for many expositions. Explanations of whole psalms in his own see of Hippo are fairly uncommon,[20] but Aurelius took advantage of Augustine's sojourns in his episcopal city, Carthage, to ask the Bishop of Hippo for a sermon on the occasion of a festival of Saint Cyprian. Such requests would be made when the bishops convened for councils during the Donatist and Pelagian controversies, but also during pagan festivals; and then the object of the sermon would often be to explain a psalm which had some bearing on the situation.

4. *The Liturgy as the Place for Expounding the Psalms*

Augustine's interpretation of the psalms was carried on above all within liturgical proclamation. In his time the liturgy of the word, which was part of the eucharistic celebration, usually included a psalm read or sung by a lector between the Old Testament reading and the New. To this psalm the congregation responded with a refrain.[21] In his commentaries Augustine sometimes alludes to this responsorial verse.[22] Similarly there are references to the gospel which the people have just heard, or to the New Testament reading or, less frequently, the

---

19. See D. De Bruyne: *"Enarrationes in Psalmos* prêchées à Carthage," in *Miscellanea Augustiniana* II, 321-325, esp. 321f.

20. See A.-M. La Bonnardière: "La prédication d'Augustin sur les Psaumes à Hippone," *Annuaire de l'École Pratique des Hautes Études. Section des Sciences Religieuses* 86 (1977/78) 337-341, esp. 339; compare the same author's Les Enarrationes in Psalmos prêchées par saint Augustin à l'occasion de fêtes de martyrs, *Recherches Augustiniennes* 7 (1971) 73-103, esp. 88-97.

21. See Exp. Ps 40,1. Compare A. Zwinggi: "Der Wortgottesdienst bei Augustinus (I)," *Liturgisches Jahrbuch* 20 (1970) 90-113, esp. 100-103; A Dohmes: Der Psalmengesang des Volkes in der eucharistischen Opferfeier der christlichen Frühzeit, *Liturgisches Leben* 5 (1938) 48-71, esp. 56f; M. Schrama: Prima lectio quae recitata est. The liturgical Pericope in light of Augustine's Sermons, *Augustiniana* (Louvain) 45 (1995) 141-156.

22. See Exp. Ps 18,II,13; 25,II,5; 29,II,1; 32,II,s.1,4; 36,s.1,12.s.3,1; 37,1; 40,1; 55,17; 57,1; 84,9; 90,s.1,3; 102,1.

Old Testament reading. Augustine generally seeks to pick out a few words and apply them in his interpretation of the psalm. The relevance of the psalm-text to reading or gospel is thereby emphasized.[23]

It cannot be determined with certainty whether Augustine's allusions to the passion of particular martyrs suggest that the Acts of the Martyrs were read in the same way as biblical readings, but in view of liturgical practice at the time it seems probable.[24]

Relatively few of the *Enarrationes* originated in eucharistic celebrations at Hippo, however. The interpretations of the psalms which were preached there are to be found primarily in Augustine's sermons on the Old Testament, whereas the *Expositions of the Psalms* mostly arose outside the ordinary liturgical cycle.[25] No direct information from Augustine is forthcoming on the subject, but the singing of the psalms at Vespers, and eventually also at Matins, especially on Saturdays, must have provided many opportunities for expounding them.[26]

The high festivals of the Church's year allowed time for only shorter sermons, so with the exception of an *Exposition of Psalm* 21(22) on Wednesday in Holy Week[27] no interpretations of the psalms resulted from these liturgical occasions.

The liturgical year left its stamp most clearly on Augustine's interpretations of the psalms at the vigils and feast days of African martyrs. The seventeen *Expositions* devoted to these occasions comprise about one-seventh of the spoken interpretations that have been preserved, and they are an indication of Augustine's endeavor to enhance the value of these festivals within the Catholic Church, in opposition to the Donatist cult of martyrs.[28]

However, it remains certain that the *Expositions of the Psalms* does not represent liturgical preaching in the sense of its themes being determined by the mysteries of the Church's year or the biblical texts prescribed for them. Since in Augustine's day the lectionary was still in the process of being gradually settled, and the fixing of texts affected in the main only the high festivals, the bishop had extensive freedom in choosing the texts, and especially the psalms. This would have been particularly the case for non-eucharistic liturgies. The selection of a

---

23. See Exp. Ps 37,1.
24. See Exp. Ps 120,13; 127,6; 137,3.7. On this practice see W. Roetzer: *Des Hl. Augustins Schriften als liturgie-geschichtliche Quelle*. Eine liturgie-geschichtliche Studie (München, 1930), 62f.
25. See A.-M. La Bonnardière: Prédication à Hippone, 337f.
26. Compare Sermon 128,6 (PL 38,716); Letter 29,11 (CSEL 34/1, 122). Compare W. Roetzer: *Schriften*, 12.
27. Exp. Ps 21,II,1.
28. See Exp Ps 32,II,s.2,9; 36,16; 40,1; 63,1; 69,1.4.9; 85,24; 88,s.1,10.27. s. 2,11.14; 102,3f; 120,1.13.15; 127,2.6; 137,3.7.14f.17; 140,1; 141,1; 144,17. See A.-M. La Bonnardière: Enarrations à l'occasion de fêtes de martyrs, 73f, 103.

psalm for the actual occasion lay with Augustine himself or, in the case of a visit to another city, with the local bishop.[29]

5. The Theological Significance of the Expositions of the Psalms

If Augustine's interpretation of the psalms continued for more than a quarter of a century, the *Enarrationes* must sum up and focus his eventful life, the theological controversies of his age, his exegetical output, and his homiletic work. The Bishop of Hippo can hardly have had any vital, theologically significant idea that did not also echo in his interpretations of the psalms and find its deployment there. As an encyclopedia of Augustine's thought the *Enarrationes* have their place close to the *Confessions* and *The City of God* as the most significant writings of the North African theologian.

Augustine's spiritually richest work, the work that perhaps represents his deepest thought, therefore ranks as an undisputed high point in patristic interpretation of the psalms. As the foremost exegete of the early Church Augustine created a complete commentary on this biblical book. Thanks to his skill in expounding them, he succeeded in extracting from the psalms depths of meaning never attained before. The proper goal of his exegesis was to make the depth of meaning accessible.

6. The Deeper Understanding of the Psalm (intellectus psalmi) as the Goal of Interpretation

In the introductory passage to his sermon on Psalm 18(19) Augustine articulates the purpose of his exposition in a vivid comparison. Songbirds are certainly able to repeat with their voices something they have been taught by human beings but have not understood, but human nature has in the plan of creation been endowed with conscious understanding. Thus the psalm words, *Blessed the people that understands the reason for its joy* (Ps 88:16(89:15)) or *Sing psalms to him with understanding* (Ps 46:8(47:7)), become the biblical motivation for the effort to attain spiritual insight into liturgical psalmody, which must not be merely perceived by the ear and performed by the voice, but understood by and pondered in the heart.[30] Augustine's struggle for understanding of the faith (*intellectus fidei*) thus reappears in his scriptural explanations as a search for understanding of the scriptures (*intellectus scripturae*).

---

29. See Exp. Ps 31,II,2; 34,s.1,1; 86,1; 138,1; 139,1. Compare A. Zwinggi: Wortgottesdienst, 96f; G.G. Willis: *St Augustine's Lectionary* (Alcuin Club Collections 44; London, 1962), 5f; A.-M. La Bonnardière: Prédication à Hippone, 337.
30. Exp. Ps 18,II,1; 37,1; 46,9; 99,3; 129,1. See R. Galdos: Psallite sapienter (Ps 46,8): *Verbum Domini* 10 (1930) 269-273.

Our understanding can approach the psalm only by degrees, however. The biblical word may be clear, evident, comprehensible (*planum, apertum, manifestum*), but it may also be dark, ambiguous, under lock and key, or full of mystery (*obscurum, ambiguum, clausum, arcanum*). Yet the biblical text offers to our minds not only various stages of difficulty, but also a progressive understanding of its depths. One and the same word of a psalm may be considered on different levels of meaning. Further varieties of understanding (*multae intelligentiae*) may succeed a simple understanding (*intellectus simplex*).[31]

To describe this innermost meaning Augustine employs the analogy of the soul concealed in the human body, so that he can speak of the soul of the psalm (*anima psalmi*);[32] but he usually designates the proper depth of meaning in the scriptural word as a mystery (*mysterium/sacramentum*).[33] Investigation of the biblical word should not be satisfied with an initial understanding, with a grasp of the literal meaning of the salvation-events as related in the psalm, but must seek to fathom its inner meaning.[34]

In the following pages we must therefore set forth the types of exposition which correspond to the various depths of meaning in the text of the psalms. It is worthwhile describing first the techniques and methods used to promote immediate understanding of the text as spoken. Then we can throw some light on the deeper theological signification.

7. The Techniques of Commentary

a) Christian adoption of classical models in the interpretation of texts

Since about A.D. 200 Christian exegesis had taken over pagan techniques and methods of textual interpretation, since the Bible was also a literary text, even though one of a special kind.[35] Augustine too, former teacher of grammar and rhetoric as he was, pressed the same fundamental methods into service for his exposition of the psalms. Inasmuch as the Bible had taken the place of the

---

31. See Exp. Ps 103,s.1,12; 34,s.2,3; 18,II,4; 43,2; 118,s.25,7.
32. Exp. Ps 104,35; 76,1.
33. See Exp. Ps 46,2; 93,1. Compare M. Pontet: *L'exégèse de saint Augustin prédicateur* (Paris, 1945), 257-272.
34. See Exp. Ps 43,2; 44,1; 77,1.
35. See C. Schäublin: Zur paganen Prägung der christlichen Exegese, in J. van Oort-U. Wickert (eds.), *Christliche Exegese zwischen Nicaea und Chalcedon* (Kampen, 1992), 148-173; H. Dörrie: Zur Methodik antiker Exegese, *Zeitschrift für die Neutestamentliche Wissenschaft* 65 (1974) 121-138; J.T. Lienhard: Reading the Bible and Learning to Read. The Influence of Education on St Augustine's Exegesis, *Augustinian Studies* 27 (1996) 7-25.

pagan classics in Augustine's educational program, the styles of interpretation developed for the latter could come in useful for illuminating the scriptures.

Fairly often his exegesis of the psalms reminds us of the interpretation of poetry as practiced by pagan grammarians, since as the Bible's poetry the psalms seemed to demand a similar approach. The form of classical commentary, freely handled, is at the base of Augustine's expositions of the psalms,[36] and this is true not only of those composed in writing, but also of those preserved as sermons. The elements of classical commentary that addressed structure and topic were adapted to serve both the particular requirements of the biblical text and the overriding homiletic purpose.

b) The structure and the common elements of the commentary

The exposition of a psalm often begins without preamble.[37] But it can also be preceded by an introduction which refers to some liturgical text the congregation has just heard—the psalm just sung, a reading, or the gospel; or it may refer to the feast being celebrated.[38] Or again, the introduction may clarify questions about the person who speaks in the psalm, or interpret its title.[39] The introduction frequently deploys a special theme or leading idea of the psalm—echoing the *skopos* or *summa* of the prologue to classical commentaries—so that this may serve as a key to the discussion and be taken up again and again later for the interpretation of individual points.[40]

c) The problem of unity of meaning in the text

In conformity with the practice of classical commentaries Augustine quoted the psalm verse by verse. A criticism frequently leveled at this technique of interpretation is that it leads to an atomizing and fragmentation on the subject matter of the text; and this criticism is undoubtedly valid for not a few of Augustine's interpretations of the psalms too. All the same, there are many references to later verses (*consequentia*) and to the overall coherence of a psalm (*contextio psalmi*),[41] numerous cross-references within the interpretation of a single psalm,[42] attention to the verses that precede and follow,[43] and statements about

---

36. On the commentary see S. Döpp-W. Geerlings (eds.), *Lexikon der antiken christlichen Literatur* (Freiburg, 1998), 381-383; on the homiletic use of it see M. Sachot: Homilie, in *Reallexikon für Antike und Christentum* 16 (Stuttgart, 1994) 148-175, especially 159.
37. See Exp. Ps 1,1.
38. See Exp. Ps 25,II,1; 26,II,1; 40,1.
39. See Exp. Ps 33,s.1,1; 85,1.
40. See Exp. Ps 48,s.1,1; 86,1; 93,1f.
41. See Exp. Ps 4,9f; 21,II,8.23.28; 26,II,13; 30,II,s.1,3; 80,12, 101,s.2,1.
42. See Exp. Ps 12,4; 26,II,9.20.
43. See Exp. Ps 36,s.1,11; 65,24; 68,s.2,21; 70,s.2,9; 118,s.2,4.

the progression of the psalm under discussion.[44] All this is an indication of the interpreter's earnest endeavor to treat the individual verse within the larger context of the whole, and to look for both the coherence and the leading idea of a psalm.[45]

The many explicit references to such a leading idea in the psalm with which he is dealing show that Augustine was able to treat it as a complete organic unity, and that he sought to understand its component elements from the overall context. Or, conversely, he would see the whole psalm illuminated by a single verse.[46] Not infrequently Augustine took even the title of a psalm (a title which for him was inspired) to be a hermeneutic key, so that he could grasp the basic thought of the psalm "from the threshold" (*a limine*), as it were.[47] Even where express mentions are lacking, the exposition often proves to be supported and determined by a leading idea.

d) Philological procedures

The techniques of classical interpretation include various philological working procedures, and these are recognizable also in Augustinian interpretation of the psalms. But problems of correct reading (*lectio*), in a text which was written in antiquity with neither division of words nor punctuation (*scriptio continua*), affect the text of the psalms only in rare cases.[48]

More significant was textual criticism (*emendatio*), for Augustine often found himself confronted by suspicious variants in the biblical manuscripts with which he had to deal. The variant readings in the Latin translation stemmed from the ambiguity of the Greek, or the difficulty of carrying its expressions over into Latin.[49] The criterion for assessing the variants in the Latin manuscripts was not the form of Hebrew text favored by Jerome, but the Septuagint version, which Augustine regarded as inspired.[50]

The third step is philological explanation of the text (*explanatio*), with regard to both formal characteristics and content. On the one hand it was a matter of commenting on vocabulary, grammar, and style; on the other of illuminating

---

44. See Exp. Ps 5,18; 30,I,1; 106,8.
45. See *City of God* 17,15 (CCL 48,579).
46. See Exp. Ps 104,35; 100,1; 132,1.
47. See Exp. Ps 53,1; 58,s.1,1; 70,s.1,2; 80,1f; 93,3. Compare M. Pontet: *Exégèse*, 272-276.
48. See Exp. Ps 3,7; 16,2; 38,16; 67,17.41; 77,6; 118,s.13,2.
49. See Exp. Ps 78,17; 16,4; 67,7.22.41; 71,8.10.17; 77,42; 89,3; 104,6; 105,2.5; 118,s.6,4; s.14,4; s.15,5.
50. See Exp. Ps 67,41; 77,18; 89,13; *Teaching Christianity* 2,1319.15,22 (CCL 32,47f); Letter 261,5 (CSEL 57,620). On the controversy with Jerome over the translation from the Hebrew see A. Fürst: "Veritas latina. Augustins Haltung gegenüber Hieronymus' Bibelübersetzungen," *Revue des Études Augustiniennes* 40 (1994) 105-126.

questions of fact, whether these concern unfamiliar customs, or modes of thought which called for explanation. For Augustine this procedure is of course directed toward and subordinate to theological understanding.

Grammatical and rhetorical matters, such as the order of words, case, number, tense, mood, conjunctions, prepositions, hyperbole, and metaphor, are dealt with only insofar as some theological or spiritual significance can be extracted from them.[51] We would look in vain in this work for any philological consideration undertaken for its own sake.

More important for Augustine than consideration of the theological implications of grammatical or rhetorical points was the illumination of unfamiliar or ambivalent words or formulations that threatened to obstruct understanding of the biblical text. As is shown by his many references to specifically biblical modes of speech (*locutiones*) in his interpretation of the psalms,[52] as also by the work he devoted to this question, *Locutionum in Heptateuchum libri septem*, Augustine was very alert to the significance of such biblical idioms. However, his attempts to explain them were often inadequate or less than appropriate, partly for lack of any extensive knowledge of Hebrew, and also because his Latin version was at two removes from the original language, being a Latin translation of the Greek translation of the Hebrew.

It was customary in classical commentaries to follow explanation of words with explanation of facts. In this respect Augustine's attention focused above all on the etymology of the names of persons, tribes, peoples, countries, and places mentioned in the psalms. These names held for him a mysterious significance which he was at pains to unlock.[53] Only by this means did it seem possible to free many statements in the psalms, which were full of concrete historical or geographical memories, from their particular place in time or confinement to a locality, and so open them up to an understanding valid for any age or place. With only a few exceptions the etymological meanings offered by Augustine in his interpretation of the psalms are to be found in Jerome's *Liber interpretationis hebraicorum nominum* and, collected and more precisely established, in his *Tractatus in psalmos*. The Bishop of Hippo undoubtedly availed himself of these works. He mentions his use of such resources, though without specifying names.[54]

Only rarely, however, did Augustine have recourse to the profane sources of wisdom recommended in his work, *Teaching Christianity*, in order to illuminate

---

51. See Exp. Ps 44,25; 44,19; 26,II,23; 31,II,15; 4,6; 8,10; 5,9; 104,21.
52. See Exp. Ps 104,18.
53. See Exp. Ps 33,s.2,2; 38,1; 41,2; 51,4; 59,2.9; 80,2. Compare S. Amsler: *Etymology and grammatical discourse in late antiquity and the early Middle Ages* (Studies in the history of the language sciences 44); Amsterdam/Philadelphia, 1989.
54. See Exp. Ps 33,s.1,4. Compare B. Altaner: Augustinus und die biblischen Onomastica, in this author's *Kleine patristische Schriften*, 312-315.

particular facts. Items of information on literature, the history of culture, medicine, botany, zoology, physics, astronomy, topography, or music are occasionally brought into play, but on the whole they are rare.[55] The specific character of the psalter, but also the interpreter's limited knowledge of the relevant disciplines, account for the striking discrepancy between the exegetical requirements formulated in *Teaching Christianity* and Augustine's concrete practice in his expositions.

The proper competence of our interpreter, and the true orientation of his interests, must be sought elsewhere. What touches him most closely is theological exposition of the psalms.

8. Hermeneutical Principles for a Theological Interpretation of the Psalms

In the task of interpreting the psalms the exegete was faced not only by the difficulties in understanding which any profane text can entail; much more important was the fact that the biblical word in the Old Testament demanded a particular approach in the time of the new covenant, one which could take into account God's economy of salvation (*dispensatio divina*). It was above all in his controversy with the Manicheans that Augustine had worked out the unity of Old and New Testaments against the backdrop of this saving plan, and emphasized the way in which past events in salvation history served as a sign, until they were revealed and fulfilled in the new covenant. Thus the relevance of the Old Testament revelation was secured for Christian understanding of the faith, through attention to its prophetic character and function as a sign. These same hermeneutical principles could be made valid for the interpretation of the psalms as well.

a) The prophetic character of the psalms

Augustine's fundamental conviction is that the psalms represent a prophecy of the new covenant, and only acquire their true and full meaning at this level of understanding:

> "*Let this be written for another generation* (Ps 101:19(102:18)). When this was written, there was little profit to be had from these events amid which someone wrote it. No, it was written to foretell the New Testament, and yet written in the lifetime of people who were still at the Old Testament stage."[56]

---

55. See Exp. Ps 47,6; 128,13; 50,12; 57,20; 41,3; 147,2; 10,3; 132,11; 32,II,s.1,5; 32,II,s.1,6; 61f.
56. Exp. Ps 101,s.1,19.

The New Testament had already testified repeatedly that the Old Testament scriptures were "written for us" (see 1 Cor 10:11; 9:10; 1 Pt 1:12; Rom 15:4). Augustine was therefore only giving concrete expression to this recognition and applying it to the Book of Psalms, which was in its entirety to be regarded as prophetic.[57] He frequently calls the psalmist a prophet,[58] who speaks prophetically.[59] The words of a psalm are often attributed immediately to the Holy Spirit as to their proper speaker, without human agency.[60]

This powerful view of inspiration had exegetical consequences: the scriptural word was to be treated as a medium of declaration ordained by God, and the meaning it contained must be thoroughly investigated from every angle.[61] The word-for-word explanation which was the fruit of this conviction must accordingly be attributed not only to the influence of classical modes of grammatical exegesis; much more did these techniques seem to be a method appropriate to the particular understanding of scripture, to be pressed into the service of biblical exposition.

b) Actualizing interpretation

The conviction that the biblical words, thanks to their inspired character and their prophetic dimension, possessed a validity and fullness of meaning that surpassed the concrete situation where they arose, led to a further exegetical consequence. The business of interpretation was not simply to engage in historical research into the original meaning of the words within the Old Testament, and to treat of the psalmist's intention, historically conditioned as this was. It had a much more important task: to unlock the meaning of the biblical words for the present day, through theological reflection and an interpretation applied to actual circumstances. Augustine was convinced that in the meeting between scriptural declarations and the faith-experience of his own time, and only there, does exposition attain its true goal.

This actualizing method was already present within the biblical tradition itself, and was thereby established as authentic for the psalms too. Furthermore it was typical of patristic exegesis, especially in the context of the homily. To that extent Augustine's method of exposition moved in paths traced already by scripture itself and by exegetical and homiletic tradition.

---

57. See Exp. Ps 107,2.
58. See Exp. Ps 3,9; 11,7; 19,1; 29,I,5; 30,I,20; 30,II,s.3,9; 103,s.2,7; compare *Teaching Christianity* 2,18,13 (CCL 32,39f).
59. See Exp. Ps 7,1; 9,3; 19,7; 29,II,1; 84,1.
60. See Exp. Ps 48,s.2,1; 57,7; 68,s.2,7; 93,9.
61. See Exp. Ps 72,1.

c) The heuristic and regulatory function of the Church's faith

What paths lead to this discernment of the Christian sense of Old Testament words? Nothing but the open revelation of the New Testament illumines the Old Testament for our understanding.[62] The faith of the New Testament, as the Church has unfolded it, has a heuristic and regulatory function with regard to the words of the Old.

Augustine's interpretation of the scriptural words he treats as signs presupposes a prior understanding, an already known horizon, as *Teaching Christianity* makes plain. He was fully persuaded that a sign (*signum*) could be understood only by someone who already had at his disposal a certain knowledge of the reality (*res*) to which the sign pointed. Otherwise the sign would remain unintelligible.[63] Thus the Church's faith, unfolding from the New Testament, forms the necessary prior understanding for correct interpretation of the symbolic words of the Old Testament.

However, the horizon provided by the New Testament is helpful not only in our discernment of the reality to which the Old Testament signs pointed. In addition to this heuristic function the faith of the Church, rooted in the New Testament, had for Augustine a regulative function also in relation to exegesis. Interpretation of the Old Testament was preserved from caprice and flights of fancy by its reference to its New Testament horizon.

The mysteries of the Christian faith derived from the New Testament permitted a retrospective understanding of the true and complete meaning of the Old Testament data. Augustine's interpretation looked back at the scripture from his standpoint in the Church's faith, to discern in its Old Testament roots and points of departure the doctrine of the faith developed in the New Testament and later tradition.

A question now arises: how far does this kind of prior understanding of the meaning of a biblical text permit us to unlock it, and how far does it threaten to close it to us? Does the orientation of exegesis to a truth known *a priori* promote our understanding of the scripture, or does scripture merely serve as an illustration of that truth, which is possibly foreign to it? Do the biblical words only provide a starting point for Augustine's reflections, which develop in accordance with a dynamism of their own and hence should scarcely be treated as scriptural interpretation? Or do the expositions of the psalms follow an inner logic, the principles of which may indeed be foreign to modern exegetical method, but are to be understood as the unfolding of what is implied in the letter?

---

62. See Exp. Ps 147,4; 138,1; 105,36.
63. See *The Teacher* 10,33 (CCL 29,192); *The Trinity* X,1,2 (CCL 50,312); *The Advantage of Believing* 13,28 (CSEL 25/1,36). Compare C. Mayer: *Die Zeichen in der geistigen Entwicklung und in der Theologie Augustins* vol II Die antimanichäische Epoche (Cassiciacum 24/2; Würzburg, 1974), 349, 437f.

That such a method remains ex-egesis, ex-planation, and not eis-egesis, the importing of meaning into the text, is for Augustine established with certainty by his faith in inspiration. On his hermeneutical premises the previously-determined object of interpretation—that is, the Church's faith as developed from the New Testament—had already been concealed in the letter of the Old Testament by the true author of the scriptures, the Holy Spirit:

> "During the Old Testament period . . . the New Testament was hidden there as fruit is hidden in the root. If you look for fruit in the root, of course you find nothing. Yet neither will you find any fruit on the branches, if it has not sprung from the root."[64]

d) The various meanings of scripture

Conviction that the Old Testament had enduring validity for faith and life even in the age of the new covenant led to various types of interpretation of the biblical text. For Augustine, exposition of scripture is fundamentally an activity carried on against the horizon of the Church's faith; what primarily matters for him is not historical investigation of the original meaning of biblical statements but their present-day understanding as it affects the specifically Christian way of life. The many-layered material in the psalms accordingly requires exegetical tools of many types if it is to be opened up in this way.

The distinction Augustine established in *Teaching Christianity* between literal and figurative senses *(locutio propria / locutio figurata)*[65] was fundamental for his practice of exegesis. *Figura* or *figurata* was Augustine's preferred term for designating a mode of speech in scripture that was not to be understood literally but in a transferred and symbolic sense.[66] For Augustine, metaphors, similes, allegory, and typology all belong to the figurative sense of scripture.

The figurative interpretation of a psalm-text may range widely. It extends from a transference of meaning that is merely extrinsic *(sensus accommodatus)* and lacks any organic connection with the scriptural word (for example, heaven = apostle), through a typological interpretation that relies on only a partial analogy between type and antitype (for example, Solomon = Christ), all the way to instances of the plenary sense *(sensus plenior)* which respects the thrust of meaning within the Old Testament statement, and brings it to a fulfillment in accord with its own inner finality (for example, Jerusalem = the Church).

The criterion for establishing whether a passage of scripture must be understood in its obvious sense *(proprie)* or symbolically *(figurate)* is not found in the

---

64. Exp. Ps 72,1; compare 72,4; 74,12; 84,4; 105,36.
65. See *Teaching Christianity* 3,24,34 (CCL 32,97).
66. See R. Bernard: *In figura*. Terminology pertaining to figurative exegesis in the works of Augustine of Hippo (Dissertation, Princeton University, 1984).

text by examining its internal evidence, but determined for Augustine by the object of exposition. His synthesis in the first book of *Teaching Christianity*[67] had found the object of exposition. This was the authoritative truth, the truth that controlled interpretation of the text: the rule of faith and the double commandment of love. Wherever a literalistic approach contradicted this truth, figurative interpretation alone was permissible.

Augustine was convinced that it was impossible to reconcile many expressions in the psalms, understood literally, with the purpose of exposition. Distasteful anthropomorphism (Ps 2:4), sensual customs in worship (Ps 67:26(68:25)), the bleak prospect of a shadowy afterlife in Sheol (Ps 87:12-13(88:11-12)), the stylized scenario of Old Testament theophanies (Ps 76:17-19(77:16-18)), confidence in the everlasting permanence of the earth (Ps 103(104):5), a doctrine of retribution in this world at variance with concrete experience (Ps 36(37):28), and God's promise to protect the physical life of his own (Ps 33:21(34:20)), which remained unfulfilled in view of the martyrs' fate—all these elements admitted of figurative explanation only.[68]

Nonetheless Augustine's interpretation paid a good deal of attention to the literal approach. Even at this level explanation of the Old Testament words in a Christian sense was frequently possible. The possibility resided not least in the literary form and poetic character of many psalms, which had been composed as formulas of prayer applicable either individually or collectively. The overtly metaphorical and archetypical idiom of these psalms made them suitable for concrete contemporary use without sweeping changes to their original sense. Yet here too through a Christian interpretation Augustine was aiming at an understanding which fitted the way of life proper to the new covenant.

The diversity of literary forms among the psalms, together with the varying acceptability of this Old Testament material to the Christian mind, demanded flexible procedures on the part of the expositor. Particular exegetical methods and distinction between senses of scripture are in the end nothing but different roads to the same goal, diverse roads chosen according to the nature of the biblical terrain.

The goal is the opening up of the Old Testament so that Christian faith can understand it. Augustine's exposition is concerned to make the text of a psalm relevant in the sense that the Old Testament words can function fully as prayer in the epoch of the new covenant; they must be taken over into this definitive stage

---

67. See G. Istace: Le livre Ier du "de doctrina christiana" de saint Augustin. Organisation synthétique et méthode mise en oeuvre, *Ephemerides theologicae Lovanienses* 32 (1956) 289-330.

68. See Exp. Ps 103,s.1,17f; 2,3; 33,s.1,10; s.2,24; 34,s.2,3; 36,s.3,7.10; 67,35; 76,20; 87,11f. Compare G.R. Evans: Absurditas in Augustine's scriptural commentary, *Downside Review* 99 (1981) 109-118; J. Pépin: A propos de l'histoire de l'exégèse allégorique, l'absurdité signe de l'allégorie, *Studia Patristica* 1 (1957) 395-413, esp. 400-404.

of salvation history in such a way that their meaning accords with the Church's faith. Augustine's interpretation of the psalms aims to transform the songs of the old covenant into a "new song" (*canticum novum*).[69]

9. Ways in Which the Text of a Psalm Could Be Made Actual

In the following pages examples are given of the application of particular interpretative methods to various biblical themes and forms of expression. Their use was directed by the faith of the Church as Augustine understood it, and intended to facilitate Christian appreciation of the words of the Old Testament.

a) Unfolding metaphors and similes

The first procedure to be considered is one much practiced by Augustine in his theological exposition of the words of a psalm: the development of its picturesque speech, the heightening of its colorful similes and metaphors. The interpreter developed his own theological explanation from the Bible's use of imagery. This could mean that he remained within the sphere of experience evoked by the words of the psalms and merely amplified it;[70] or he might associate with those often polyvalent or strange images new content, not based on the text of scripture or even in conflict with its imagery.[71] Where the images and similes of the Bible are confined to one pregnant saying, the Old Testament sketch is often filled out by Augustine with Christian colors and taken further.

For example the lament, *You have brushed my soul away like a spider's web* (Ps 38:12(39:11)), becomes when amplified by Augustine a sign of the human condition since the fall. The sentence pronounced on evildoers, *They will wither swiftly like grass, and quickly fall like plants in the meadow* (Ps 36(37):2), is contrasted with the picture of believers whose life is rooted in God, so as to produce eventually a flower that cannot fade.[72] The confession that *You are a strong tower against the enemy* (Ps 60:4(61:3)) is used to suggest a Christian's spiritual warfare.[73] Scenes from the days of the martyrs illustrate the saying, *Our soul is like a bird escaped from the fowler's net* (Ps 123(124):7).[74] A hymn reflecting on past deliverance, *We passed through fire and water, but you brought us through to a place of rest* (Ps 65(66):12) is a sign of Christian initia-

---

69. See Exp. Ps 32,II,s.1,8; 149,1.
70. See Exp. Ps 36,s.1,3s.2,12; 57,16; 90,s.1,5; 102,22; 143,11.
71. See Exp. Ps 17,30.34; 35,10; 37,10; 38,9; 54,8.24; 68,s.2,8; 119,5.
72. See Exp. Ps 36,s.1,3; 38,18.
73. See Exp. Ps 60,5.
74. See Exp. Ps 123,12.

tion, of our purifying journey on earth and of its heavenly fulfillment.[75] The imprecation against the wicked, *They shall be like grass on the rooftops that withers before it can shoot; never will the mower take a handful of it, or the binder an armful* (Ps 128(129):6-7) is illustrated by the scenario of the final judgment of the world.[76]

Augustine had a predilection for picturesque and symbolic modes of speech, which is reflected in his *Confessions* and his other preaching. In the poetic imagery of the psalms this preference found an inexhaustible reservoir, on which he drew to work out more receptively or more creatively the evocative power or associations latent in the biblical words.

b) Theological and philosophical interpretation of the Old Testament's picture of God

The reader of the psalms encountered not only pictures which, by reason of the archetypical character or their flexible mode of speech, could be developed without difficulty. More prominent were the numerous idiomatic and metaphorical elements in biblical statements which could not without more ado be reconciled with the Church's accustomed usage. Above all the picture of God presented by the psalms posed for the Christian reader the problem of finding an interpretation that would correspond to his or her own outlook of faith and thought. Two problematic areas appear: formulations which evoke polytheistic ideas, and manifold instances of anthropomorphism.

In archaic styles of expression employed by the psalms, or in their polemic against idolatry, references are made to divine beings alongside or subordinate to the "Most High God." These are generally interpreted by Augustine as pagan idols and demons (see, for example, the declaration already made by Psalm 95(96):5 itself: *All the gods of the heathen are demons*).[77]

The numerous anthropomorphisms, occasioned by the poetic character of the psalms and their metaphorical style, called still more loudly for a clarification that would enable Augustine to confront the Manicheans on one side, and on the other the anthropomorphists who had spread widely during the fourth century. His repeated warnings about possible misunderstanding of the words of the psalms reveal the severity of the problem.[78] With the help of a figurative explanation of Genesis 9:6 imparted to him by Ambrose. (*He made man in the image of God*), Augustine had freed himself from the Manichean rejection of the anthropomorphic picture of God offered by the Old Testament. That same

---

75. Compare *The Christian Combat* and see Exp. Ps 65,17.
76. See Exp. Ps 128,11.
77. See Exp. Ps 85,12; 95,5f; 96,14; 135,3.
78. See Exp. Ps 120,11; 30,II,s.1,7; 2,3; 87,2; 89,12.14.

method of interpretation had therefore to be used in the expounding of the psalms too, if he was to encourage the "carnally-minded" (*carnales/animales*) within the Church to a more spiritual understanding of God.[79]

Where the Bible speaks of parts of the body or organs of perception as belonging to God, Augustine holds that these are primarily to be understood as his powers of action (*potentiae operationum*).[80] Thus God's hand or arm signifies his might as revealed in creation and history; God's ear means his compassionate power to hear us; his eyes are his love; his countenance is his presence and power to reveal himself to human beings.[81]

Although these interpretations may well correspond to the intention of the psalmist in using such expressions, Augustine with the philosophical presuppositions of his own picture of God could not simply go along with the Old Testament's artless realism concerning emotions in God. His conviction that immutability was the fundamental characteristic of God's essence prevented him from accepting unaltered the unmistakable liveliness of the God depicted in the Bible, his emotionality and activity. It often seemed possible to avoid overstepping the limits imposed by philosophy on theological thought[82] only by tortuous and strained expedients, such as transposing divine emotions like regret onto human beings.[83] Even the many colorful pictures of theophanies painted by the psalms (Ps 17(18):7-16; 28(29):3-10; 76:17-19(77:16-18); 113(114):3-8) could represent for Augustine only figurative descriptions of the mighty manifestation of God's action, the cosmic echo of which was subsequently interpreted in anthropomorphic fashion in the imagery of the psalms. The convulsions of nature become a reflection of the irresistible strength of the message of faith addressed to human beings.[84]

c) The treatment of history as typological and exemplary

Since the locus of God's revelation was the history of his chosen people, the faith and hope of Israel lived most deeply from that history. Inevitably, therefore, allusions of every possible kind are made in the psalms to the various historical traditions. History is recalled in praise, lament and didactic psalms, so that hope for the present and orientation for the future may be gained from it.

---

79. See R.J. Teske: Spirituals and Spiritual Interpretation in Augustine, *Augustinian Studies* 15 (1984) 65-81, especially 70-73.
80. See Exp. Ps 9,33.
81. See Exp. Ps 18,II,3; 76,17; 30,II,s.1,7; 31,I,8; 10,11.
82. See esp. W. Pannenberg: Die Aufnahme des philosophischen Gottesbegriffs als dogmatisches Problem der frühchristlichen Theologie, *Zeitschrift für Kirchengeschichte* 70 (1959) 1-45.
83. See Exp. Ps 105,35; 109,17; 131,18. Compare J.M. Hallman: The emotions of God in the Theology of St. Augustine, *Recherches de Théologie ancienne et médiévale* 51 (1984) 5-19.
84. See Exp. Ps 17,7-16; 28,3-10; 67,9-12; 76,18-20; 113,s.1,6-11.

This meant that allusions to history, often very general in character or restricted to passing references, offered plenty of scope for later actualization. Augustine's desire was to demonstrate through the prophetic nature of the psalms their intimations of the future, and hence their relevance and actuality for later generations living under the new covenant. In those passages of the psalms that dwelt on history he found plenty of starting points.

In the light of this interpretation the exodus, the entry into the promised land, the sojourn in exile and the return had a dimension of meaning for the future over and above their significance in the past. Augustine frequently returns to the Pauline principle that *All these things happened to them, but with symbolic import (in figura)* (1 Cor 10:11), in order to bring the story of past events to bear on contemporary experience of salvation. The historical events related in the psalms are only a husk, under which the real mysteries lie hidden.[85] These past occurrences remain relevant for Christian consideration only to the extent that they prefigured the new order of salvation. Even in Old Testament times history was not related for its own sake; rather it served for the most part as a paradigm. Since those descriptions were exemplary and not completely time-bound, they provide a valid means of expressing the Church's experience of history as well.

d) Allegorical and metaphorical treatment of creation

Clearly connected with God's salvific activity in the psalms are his creative deeds. But the biblical description of them raised no small problems for understanding. The cosmic reverberations of a mighty theophany (*the mountains melted away like wax before the presence of the Lord*, Ps 96(97):5), the anthropomorphic face of glad creation (*Let the heavens rejoice and earth be glad . . . The fields and everything in them will make merry, and all the trees of the forest shout for joy*, Ps 95(96):11-12), reminiscences of the myth of chaotic conflict (*He gathers the waters of the sea together as though into a bottle, storing up the depths in his treasure-houses*, Ps 32(33):7), or the archaic idea of the world's architecture (*The round world is the Lord's . . . he founded it on the seas*, Ps 23(24):1-2)—these are a few examples. They seemed to allow of figurative exegesis only, if such descriptions were to be accessible to the faith-experience of Augustine's contemporaries.

However, it was not only passages marked by an archaic or anthropomorphic idea of the world and God which made it imperative to resort to figurative interpretation, and so pass beyond their literal meaning. Other descriptions of God's creative work, which were less time-conditioned, seemed scarcely able to awaken Augustine's interest at the level of their literal sense, because owing to

---

85. See Exp. Ps 113,s.1,1.3; 134,20; 84,4; 7,1.

his anti-Manichean bias the cosmic dimension of redemption had remained largely foreign to his thought.[86] Only as a mirror of human existence and the Church's life did creation seem meaningful to him; only under the aspect of its character as a sign could he treat of it in the text of scripture. Almost without exception his consideration of the Old Testament cosmos kept to this perspective and was carried through by means of allegorical and figurative exegesis.

Thus the sky, which already in the psalms proclaimed the glory and righteousness of God, is a symbol of evangelists, prophets, and preachers.[87] The earth is a symbol either of transient, earthly-minded humanity, or of the thirst for grace.[88] The mountains represent prophets, evangelists, apostles, preachers, and saints in the Church, firmly established by God, towering high and radiant with the light of Christ;[89] but they also symbolize the pride and arrogance of the great people in this world, who quake before God's power.[90] When sea or water is mentioned the idea of menace dominates: Augustine here finds hints of the world, the godless and sinful, pagan peoples, persecution and rampant desire.[91] Alternatively springs and rivers, on account of their positive connotations in the psalms, may especially provide an image of prophets, evangelists, and preachers, who dispense life.[92] In other contexts, though, as when the rivers of Babylon or the Jordan are in question, they symbolize the fleeting nature of life.[93] The animal kingdom is treated in the psalms partly in a realistic way as praising the creative power of God, and partly as invested with metaphorical and symbolic character; but Augustine interprets it figuratively, applying its symbolic content, as currently understood, to human beings.[94]

Augustinian allegory constantly depends on the drawing of analogies between what is said and what is meant, between the word of a psalm and its transposed meaning, which permits him to work out the many-sided connotations of the poetic text. This allegorizing procedure is certainly preserved from random associations by the criteria for analogy and the context, but many of his interpretations can be regarded as no more than accommodation of the scripture, as attempts to make extrinsic realities fit its original meaning. But for Augustine it is precisely these realities—and ultimately the quest for the true destiny of human beings—that enjoy priority over any other speculations: "The investigation of this world seems to me to have scarcely anything to do with the attain-

---

86. See Th. E. Clarke: St. Augustine and cosmic redemption, *Theological Studies* 19 (1958) 133-164.
87. See Exp. Ps 18,I,2; 18,II,2; 49,13; 67,10; 88,s.1,3.6.12.
88. See Exp. Ps 67,9; 81,7; 134,16; 94,9; 103,s.1,17.
89. See Exp. Ps 35,9; 45,6; 64,10; 71,5.18; 79,9; 86,1.
90. See Exp. Ps 82,12; 94,8; 96,9.
91. See Exp. Ps 23,2; 28,3; 32,I,7; 64,9.11; 73,15; 76,18.21; 77,13; 80,11.
92. See Exp. Ps 17,16; 64,14; 73,17; 106,13.
93. See Exp. Ps 23,2; 65,11; 109,20; 136,3f.
94. See Exp. Ps 8,12f; 64,18; 73,4; 103,s.3,5.16.18; 146,18.

ment of a blessed and happy life. Even if the inquiry yields some joy, we must still fear lest it take up time that should be spent on more important matters."[95]

e) The correction in a Christian sense of deficient declarations on faith and morality

Augustine's requirement that Old Testament sayings must be understood "by Christians in a Christian way" (*christiane a christianis*)[96] acquired greater importance in the case of two more extensive complexes of themes which called for correction. First there were inadequate eschatological statements and, second, the quite frequent cursing psalms; both raised problems of understanding if they were to be brought into conformity with the rule of faith and moral principles. A number of factors hindered Augustine from perceiving the psychological and historical conditioning that affected such passages, and their polemical and hyperbolic forms of expression; he was therefore unable to illuminate them adequately. Among these limiting factors were his faith in unlimited inspiration, his persuasion that all utterances in holy scripture were of equal value, a defective understanding of the progress of revelation from Old to New Testament, and his homiletic purpose of ensuring that the words of the Old Testament should be comprehensible and effective for present hearers.

How then did Augustine attempt to harmonize with the Church's eschatological faith the many palpable assertions to be found in psalms of lament, but in thanksgiving psalms too, that only a shadowy continuation of life awaits us after death? The despairing cry in that gloomiest of psalms, *Will anyone recount your mercy in the grave, or your faithfulness in the land of the lost? Will your wondrous deeds be known in the darkness, or your righteousness in the land of oblivion?* (Ps 87:12-13(88:11-12)) could in Augustine's eyes be understood only as a figurative description of the spiritual death that results from sin, not as an eschatological statement about our fate beyond this life.[97] Similarly in Psalm 38:14(39:13) the despairing presumption of eternal extinction in death (*Forgive me, so that I may find some cool refreshment, before I go away to be no more*) could not be taken by Augustine to mean that human existence is to be totally snuffed out, but only as a confession that in comparison with God's fullness of being, all creaturely and ephemeral existence should more properly be seen as not-being than as being.[98] Finally the cry, *What use is there in my blood, if I sink*

---

95. Letter 11,2 (CSEL 34/1,26). On the allegorical and symbolic treatment of the world see
    J.-M. Le Blond: *Les conversions de saint Augustin* (Théologie 17; Paris, 1950) 285-294.
96. Sermon 41,6 (CCL 41,500).
97. See Exp. Ps 87,11f.
98. See Exp. Ps 38,22.

down into corruption? (Ps 29:10(30:9)) is corrected into an allusion to bodily resurrection at the end of time.[99]

These examples demonstrate how Augustine tried to harmonize the Old Testament's declarations about the final destiny of human beings with the eschatological faith of the Church, and so to make them available for use in Christian prayer. For him it was irrelevant to ask whether this interpretation went beyond the perspectives of Old Testament prayer. That Augustine considered himself authorized by Christ's resurrection to go beyond them is clear from the answer he gave to the psalmist's question, *What man is there who will live but not see death? Shall anyone pluck his soul from the grasp of hell?* (Ps 88:49(89:48)). He pointed to the unique destiny of the risen Christ.[100]

With regard to the cursing psalms, and other psalms which include imprecations and threats, Augustine made use of several techniques to blunt the contrast—a contrast of which he was fully aware—between them and Christ's command to love one's neighbor.[101] Very frequently the imprecation was explained as a prophecy of the future fate of the wicked, and justified by the demands of God's righteousness; in this sense the fulfillment of the prophecy should be regarded as matter for rejoicing.[102] But often psalm passages of this kind were interpreted positively as wishes, prayers for the conversion of sinners.[103] It is true that in either case the Old Testament wording could by this procedure appear to be brought to its fulfillment in the spirit of the gospel and made viable for Christian prayer, but the discrepancy between this interpretation and the original intention of the psalmist remains unmistakable. To justify his reversal of the intention, however, Augustine was able to make a distinction: hatred was to be seen as directed not against the sinner but against the sins.[104] The anticipation that calamity might fall back upon the evildoers themselves, expressed in many psalms, was explained by Augustine with an allusion to the destructive effect of wickedness on the soul and the tendency of wrongdoers to become entangled in their sins.[105]

More important for Augustine's methods of interpretation is the concrete identification of the "enemies" mentioned not only in the cursing psalms but in psalms of lament as well. Augustine interpreted "enemy" in concrete fashion (as a persecutor of the Church), or in the light of contemporary events (as a schis-

---

99. See Exp. Ps 29,II,19.
100. See Exp. Ps 88,s.2,10.
101. See Exp. Ps 69,3; 34,s.1,8; 78,14; 103,s.4,19; 138,27. Compare H. Weber: Die Fluchpsalmen in augustinischer Sicht, *Theologie und Glaube* 48 (1958) 443-450; C. Mielgo: Interpretatación agustiniana de algunos salmos dificiles, *Estudio Agustiniano* 22 (1987) 261-281, esp. 274-278.
102. See Exp. Ps 5,13; 27,1.4; 34,s.1,8f; 51,8.
103. See Exp. Ps 103,s.4,19; 6,13; 34,s.1,8; 39,25.
104. See Exp. Ps 138,28; 78,14.
105. See Exp. Ps 7,17f; 9,15; 34,s.1,11; 36,s.2,3.

matic), or abstractly (as depravity), or generally (as sinners), or in a spiritual sense (as Satan). In the perspective of the psalms themselves the enemies of the chosen people could be regarded on theocratic grounds as ultimately the enemies of God, and the enemies of the individual as the prototypical Evil One who separates us from God; hence Augustine's extension of this idea seems in no way irreconcilable with the ultimate intention of the psalmist. Rather does it forcefully indicate, at the level of the new covenant, the hostility against God which, in its diverse manifestations, increased with Christ's appearance; and the resolve against evil on the part of the one who prays is given powerful expression through the idiom of the psalms.

f) The interiorizing and spiritualizing of historical, liturgical, and soteriological statements

The process of transposing biblical words from the material and bodily realm into the spiritual sphere, from the external to the inner world, had begun in the Old Testament itself. Furthermore there were similar reinterpretations of the Old Testament in the New, especially Matthew 5:21-45. This tendency to reinterpret was taken up by Augustine and intensified in consequence of the influence of Neoplatonism on his mind and of the Pauline doctrine of the inner person.[106]

Which of the realities proclaimed by the psalms underwent this spiritualizing and interiorizing treatment? Three complexes of themes stand out. Reminiscences of salvation history concerning the exodus and the other events of Israel's history, cultic arrangements with regard to music and the offering of sacrifices, and finally the experience of God's presence in blessing and in rescuing his people from some particular distress—all these figure in the psalm passages which underwent spiritualizing and interiorizing treatment at Augustine's hands.

The attitude of Israel toward God as depicted in the comprehensive meditation on its history found in Psalm 77(78) represented for Augustine what can take place constantly in human experience on a spiritual plane.[107] Similarly the recollection of being freed from Babylon (*You reversed Jacob's captivity* Ps 84:2(85:1)) was transposed from the external and historical into the inner and moral sphere with the help of Pauline metaphors on slavery to sin.[108] The great thanksgiving hymn of different groups of pilgrims who celebrated their rescue from various dangers (Ps 106(107)) likewise becomes through Augustine's

---

106. See C. Dagens: L'intériorité de l'homme selon saint Augustin, *Bulletin de littérature ecclésiastique* 88 (1987) 249-272; A. Solignac: Homme intérieur, in *Dictionnaire de Spiritualité ascétique et mystique* 7/1 (Paris, 1969) 650-658.
107. See Exp. Ps 77,11,13f.27.31.
108. See Exp. Ps 84,4f

explanation a description of the spiritual and interior hazards which threaten the life of believers at the various stages of their spiritual journey.[109]

In comparable fashion Old Testament liturgy, as reflected in the psalms, is transposed to a spiritual and interior plane by means of figurative interpretation. The pilgrimage to Zion, to the sanctuary, the climb up to the earthly Jerusalem, is understood, especially in the Gradual Psalms (the "Psalms of Ascent"), as a spiritual climb to God and to the heavenly Jerusalem. The statement in a psalm that *God arranges ascents in the believer's heart* (Ps 83:6(84:5)) demanded such an interpretation in Augustine's view.[110]

In conformity with older patristic exegesis the musical instruments used in the worship of God in the Old Testament, especially the psaltery and the lyre, were given an interior meaning, which attempted to bring the cultic customs of a remote age nearer to the practice of Christian prayer.[111] Moreover even the Old Testament's sacrificial usage could be spiritualized and interiorized by means of figurative interpretation. The obvious criticism of merely external cultic practices found in various psalms, along with their ideas on inward sacrifice, needed only to be taken up anew and deepened in the light of the New Testament.[112]

A spiritualizing and interiorizing approach was required for one last complex of themes: the declarations in the psalms about God's blessing and assistance. In the former instance correction of a generally material outlook was required; in the latter, confidence and gratitude with regard to the preservation of bodily life were brought into harmony with the experience of martyrdom in particular. Augustine often cited the body-soul antithesis in order to establish the validity of such expressions in the psalms, not for physical life, but for the soul's safeguarding of its unbroken faith.[113]

g) Opening up the fullness of meaning

Augustine's exposition was frequently able to take the literal sense of the psalm words as a basis, and without resorting to any figurative interpretation to deepen it decisively, so that the psalms' declarations were considered and understood in the light of the Church's faith. This was especially the case with God's saving deeds—protection, ennoblement, and redemption—and with the good

---

109. See Exp. Ps 106,3.
110. See Rom 7:22-25 and see Exp. Ps 83,10; 123,1; 120,3; 121,11; compare G. Madec: Ascensio, ascensus, in C. Mayer (ed.), *Augustinus-Lexikon* 1 (Basel, 1991-1994) 465-475.
111. See Ps 106(107) and see Exp. Ps 32,II,s.1,5; 32,I,2; 42,5; 56,16; 67,34; 70,s.2,11. Compare H. Rondet: Notes d'exégèse augustinienne. Psalterium et cithara, *Recherches de science religieuse* 46 (1958) 408-415.
112. See Exp. Ps 28,2; 50,21; 44,27; 49,15-21; 53,10; 55,19; 65,20.
113. See Exp. Ps 26,II,21; 33,s.2,8f.22.24; 17,20; 35,17; 36,s.2,3.s.3,13; 53,8; 54,6; 55,19; 90,s.1,10.

things of salvation which God brought into being—health, life, fullness of days, joy, peace. The articulation of these realities in the psalms lent itself to a deeper and fuller understanding, which both took account of the psalmist's intention and surpassed it.[114]

Because Augustine explained all these notions in the light of the mystery of Christ's resurrection, and understood them as referring to eternal life beyond the reach of death, the Old Testament words took on a deeper and fuller meaning, which was nonetheless thoroughly conformed to their literal sense, since the literal sense itself testified to a longing for unlimited life. Moreover it was only from the faith of the Church that the light of this fuller meaning could dawn upon the words of the Old Covenant. Only gradually, and only late in Old Testament times, did hope for salvation call out for true life beyond the threshold of death. The same truth can be demonstrated with regard to other themes and key concepts in the psalms, such as mercy, truth, righteousness, law, sin, pilgrimage, hope, and yearning.

Modern biblical scholarship has coined the term "plenary sense" (*sensus plenior*) for this type of interpretation. The plenary sense is the prolongation and deepening of that fullness of the literal sense already present in the original wording, and so it brings to the literal sense its authentic value. The majority of Augustine's expositions of the psalms can be measured against this concept and classified as examples of the plenary sense, since his exegesis, conducted in the light of the entirety of revelation, was able to unlock the finality hidden in the words at their Old Testament level of meaning. The significance that Augustine extracts from declarations in the psalms is often present in them, at least virtually. Many of his actualizations of the biblical word lead to no alien meaning, but bring to its true value an aspect of the fullness of meaning already locked into the letter, and make it available for his own day.

10. The Psalms as a Mirror and Remedy of Salvation for the Soul

a) Existential and anthropological interpretation

In his *Confessions* (IX,4,6; IX,10,33) Augustine gave a picture of the early stages of the conversion of his mind and will, and related how he owed the transformation of his inner attitudes, affections and feelings to the psalms.[115] From his personal history he was aware that his experience had been clarified for him

---

114. See Exp. Ps 3,2.8; 5,1; 16,13; 17,49; 19,7; 20,I,5; 22,6; 26,II,7; 27,7; 29,I,3.6.12; 36,s.1,12; 60,8; 70,s.1,8; 71,8; 83,17; 102,8.
115. See H.J. Sieben: Der Psalter und die Bekehrung der VOCES und AFFECTUS. Zu Augustinus, Conf. IX,4,6 und X,33, *Theologie und Philosophie* 52 (1977) 481-497.

and his affective life healed by the psalms, and that in the biblical words he had discovered a medium of expression adequate to his own soul. This existential and anthropological estimate of the psalms came into play in the *Enarrationes* as well. Augustine designates the function and effect of the psalms by the terms "mirror" and "remedy" (*speculum et medicamentum*) in order to indicate their diagnostic significance and their power to bring psychological healing.[116]

b) The diagnostic properties of the psalms

Precisely because of the poetic character of the psalms, experiences which were originally individual and personal, concrete and unique, attain universal and timeless validity. In their poetry are expressed not an unrepeatable experience, not a transitory state of mind, but the pain, anxiety, longing, and joy of men and women, the experiences that are simply human. The variety of poetic language that articulates these experiences in the psalms renders them timeless and typical, and hence permits individual appropriation.

But this raises the question whether the mirror of the psalms, manufactured from materials derived from the Old Covenant, is capable of reflecting a true likeness to anyone who lives under the dispensation of the new covenant. Admittedly there are many psalms of sapiential character which depict the human condition in terms valid for any age. But are there not just as many psalms whose reflective surfaces contain too slight a content of silver, and shine so dimly, that they are incapable of mirroring the renewed Godlikeness of the baptized?

Augustine's primary answer to the problem was that the declarations of the psalms are read at differing levels of understanding. The biblical words may sometimes describe what is eternal in human beings without reference to time (*Many say, "Who has anything good to show us?"* Ps 4:7(6)); they may offer the Christian who prays a retrospective understanding of his or her own story of conversion (*O God, in converting us you give us life:* Ps 84:7(85:6)). But they may also give expression to the present situation of those who, already baptized, still bear the traces of the old humanity (*Lo, how old you have made my days!* Ps 38:6(39:5)). In Augustine's view it was precisely those psalms in which Adam's voice is heard that are particularly suitable for Christian prayer. According to his anthropology our rebirth into new life in no way signifies the complete conquest of the old nature. Those psalms are therefore not to be disowned even under the regime of the new covenant.[117]

---

116. See Exp. Ps 123,3; 36,s.1,3; 106,1; 118,s.4,3.
117. See Exp.Ps 38,9; 37,15.

His overriding concern is thus the interpretation of Old Testament terms in the fullness of meaning revealed by Christianity. By means of an abundant orchestration from the New Testament, dependent especially on Pauline theology, concepts such as poverty, pilgrimage, conversion, confession, righteousness and mercy are taken further along the line of their Old Testament content, deepened, and unlocked to reveal their plenary sense.

During the period of his conversion Augustine had seen his own existence interpreted by the psalms; but conversely his own story became an exposition of the biblical words. Augustine's theological meditation, ripened by his own experience of life, enriched the picture of the human condition offered by the psalms with color and sharp definition derived from his own experience and conformable to the new covenant. The biblical picture of human beings was thus capable of displaying both the depth of God's absence, which the expositor had plumbed himself, and also the intensity of God's nearness; and only in such light did they become fully visible. Transposed into the final stage of the economy of salvation, and filled out by the expositor's knowledge of life, the psalms could now present to the eyes of human beings under grace a true picture of themselves, and so offer the community which prayed the psalms the possibility of making them its own.

c) The therapeutic significance of the psalms

If the psalms reflected the life of human beings before God in all its aspects, they also exerted a powerfully transforming effect on hearers and prayers, in Augustine's view. The psalms offered to men and women not only a reflection which served as a diagnosis of their condition before God; they also, more especially, offered a therapy for human affective life bereft of its primordial harmony. Augustine's exposition of Psalm 93(94) exemplifies this double function. The psalm is a song of lament which primarily articulates the suffering of a righteous person at the doings of the wicked, and it bears traces of the wisdom tradition. The inspired words of the psalm make their own the thoughts of one under attack and tempted, and echo his perplexed questions:

> Meanwhile the wicked triumph, the wicked exult, the wicked blaspheme and commit all manner of crimes. . . . Does this upset you? The psalm grieves with you, and asks questions with you, but not because it does not know. Rather does it ask with you the question to which it knows the answer, so that in it you may find what you did not know. Anyone who wants to console someone else acts like this: unless he grieves with the other, he cannot lift him up. First of all he grieves with him, and then he strengthens him with a consoling word. . . . So too the

psalm, and indeed the Spirit of God, though knowing everything, asks
questions with you, as though giving expression to your own words.[118]
    The next step is to assimilate oneself to the words of the psalm, in order to
find, through the wisdom they contain, healing for one's own ills:

> Look how the psalm corrects itself: allow yourself to be corrected along
> with it. It was to that end that the psalm adopted your complaint. What
> did you say? *How long will sinners gloat, O Lord, How long?* The psalm
> took on your words, so now you take on the words of the psalm. And
> what does the psalm say? *The Lord has become a refuge for me.*[119]

Thus the therapeutic method of the divine physician relies on a "wonderful
exchange" (*admirabile commercium*). The words of the psalms adjust themselves to the patient, who obtains healing by adjusting himself on his own part to
the inspired words. This indication of their therapeutic character is a common-
place in patristic understanding of the psalms. Thus Augustine treats the psalms
as a medicinal potion administered by the divine physician and presented to the
mouth of the sick person's heart through his hearing.[120] As Augustine described
in his *Confessions* (X,28,39) the transformation of his disturbed affective life by
the psalms, so too is his explanation of them in the *Enarrationes* directed to the
healing of the affections.

The conversion of the affections

    The Bishop of Hippo's mature position with regard to the classical doctrine
on human affective life (a doctrine derived from Platonic-Aristotelian and also
Stoic sources) was summarized in Book XIV of *The City of God* as follows:
"The citizens of God's holy city have all their affections rightly ordered" (*omnes
affectiones rectas habent*).[121] In his expositions of the psalms too Augustine crit-
icizes the ideal of "apathy," which he characterizes as a "numbness" (*stupor*)
and impossible in this life.[122] The language of the psalms pointed to the regula-
tion of the affections in human life. On the other hand Augustine followed
ancient thought in speaking of a "sickness of the soul," manifested in the distur-
bances (*perturbationes*) of affective life. For him, the psalms demonstrated the

---

118. Exp. Ps 93,9.
119. Exp. Ps 93,27.
120. Exp. Ps 36,s.1,3.9; 74,1; 93,2; 48,s.1,1.
121. City 14,9 (CCL 48,426). Compare M. Fiedrowicz: "Cives sanctae civitatis Dei omnes
      affectiones rectas habent" (civ. 14,9). Terapia delle passioni e preghiera in S. Agostino, in
      L'Etica cristiana nei secoli III e IV: Eredità e confronti, XXIV Incontro di studiosi
      dell'antichità cristiana, Roma 4-6 maggio 1995 (Studia Ephemeridis Augustinianum 53;
      Roma, 1996) 431-440.
122. See Exp. Ps 55,6. Compare G.J.P. O'Daly-A. Zumkeller: Affectus, in C. Mayer (ed.),
      Augustinus-Lexikon 1 (Basel, 1991-1994) 166-180, esp. 170f.

right orientation of the affections, in conformity with God's order. What is required is that the affections be straightened out, not extinguished.

Laments and jubilations in the psalms articulate the whole gamut of human emotions. It was precisely Augustine's conviction that the biblical words were inspired[123] that enabled him to discover the necessary correction of such affections in the movement, typical of many psalms, from lament to trust and thanksgiving.[124] If the emotional language of the psalms gives expression to rightly oriented affections—if indeed the psalm itself includes an *affectus*[125]—this same emotion should be aroused in the hearers: *May this same feeling arise in you!*[126]

The affections were to be elicited, though, not only by a passive hearing of the words of the psalm, but by actively putting them into practice.[127] This is why Augustine constantly adds the characteristic formula, "Let him say" (*dicat*) or a variant of it to his exposition: *"You have redeemed me, Lord God of truth."* The people redeemed by its Lord's passion . . . must also say, *"You have redeemed me, Lord God of truth."*[128]

The making real of the psalm words which Augustine demands implies not only recitation with the lips but inner conformity. And attunement to the psalmody is required not only where the objective statements of the psalms and one's own experience happen to coincide.[129] Far more important is it to take one's tone from the psalm when one's soul is badly out of tune with it. As a consequence of the painful striving for affective adjustment to the psalms the inspired words may effect a transformation of the one who prays.[130]

If Augustine attributed to the psalms a corrective function with regard to the affections, this does not mean that joy must necessarily be evoked in the heart in place of sadness, or hope in place of fear, by means of the psalm's words. Even obviously negative emotions like sadness, fear or desire are legitimate for him, since the inspired words expressly testify to them. The person who prays the psalms must be conformed to these words too.[131] The decisive point is that the affections must be oriented aright. What Augustine demands is the conversion of the affections, their straightening out toward God.[132]

---

123. See Exp. Ps 26,II,1.
124. See Exp. Ps 93,27.
125. See Exp. Ps 86,1; 128,3; 85,10; 70,s.1,1.
126. Exp. Ps 62,17.
127. See Exp. Ps 69,2; 123,3; 32,II,s.1,1; 39,20; 50,6.
128. Exp. Ps 30,I,6; see also 3,9; 10,6; 33,s.II,3; 42,4; 30,II,s.1,5.10.
129. See Exp. Ps 45,2; 54,4; 85,19; 123,3.
130. See Exp. Ps 103,s.4,19; 51,6; 130,3; 119,9; 101,s.1,2; 37,1; 68,s.1,2; 70,s.1,1; 33,s.2,5; 40,6.
131. See Exp. Ps 30,II,s.3,1.
132. See Exp. Ps 79,13. Compare G. Madec: Conversio, in C. Mayer (ed.), *Augustinus Lexikon* 1 (Basel 1991-1994) 1282-1294, esp. 1286f.

An illustration: the four principal passions

Let us illustrate this from the classical schema of the four principal passions. The psalmist's confession, *My soul thirsts for you* (Ps 62:2(63:1)) gives the expositor a chance to contrast a wrongly aimed desire for the good things of this world with the true direction of desire toward God.[133] Similarly the promise, *He appeases your longing with good things* (Ps 102(103):5, is used to highlight the need for an ordering of love (*ordo amoris*) in our search for the good that will truly fulfill us, and to demonstrate to the soul that its highest good, the good for which it is made, is God himself.[134]

According to the classical doctrine of the passions the opposite of desire is fear. In this instance too we meet a reversal. If the passion of fear is directed toward God alone, the human person loses all fear of creatures: *The Lord is . . . my salvation, whom shall I fear?* (Ps 26(27):1).[135] The call to fear God is raised by many a psalm, and for Augustine it becomes an appeal to make this liberating conversion complete. The plea, *Free my soul from fear of the enemy* (Ps 63:2(64:1)) therefore becomes a prayer not to lose one's eternal soul as a consequence of wrongly directed fear of creatures. Once again we find a reversal of fear.[136]

Desire and fear are directed toward a future good or evil that is absent; joy and sadness arise from the experience of their presence. To the joy in God trumpeted in many psalms (*I will rejoice and exult in you,* Ps 9A:3(2)) Augustine opposes misdirected enjoyment of the world, in order to signal through the antithesis the right ordering of this emotion.[137] In this changeable world God alone, the unchangeable good, can give that "surer joy" we most deeply seek.[138] Once again in the psalm formulas Augustine finds pointers to the *conversio* which redirects the wrongly oriented passion toward its proper goal, and so heals the soul's sickness: *O God, in converting us you will give us life, and your people will rejoice in you* (Ps 84:7(85:6)).[139]

Finally Augustine treated sadness as the emotion which gives appropriate expression to the pilgrim status of human beings. The sadness of soul experienced by the psalmist (*O my soul, why are you sorrowful, and why do you disquiet me?* Ps 41:6(42:5)) remains normative for human existence until perfect union with God is attained.[140] This sadness conforms to the right order of

---

133. See Exp. Ps 62,5.
134. See Exp. Ps 102,8.
135. See Exp. Ps 26,II,3-5.
136. See Exp. Ps 63,2.
137. See Exp. Ps 9,3; 96,19; 94,2.
138. See Exp. Ps 85,7.
139. See Exp. Ps 84,8; 74,1.
140. See Exp. Ps 41,10.

things, since it proves that human beings have not forgotten their transcendent destiny, their true home in the heavenly Jerusalem: *By the rivers of Babylon we sat and wept, as we remembered Zion* (Ps 136(137):1).[141]

These examples show how in Augustine's view the recitation of the psalms leads to conformity with their sentiments, and how this conformity in its turn effects the conversion and rectification of one's own affections.

The existential and anthropological method of exposition here discussed, which treats the Book of Psalms as a mirror of the soul and a remedy for its healing, was characteristic above all of Augustine's first encounter with the world of the psalms, attested already for the year 386. Not only the use of them in the *Confessions*, but also his praying of the penitential psalms on his deathbed, prove that this level of interpretation was a constant feature of his spirituality, one which is fundamental for his *Expositions of the Psalms* as well.

The background to this interpretation of the psalms has been considered in relation to Augustine's personal history; but along with this we must examine the Christological dimension of his search for God,[142] the road "from his speculative, private life, focused on himself, to the preaching life of a priest and bishop who lived only for the Church."[143]

11. The Psalms as a Prophecy of Christ and the Church

a) The hermeneutical presuppositions of a Christological and ecclesial interpretation

Through understanding the psalms as a prophecy of the mystery of Christ in his totality—of Christ, head and body (the *totus Christus*)—Augustine had found a hermeneutical key for expounding them, which enabled him to plumb the utmost depths of the Old Testament words and make them immediately available to Christian understanding. In so doing he was following the practice of the New Testament writers. Considered in the light of the New Testament the psalms were shown up in new contours, which reflected the mystery of Christ. But this mystery itself was more richly understood when expressed in the prayers of the Old Covenant. The psalms that were interpreted Christologically became "as clear as the

---

141. See Exp. Ps 136,4f.

142. See G. Madec: Christus, in C. Mayer (ed.), *Augustinus-Lexikon* 1(Basel, 1991-1994) 845-908.

143. H.U. v. Balthasar: Einführung zu: *Augustinus. Das Antlitz der Kirche* (Einsiedeln,[2] 1955), 11. Compare F. Refoulé: Sens de Dieu et sens de l'Église chez saint Augustin, *Nouvelle Revue Théologique* 78 (1956) 262-270.

gospel,"[144] but conversely the representation of Christ given by the gospels was filled out by the psalms understood as the voice of Christ.

The fundamental point for Augustine's interpretation of the psalms is that he understood them as a prophecy of Christ. The psalmist's prior knowledge of the fate of Christ permitted him to choose words in such a way that they would be fully capable of expressing the mystery of Christ.[145] Already with the first psalm Augustine's exposition clearly formulates this ultimate Christological reference.[146] Their bearing on Christ, their transparency to Christ, becomes the criterion for correct understanding of the psalms, an understanding to be attained in no other way than by recognizing the presence of Christ in them (*intellectus Christi*).[147] Augustine repeatedly reminds his hearers that what matters is to seek Christ and recognize him in the psalms:

> We must apply it all to Christ, if we want to keep to the path of correct understanding. . . . Whatever doubts a person has in his mind on hearing God's scriptures, let him not move away from Christ. When in those words Christ has been revealed to him, let him understand that he has understood; but before he attains to this understanding of Christ, let him not presume to think he has understood.[148]

That prophetic speech was, however, obscured by figurative language, until the incarnation drew aside the veil from the Old Testament writings, and the truth hidden within them became visible.[149]

It is important, though, that Augustine complemented the Christological orientation of his hermeneutical criterion by including the Church, and explained that the Church together with Christ is the central content of holy scripture: "Christ and his Church, that total mystery with which all the scriptures are concerned."[150] In the context of anti-Donatist polemic he even formulated the principle that the ecclesial mystery is the more evident: "The prophets spoke more clearly about the Church than about Christ."[151]

b) *Different perspectives in interpretation*

Now, what routes are there from the text of the psalms to the mystery of Christ and the Church? Augustine followed the pattern customary in early Christian exegesis, which interpreted the psalms either as a word to Christ (*vox*

---

144. Exp. Ps 21,I,2.
145. See Exp. Ps 62,1; 87,3; 93,8.
146. See Exp. Ps 1,1.
147. See Exp. Ps 96,2; 98,9f.
148. Exp. Ps 96,2.
149. See Exp. Ps 98,1; 70,s.2,9; 21,II,15; 45,1; 64,6.
150. Exp. Ps 79,1; compare *City of God* 16,2 (CCL 48, 500).
151. Exp. 30,2,s.2,8f.

ad Christum), or as a word about Christ (*vox de Christo*), or as a word spoken by Christ himself (*vox Christi*), or in an ecclesiological perspective as a word about the Church (*vox de ecclesia*), or finally as a word spoken by the Church (*vox ecclesiae*).[152]

This scheme represents only a subsequent systematization of the possibilities of Christological and ecclesiological interpretation. In practice the various perspectives intermingle, so that often one and the same psalm speaks to God, speaks about God, and represents God himself as speaking. The same is true for the people of Israel, which made itself heard within the psalms in a variety of forms. Nonetheless this scheme is well adapted to the working out of the different emphases in Augustine's exegesis of the psalms.

c) The psalm as a word to Christ

In an ample reflection on the place of Christ in the practice of prayer Augustine expressly warned that the Son must not be excluded from prayer to the Father.[153] Following the example set by the New Testament and patristic tradition,[154] Augustine understood various psalms or portions of psalms as prayers to Christ.[155] Thus it comes about that the God invoked in the psalms is invested with the traits of Christ, as when the prayer is for forgiveness,[156] or thanksgiving for it, when it implores God to intervene in situations of distress or persecution,[157] when it calls upon God to see justice done,[158] or expresses hope for his present aid.[159] This is bound up with the awareness that reconciliation between God and humanity will be definitively achieved only through Christ's death on the cross,[160] that all hope is founded on his resurrection,[161] and that with his return at the end of time all the powers of evil will be finally defeated.[162]

---

152. See B. Fischer: *Die Psalmen als Stimme der Kirche*. Gesammelte Studien zure christlichen Psalmenfrömmigkeit, ed. A. Heinz (Trier 1982) 15-35; J. Trublet: Psaumes, in *Dictionnaire de Spiritualité ascétique et mystique* 12/2 (Paris, 1986) 2504-2562, esp. 2554-2559; L. Scheffzcyk: "Vox Christi ad Patrem—Vox Ecclesiae ad Christum. Christologische Hintergründe der beiden Grundtypen christlichen Psalmenbetens und ihre spirituellen Konsequenzen," in H. Becker-R. Kaczynski (eds.), *Liturgie und Dichtung* vol. II (St. Ottilien, 1983) 579-614.
153. Exp. Ps 85,1.
154. See B. Fischer: *Psalmen*, 24-28; J. Trublet: Psaumes, 2558f.
155. See K. Baus: Die Stellung Christi im Beten des heiligen Augustinus, *Trierer theologische Zeitschrift* 63 (1954) 321-339.
156. See Exp. Ps 84,4-7.
157. See Exp. Ps 69,8f; 82,2f.
158. See Exp. Ps 7,2f.5-8; 20.
159. Exp. Ps 55,4-6; 70,s.1,3; 90,s.2,3-9.
160. See Exp. Ps 19,1-7; 64,3-9; 129,3.
161. See Exp. Ps 65,1-9.
162. See Exp. Ps 79,13.

d) The psalm as a word about Christ

In cases where the psalms were not expressly understood as a prayer to Christ or as the voice of Christ himself, or did not admit of such understanding, patristic tradition followed the New Testament's lead in choosing between two possible ways of applying the biblical text to Christ. Either the transfer to Christ of titles designating God in the third person, especially the title "Lord" (*Kyrios*), or the Christological interpretation of other key concepts, images, and symbolic representations, made it possible to treat the psalms as a word about Christ.[163]

Christ as "Lord and God"

Where Christological applications of particular verses, or of whole psalms, were already part of patristic tradition, Augustine took the same route. This was the case with the verses *He is like a bridegroom coming forth from his tent* (Ps 18:6(19:5));[164] *Away with your gates, you princes! But you, everlasting gates, lift yourselves up, and the King of glory will enter* (Ps 23(24):9);[165] or again with the whole of Psalm 109(110).[166] Augustine followed tradition to find in these Old Testament words pointers to the mystery of Christ's incarnation, death, resurrection, glorification, and return at the end of time.

In the figure of Christ many soteriological declarations concerning God's dealings with humankind—help, guidance, mercy, strengthening, ennoblement, setting free and protection, preservation from death and destruction—find concrete verification beyond compare.[167] Augustine reads the psalms in the light of the Christian confession of faith. Wherever a psalm verse seems capable of evoking one of the mysteries of Christ, Augustine transfers the corresponding article of faith to the Old Testament words, usually backing this up with suitable New Testament quotations. Thus the statement in the psalm is made concrete and verified in a Christological sense. Against this background exhortations to love God, or testimonies to God's trustworthiness, take on a new, Christological motivation in Augustine's eyes, since they become the response to the experience of salvation granted in Christ.[168]

In the cases where whole psalms are given a Christological interpretation, Augustine shows steady awareness of the categories of Old Testament psalms. The hymns celebrating God's kingship (Pss 46(47), 92(93), 95(96), 98(99))[169]

---

163. See B. Fischer: *Psalmen*, 23; J. Trublet: Psaumes, 2556-2558.
164. See Exp. Ps 18,II,2-10.15.
165. See Exp. Ps 23,1.9f.
166. See Exp. Ps 109.
167. See Exp. Ps 40,2f.5; 36,s.2,6.15.17; 102,11; 145,17; 40,2; 120,13.
168. See Exp. Ps 63,18; 145,1f; 146,20; 150,4.
169. See Exp. Ps 46,3-13; 92,2-7; 95,2.11.14f; 96; 98,2-6.

are especially applied to Christ's universal lordship and his return as judge of the world. But other psalms too that concern the king (Ps 113(114)),[170] or descriptions of theophanies (Ps 28(29))[171] or recollections of God's dealings with his people in the history of salvation (Ps 67(68)),[172] become the background on which Augustine paints in bright colors a portrait of Christ as Lord of the Church and mighty conqueror of all the powers at enmity with God. This aspect of Augustine's interpretation can be regarded as a reflection of Christian piety in a Church that was part of the empire, marked by the triumph of Christian faith over paganism and particularly eager to reverence Christ as the King of glory (*rex gloriae*).[173]

Christ in images, similes, and symbolic representations

Christological interpretation of various key concepts and images found in the psalms had begun already in the New Testament with the designation of Christ as the cornerstone (Ps117(118):22; Mt 21:42; Acts 4:11; 1 Pt 2:7). Augustine discovered further and fuller possibilities of association that could link the world of the psalms into Christ's mysteries. The way, the fountain, the sun, light, bread, the door or gate—all these become a many-faceted reflection of Christ. His figure is enhanced by the dynamism inherent in these images in the context of their own times,[174] but conversely the fullness of Christ's saving mystery lights up the images.[175]

There are in addition various abstract concepts understood in a plenary sense, and representations interpreted typologically. Peace, justice, mercy, truth, wisdom, and the word receive their fullness of meaning in Christ.[176]

A further form of Christian rereading of the psalms was the investing of individual persons with a typological significance in relation to Christ, in whom they receive their full meaning. Accordingly the figure of a holy person or a righteous man includes the traits of Christ who, being the sole holy and righteous one, has power to make others righteous.[177] Similarly the mention of a king can be applied to Christ, and particularly to the inscription over his cross, his future coming as judge and his guidance of creation.[178] The figures of the anointed, the

---

170. See Exp. Ps 113,s.1.
171. See Exp. Ps 28.
172. See Exp. Ps 67.
173. See Exp. Ps 46,4; 92,7; 95,2; 96,9.11; 98,2.4.6. Compare P. Beskow: *Rex gloriae*. The kingship of Christ in the early Church (Uppsala, 1962).
174. See Exp. Ps 84,9; 118,s.6,3; s.20,1; 113,s.1,11.
175. See Exp. Ps 35,15; 66,5; 85,15; 97,2.
176. See Exp. Ps 33,s.2,19; 118,s.12,5; 118,s.13,1; 39,18; 103,s.3,25; 118,s.13,2.
177. See Exp. Ps 4,4; 10,12; 30,II,s.3,5.
178. See Exp. Ps 20,2; 23,7.9f; 44,5; 62,20; 67,15; 71,2; 149,6.

poor, and the innocent are likewise interpreted of Christ, who came to enrich men and women through his poverty, and as the sinless lamb to forgive the sins of all.[179] Finally personal names, especially those of Solomon and David, were transferred to Christ, the author of peace, the true shepherd and the universal Lord.[180]

All these images, ideas, and symbolic representations shed light on new aspects of the mystery of Christ's person, though the profundity of that mystery became all the clearer by contrast with such representations. Conversely these pictures of Christ proved to be a key to understanding the reality poetically presented in the psalms, which are a microcosm of the Bible.

e) The psalms as a word about the Church

The people of God and Jerusalem as symbolizing the Church

Apart from figurative and allegorical explanations of the moon, a dove, a ship, a winepress, a vine, and the daughter or bride of the king,[181] it was predominantly the declarations about God's people in the Old Testament that Augustine applied to the Church.[182] Not infrequently he admonished his hearers, "Do not regard yourselves as strangers to this," when the text of a psalm spoke of the people of the Old Covenant, of Abraham, Isaac, and Jacob.

What kind of theological arguments made such a transfer and identification possible? Augustine had recourse to various Pauline teachings, sometimes pointing out that the noble olive tree remained alive and flourishing in spite of the breaking off of some branches and the grafting in of others (see Rom 11:16-24), or asserting that Christians, by belonging to Christ through their faith, constitute Abraham's posterity (see Gal 3:29), and fulfill the universal promise made to him (see Gal 22:18).[183]

In addition to these complexes of words in the psalms which applied to God's chosen people, and were interpreted by Augustine as declarations about the Church which had sprung from the Jews, the true Israel, there were also in the psalms universal perspectives, such as the comprehensive claims about Yahweh's sovereignty, or the world-ruler status of the king in Jerusalem. These could be seized upon and applied to the Church drawn from the Gentiles. Since the election of Israel was intended ultimately to serve the salvation of all the peoples of the earth, this universal concept of salvation could without difficulty

---

179. See Exp. Ps 2,1; 17,51; 88,s.2,13; 81,3; 108,19; 63,6.
180. See Exp. Ps 126,1f; 77,43; 88,s.1,21-29.
181. See Exp. Ps 8,9; 67,17.20; 103,s.4,5; 8,1; 79,1.8-13; 44,24-33.
182. See Exp. Ps 28,11; 84,11; 105,37; 78,17.
183. See Exp. Ps 134,7; 148,17; 113,s.1,2.

be given its full value through application to the Church, and the Christian Church could be treated as the place where the promise made to the fathers in ages long past was fulfilled.[184]

What starting points did the psalms provide for such ideas? In the first place, those saving acts, and the summons of the heathen to praise God, could be taken over immediately. Moreover with the help of figurative exegesis it was possible to apply to the conversion of the pagans words originally referred to their defeat and annihilation. Augustine repeatedly stressed that in the measure that unbelief and the worship of false gods were being conquered by the preaching of the gospel, these prophetic and eschatological assertions were being proved true.[185] Associated with these ideas about the pagans were the expectations of God's universal sovereignty articulated in the psalms by such formulas as "the round earth" (*orbis terrarum*), "the ends of the earth" (*fines terrae*), or "all the earth" (*omnis terrra*). These could be given their full value through application to the Church, in order to show that even the Old Testament had given witness to the Church's worldwide extension.[186] This point was often useful in anti-Donatist polemics.

Since Zion and the city of Jerusalem, the holy mountain and the temple, ranked as the focus of God's saving presence, Augustine's explanation of the psalms followed the path already traced by early Christian tradition and treated the Church as the true Zion and the true Jerusalem, inasmuch as only in the Church could God's salvific presence be experienced, and only there could the response of faith-filled worship of God be offered.[187] But Augustine's view of the prophecy of the Church was not confined to a place where God was present; he frequently understood the prophecy to mean the assembly which worships God in that place, and is the proper subject of the fear and praise of God.[188]

The city of God in the psalms

In pursuance of the idea of the city of God Augustine had derived his own conviction from the message of the psalms.[189] It is therefore understandable that his *Expositions of the Psalms* can in many respects be described as a commen-

---

184. See Exp. Ps 30,II,s.3,9; 149,3.
185. See Exp. Ps 85,13; 46,3-5.10; 58,s.1,11.17.
186. See Exp. Ps 23,2; 44,32; 46,3; 47,10; 56,13.
187. See Exp. Ps 86,5; 75,3; 149,5; 77,41; 131,21; 136,19; 78,6; 125,3.9; 101,s.1,17; s.2,4; 10,7; 28,9; 95,10; 137,4; 26,II,13.
188. See Exp. Ps 21,I,26; 34,s.2,10; 106,13; 108,32; 88,s.1,6; 18,I,10; 21,II,24; 112,1.
189. See *City of God* 11,1 (CCL 48,321).

tary on his other work, *The City of God*, in that various expositions prepare, or fill out, or draw together what was there developed.[190]

What points of departure are to be found in the psalms for this theme? The principal ones are provided by a string of prominent terms which in particular passages of the psalms open up a perspective either on the two *civitates* or on the opposition between them. City, Zion, Jerusalem, exile in a foreign land, captivity, ingathering—all these are taken up by Augustine as cues. With their help he establishes his doctrine of the *civitates* under its various aspects: their mutual opposition on earth and separation at the end of time, their mingling within the Church, the uniting of humankind, now exiled in a foreign land, with the fellowship of the angels. All this could be illuminated by the symbolism and metaphorical speech of the underlying psalm-verses.[191]

In other cases entire psalms could be interpreted in the light of this antagonism that runs through sacred history. Such were Psalms 61(62), 64(65), 86(87), 113(114), 121(122), 125(126), 136(137), 147(147B) and 148. It was not only prophetic and eschatological prospects on the significance of God's city for universal salvation that Augustine could adopt and take further. Recollections of the exodus events and the experiences of exile, the divine choice of Jerusalem, pilgrimage customs and the temple cult, were broken free from their historically contingent setting and their confined locality to become the means of representing the opposition between the two cities, an opposition found in all ages and all places.

Spiritualization, interiorization, and eschatological reference are the ways which lead from a once-only and locally restricted reality to one universally valid. The rich symbolism of the psalms often imparts to this theological idea a possibility of expression which without this medium it might never have attained.

f) The psalms as the voice of Christ

The prosopological method of interpretation

In addition to the styles of Christological interpretation of the psalms hitherto discussed, Augustine made use of so-called prosopological exegesis.[192] Patristic

---

190. See A.Lauras-H. Rondet: Le thème des deux cités dans l'oeuvre de saint Augustin, in H. Rondet (ed.), *Études augustiniennes* (Théologie 28; Paris, 1953) 99-160, esp. 114; M. Fiedrowicz: Könnte ich dich je vergessen, Jerusalem? Der Gottesstaat im Spiegel der Psalmendeutung Augustins (Augustinus heute 8; Würzburg, 1997).

191. See Exp. Ps 45,8; 47,3; 146,4; 118,s.8,1; 105,36f; 106,3.

192. See M. J. Rondeau: *Les commentaires patristiques du Psautier (IIIe—Ve siècles)* vol II (Orientalia Christiana Analecta 220; Roma 1985) 365-388; *idem*: L'Élucidation des interlocuteurs des Psaumes et le développement dogmatique (IIIe—Ve siècle), 9n H. Becker R. Kaczynski (eds.), *Liturgie und Dichtung* vol. II (St. Ottilien, 1983) 509-577, especially 568-572.

commentary on the scriptures had taken this practice over from the ancients, in particular from the exposition of Homer and Plato.[193] When it was applied to the psalms, the principal endeavor was to identify the different partners in the dialogue. Prosopological exegesis attempted to make clear who was the proper speaker in a psalm, and whether he was speaking in his own name or in the name (*ex persona / ex voce*) of someone else. Not unless this could be clarified would the true understanding of a psalm be available, since the character of a speaker would penetrate the words and endow them with specific meaning. This meaning is opened up only where the word in question is interpreted entirely with respect to the mind of the speaker.

The witness of the New Testament had already put many words from the psalms into the mouth of Christ, who imparted to them a new fullness of meaning. In the same way early Christian tradition discovered in many other words of the psalter an utterance of Christ himself, which helped it to reach a deeper knowledge of his mystery.[194] Prosopological exegesis aims to define the various ways in which it is possible to understand Christ as the speaker in the psalms.

Augustine's Christology and soteriology were determined by the traditional notion of the "wonderful bargain" (*admirabile commercium*).[195] This concept required a throughgoing participation by the Redeemer in human life, in order to make it possible for human beings to share in the immortal life of God.[196] Against the background of this soteriological principle, interpretation of the psalms is inspired by a desire to demonstrate Christ's unreserved sharing in our weakness, and to carry prosopological definition through in a way that is as fully Christological as possible.

For Augustine a comprehensive Christological rereading of the psalms was very possible because he heard in them "the voice of the whole Christ" and therefore could notably broaden the spectrum of possibilities for the interpretation of a psalm. The doctrine of the "whole Christ" (*totus Christus*) is expressly designated as the key to a correct understanding in faith of many psalms.[197]

To describe this prosopological approach Augustine uses many stereotyped formulas, such as "Sometimes Christ speaks in his own name, sometimes in

193. See M. J. Rondeau: *Commentaires*, 21-93.
194. See A. Rose: *L'influence des Psaumes sur les annonces et les récits de la passion et de la résurrection dans les Évangiles*, in R. de Langhe (ed.), *Le Psautier. Ses origines, Ses problèmes littéraires. Son influence*. Études présentés aux XIIe journées Bibliques 29-31 août 1960 (Orientalia et biblica Lovaniensia 4; Louvain, 1962) 297-356; J. Trublet: *Psaumes*, 2554-2556; B. Fischer: *Psalmen*, 21-24.
195. See W.S. Babcock: *The Christ of the Exchange*. A Study of Augustine's Enarrationes in Psalmos (Dissertation, Yale University, 1971).
196. See Exp. Ps 52,6; 30,II,3; 58,s.1,7.10; 60,3; 66,9; 70,s.2,10; 102,22; 118,s.16,6; 146,11; 148,8.
197. See Exp. Ps 90,s.2,1; 140,7; 142,3; 143,1.

ours" (*Christus aliquando loquitur ex se, aliquando ex nobis*), or "Now he speaks in the name of his members, now in his own person" (*modo loquens ex membris suis, modo loquens ex persona sua*).[198] But alongside such distinctions there are formulations that betoken a more powerful union, expressions that do not ascribe some word of a psalm to Christ *or* the Church, but will have it spoken by Christ as Head and body inseparably.[199]

The psalms as Christ speaking in his own name

In some psalms or psalm verses Augustine discovered indications of the mystery of Christ's death and resurrection. This made it possible for him to treat those words as a prayer made by Christ in his own name (*ex persona sua*). If it seems that other mysteries of Christ's life were pushed into the background, this is not least a consequence of the fact that the psalms which were most suitable for such prosopological exegesis were primarily psalms of individual petition and lament. These lent themselves to a Christological interpretation, directed especially toward demonstrating the fulfillment of these words in the historical figure of Christ. The lament of the psalmists over betrayal, persecution and oppression,[200] their hope for divine assistance[201] and their jubilant thanks for the deliverance they have experienced from all afflictions,[202] become when interpreted as Christ's own prayer part of his utterance of himself. This complements the more narrative character of the reports of his passion and resurrection in the gospels by adding to these a view from within, a view of the events from the standpoint of Christ himself. Thus a new perception of the mysteries of his passion and resurrection becomes possible.

It comes about, therefore, that just as the many psalm words which Christ adopted or which were applied to him become an expression of the secret of his person, so too the Old Testament words themselves receive from this prayer of Christ their own ultimate depth of meaning, through being fulfilled in his experience. What persecution and abandonment mean, what deliverance and life are at their deepest, is evident henceforth in the light of Christ's passion and resurrection. Thus prosopological exegesis proves itself to be the way to the plenary sense of the biblical words.

However, the view of the psalm-verses as capable of immediate interpretation as Christ's voice remains limited. In such prayers it is not only complaints under external oppression that are voiced, not only laments in the face of inva-

---

198. See Exp. Ps 39,5.12; 37,6; 74,4; 118,s.16,6; s.22,3; 138,2; 142,3.
199. See Exp. Ps 62,2; 37,6; 39,10; 59,1.
200. See Exp. Ps 70,20; 34,s.2,2-5; 37,16-21; 40,1; 58,s.1,8; 63,3-8; 68,s.1,9. s.2,5.9; 108.
201. See Exp. Ps 10,12; 15,9f, 30,I,1-6; 30,II,11.
202. See Exp. Ps 3,1-8; 4,2; 27,7; 29,I,10; 29,II,12.19-22; 40,12f; 56,8-12; 63,3; 85,17; 138,4.25.

sive power and affliction from external human sources; much more insistently is heard in them the voice of inner oppression by guilt, sin and Godforsakenness. And this seems to call in question an unrestrictedly Christological interpretation of the psalms.[203] Even though the experience of a suffering righteous man—weakness, pain and distress—can be understood on Christ's lips as the basis of the kenotic argument of Philippians 2:6-8, the confession of personal enslavement to guilt requires a more solid theological foundation, if such words are still to remain open to interpretation as Christ's voice.[204]

The psalms as Christ speaking in our name

In order to maintain the most comprehensive Christological interpretation he possibly can, Augustine sets the prayer of Christ in the psalms in a soteriolgical and ecclesiological perspective. Not only does Christ turn to the Father in his own name with the words of the psalms on his lips; he also prays to the Father in the name of all men and women. It is to be noted in this connection that the frequently used word "for" (*pro*) carries the full weight of meaning contained in the notion of "representation." It is not to be understood only of the external pleading of an intercessor,[205] but as indicating one who speaks in the name of another person.[206] This becomes clearer where Augustine uses such formulas as "Christ speaks in our name" (*ex persona nostra*), or "in the name of the body" (*ex persona corporis*), or "in the name of his members" (*ex membris*).[207] These prosopological formulas have an unmistakably representative and inclusive connotation.

Augustine was convinced that it was the glorified Christ who made use of the words of the psalms in order to appear before the Father on our behalf. His promise to remain with his Church (see Mt 28:20), the identification of the body with Christ himself (see 1 Cor 12:2), and finally the Pauline concepts of the filling-up of the sufferings of Christ (see Col 1:24) and of his life in the individual believer (see Gal 2:20) all indicated that even though the Lord is glorified his passion goes on (*Saul, Saul, why are you persecuting me?* Acts 9:4), and therefore so does his praying of the psalms of petition in the name of his body.

On the other hand Augustine interpreted many words in the psalms as the prayer of the earthly Christ in the name of his body.[208] He took his stand on Christ's assertion of identification with his members in Matthew 25:40, and has

---

203. See Exp. Ps 4,2; 85,1; 140,3.
204. See Exp. Ps 30,II,s.1,4.
205. Thus Exp. Ps 3,8; 85,5.
206. See Exp. Ps 40,6; 37,6; 142,7.
207. See Exp. Ps 39,5; 140,3.7.
208. See Exp. Ps 40,1.

Christ promising, "Whenever one of my members prays so, I pray so."[209] Christ entered into the human condition and made its words his own;[210] from the midst of humanity he addressed these words to the Father,[211] so that by means of the words men and women may be mysteriously present in Christ[212] and be carried to the Father in the impetus of Christ's prayer.[213] The characteristic formula, "in him," indicates the inclusive dimension of Christ's prayer, which ultimately depends on the inclusion of all humanity in the human nature of Christ.[214]

In cases where Christ was envisaged as speaking in his own name it was enough simply to indicate his assumption of human nature,[215] but the many confessions of guilt in the psalms (Ps 21:2b(22:1b); 37:4(38:3)) and the cries of abandonment (Ps 21:2a(22:1a)) demanded sharper definition of that human nature of Christ. In these cases Augustine points out that Christ is speaking "in Adam's name" (*ex persona Adae*), whose mortal flesh he shared by his birth from Mary, so that on the cross the old humanity was crucified with him (see Rom 6:6).[216] As he had taken on himself "the likeness of sinful flesh" (Rom 8:3) in the incarnation, so Christ in his cry of abandonment on the cross also made "the voice of a sinner" his own.[217] The "for your sake" (*propter te*) of the incarnation is carried further into the "on your behalf" (*pro te*) of his prayer; and his "dying for us" (*mori pro nobis*) is anticipated by his "speaking in us" (*loqui in nobis*).[218]

An important part of Augustine's thought is that the Church was already present in Christ's prayer. His exegesis of the frequently quoted verse of Psalm 21 (21:2(22:1)) shows that for Augustine the cry of Christ on the cross was not only raised "in Adam's name" but had an ecclesial dimension too, in that Christ directed those words to the Father "in the name of his body" equally (*ex persona corporis*). By identifying the Church with even the earthly body of Christ Augustine was able to discover a mysterious involvement of humanity in the event of the cross. We were there (*nos ibi eramus*).[219]

An interesting point is Augustine's conviction that Christ's prayer-life had an anticipatory character with regard to ours (*praefiguravit nos in se*), so much so

---

209. See Exp. Ps 140,7; compare 68,s.1,10.
210. See Exp. Ps 26,II,1; 30,II,3; 62,17.
211. See Exp. Ps 85,1.
212. See Exp. Ps 85,1; 32,II,s.1,2; 54,4.
213. See Exp. Ps 4,2; 21,II,4; 63,18; 103,s.3,11.
214. See T.J. v. Bavel: *Recherches sur la christologie de saint Augustin*. L'humain et le divin dans le Christ d'après saint Augustin (Paradosis 19; Fribourg, 1954) 74-78.
215. See Exp. Ps 15,1; 29,II,4.
216. See Exp. Ps 21,I,1f; 68,s.2,11; 70,s.1,12; 68,s.1,2.
217. See Exp. Ps 49,5.
218. See Exp. Ps 29,II,4; 142,3; 62,17; 56,5.
219. See Exp. Ps 21,II,3; 40,6; 37,6; 68,s.1,2.

that the later fate of the Church was already manifested in it.[220] This in no way means that Christ's life had a significance for the future Church by way of example only. It is not simply a case of the Church focusing on Christ's earthly existence; much more does the Church condition that existence. Augustine often stresses that Christ acted in this way or prayed in that way because at some future date a situation would come about in the Church where the faithful would need to be strengthened by the exemplary conduct or prayer of Christ. For Augustine it is especially the misfortunes of the Church, its experience of finding its prayers not heard, and the fate of its martyrs, that already had their effects on the prayer of Christ and gave it an anticipatory and prefigurative character.[221]

g) The psalms as the voice of the Church

In addition to those psalms which were primarily interpreted as the voice of Christ, there are not a few in which Augustine heard the voice of the Church.[222] In chronological terms it can be demonstrated that the ecclesiological interpretation tended to take up more and more space.

From the angle of qualitative exegesis as well, however, an advance can be marked. In his first commentaries Augustine brought into play the traditional exegetical principle that the words of the Bible are to be regarded "either as those of the Church or as those of the soul" (*ecclesia vel anima*). This he did either by allowing the individual and moral interpretation to follow a typological exposition,[223] or by treating a psalm from a shifting viewpoint, moving easily between "voice of the Church" and "voice of the soul."[224] But in his later practice of interpretation the voice of the Church takes front rank, being understood as the principal subject of the psalm's prayer. Into this the individual who prays can and must insert himself by reason of belonging to the body of Christ.[225]

Moreover the priority of the Church as praying subject over the praying individual is often made clearer by Augustine's habit of describing the Church as the only sphere of experience within which an understanding of the psalm's words becomes at all possible for the individual. Only through membership of Christ's body can the praying individual enter fully into the experience articulated in the psalm and make it his own.[226]

---

220. See Exp. Ps 60,3.
221. See Exp. Ps 60,3; 68,s.1,3; 21,II,4; 103,s.3,11; 42,7; 68,s.1,8; 140,6.
222. See Exp. Ps 3; 5; 6; 9; 22; 24; 25; 41; 42; 43; 47; 55; 59; 60; 64; 65; 83; 93; 102; 103; 110; 114; 117; 119; 121; 122; 123; 128; 130; 139; 143; 147.
223. See Exp. Ps 3,10.
224. See Exp. Ps 6.
225. See Exp. Ps 139,2f; 143,13; 42,1; 52,1; 60,1; 103,s.1,2f; 128,3; 130,3; 137,1; 143,3.
226. See Exp. Ps 47,7; 54,3; 101,s.1,10; 52,1; 59,1; 74,4; 100,3; 101,s.1,5; 127,3.9; 139,3.

As he came more and more frequently to designate the Church as the "one man" (*unus homo*), Augustine could the more readily identify the "I" who speaks in the psalms with the voice of this one individual.[227] Accordingly not only could collective songs of thanksgiving or lament, hymns, songs of Zion and pilgrimage psalms be read as the Church's self-utterance; so above all could individual laments, and occasionally songs of personal thanksgiving and confidence. All these could be heard as the praying voice of the Church, as descriptions of its distress under persecution, heresy and the destructive power of sham Christians, but also as an expression of its journey of conversion, its longing for God and its gratitude for the help it has received.

The psalms give expression to the fortunes of God's people in the Old Testament as well as to the variable lot of the individual within it. In Augustine's exegesis, therefore, those words became a formula of prayer in which the Church could discover and express its own experience of the journey of faith. The Church thereby gained personality, to an extent it had never done in earlier ecclesiological tradition, even in the descriptions of it as bride and mother.[228] Indeed, it was precisely the promotion of the Church as the praying subject over the individual prayer that showed how completely the Church had personal traits for Augustine. In this way it was possible for exposition of the psalms to enrich and deepen ecclesiological reflection as well.

The converse was also true: this ecclesiological horizon added depth to the interpretation of the psalms. In Augustine's view the psalms needed this life of the Church, conceived in personal terms, as their hermeneutic sphere, if they were to develop their full resonance and reveal their richest meaning. Only particular situations in the life of the Church permitted the deeper sense of some psalm words to be recognized.

In this way the words of the psalms became the inspired language of a dialogue carried on between bride and Bridegroom, a dialogue that is the source of all spirituality, liturgy and theology.

h) The psalms as the voice of the whole Christ

The proper subject of prayer in the psalms has not been completely described according to Augustine, however, in the foregoing prosopological definitions of the psalms as the prayer of Christ or that of his Church. More and more clearly in his expositions[229] the idea surfaces that Christ can only be the true bearer of the

---

227. See Exp. Ps 60,1; 102,1; 103,s.1,2; 117,3; 119,7; 122,2.
228. On the theme of the Church's personality see Y. Congar: La personne "Église," *Revue Thomiste* 71 (1971) 613-640.
229. See Exp. Ps 3;16; 17; 29,I.II; 34; 39; 40; 52; 54; 56; 58; 61; 62; 63; 68; 69; 70; 74; 85; 87; 90; 91; 101; 108; 118; 138; 140; 141; 142.

prayer if he is understood as "the whole Christ" (*Christus totus*), as "one human being" (*unus homo*) in the unity of a Head and body. This concept of the "one human being" expresses organic unity, which closely corresponds to the Old Testament idea of corporate personality.[230]

This unity of Head and body, bride and Bridegroom, Christ and the Church, is the focal point of Augustine's personal interest in expounding the psalms.[231] The constantly changing patterns of Christ's presence in the Church, and of the Church's in Christ, allowed the expositor to understand all the words of the psalms in equal measure as the prayer of Christ in his totality.[232] However the particular prosopological definition may turn out, for Augustine the decisive principle remains: "Christ is speaking."[233]

i) The mystery of redemption in the light of prosopological exegesis

As an analysis of Augustine's key ideas demonstrates, his constant concern was to make the mystery of redemption transparent through the biblical words. The essential principle may now be summarized.

Where the content of a psalm offered the possibility of discovering the voice of Christ, speaking in his own name in some historical situation, Augustine seldom lets slip the chance of doing so. Thus Christ's cries of distress in his passion, and his thanksgiving in his resurrection, are audible in many psalms. Even confessions of guilt and cries of abandonment remain understandable as Christ's words provided that they are taken in a soteriological sense as the voice of Christ speaking "in our name" or "in the name of his body."

Christ adopted as his own the voice of Adam, the voice of the old man, the voice of humanity in need of redemption, so that the whole of humankind could already be present and included in his own prayer to the Father.[234] But he also did this in order to provide for them an exemplary form of prayer into which they could insert themselves, and so be enabled to learn, in this perfect act of prayer, the right attitude before God.[235] Hence Augustine's frequently emphasized phrase, "for us" (*pro nobis*), with reference to Christ's prayer is marked by the

---

230. See Exp. Ps 118,II,10; 101,s.1,2; 61,4; 58,s.1,2; 138,2. Compare H.W. Robinson: The Hebrew Conception of Corporate Personality, in *Beihefte zur Zeitschrift für alttestamentliche Wissenschaft* 66 (1936) 49-62. On the Old Testament idea of "the greater I" as a biblical foundation for the Augustinian doctrine of the *totus Christus*, see H. Mühlen: *Una mystica persona* (Paderborn,³ 1968) 75, 91.
231. See Exp. Ps 40,1; 90,s.2,1; 140,3; 138,21.
232. See Exp. Ps 30,II,s.1,4; 62,2.17; 85,1.
233. See Exp. Ps 140,3; 37,6; 138,2.21.
234. See Exp. Ps 21,II,3; 85,1.
235. See Exp. Ps 30,II,s.1,3; 56,5.

notion of inclusive representation, as well as by the principle of exemplary character.[236]

Augustine seeks in many cases to unlock as examples for the prayer of the Church even those psalms and psalm-verses which are principally understood only as "the voice of Christ speaking in his own name." Statements about persecution and oppression are often explained in a twofold sense, as the passion of the Head and the passion of the body. What Christ underwent, the Church undergoes now, whether in its martyrs or in other forms of contemporary affliction. One and the same word in a psalm thus becomes "the voice of the Head and of the body."

Here too Augustine often highlights the exemplary function of Christ's prayer, which becomes a form of prayer into which the Church must enter in order to find comfort and confidence in its own trials.[237] In his cry of forsakenness on the cross Christ gave utterance to Adam in his estrangement from God; but, more than that, in his confession of guilt he made it possible for all sinners to enter into this confession. Similarly Christ's articulation of horror in the face of death, but also his obedience to God in approaching his passion, serve as examples to show the Church which follows him in suffering the right way to pray, and thereby also the fundamentally right attitude before God in the midst of its own distress.[238]

The principle that Christ's prayer functions as an example is applicable also to a wider category of verses in the psalms. Where the passion-sayings of Christ and the Church are concerned, the time-scheme is "Once . . . now." But in a similar way the sayings in the psalms about the resurrection, when interpreted as uttered by Christ and the Church, fit the time-scheme "Now . . . later."[239] As in the present the Church carries on the passion once undergone by Christ, so will the Church be able later to make its own the thanksgiving for resurrection fulfilled already in its Head. Thus as his body it will make those thanksgiving psalms its own prayer of praise.[240]

As Christ's prayer made the words of humankind its own, so too must men and women make these words of Christ their own, in order to find anew the right basic attitude in God's presence by following Christ in his prayer. Thus the prayer of the psalms becomes a means of being conformed to Christ, becomes a

---

236. See Exp. Ps 40,6; 70,s.2,10; 63,18; 87,1.3; 140,3.6. Compare J.A. Goenaga: *La humanidad de Cristo figura de la Iglesia: Estudio de teologia espiritual agustiniana en las Enarrationes in Psalmos* (Madrid, 1963) 139-148; W.S. Babcock: *Christ of Exchange* 180-194.
237. See Exp. Ps 34,II,s.2,1; 31,II,26; 87,3.
238. See Exp. Ps 93,19; 103,s.3,11; 32,II,s.1,2; 31,II,26.
239. See Exp. Ps 29,II,11f; 85,23; 90,s.2,4.
240. See W.H. Marrevee: An Ecclesial Dimension in Augustine's Understanding of the Ascension of Christ, *Revue de l'Université d'Ottawa* 37 (1967) 322-343.

way of following Christ (*imitatio Christi*) which is not an external copying of an example, but entails an inner transformation in the accomplishment of the prayer.[241]

Because Christ articulated his passion and resurrection in the words of the psalms, these mysteries became communicable and made it possible for the Church, through praying the same words, to enter into these mysteries too. If the paschal mystery lives in the words of the psalms, it is capable of being made present again age after age, so as to draw those who pray into participation, and to endow the figure of Christ with its true dimension as *totus Christus*.

The idea of the whole Christ had the capacity to bring the various levels of interpretation and the exegetical perspectives into correlation and to render them transparent to each other. This is true of Christological interpretations that refer to historical events, soteriological expositions, ecclesiological and actualizing applications. In spite of all prosopological variations the identity of the person who is speaking—Christ in his totality as Head and body—is thus maintained. Indeed, it is only by means of this variation that the figure of Christ without curtailment and in all its fullness of meaning comes into view.[242] The figure of the whole Christ embraces the entire play of variable interpretation so obvious in Augustine's exposition of the psalms: the contraction and broadening, the narrowing of concentration to the voice of the Head and its widening to the voice of the body, the powerful interweaving of the notions of inclusion and exemplary causality, of anticipation and imitation. Only the figure of the whole Christ could save so complex a technique of interpretation from breaking apart into its several elements.

In the measure that the words of the psalms reflect this mystery, they find their true meaning for Augustine, since no individual is capable of fathoming all the human experiences poetically orchestrated in the psalms, or of filling them with life. Only the figure of the whole Christ, which spans all parts of the world and bestrides all ages, is able to do that. But in those words the mystery itself meets with an incomparable form of expression. Because the psalms sing of so vast a range of human experiences, they are capable of illuminating with power and life all the vicissitudes the whole Christ will encounter throughout history.

Very striking is the fact that the majority of the psalms that are interpreted through the idea of the *totus Christus* belong to the category of individual laments. Nevertheless it is not only the themes of such psalms—affliction, trust, thanksgiving for God's assistance—that make them fit to articulate Christ's life, whether the life of the Head or that of the body. Their suitability derives far more from their formal structure: the "I" who is heard in these psalms speaks for both

---

241. See Exp. Ps 68,s.1,2.
242. See Exp. Ps 90,s.2,1. Compare H. Mühlen: *Una mystica persona*, 86.

the unique figure of Christ and the unity of his body, but it is also the voice of Head and body together, the voice of the "one man."[243]

j) The advance in theological understanding offered by prosopological exegesis

The result was that the risky wholesale interpretation of the psalms in reference to Christ, as Augustine understood it, proved repeatedly to be a gain in knowledge of Christ. If at first it seemed likely that some words in the psalms would threaten the personal mystery of the God-man, nonetheless the mode of understanding entailed by the prosopological option for the "voice of Christ" led to a deeper understanding of Christ's person, seen in its true dimensions only as "the whole Christ." The principles of inclusivity, exemplary function and prefiguration broadened the range of psalm words that could be interpreted as utterances of Christ, and gave a soteriological and ecclesiological dimension to Christ's prayer. Though Augustine's reflection on the mystery of the "whole Christ" was principally conducted within his exposition of the psalms, the heuristic value of patristic exegesis for theological thought was thereby demonstrated.

That such exegesis is in no way alien to biblical thought is proved by the concept of corporate personality, which can be regarded as the Old Testament's correlative to Augustine's idea of the *totus Christus*. If that Old Testament concept and the Augustinian idea were both manifested precisely in the "I" of the psalms, that only goes to show how fully Augustine through both intuition and reflection understood how to take up and prolong the theology contained in the psalms. Augustine's originality within the patristic tradition of exegesis may be seen especially in this broadening of Christological understanding of the psalms to embrace ecclesiological perspectives, and its synthesis in the idea of the *totus Christus*.

12. The Psalms as the Song of the Eternal City of God

a) The transcendent and eschatological dimension of the psalms

The psalms offer not only a timeless reflection of men and women and a therapy for their affective life, nor are they only a prophecy about Christ and the Church fulfilled in the past and the present. Rather do the biblical words have a transcendent and eschatological dimension, which exposition does its best to unlock.

---

243. See Exp. Ps 40,1.

Augustine's thinking was increasingly marked by a basic conviction about the last things. In contrast to his earlier writings, his later work tended ever more strongly to defer blessedness until the hereafter, and to distinguish more and more sharply between the Church on earth (*ecclesia terrestris*) and the Church in heaven (*ecclesia caelestis*). With advancing age the bishop became increasingly conscious of the distance in space and time which characterized the relationship of bride and Bridegroom, Head and body, heavenly and earthly Jerusalem, God and humankind, in this in-between period (*interim*).

A tendency in his interpretation that focused on eschatological and transcendent realities—expectation of events at the end of time, and our ultimate mode of existence in eternity—was only the exegetical consequence of this insight on Augustine's part. To interpret the psalms in function of this time-scheme served to endow them with a significance that corresponded to faith and experience under the new covenant, a significance that took account of the tension between the "already" and the "not yet."

Augustine had earlier described the relationship between Old and New Testaments principally by the pattern of promise-fulfillment, or veiled-unveiled, in order to contemplate the mysteries of Christ and the Church as depicted in advance. But he was equally conscious of the abiding regime of promise which characterized the New Testament itself, the eschatological fulfillment of which is still outstanding.[244] Hence the words of the Old Testament refer to an eschatological reality over and above their preliminary fulfillment in the New Testament, and provide the person who prays with a form of expression still valid in the time of the new covenant.[245]

Here again the principle of reciprocal illumination, already noticed in other connections, holds sway. The eschatological realities known in the light of the New Testament lead to discovery of their prefigurations in the Old Testament; but conversely these foreshadowings serve to enrich the eschatological faith of the Church with imagery from the psalms, and to bring it to articulation in forms of prayer.[246]

At the Old Testament stage of revelation, from which the psalms sprang, there was neither express hope for life after death nor any clear comprehension of immortality. This posed a problem for the Christian exegete: how could biblical words testify to a hope that was not accessible before Christ's resurrection?

Convinced of the prophetic character of the Old Testament words, and of the legitimacy of presupposing the beginnings of the resurrection-faith of later ages in the time of the psalmists, Augustine read the psalms in the light of Christian escha-

---

244. See Exp. Ps 89,10; 67,20.
245. See Exp. Ps 129,6; 88,s.2,14.
246. See Exp. Ps 93,27.

tology. Whatever appeared to him in this light to be an Old Testament prefiguration of the Church's faith was interpreted as a witness to Christian hope.

b) The psalms in the period of tension between promise and fulfillment

Faced with not a few difficulties that resulted from the approach to interpretation just described, Augustine resorted to various expository schemes in order to
achieve harmony between the biblical words and the faith of the Church. To
begin with, the psalmist's experience of salvation in the present (*He has delivered my soul from death,* Ps 114(116):8) had to remain as a pointer to an eschatological fulfilment[247] in the plenary New Testament sense. But where contingent
experiences were articulated in the psalms (*Lo, how old you have made my days!*
Ps 38:6(39:5)) it was right to open these verses up to the Christian perspectives
of hope.[248] To this end the exegete constantly made use of the characteristic
antitheses, "now . . . then" (*nunc . . . tunc*), "here . . . there" (*hic . . . ibi*), "in hope
. . . in reality" (*in spe . . . in re*), or of the concepts "not yet" (*nondum*) and
"meanwhile" (*interim*), to bring the meaning of the psalms into approximation
with the ways in which a praying Christian could understand them.

c) The triumph of iniquity, and the answer given by the psalms

It was especially the theme of the suffering of the righteous under the
onslaught of the godless, developed in so many psalms, that Augustine transposed both to the concrete situation of the Church at large and to the timeless
problem of theodicy. In the process, however, a change brought about through
the vindicating intervention of God, as hoped for by the psalmist, was referred
by the expositor to the final judgment of the world. In the face of the undiminished activity of the wicked in his own times, Augustine could allow to the many
assertions in the psalms about their fate (*The Lord . . . destroys all sinners* Ps
144(145):20) an eschatological fulfillment only.[249] The contrast between the
immediate sense of the psalm words and contemporary experience left the
expositor no choice but to transpose to the end of the world the Old Testament's
expectations of an imminent intervention by God.

d) The psalms as a witness to eternal life

In a few psalm verses there was articulated an incipient hope for enduring life
with God, not to be violated even by death. Augustine led these biblical expres-

---

247. See Exp. Ps 114,7; 41,11; 70,s.2,10; 84,10; 85,16; 99,8; 127,10; 146,8; 147,20.
248. See Exp. Ps 38,9; 37,10.15; 38,21; 41,5f.10.12; 49,22.
249. See Exp. Ps 6,12; 30,II,s.3,5; 36,s.1,11.s.2,2.s.3,14; 43,6; 51,12; 53,7; 67,3.

sions to their plenary sense in the light of Christ's resurrection. It often happened that the way to such an interpretation had been decisively opened by the augmented hope in an afterlife attested to by the Septuagint, as opposed to the original Hebrew text, and accepted in the Latin versions.

The confession, *God will indeed save my soul from the grasp of hell, when he takes up my cause* (Ps 48:16(49):15), may be regarded as an intuitive expectation, grounded in the logic of faith and formulated in symbolic language, of a fellowship with God that lasts beyond death. Augustine unlocked its full meaning in view of Christ's example.[250] The same holds for the verse, *Even my flesh shall rest in hope. You will not leave my soul in hell, nor allow your holy one to suffer corruption* (Ps 15(16):9-10). Here too Augustine was able to make the psalmist's confession, which in the Greek version was already an expectation of an enduring fellowship with God, into a testimony to Christian faith in the resurrection.[251] And finally the confession, based on the Septuagint, that *my heart has hoped in him, and I have been helped. My flesh has blossomed anew* (Ps 27(28):7), becomes in Augustine's interpretation Christ's thanksgiving for his resurrection.[252]

Apart from these verses, so eminently suitable as a medium for expressing Christian eschatology, Augustine understood how to interpret other groups of ideas in an eschatological sense. These included soteriological concepts (life,[253] salvation,[254] peace,[255] joy[256]), temporal indications (morning,[257] for ever[258]), and places (the temple, Jerusalem[259]). Thus the ultimate purpose and fullest meaning of these sayings could be opened up—undiminished, enduring fullness of life in abiding with God.

e) Contemplation of God and praise of God in the heavenly Jerusalem

Augustine found the essential fulfillment of eternal life—contemplation and praise of God—described already in the psalms: to live in the Lord's house all the days of my life, that I may contemplate the Lord's delight (Ps 26(27):4) *Blessed are they who dwell in your house; they will praise you for ever and ever* (Ps 83:5(84:4)).[260] This latter verse, originally intended mostly for priests and

---

250. See Exp. Ps 48,s.2,5.
251. See Exp. Ps 15,9f.
252. See Exp. Ps 27,7.
253. See Exp. Ps 118,s.19,4; 40,3; 103,s.4,17; 145,7.
254. See Exp. Ps 41,11; 146,6.
255. See Exp. Ps 33,s.2,19; 75,5; 84,10.
256. See Exp. Ps 85,16; 99,8.
257. See Exp. Ps 58,s.2,10; 29,I,6; 29,II,16; 48,s.2,4; 89,15; 100,13.
258. See Exp. Ps 111,5; 44,33; 11,8; 30,II,s.1,5; 36,s.3,9; 48,s.2,11.
259. See Exp. Ps 121,2f; 134,26; 136,17.
260. See Exp. Ps 26,I,4; 26,II,6-8; 83,8.

Levites, runs through the whole of Augustine's expositions of the psalms like a refrain; he cites it twenty-one times. It is thus freed from the context of Jerusalem's worship theology and universalized, to permit a chiming in of the inspired word with a basic theme of Augustinian thought: the fulfillment of our desire for happiness in the eternal praise of God. How deeply the language of the psalms stamped and shaped Augustine's eschatological ideas is shown by the frequency with which this verse is cited in his other work. It was the means whereby the motif of blessedness in his thought attained an ecclesial and liturgical dimension, to discover the fulfilment of every created being in the eternal "Alleluia" of the heavenly Jerusalem.

13. Summary

The discovery of the wisdom of Christ in the psalms

As the psalms are a microcosm of the Old Testament, so the *Expositions of the Psalms* can be treated as a microcosm of Augustinian thought. As in the Book of Psalms are to be found the history of the people of Israel, the theology and spirituality of the Old Covenant, and a treasury of human experience expressed in prayer and poetry, so too does the work of expounding the psalms recapitulate and focus the experiences of Augustine's personal life, his theological reflections and his pastoral concerns as Bishop of Hippo.

The ability to unlock the fullness of the meaning of many of the words in the psalms derived not least from a special affinity on Augustine's part with the world of the psalms, from a connatural sensitivity to the soul of the psalmist. This enabled Augustine to relive sympathetically the psalmist's experiences and make them his own, and at the same time to enrich them from the substance of his own soul and allow them to become its expression. Augustine's ability to extract such meaning from the psalms sprang from the riches of his personality. His human greatness ripened and broadened in his office as a bishop of the Catholic Church to take the measure of the mystery of the *totus Christus* in all its length and breadth and height and depth (see Eph 3:18) in the biblical words.

It seems to have been reserved for the Bishop of Hippo to give full value to the idea of the "whole Christ" for exegesis of the psalms. The concept embraced the whole of history, and made it possible to extract from this book of holy scripture aspects which only the perspective of universal history can yield. Neither the short life-span of the praying individual nor the restricted history of Israel, but only the "whole Christ" who bestrides the ages was sufficient to contain and fully assimilate the gamut of individual and communal experiences poetically recorded in the psalms, from the lament of the *De profundis* to the jubilant *Alleluia!* Pilgrimage and war, exile and temple, critique of the cult and priestly sacrifice, royal dignity and levitical service, illness and ecstasy, betrayal and brotherly concord were so united in this central figure that the reality of these experiences, spiritually understood, became the expression of a single life which stretches from the morning of creation until the last day, to be consummated in eternity.

Considered as the voice of the "whole Christ" the psalms are not primarily a collection of literary texts that grew through an historical period, but the living prayer of a community, interpreted and enriched by the faith-experiences of countless generations. For Augustine the Church is therefore the all-embracing subject in whose memory the deepest meaning of the psalms, the "wisdom of Christ," is preserved and brought to mind.[261]

This memory of the Church, its tradition of prayer and practice of prayer, is now the proper place of understanding for the individual expositor of scripture. Augustine's own horizon of understanding was broadened by his acceptance of his place within the Church which he recognized as the *totus Christus*. Through participation in this greater subject, in whom the faith-experiences of countless praying people had been nourished by the psalms and preserved, Augustine obtained an access to the psalms which opened to him a dimension of the biblical words visible only in this perspective of the Church's appropriation of them throughout history. It was not least through his experiences in his episcopal office that the expositor had gained intimate familiarity with the mystery of the "whole Christ," an intimacy which helped him to maintain and explain the hidden references to the mystery in the psalms.

Augustine's exposition of the psalms aimed to transform the songs of the Old Covenant into a "new song" (*canticum novum*) by actualizing them. The singing of this new song conforms men and women more and more fully to the mystery of Christ, and thus also builds up the figure of the "whole Christ."

Augustine had seen the spiritual interpretation of the Old Testament typified in the miracle of the wine at Cana.[262] In a similar way, thanks to his skill in exegesis, the psalms too took on a new savor and a fuller meaning, since his exposition made it possible to taste the "wisdom of Christ" in their words.[263] This Augustinian charism for the spiritual interpretation of scripture, and especially of the psalms, was seized on by a Vesper hymn used for the feast of the saint, found in a twelfth-century manuscript:[264]

---

261. See Exp. Ps 21,I,15.
262. *See Homilies on the Gospel of John* 9,5 (CCL 36,93).
263. See Exp. Ps 21,I,15.
264. C. Blume (ed.), *Die Hymnen des Thesaurus hymnologicus H.A. Daniels (Analecta hymnica medii aevi* 52; Leipzig, 1909) 110.

Quae obscura prius erant,
nobis plane faciens,
Tu de verbis Salvatoris
dulcem panem conficis.
Et propinas potum vitae
de Psalmorum nectare.[265]

Michael Fiedrowicz

---

265. You made us see it clearly, / the truth so dark at first. / Fresh bread from Christ you baked us, / his words explained, rehearsed, / and stole the psalmist's nectar/to slake our spirits' thirst.

Exposition of Psalm 1[1]

Verse 1. Christ Jesus and the spiritual way

1. *Blessed is the person who has not gone astray in the council[2] of the ungodly.* This statement should be understood as referring to our Lord Jesus Christ, that is, the Lord-Man.[3] *Blessed is the person who has not gone astray in the council of the ungodly,* as did the earthly man who conspired with his wife, already beguiled by the serpent, to disregard God's commandments.[4] *And has not stood in the way of sinners.* Christ most certainly came in the way of sinners by being born as sinners are; but he did not stand in it, for worldly allurement did not hold him. *And has not sat in the seat of pestilence*: he did not want an earthly kingdom and the pride that goes with it. Such pride is rightly understood as the seat of pestilence because there is hardly anyone who is free of the love of wielding power or does not long for human glory. For a pestilence is a disease which has spread widely and overwhelms all, or nearly all. Alternatively, the seat of pestilence might more appropriately be understood as harmful doctrine, the dissemination of which creeps like a cancer.[5] What is more, the order of the words, "gone astray," "stood," "sat," should be examined closely; for he[6] "went astray" when he drew back from God, he "stood" when he was seduced by sin, he "sat" when, once established in his pride, he could not return unless set free by

---

1. This *Exposition*, like many of those on Psalms 1-32, is impersonal in tone, a piece written rather than preached. Augustine's tone is markedly different in those *Expositions* which were sermons to the people. The first of these is *Exposition* 2 of Psalm 18.
2. Or "counsel": the Latin *consilium* can mean either an assembly of people who deliberate, or the advice they give. The former sense is more appropriate to the psalm in general, and to its fifth verse in particular; the latter is preferable a few lines below, where Adam is in question.
3. *Hoc est [de] homine dominico*; he is being a little over-scrupulous about his language, making it quite clear that he limits the reference to the human nature of Christ. In *Revisions* I,19,8, where Augustine is reviewing his two books on the Sermon on the Mount, he says that in Book II,6, he used this expression, *homine dominico*. "But I do not see," he continues, "whether the one who is the mediator between God and men, the man Christ Jesus (see 1 Tm 2:5) is properly to be called *homo dominicus*, the Lord's man, since he is, of course, *Dominus*, the Lord. But what person in his, the Lord's, holy family [that is the Church] cannot be called a *homo dominicus*? And indeed I used this expression, because I found it in some Catholic commentators on the divine scriptures [the Maurists refer to Athanasius and Epiphanius]; but wherever I used it, I would rather I had not done so."
4. See Gn 3.
5. See 2 Tm 2:17.
6. Adam.

him who neither walked in the council of the ungodly nor stood in the way of sinners nor sat in the seat of pestilence.

Verse 2. Slave and free in the spirit

2. *But in the law of the Lord was his will, and on his law will he reflect day and night.* As the apostle says, *The law is not imposed on a righteous person* (1 Tm 1:9); but it is one thing to be in the law, something else to be under the law. Whoever is in the law acts according to the law; whoever is under the law is acted upon according to the law. The former, therefore, is free, the latter a slave. What is more, the law which is written and imposed on the one enslaved is one thing, whereas the law which is discerned with the mind by the one who does not need the law is another.

He will reflect day and night: this could be understood as "without ceasing," or else "by day" means in joyfulness, "by night" in tribulations. For it is said, *Abraham saw my day, and rejoiced* (Jn 8:56); and of tribulation it is said, *Even into the night my inward parts rebuked me* (Ps 15(16):7).

Verse 3. Christ the tree by the running waters

3. *He will be like a tree planted alongside the running waters.* This may refer to Wisdom itself, who deigned to assume humanity for our salvation, so that it is the human Christ who is planted like a tree by the running waters; for what is said in another psalm, *the river of God is brimming with water* (Ps 64:10(65:9)), can also be taken in this sense. Or again, it can be referred to the Holy Spirit, concerning whom it is said, *He himself will baptize you with the Holy Spirit* (Mt 3:11); and in another place, *If anyone is thirsty, let him come and drink* (Jn 7:37); and again, *If you knew the gift of God, and who it is who is asking you for water, you would have asked of him, and he would have given you living water. Anyone who drinks of the water I shall give will never be thirsty, for it will become in that person a fountain of water springing forth to eternal life* (Jn 4:10, 13-14). Another possibility is that *alongside the running waters* means, because of the sins of the peoples, partly because waters mean peoples in the Book of Revelation;[7] and partly because the running stream is not implausibly understood as "falling," something which is applicable to wrongdoing. That tree, therefore, is our Lord, who draws those who are in the way[8] from the running waters, that is, from the peoples who sin. By drawing them into the roots of his discipline he *will bring forth fruit*; that is, he will establish churches, but *in due time*, that is, after he has been glorified by his resurrection and ascension into heaven. Once the

---

7. See Rv 17:15.
8. The way of sinners (v. 1), in which he did not stand.

Holy Spirit had been sent to the apostles, and once they had been established in their faith in him and sent out to the peoples, he bore the churches as his fruit.

His leaves will not fall off: this means that his word will not be ineffectual; although *all flesh is but grass, and human glory like the flower of grass; the grass is dried up and the flower is fallen, yet the word of the Lord abides for ever* (Is 40:6-8). *And whatever he does will prosper*, namely, whatever the tree bears, its fruits and leaves, which stand for deeds and words.

Verse 4. Pride and the inner man

4. *The ungodly are not like this, but like dust which the wind sweeps away from the face of the earth.* Here the word "earth" is to be understood as that steadfastness in God of which it is said, *The Lord is my allotted inheritance; indeed my inheritance is glorious to me* (Ps 15(16):5.6). Accordingly scripture says, *Wait for the Lord and heed* [9] *his ways, and he will exalt you to possess the earth for your inheritance* (Ps 36(37):34); and similarly, *Blessed are the gentle, for they will inherit the earth* (Mt 5:4). We can find an analogy for this. As this visible earth nourishes and sustains human life outwardly, so that other invisible earth[10] nourishes and sustains our inner being. From the face of this earth the ungodly are swept away by the wind, that is, by pride, because it puffs them up (see 1 Cor 8:1). Someone who was on guard against this, being inebriated by the bounty of God's house and intoxicated by its torrent of pleasure, prayed, *Let not the foot of pride come near me* (Ps 35:12(36:11)). From this earth pride cast forth him who said, *I will set my throne in the north, I shall be like the Most High* (Is 14:13-14).[11] From the face of this earth he too was cast forth by pride who, after agreeing to taste the forbidden fruit in order to be like God, hid himself from the face of God.[12] That this earth is where our inner life belongs, and that we are cast forth from it by pride, is most clearly understood from the text, *What business have earth and ashes to be proud? Even in life he has thrown away his inmost parts* (Sir 10:9-10).[13] It is not unreasonable to say that "he was cast out" from the place whence he cast himself out.

---

9. Reading *observa* instead of the text's *obsecra*, "entreat," which makes no sense and could be the slip of a copyist.
10. That is, "the Lord, my allotted inheritance."
11. A text from a passage which refers immediately to the king of Babylon, but which from the beginning tradition has applied to Satan; see Lk 10:18, Rv 12:3-9.
12. See Gn 3:8.
13. The text is obscure, but apparently the original means that even in their lifetime human beings begin to suffer bodily decay. Augustine uses it differently.

Verse 5. The distinction between the ungodly and sinners

5. *Therefore the ungodly do not rise in the place of judgment.* Obviously not, because they are whirled away from the face of the earth like dust. Rightly did the psalm say that the very thing the proud crave, namely, to exercise judgment, is taken away from them. The point is made more clearly in the following clause: *nor sinners in the assembly of the just.* It is usual that what is said in the first half of a verse should be repeated more clearly, as it is here. Thus those who are now called *sinners* are to be identified with *the ungodly,* and the earlier phrase, *in the place of judgment,* is here expressed as *in the assembly of the just.* Or, at any rate, if the ungodly are one thing, and sinners another, in the sense that every ungodly person is a sinner, but not all sinners are ungodly, still *the ungodly do not rise in the place of judgment.* That is to say, they rise indeed, but not to be judged, because they have already been consigned to most sure and certain punishment. Sinners, on the other hand, do not rise *in the assembly of the just* in order to exercise judgment, but perhaps rather that they may be judged. Hence it is said of them, *The work of each one will be disclosed for what it is, for it will be revealed by fire. If the work anyone has put into building survives, that builder will be rewarded. If anyone's work is burnt up, he will suffer the loss; but he himself will be saved indeed, though it be through fire* (1 Cor 3:13-15).

Verse 6. God's knowledge and being

6. *For the Lord knows the way of the just.* As the proverb says, "Medicine knows health but does not know diseases," and yet diseases too are diagnosed by medical skill; so too it can be said that the Lord knows the way of the just, but does not know the way of the ungodly. This does not mean that there is anything the Lord does not know, but he did say to sinners, *I never knew you* (Mt 7:23). However, to say, *the way of the ungodly will perish,* is substantially the same as saying, "The Lord does not know the way of the ungodly"; but it makes the point clearer that to be unknown to the Lord is to perish, and to be known by him is to remain. Thus being corresponds to God's knowledge, and non-existence to not being known, for the Lord said, *I AM WHO I AM. Thus shall you say to the children of Israel, HE WHO IS has sent me to you* (Ex 3:14).

Exposition of Psalm 2

Verses 1-3. The raging of the nations

1. *Why have the nations raged, and the peoples devised futile schemes? The kings of the earth have arisen, and the rulers conspired together against the Lord and against his Christ.* The question "Why?" is asked as if to suggest "in vain," for they have not accomplished their end, that Christ be destroyed. This is said with reference to Christ's persecutors, who are spoken of also in the Acts of the Apostles.[1]

2. *Let us burst their chains asunder, and throw their yoke away from us.* Although this might be understood otherwise, it is most suitably taken to refer to those who, he said, were devising futile schemes. The meaning, then, of *Let us burst their chains asunder, and throw their yoke away from us* is, "Let us do our utmost to ensure that the Christian religion does not fetter us[2] and is not imposed on us."

Verse 4. God's derision

3. *He who lives in heaven will laugh them to scorn, and the Lord will mock them.* The opening clause is repeated, for instead of the initial *He who lives in heaven* we have another expression, *the Lord*; and instead of *will laugh them to scorn* the psalm uses *will mock.*[3] None of this, however, is to be understood in a bodily sense, as though God laughed with his cheeks or expressed mockery with his nose; it must be referred to the capacity which he gives to his saints. They foresee what is to come, that the name of Christ and his lordship will spread to future generations and be acknowledged among the nations; and so they are enabled to understand that those others have devised futile schemes. This capacity, whereby such things are foreseen, is God's laughter and derision. *He who lives in heaven will laugh them to scorn*: if we understand heaven to be the

---

1. See Acts 4:25-27.
2. *Ut non nos alliget*: the verb is kin to *religare*, to bind, make fast, whence, probably, the noun "religion" is derived.
3. *Subsannabit*, to mock or deride with gestures. In the following lines Augustine refers it to the nose, as, perhaps, something that is "looked down."

71

souls of the saints, it is through them that God, who knows quite well in advance what is to happen, will deride and mock his enemies.

Verse 5. God's anger

4. *Then he will speak to them in his anger, and in his rage he will throw them into disarray.* The psalm now shows more clearly how he speaks to them by saying, *He will throw them into disarray.* His *anger* is the same thing as his *rage.* However, the Lord God's anger and rage should not be thought of as any disturbance in his mind, but as the power by which he most justly punishes, for the whole creation is subjected to him and at his service. Something which is particularly to be remembered and borne in mind is expressed in the Wisdom of Solomon: *You judge in tranquillity, O Lord of might, and govern us with great forbearance* (Wis 12:18). God's anger, then, is the emotion which occurs in the mind of someone who knows God's law, when it sees that same law being transgressed by a sinner. Through this emotion in the souls of the just many things are avenged. God's anger could also reasonably be interpreted as the very darkening of the mind which befalls those who transgress God's law.

Verse 6. Christ rules over Zion, the Church

5. *Yet I have been established by him as king over Zion, his holy mountain, preaching the Lord's decree.* This statement is obviously put into the mouth of our Lord Jesus Christ himself. But as for Zion, if it means "Lookout Post," as some translate it, we should understand it as nothing other than the Church, whose gaze is daily lifted with longing toward the contemplation of God's glory, as the apostle[4] says, *We, with unveiled faces, contemplate the glory of the Lord* (2 Cor 3:18). This, then, is the meaning: "I have been established by him as king over his holy Church, which he calls a mountain because of its lofty dignity and stability." *I have been established by him as king,* I, whose chains they were plotting to burst asunder, whose yoke they planned to throw away. *Preaching his decree:* yes, who does not experience this, when it is being done repeatedly, day after day?

Verse 7. The eternal Son of God

6. *The Lord said to me, You are my Son, today have I begotten you.* It might seem that the day on which Jesus Christ was born in human form is here spoken of prophetically; but the statement is more probably to be referred to his eternal

---

4. Paul, as habitually in Augustine.

birth. The word *today* signifies the present, and in eternity there is nothing which is past, as though it had ceased to be, nor future, as though not yet in existence; there is present only, because whatever is eternal always is.[5] By this phrase, *today have I begotten you*, the most true and Catholic faith proclaims the eternal generation of the Power and Wisdom of God,[6] who is the only-begotten Son.

Verse 8. The salvation of all nations

7. *Ask of me, and I will give you the nations as your heritage.* This verse, on the contrary, is to be understood in a temporal sense, of the manhood he took upon himself, he who offered himself as a sacrifice to supersede all sacrifices, and intercedes for us still (see Rom 8:34). The words, *ask of me*, then, may be referred to the whole temporal dispensation made for the benefit of the human race, namely that the nations are to be joined to the name of Christ and so redeemed from death, and become God's possession. *I will give you the nations as your heritage* means "May you possess them for their salvation, and may they bear for you spiritual fruit." *And the ends of the earth for your possession*: here the same idea is repeated. *The ends of the earth* replaces *nations* to make it clearer that all nations are envisaged, and *your possession* is used instead of the previous *your heritage*.

Verses 9-10. Spiritual rule over the earth

8. *You will rule them with an iron rod*, that is, with unbending justice, *and you will dash them to pieces like a potter's vessel*, that is, you will dash to pieces in them earthly desires and the muddy preoccupations of the old man[7] and whatever has been contracted or implanted from the slime of sin.

And now . . . it is speaking to these "kings" who are renewed already. You whose grimy garments have been destroyed, those carnal implements of delusion which belong to your former life, *understand now*; you are already kings; you are strong enough to subdue whatever in you is servile and brutish, and strong enough to fight, not like people beating the air, but chastening your bodies and bringing them into subjection.[8] So *be instructed, all you who judge the earth*. The same idea is expressed twice: *be instructed* has the same meaning as *under-*

---

5. The radical difference between the eternal "now" of God, and the slippery elusiveness of time which characterizes the life of creatures, fascinated Augustine all his life. For a prolonged meditation on it, compare his *Confessions*, Book XI.
6. See 1 Cor 1:24.
7. See Gn 2:7; the fashioning of Adam from the earth is evoked in the following words. The "old man" is in Saint Paul's teaching the whole human being, mind as well as body, before regeneration by grace.
8. See 1 Cor 9:26,27.

stand, and *you who judge the earth* as *kings*; for by those who judge the earth he means spiritual persons. Whatever we judge is beneath us, and whatever is beneath a spiritual person is rightly called "earth" because it is impaired by earthly taint.

Verse 11. The understanding of kings

9. *Serve the Lord in reverence*. This is said lest the previous address, "you kings who judge the earth," might tempt you to arrogance. *And rejoice before him with awe*: most appropriately is "rejoice" added, in case the exhortation, *serve the Lord in reverence* might induce gloom; but then, to ensure that such an invitation does not itself lead the hearers into rashness, the psalm adds, *with awe* to urge caution and the careful preservation of holiness.

And now, you kings, understand can also be interpreted as follows: "Now that I am established as king, do not be despondent as though your pre-eminence had been taken from you; but understand rather and be instructed." It is to your advantage that you be subject to him by whom understanding and instruction are given to you. It is also to your advantage not to exercise lordship irresponsibly, but to serve the Lord of all with reverence, and rejoice in most certain and most pure blessedness, while exercising due caution and consideration to avoid falling away from it through pride.

Verse 12. The way of righteousness

10. *Take hold of discipline, lest the Lord at some time grow angry and you disappear from the righteous path*. This injunction expresses the same senti- ment as *understand and be instructed*, for to understand and accept instruction is the same thing as to take hold of discipline. Nevertheless in the exhortation to *take hold of* there is a clear hint of protection and defense against everything that could harm us unless we lay hold of discipline with great care. *Lest at some time the Lord grow angry* is phrased with some uncertainty, not in relation to the vision of the prophet, to whom it is certain, but in relation to those who are being given the warning; because those to whom God's anger is not openly revealed are accustomed to think of it as uncertain. They must say to themselves, "Let us take hold of discipline, lest at some time the Lord grow angry and we disappear from the righteous path."

How we are to take the phrase, "lest the Lord grow angry" has been explained already. *And you disappear from the righteous path*: this is a great punishment which is feared by those who have any experience of the sweetness of justice, for whoever disappears from the way of righteousness will wander in great distress through the paths of iniquity.

Verse 13. God's sudden anger

11. *When his anger flares up quickly, blessed are those who trust in him.* When the punishment comes that is being prepared for the ungodly and sinners, not only will it not reach those who trust the Lord, but it will also help toward the provision and raising up of a kingdom for them. The psalm did not say, *"When his anger flares up quickly* all those who trust in him will be untroubled," as though all they could expect would be to escape punishment; it called them *blessed*, for in blessedness is the pinnacle and crown of all good things. As to his use of *quickly*, I think it means that God's anger will be something sudden, while sinners will think it far away and in the distant future.

Exposition of Psalm 3

Verse 1. David and Abessalon, figures of Christ and Judas

1. *A psalm of David when he was in flight from the face of Abessalon,*[1] *his son.*
That this psalm should be understood as spoken in the person of Christ is
strongly suggested by the words, *I rested, and fell asleep, and I arose because
the Lord will uphold me* (Ps 3:6). For this seems more in tune with the Lord's
passion and resurrection than with the particular story in which we are told about
David's flight from the face of his own son who was at loggerheads with him.[2]
And because scripture says of Christ's disciples, *The bridegroom's children
cannot fast as long as the bridegroom is with them* (Mt 9:15), it need not surprise
us if David's undutiful son foreshadows the undutiful disciple who betrayed
Jesus. The statement that he fled from his face could be understood to refer to the
historical occasion when, on Judas' departure, Jesus withdrew in the company
of the others to the Mount of Olives. But it also has a spiritual interpretation as
follows: the Son of God, that is, the power and wisdom of God,[3] deserted the
mind of Judas, when the devil took possession of him deep within. The phrase,
and the devil entered his heart (Jn 13:2.27), is rightly understood as Christ's
having fled from his face. This is not because Christ gave way to the devil but,
rather, as Christ left, the devil took possession. Such a departure is, I think,
referred to as flight in this psalm because of its speed. It is represented also by the
Lord's saying, *What you do, do quickly* (Jn 13:27).

We speak like this too in everyday conversation. We say, "It has escaped
me," of something which will not come to mind, or again of a very learned
person we say, "Nothing escapes him." That is why the truth escaped Judas'
mind when it stopped enlightening him. Abessalon, according to some inter-
preters, means "a father's peace." It may seem strange that it could mean "a
father's peace," either in the story in Kings,[4] when Abessalon waged war against
his father, or in the New Testament story where Judas was the one who betrayed
the Lord. But in the first story, those who read carefully see that in that particular

---

1. The reading of the best manuscripts. The editors substitute *Absalom*.
2. See 2 Sm 15-18.
3. See 1 Cor 1:24.
4. Augustine refers to 1,2,3,4 Kings. Today we refer to the same books as 1,2 Samuel and 1,2
Kings.

war David had made his peace with his son, for he certainly mourned his death with intense grief, saying, *Abessalon, my son, if only I could have died in your stead!* (2 Sm 18:33). Similarly in the New Testament story, we see the endless and quite amazing patience of our Lord. He put up with Judas for a very long time, as though he were good, although the Lord was not unaware of what Judas was thinking. Moreover he admitted Judas to the feast at which he entrusted the sacrament[5] of his body and blood to his disciples and handed it over to them. And at the very moment of betrayal he accepted Judas' kiss. From all this it is clear that Christ offered peace to his betrayer, even though Judas was devastated by the internal war of so wicked a scheme. This is why Abessalon is called "a father's peace." His father had the peace which he did not have himself.

Verses 2-3. Judas again

2. *Lord, how numerous are they who afflict me!* So many are they that even from the number of the disciples there was not lacking one to join the number of Christ's persecutors. *Many rise up against me; many say to my soul, "He can find no salvation in his God."* It is clear that, had they not disbelieved in the possibility of his rising from the dead, they surely would not have killed him. This is the point of their taunts, *Let him come down from the cross, if he is the Son of God*, and, *Others he saved, himself he cannot save* (Mt 27:42). Neither would Judas have betrayed him, had he not been of the number of those who despised Christ and said, *He can find no salvation in his God.*

Verse 4. Incarnation

3. *But you, Lord, are my support.*[6] This is said to God from the perspective of the human nature, because the taking on of manhood is the Word made flesh. *My glory*: even he whom the Word of God took on, in such a way that God became one with him, calls God his glory. The proud should listen and learn. They should take note, they who do not want to listen when they are told, *What have you that you did not receive? And if you did receive it, why boast as though you had not?* (1 Cor 4:7).[7] *And you lift up my head.* I think that this should here be understood of the human mind itself, because it is not inappropriate to refer to it as the head of the soul which inhered in and, so to speak, grew together with the

---

5. *Figuram*. Another reading is *mysterium*.
6. The Latin noun *susceptor* is related to the verbal form *suscipio*, which can mean "I take up the cause of" or "I take something up and make it my own." Often this second meaning refers to the way a father in Roman society would acknowledge a new-born child as his own.
7. The point he is making is clearer in Latin, where "why boast?" is *quid gloriaris?*

surpassing excellence of the Word who took humanity to himself, so much so that it was not laid to one side even in the great humility of the Passion.

Verse 5. Prayer as silent shouting

4. *With my voice I have cried to the Lord.* That is, not with the voice of my body, which is produced with the noise of reverberating air, but with the voice of the heart, which is unheard by other people but makes a noise which to God is like shouting. It was by speaking in such a voice that Susanna was heard.[8] The Lord himself taught that it was with such a voice that prayer should be made behind the closed doors of one's bedroom,[9] that is to say, in the recesses of the heart, without any noise. It cannot easily be asserted that prayer offered in this kind of voice, without any sound of words coming from the body, is less real prayer; because if thoughts alien to the intention of the person praying intrude, we cannot honestly say, *with my voice I have cried to the Lord,* and this is just as true when we are praying silently in our hearts. Nor can it rightly be said except when the soul, bringing into its prayer nothing fleshly and no fleshly aspirations, speaks to the Lord, in the place where he alone hears. And this is even called shouting, because of the strength of our intention. *And he heard me from his holy mountain.* We find the Lord himself spoken of as a mountain by the prophet; as scripture tells us, the stone cut without hands grew to the size of a mountain.[10] But this cannot be understood with reference to the Lord's own person, unless perhaps he wanted to speak like this: "Out of myself, as if from his holy mountain, he heard me, because he dwelt in me," that is, in this very mountain. But it is clearer and more straightforward if we understand it as saying that God has heard from the place of his own justice; for it was just that he should raise again from the dead the innocent one who had been killed, the innocent one to whom evil had been repaid for good, and should repay his persecutors their due. So we read, *Your justice is like God's mountains* (Ps 35:7(36:6)).

Verse 6. Christ's willing sleep

5. *I rested and fell asleep.*[11] It is not inappropriate to notice that the use of the "I" expresses the idea that Jesus underwent death of his own volition in accordance with his statement, *For this the Father loves me: because I lay down my life that I may take it up again. No one takes it away from me; I have the power to*

---

8. See Dn 13:44.
9. See Mt 6:6.
10. See Dn 2:34-35.
11. Variant readings include *somnium coepi,* "I have begun a dream," and *soporatus sum,* "I have fallen into a deep sleep."

lay it down, and I have the power to take it up again (Jn 10:17-18). What Christ said was this: you did not arrest me and put me to death as though against my will; no, *I rested and fell asleep, and I arose because the Lord will uphold me.* The scriptures contain countless examples of "sleep" being used to mean "death." For example, the apostle Paul says, *I would not have you ignorant, brothers and sisters, about those who have fallen asleep* (1 Thes 4:12). Nor need anyone ask why *I fell asleep* is added after *I rested* had already been said. The scriptures have frequent repetitions like this. I have earlier shown that there are many in the second psalm. But some manuscripts have *I have slept and fallen into a deep sleep.* And different translations express it differently, depending on their interpretation of the Greek original. Or perhaps resting can be understood of one who is dying, and sleep of one already dead, so that resting is the transition to being asleep, as waking up is the transition to being awake. Nor should we think that such repetitions in the holy books are worthless rhetorical flourishes. *I rested and fell asleep* is rightly understood as "I gave myself over to suffering, and death followed."

It continues, *And I arose, because the Lord will uphold me.* The way in which the psalmist has in one and the same sentence used both past and future tenses is particularly worth noticing. He said, *I arose,* which is in the past tense, and *he will uphold me,* which is in the future. He certainly would not have been able to arise without such support. But in prophecy the future is quite rightly mixed with the past, because those things which are prophesied as still to come are in the future as far as time is concerned, but with regard to the knowledge of those prophesying, they are already to be considered as over and done. Verbs in the present tense are also mixed in. They will be dealt with in their proper place, when they occur.

Verse 7. How scripture expresses God's speaking

6. *I shall not fear the thousands of people surrounding me.* It is recorded in the gospel how great a multitude stood around Christ as he suffered on the cross. *Arise, Lord, save me, my God.* The plea, *arise,* is not addressed to a God who is asleep or lying down, but it is conventional in holy scripture to attribute to the person of God what he effects in us. This does not, of course, hold in every instance, but only where it is appropriate to say so, as when he himself is said to speak, when by his gift prophets speak or apostles or other messengers of the truth. This is why we find a phrase like this: *Do you presume to interrogate Christ, who speaks through me?* (2 Cor 13:3). He does not say, "interrogate him by whose enlightenment or command I speak"; he directly attributes that very utterance to him by whose gift he was speaking.

Verse 8. Spiritual teeth

7. *Because you have struck down all those who oppose me without good cause.* This should not be punctuated as if it were one sentence: *Arise, Lord, save me, my God, because you have struck down all those who oppose me without good cause,* for it was not because he smote his enemies that he saved him, but rather, having first saved him, he struck them down. Therefore it refers to what follows. It means *because you have struck down all who oppose me without good cause, you have broken the teeth of sinners.* In other words, in striking down all those who oppose me, you have broken their teeth. The punishment of those who block the way is that their teeth are broken. These represent the words of sinners, which tear apart the Son of God with their curses. They are brought to nothingness, as though to dust. We should understand teeth as words of cursing. Paul the apostle speaks about teeth in this way: *If you bite each other, take care that you are not gobbled up by one another* (Gal 5:15). The phrase, "the teeth of sinners," can also be understood as those sinful leaders by whose authority a person is cut off from the community of those who live upright lives, and is incorporated, so to speak, into those who live corruptly. Opposed to these teeth are the teeth of the Church, by whose authority believers are cut clean away from the error of the heathen and of a whole range of heterodox opinions, and are brought over into that society which is Christ's body. Peter was told to slaughter animals and eat them with teeth like this,[12] which means to kill in the Gentiles what they were and change it into what he himself was. And of these teeth of the Church it is said, *Your teeth are like newly-shorn flocks, coming up from their washing. All of them bear twins; there is never a barren one among them* (Sg 4:2; 6:5). These are the people who teach correctly and live in accordance with what they teach, the people who do what scripture says, *Let your deeds shine before men and women in such a way that they bless your Father who is in heaven* (Mt 5:16). The integrity of these people makes a profound impact on others, who believe in the God who speaks and works through them. They separate themselves from the world to which they were once conformed and cross over to join the members of the Church.[13] And for this reason it is right to describe those teeth, through which these things happen, as shorn sheep, because they have set aside the burdens of earth-bound cares. Rising from the sheep-dip, from the washing away of the filth of the world through the sacrament of baptism, all give birth to twins, for they fulfill the twin commandments of which it is said, *On these two commandments depend all the law and the prophets* (Mt 22:40): they love God with all their heart and with all their soul and with all their mind, and their neighbor as themselves. There is not one among them who is barren,

---

12. See Acts 10:13.
13. An early hint of a distinction which becomes a part of the argument of his *City of God.*

because they yield to God fruits such as these. *You have broken the teeth of sinners* should, therefore, be understood in the sense, "you have brought to nothing the chief sinners, by striking down all who oppose me without good cause." For it was the leaders who, according to the gospel story, persecuted him, while the inferior rabble held him in honor.

Verse 9. Salvation is from the Lord alone

8. *Salvation is the Lord's, and may your blessing be upon your people.*[14] In a single sentence the psalmist has taught people what to believe and he has prayed for believers. When he says, *Salvation comes from the Lord* , he is addressing everyone. But he does not go on to say, "And may his blessing be over his people," as though the whole verse were addressed to everyone; at this point it turns into a prayer to God himself, on behalf of the very people who have just been told, *salvation is of the Lord.* What is the psalmist saying, then, if not, "Let nobody presume on himself, because it is for the Lord to save from the death of sin"? So Paul asks, *Who will deliver me from this death-ridden body, wretch that I am? Only the grace of God, through Jesus Christ our Lord* (Rom 7:24-25). Do you then, Lord, bless your people, who hope for salvation from you.

Prayer of the whole Christ

9. This psalm can also be understood with reference to the person of Christ in another way, namely, that the whole Christ is speaking:[15] Christ in his totality, I say, in concert with his body of which he is the Head, according to the apostle Paul who says, *You are Christ's body, and his limbs* (1 Cor 12:27). Therefore he is the Head of this body. That is why Paul says elsewhere, *By doing the truth*[16] *in love, let us grow in every respect in him who is the Head, Christ, from whom the whole body is united and consolidated* (Eph 4:15-16). Therefore in these prophetic words the Church is speaking together with its Head, the Church beset by the storms of persecution throughout the whole earth, as we know to be the case already. *Lord, how numerous are they who afflict me! Many rise up against me*, intent on destroying the Christian name once for all. *Many say to my soul, "He can find no salvation in his God."* They could not hope to destroy the

---

14. The same verse is treated in Exposition of Psalm 70, 16 and Exposition of Psalm 145, 9.
15. A key idea of Augustine's. Christ prays, Head and members; Christ is served in the person of his members.
16. *Veritatem facientes in caritate.* The expression "to do truth" is awkward in English, but attempts to capture the meaning in the Greek of Ephesians and Augustine's Latin version. "Truth" is originally what is genuine, reliable, real, and trustworthy; it is a moral quality of God, and by derivation of human beings also. An aspect of this is truthful speech.

Church, which is already branching out far and wide, unless they did not believe it to be to under God's care and protection. *But you, Lord, are my support*: in Christ, of course. For in the human Christ Jesus, the Church has been taken up by the Word, who *was made flesh and has dwelt among us* (Jn 1:14), because God has made us sit together with him even in the heavenly places.[17] Where the Head goes first, the other limbs will follow, for who will separate us from the love of Christ?[18]

The Church, therefore, is right to say, *You are my support, my glory*, for it does not attribute its pre-eminence to itself, since it understands by whose grace and mercy it is what it is. *And you lift up my head*. This, of course, refers to the one who is the firstborn from the dead[19] and who ascended into heaven. *With my voice I have cried to the Lord, and he heard me from his holy mountain*: this is the prayer of all the saints, the sweet savor which rises in the Lord's sight; for even now the Church is being heard from that mountain which is its Head, or from that justice of God by which his elect are set free and their persecutors punished.

Let God's people also say this: *I have slept and taken rest, and I arose because the Lord will uphold me*; let them pray so, that they may be joined and connected to their Head. For to this people it is said, *Arise, sleeper, and rise from the dead, and Christ will take hold of you*. (Eph 5:14).[20] This is because God's people are gathered in from among sinners, about whom it is said more generally, *Those who sleep, sleep by night* (1 Thes 5:7). Let God's people also say, *I shall not fear thousands of people surrounding me*, heathen peoples, that is, closing in, bent on extinguishing the Christian name everywhere if they possibly can. But why should they be feared, when the warm glow of love is kindled by the blood of those martyred for the sake of Christ, as if by oil? *Arise, Lord, save me, my God*: the body can say this to its Head; for the body is saved by the raising of him who ascended on high, led captivity captive, and gave gifts to humankind.[21] This is said by the prophet, giving expression to God's predestined purpose until the ripe harvest, spoken of in the gospel,[22] brought our Lord to earth;[23] its salvation was to be found in the resurrection of him who condescended to die for us.

Because you have struck down all those who persecute me without good cause, you have broken the teeth of sinners. The Church reigns even now, and

---

17. See Eph 2:6.
18. See Rom 8:35.
19. See Col 1:18.
20. The best reading in the original Greek of this verse is, "Christ will enlighten you," with probable reference to baptism. A variant reading is "you will touch/grasp/attain to Christ." Augustine's Latin version *continget te Christus* seems to reflect a hybrid reading.
21. See Ps 67:19(68:18); Eph 4:8.
22. See Mt 9:37.
23. Or "shed our Lord into the earth," with reference to Jn 12:24-25.

the enemies of the Christian name have been struck down and thrown into disarray; and either their abusive words or their leaders, whichever interpretation you prefer, have been reduced to oblivion. Believe, therefore, all of you, that *salvation comes from the Lord*; and we beg you, Lord, that *your blessing may be on your people*.

Individual application

10. Each one of us can also say, when a whole host of vices and desires leads the struggling mind under the law of sin, *Lord, how numerous are they who afflict me! Look how many rise up against me!* Usually it is amid the rising tide of misfortunes that loss of hope for the recovery of health sets in. It is as if these very ills were taunting the soul, or even as if the devil and his angels were working through poisonous suggestions to make us lose hope. So this saying contains a very great truth: *Many say to my soul, "He can find no salvation in his God." But you, Lord, are my support*. For this is the basis of my hope, that God has deigned to take on human nature in Christ. *You are my glory*: this is said in accordance with the rule that nobody should attribute anything to himself. *And you lift up my head*. This could mean either Christ himself who is the Head of all of us, or the spirit of each one of us, because our spirit is the head of soul and flesh. For *the head of the woman is the man, and the head of the man is Christ* (1 Cor 11:3). And the mind is lifted up when it can already be said, *With my mind I submit to God's law* (Rom 7:25), in the hope that the other parts of human nature may be finally pacified and subdued,[24] when by the resurrection of the flesh death is swallowed up in victory. *With my voice I have cried to the Lord*, with that innermost and most fervent voice, *and he heard me from his holy mountain*, from him, that is, through whom he came to our aid, and by whose mediation he hears us. *I rested and fell asleep, and I arose because the Lord will uphold me*. Who among the faithful cannot say this, remembering the death he died by his own sins and the gift of rebirth? *I shall not fear the thousands of people surrounding me*. Apart from those which the Church worldwide has borne and continues to bear, every individual also has temptations; they besiege us and make us say, *Arise, Lord, save me, my God*, or, in other words, "Make me arise." *Because you have struck down all who oppose me wthout good cause*: this is rightly expressed as a prophecy of predestination with reference to the devil and his angels, who not only rage against the body of Christ as a whole, but also against each one individually. *You have broken the teeth of sinners*. Each one of us has those who speak ill of us; and each of us also has those who try their

---

24. *Cetera hominis pacata subdantur*. A variant reading has *peccata*: "the other sins of a person."

hardest to lure us into vices in an attempt to cut us off from the body of Christ. But *salvation is from the Lord*. Pride is to be avoided and we must say, *My soul has clung to you* (Ps 62:9(63:8)). And *may your blessing be over your people*, that is, over every one of us.

Exposition of Psalm 4

Verse 1. Psalms and songs

1. *To the end, a psalm, a song of David*, so is the psalm entitled. Now *Christ is the end of the law, bringing justification to everyone who believes* (Rom 10:4). This "end" means perfection, not annihilation. But whether every song is a psalm, or rather every psalm a song, or whether there are certain songs which cannot be called psalms, and certain psalms which cannot be called songs, is a valid question. We must take heed of scripture, for perhaps "song" may mean only joy. Those which are sung to the accompaniment of the psaltery[1] are called psalms. The historical books tell us that David the prophet used the psaltery as part of a great mystery.[2] Here is not the place to examine this question, because it requires a protracted investigation and a lengthy discussion. Now, in the meantime, we ought to prepare ourselves for the words of the Lord-Man[3] after the resurrection, or those of any member of the Church who believes and hopes in him.

Verse 2. How God enlarges the heart

2. *When I called on him he heard me, the God of my vindication.* When I called, God, from whom my righteousness derives, heard me, says the psalmist. *When I was hard beset you led me into spacious freedom*; that is, from the cramped conditions of sorrow you have led me into the broad open fields of joy and gladness. For sorrow and distress beset the soul of everyone who works evil;[4] but contrast what Paul says: *We even rejoice in our sufferings, knowing that suffering fosters endurance*, right to the point where he ends, *because the love of God has been poured out into our hearts through the Holy Spirit who has been given to us* (Rom 5:3-5). His heart does not live in a poky little room, even though his persecutors pile in against him from without, trying their best to drive him into a corner.

---

1. See his discussion of psalteries and lyres in Exposition of Psalm 42,5; Exposition of Psalm 80,5.
2. See 1 Chr 13:8; 16:5.
3. See note on this expression, *homo dominicus*, at Exposition of Psalm 1,1.
4. See Rom 2:9.

In grammatical terms there is a change of person, a sudden shift from the third, where the psalmist says, *He heard*, to the second, where he says, *You led me into spacious freedom*. If it is not done simply for the sake of variety and elegance of style, I wonder why he wanted in the first case to show everyone that he had been heard, and in the second to address the one who heard him. Perhaps it was because after he had indicated how in the enlargement of his heart he had been heard, he preferred to talk with God; for this was another way of showing what it means to have our heart enlarged, to have God poured into our hearts already: it means that we can converse inwardly with him. This is quite reasonably understood to refer to a person who believes in Christ and has been enlightened. When applied, however, to the person of the Lord-Man, whom the Wisdom of God took to himself, I do not see how this can hold, for he was not at any time abandoned by Wisdom. But as his plea is, when properly understood, an indicator of our infirmity, so also can the same Lord speak for his faithful when the psalmist speaks about the sudden enlarging of the heart. The Lord took their person upon himself when he said, *I was hungry, and you did not feed me; I was thirsty, and you gave me nothing to drink*, and so forth (Mt 25:42). That is why here too he can say, *You led me into spacious freedom*, speaking on behalf of one of his littlest ones who converses with God, and has God's charity scattered abroad in his heart through the Holy Spirit, who has been given to us.

Have mercy on me, and hearken to my prayer. Why does he ask again, when he has already made it clear that he has been heard and enlarged? Perhaps for our sakes, because the text, *If we hope for what we do not see, we wait for it in patience* (Rom 8:25), is talking about us? Or is it so that what has been begun in the one who believes may be brought to fruition?

Verse 3. Truth and permanence

3. *How long will you be heavy-hearted, human creatures?* Let us imagine your delusion has lasted, someone suggests, until the arrival of the Son of God. But why, then, are you still heavy-hearted? When will you have done with spurious things, if you do not do so even when the Truth is present? *Why love emptiness and chase falsehood?* Why do you wish to be blessed by the most worthless things? Truth alone makes people blessed, the truth by which all things are true. For vanity is the preserve of those who exercise vanity,[5] and *all things are vanity. What more of wealth does a person gain by all his toil, all his labor under the sun?* (Eccl 1:2-3). Why therefore are you shackled to the love of temporal things? Why do you pursue things that are ultimately inconsequential

---

5. *Vanitantium*. The variant reading *vanitatum* seems too obviously derivative from the ensuing quotation.

as if they were of paramount importance? This is no more than vanity and lying. For you want all those things which pass away like a shadow to stay with you on a permanent basis.

Verse 4. The diapsalma

4. *And be sure of this: the Lord has glorified his Holy One.* Who is this, if not the one he raised from the depths and set at his right hand in heaven? The human race is admonished to turn to God, even at the eleventh hour, from its love of this world. But if the further addition of the conjunction *and* worries anyone (when he says, *And be sure of this . . .*), it is easily seen that in scripture this mode of expression is common to the language in which the prophets spoke. You often find an opening phrase like this: *And the Lord said to him*, or *And the word of the Lord came to him*. This tagging on by means of a conjunction, when there was no earlier sentence to which the sentence following can be connected, in some strange way perhaps shows the connection of the articulated expression of truth with that vision which takes place in the heart. It could be said in the present instance that the previous sentence, *Why love emptiness, and chase falsehood?* is a way of saying, "Do not love emptiness, and do not chase falsehood"; and then after it has been expressed in this rather oblique way, there follows in a very direct way of speaking: *And be sure of this: the Lord has glorified his Holy One.* But the insertion of the diapsalma[6] argues against this being joined with the previous sentence. It is not clear whether diapsalma is a Hebrew word, as some would like us to understand it, and means "So be it," or a Greek word, meaning a break in singing (so that the psalma would be what is sung to the psaltery and the diapsalma a period of silence inserted into the singing; just as the sympsalma means a uniting of voices in singing, so the diapsalma would be the separation of those voices, where a pause or disruption of continuity is marked). But whether it is either of these or another possibility again, this in any case is likely, that the sense cannot be continued and carried on without interruption, where the diapsalma is inserted.

God's listening

5. *The Lord will listen to me, when I cry to him.* I believe that here we are being warned to invoke God's assistance with great earnestness of heart, with the cry from within which does not come from the body. This is because, just as we should give thanks for light God sheds on this life, so we should pray for rest after this life. Whether this is said in the person of a faithful preacher of the

---

6. A pause.

gospel, or in the person of the Lord himself, we are to take it thus: "The Lord will hear you, when you cry to him."

Verse 5. The positive use of anger

6. *Be angry, and do not sin.* The psalmist began to wonder, Who really deserves to be heard, or how is it that the sinner cries out to the Lord and his crying is not in vain? That is why he says, *Be angry, and do not sin.* This can be understood in either of two ways:

(1) Even if you are angry, do not sin. This means: even if there wells up a strong emotional reaction, which we cannot altogether help, because of our sinful inheritance, at any rate do not let reason and the mind collude with it. The mind has been reborn within and conformed with God. The upshot of this is that with the mind we serve the law of God, even if still in the flesh we serve the law of sin.[7]

(2) Go on, repent! That is, be angry with yourselves about past sins and do not sin anymore in future.

What you say, in your hearts; to this should be added, "say," to complete the sentence like this: "What you say, say it in your hearts!" That is, do not be the people of whom scripture says, *With their lips they honor me, but their heart is far from me* (Is 29:13; Mt 15:8; Mk 7:6). *Be pierced in your own rooms.* The second part of this means the same as the phrase used already, *in your hearts*; it refers to the private room of which the Lord too advises us: he tells us to pray within, the doors firmly closed.[8] The command, *Be pierced*, may refer to the pain of repentance which the soul inflicts on itself by way of punishment, rather than being condemned and tormented by the judgment of God; or else *be pierced* is a wake-up call, prompting us to rise from sleep as though prodded with goads, so as to see the light of Christ. But some say that "be open" rather than "be pierced" is the better reading, because in the Greek psalter the word is κατανοίγητε, which refers to the broadening of the heart which makes it open to receive the love shed abroad by the Holy Spirit.

Verse 6. The sacrifice of justice

7. *Offer a sacrifice of justice, and hope in the Lord.* He says the same thing in another psalm: *A sacrifice to God is a troubled spirit* (Ps 50:19(51:17)). That is why in the present context the sacrifice offered through repentance is not unreasonably taken to be a sacrifice of justice; for what is more just than that each one

---

7. See Rom 7:25.
8. See Mt 6:6.

of us should be angry at our own sins rather than at those of others, and offer ourselves in sacrifice to God by punishing ourselves? Or are the just works which one does after repentance the sacrifice of justice? The interpolation of the diapsalma possibly suggests the passage from the old life to the new life. This means that, once the old person has been destroyed or enfeebled by repentance, a sacrifice of justice is offered to God consonant with the rebirth of the new person. The mind, now washed clean, offers itself and places itself on the altar of faith, to be consumed by the divine fire, that is, the Holy Spirit. This, then, is what *offer a sacrifice of justice, and hope in the Lord* means: "Live uprightly, and hope for the gift of the Holy Spirit, that the truth in which you believe may enlighten you."

Verse 7. Enjoyment of the good

8. Nonetheless, *Hope in the Lord* is used without further explanation as yet. What things other than good things are the object of this hope? Yet because every single individual wants to ask God for the good thing which he personally loves, it is not easy to find those who love the good things within. By this I mean those which belong to the inner person, the good things which alone are to be loved. The rest, on the contrary, are to be used to fulfill our everyday needs[9] rather than being enjoyed as objects of delight; and so after saying *Hope in the Lord*, the psalmist was quite right to add, *Many say, "Who has anything good to show us?"* This is the chatter, the daily questioning of all foolish and unjust people. Some of them crave peace and tranquillity in this earthly life, yet do not find it because people are so tiresome. So blind are they to what is really happening that they have the cheek to find fault with the way things are[10]; wrapped up in their sense of their own goodness, they think the present times worse than the past. Or again, there are those who entertain doubts or despair of that future life which is promised to us. They often say, "Who knows if it's true? Who has ever come back from the dead to tell us about these things?"

Therefore in a quite wonderful and yet concise way the psalmist shows to those who see within, the good things which are to be sought. By way of reply to the questioning of those who say, *Who has anything good to show us?* the psalmist says, *The light of your countenance is stamped upon us, O Lord*. This light is the complete and true good of humankind; it is seen not with the eyes but with the mind. The psalmist's phrase, *stamped upon us*, suggests a coin stamped with the king's picture. For the human individual has been made in God's image

---

9. Augustine famously distinguished between the goods which are useful or necessary as means to something else, and those which are to be enjoyed for themselves. To the former the verb *uti* is appropriate, to the latter *frui*. The latter only are worthy of love.

10. *Ordinem rerum.*

and likeness,[11] something which each has corrupted by sinning. Therefore true and eternal goodness is ours if we are minted afresh by being born again. And I believe that our Lord's exhortation when he saw Caesar's coin, *Render to Caesar what is Caesar's, and to God what is God's* (Mt 22:21), refers to this, as some have aptly understood it. It is as if Christ said: "Just as Caesar demands from you the mark of his likeness, so too does God; and just as money is rendered to Caesar, by the same principle the soul is rendered to God, illuminated and marked by the light of his face."

You have given joy to my heart. Joy, therefore, is not to be sought outside oneself, by those who, still heavy in heart, love emptiness and chase falsehood. Rather, it is to be sought within, where the light of God's face is stamped. For Christ dwells in the inner person, as the apostle says;[12] and to Christ belongs the capacity to see the truth, for he said, *I am truth* (Jn 14:6). When the apostle asked, *Do you presume to interrogate Christ, who speaks in me?* (2 Cor 13:3), it was not a case of Christ speaking to him outwardly; Christ spoke within him, in his very heart, in that inner room where we ought to pray.[13]

Verses 8-9. The simple spiritual good

9. But those who chase after temporal things, who are certainly many, know nothing to say other than, *Who has anything good to show us?* They cannot see the good things that are true and certain within themselves. Therefore the additional phrase which follows, *from their seasons of wheat and wine and oil they have been multiplied*, is very appropriately applied to them. The insertion *their* is not redundant, for God also has his wheat, and there is indeed living bread which comes down from heaven.[14] He has his wine too, for scripture says, *They will be inebriated by the rich abundance of your house* (Ps 35:9(36:8)). God has oil as well. This is what is said about it: *With oil you have richly anointed my head* (Ps 22(23):5). But those who say in great numbers, *Who will show us good things?* and yet do not see that the kingdom of God is within them,[15] are *multiplied from their seasons of corn, wine and olives.* For increase does not always mean plenty; it can also mean poverty. When the mind is given over to temporal pleasures, is always burning with desire and cannot be satisfied, when it is stretched this way and that by all sorts of conflicting and miserable thoughts, it does not allow itself to see the good which is uncompounded. This is the sort of mind of which it is said, *The corruptible body weighs down the soul, and this earthly*

---

11. See Gn 1:26.
12. See Eph 3:17.
13. See Mt 6:6.
14. See Jn 6:51.
15. See Lk 17:21.

dwelling oppresses a mind that considers many things (Wis 9:15). Such a mind, filled with countless images, is so distended by the rise and fall of temporal goods, that is to say, by the succession of its wheat, wine and olives, that it is incapable of fulfilling the command, *think about the Lord in goodness, and seek him in simplicity of heart* (Wis 1:1). For the proliferation of which we speak is at the opposite end of the spectrum from that simplicity. And that is why the person of faith rejoices and says, *In peace, in Being-Itself, I will rest and fall asleep,*[16] leaving aside those many people who are completely fragmented by their desire for temporal things and ask, *Who has anything good to show us?* when all the time these things are to be sought on the inside, in simplicity of heart, rather than on the outside, by using the eyes. Believers rightly hope for a complete separation of the mind from mortal things and for the opportunity to forget the miseries of this world. This is fittingly and prophetically described by the terms rest and sleep, which is where the greatest peace can be disturbed by no commotion. But this is not within our grasp at present, in this life. Instead it is something to be hoped for after this life. This is something which even the verbs themselves, which are in the future tense, show; for what is said is neither, "I rested and fell asleep," nor, "I rest and fall asleep," but *I will rest and fall asleep.* Then this corruptible nature will be clothed in incorruption and this mortal nature will be clothed in immortality; then will death be swallowed up in victory.[17] This is what lies behind the text, *if we hope for what we do not see, we wait for it in patience* (Rom 8:25).

Verse 10. Multiplicity and singleness

10. That is why, in tune with this, the psalmist adds the final verse and says, *Because you, Lord, through hope have established me in unity.*[18] He did not say, "You will establish me," but, *You have established me,* for in him this hope is already grounded, and in him most certainly this hope will be fulfilled. And the psalmist is right to say, *in unity,* by contrast to the many who are fragmented by the seasons of their wheat and wine and olives, and ask, *Who has anything good to show us?* This proliferation perishes. It is singleness which is held dear among the saints of whom it is said in the Acts of the Apostles, *The multitude of believers had but one mind and one heart* (Acts 4:32). Single, therefore, and

---

16. *In pace, in idipsum, obdormiam et requiescam.* The Latin seems to mean "In the selfsame . . . "; but in his meditation on this psalm after his conversion, described in his *Confessions* IX,4,8-11, Augustine takes it to be a mysterious name for God, Being-Itself, evoking the revelation of the divine name to Moses, Ex 3:14.
17. See 1 Cor 15:54.
18. The adverb *singulariter* could be applied to God's action: "You alone have established me;" but here and in *Confessions* IX,4,11 Augustine takes it to be the antithesis of multiplicity and dispersion in ourselves.

simple, withdrawn from the multitude and crowd of things which are born and die, we ought to be lovers of eternity and unity if we desire to become one with our God and Lord.[19]

---

19. There is thus a double contrast running through these last two paragraphs: 1) the temporal, material harvests, which are the joy of "the many," are contrasted with the spiritual bounty of God's wheat, wine, and oil in a veiled reference to the sacraments; 2) the multiplicity and dispersion of these "many" who find their joy in perishable good things is set over against the unity and eternity of the saints who find joy in God.

Exposition of Psalm 5

Verse 1. The Church's inheritance is God, and God's is the Church

1. The title of the psalm is: *For her who receives the inheritance*. The feminine pronoun is used of the Church, which receives eternal life as its inheritance through our Lord Jesus Christ, so as to possess God himself, and so as to be blessed by holding fast to him, in accordance with the promise, *Blessed are the gentle, for they will inherit the earth* (Mt 5:4). What earth is meant other than that of which it is said, *You are my hope, my portion in the land of the living* (Ps 141:6(142:5))? And this expression is even clearer: *The Lord is my allotted inheritance and my cup* (Ps 15(16):5. Alternatively the Church itself is referred to as God's inheritance, as in the following text: *Ask of me, and I will give you the nations as your inheritance* (Ps 2:8). Therefore God is said to be our inheritance because he himself feeds us and supports us. We also are spoken of as God's inheritance, because he himself takes charge of us and rules us. That is why the voice in this psalm is that of the Church called to its inheritance, so that it in turn may be the Lord's inheritance.

Verse 2. The inner cry of the Church

2. *Hear my words, Lord.* Being so called, the Church calls upon the Lord so that, with his help, she may pass through the vileness of this world and reach him. *Understand my cry*: the psalmist gives a very clear idea of what this cry is. Inasmuch as it is something interior, from the chamber of the heart, it reaches God without any bodily sound, for when the voice of the body is heard, it is the voice of the spirit that is understood. This may also be what it means for God to hear. He does so not with the ear of the body but by the presence of his majesty.

Verse 3. The Trinity, one God

3. *Give heed to the voice of my petition*, that is, to the voice which the psalmist asks God to understand. He has already suggested what sort of voice this is when he said, *Understand my cry*. Now he continues, *Give heed to the voice of my petition, my king and my God*. The Son is God and the Father is God, and Father and Son together are one God. If we ask about the Holy Spirit, no other reply is possi-

ble than that he is God. And when Father, Son and Holy Spirit are spoken of all together, nothing other than one God is to be understood. Nonetheless the scriptures tend to use the title, "king," of the Son. Therefore, in line with what scripture says, *The way to the Father is through me* (Jn 14:6), the order, *my king* and then *my God*, is correct. However the psalmist did not say, *Give heed*, in the plural, but in the singular. For it is not two or three gods that the Catholic faith preaches, but the Trinity itself, one God. It is not the case that the same Trinity can be spoken of now as the Father, now as the Son, now as the Holy Spirit, as Sabellius believed.[1] No—the Father alone is the Father, and the Son alone is the Son, and the Holy Spirit alone is the Holy Spirit, and this Trinity is none other than the one God. After saying, *From whom are all things, through whom are all things, in whom are all things*, thereby hinting at the Trinity, the apostle did not add, "To them be the glory," but, *To him be the glory* (Rom 11:36).

Verse 4. God hears the Church

4. *I will pray to you, Lord, and in the morning you will hear my voice.* How can it be that, whereas the Church said above, *Hear*, as if she wanted to be heard immediately, now she says, *In the morning you will hear me*, as opposed to *Hear*; and further says, *to you I will pray*, rather than, "to you I pray"? The same holds for what follows: *in the morning I will stand before you and I will see*, rather than, "I stand before you and see now." What is the point of this change? Perhaps the earlier prayer marks the act of praying itself, but, shrouded in darkness amidst the storms of this age, the Church realizes that it does not see what it longs for, and yet does not give up hoping. For the hope which is seen is not hope.[2] However, the Church understands why it does not see, because the night is not yet over. The night represents the darkness which our sins have deserved. That is why the Church says, *I will pray to you, Lord*; that is, because you to whom I will pray are so great, *in the morning you will hear my voice.* You are not one who can be seen by those from whose eyes the night of sins has not yet withdrawn. Therefore once the night of my wandering is over, and the darkness which I brought upon myself by my sins has receded, you will hear my voice. Why, then, did the Church not use the future, *you will hear*, in the earlier instance, but instead the imperative: *Hear*? Was it because after it had cried, *Hear*,

---

1. Sabellius (early third century) was associated with the Modalist wing of the Monarchian heresy. Monarchianism was concerned to safeguard the absolute unity of the Godhead, and was therefore in itself capable of orthodox interpretation, but it became linked with heretical views. The Modalist version preached by Noetus, Praxeas, and Sabellius held that the Persons are not distinct substances in the Godhead; the one God manifests himself in different "modes" to which the names "Father," "Son," and "Spirit" are assigned.
2. See Rom 8:24.

and was not heard, it realized what must pass away in order that it may be heard? Or is it that the Church was indeed heard on the earlier occasion but does not yet understand that it has been heard, because it does not yet see him by whom it has been heard? So when it says now, *You will hear in the morning*, the Church means: "in the morning I will understand that I have been heard." Isn't it like the way we say, *Arise, Lord*, when what we mean is, "make me arise"?[3] (Well, that may refer to Christ's resurrection.) Undoubtedly the statement, *The Lord your God tests you in order to know if you love him* (Dt 13:3), cannot properly be taken otherwise than to mean, "in order that through him you may know, and it may be made clear to you how much progress you have made in his love."

Verse 5. Seeing God

5. *In the morning I shall stand before you, and contemplate.* The words, *I shall stand*, can mean nothing other than "I shall not lie down." For what else is lying down but to rest content in the earth and to seek one's blessedness in earthly pleasures? *I shall stand before you*, says the psalm, *and I will contemplate*. We should not cling to earthly things if we want to see God, who is seen with a pure heart. *You are not a God to tolerate iniquity. The wicked person will not live close by you, nor will the unjust remain before your eyes. You hate all those who work iniquity; you will destroy all those who speak a lie. A bloodthirsty and deceitful person is loathsome to the Lord.* Injustice, ill will, falsehood, murder, deceit, and anything else of this sort, are what constitute the night. Once this night has passed, morning comes, so that God may be seen. Accordingly the psalmist has set forth the reason why he will stand and will see in the morning, by saying, *Because you are not a God to tolerate iniquity*; for if God were such as to want iniquity, he could be seen by the unjust as well. This would do away with the idea that God is to be seen in the morning, that is, when the night of iniquity has passed.

Verse 6. The habit of sinning and blindness

6. *The wicked person will not live close by you*: that is, will not see in such a way as to cling to you. That is why it continues, *nor will the unjust remain before your eyes*. This is because their eyes, that is to say, their mind, is beaten back[4] by the light of truth because of the darkness of their sins. Owing to their habit of sinning they cannot endure the bright light of true understanding. Therefore even

---

3. See Ps 3:7.
4. *Reverberatur.* He uses the same verb in *Confessions* VII,10,16, when describing his attempt at Platonic ecstasy: "Your rays beamed intensely upon me, beating back my feeble gaze, and I trembled with love and dread." In the present paragraph he echoes his own experience.

those who see from time to time, that is, those who sometimes understand the truth, are still unjust, because through loving those things which distract their attention from the truth they do not remain in it. They carry their own night around with them: that is, not only the habit, but also the love, of sinning. If this night passes, that is, if they cease to sin, and the love itself and the habit are put to flight, then the morning comes in such a way that they not only understand but also hold tight to the truth.

Verse 7. Telling lies and concealing the truth

7. *You hate*[5] *all those who work iniquity.* The hatred of God is to be understood from that way of speaking by which every sinner hates the truth. For it seems that the truth also hates those whom she does not allow to remain with her. However, those who are not strong enough to endure her do not remain. *You will destroy all those who speak a lie,* for this is the opposite of the truth. But if anyone thinks that there is any substance or nature contrary to the truth,[6] let that person understand that lying belongs to what has no being, rather than to what is. For if what is is spoken, truth is spoken, but if what is not is spoken, it is a lie. Therefore, the psalmist says, *You will destroy all who speak a lie,* because by withdrawing from what is, they slide away toward what is not. Many lies admittedly seem to be told for the safety or advantage of someone, and motivated not by ill-will but by kindness, like the lie told by those midwives in Exodus who gave a false report to the Pharaoh to ensure that the babies of the children of Israel would not be killed.[7] But even such things are praised not because of what happened but for the presence of mind[8] shown. Why so? Because those who lie only in this way will deserve one day to be freed from lying altogether, for in those who are perfect, not even lies of that sort are to be found. They were told, *This is what should be on your lips: yes meaning yes, no meaning no; anything more than that is from the evil one* (Mt 5:37). Not without good reason is it written elsewhere, *A lie in the mouth kills the soul* (Wis 1:11). Otherwise someone might think that the perfect and spiritual person ought to lie for the preservation of this temporal life, by the death of which no one's soul is killed, either the perfect spiritual person's or anyone else's.

---

5. Some manuscripts here add "Lord."
6. Manicheanism, the radically dualistic theosophy to which Augustine had subscribed in his youth, held that evil and good were two aboriginal realities in conflict with each other. Augustine's long struggle to understand the nature of evil reached a turning-point when he came to think of evil as non-being, a lack where goodness ought to be.
7. See Ex 1:19.
8. *Indole.* A number of manuscripts have *in dolo,* in deceit. Augustine deals extensively with these questions in his treatises *Lying* and *Against Lying.*

But it is one thing to lie, another to cloak the truth, since it is one thing to say what is false, another to keep silent about what is true. If someone, for example, does not want to betray another person even to the death we can all see, he ought to be willing to conceal the truth, but not to tell a lie. This means that he neither betrays nor tells a lie, and avoids killing his own soul for the sake of another's body. But if he is not yet able to do this, then he should tell only those lies which are unavoidable, like those in the example above. In this way he will deserve to be freed even from those lies, if they are the only ones left, and to receive the strength of the Holy Spirit, through which he may despise whatever has to be endured for the truth's sake.

There are two types of lies to which there is no great blame attached, and yet they are not completely without blame: when we are joking and when we are lying to be helpful. The first type, spoken as a joke, is not very harmful precisely because it does not aim to deceive. The person to whom it is said knows that it was said as a joke. And the second is fairly innocuous precisely because it retains a certain amount of kindly goodwill. In fact that which has no duplicity at its heart cannot even be called a lie. Take the following example: a sword is given to someone for safekeeping and he promises to return it whenever the person who entrusted it to him asks for it back. If, then, the original owner who asks for it back has gone mad in the meantime, it is clear that he should not give it back to him there and then, but wait until his sanity is restored, in case he goes out and kills himself or other people. In this case there is no duplicity of heart, because the person to whom the sword was entrusted, when he promised that he would return it at the owner's request, did not imagine that he would ask for it back in a state of madness. Even the Lord himself concealed the truth when he said to his disciples, who were not yet strong enough for the whole story, *I have many things to tell you, but at present you are not able to bear them* (Jn 16:12), and so did the apostle Paul when he said, *Not as spiritual persons could I speak to you, but only as carnal* (1 Cor 3:1). From this it is clear that it is not culpable sometimes to keep the truth quiet. But we have no evidence that perfect disciples have ever been allowed to make false statements.

Verses 7-8. *The Church rejoices to receive mercy*

8. *A bloodthirsty and deceitful person is loathsome to the Lord.* This may quite rightly be seen as a repetition of what the psalmist said above: *You hate all those who work iniquity, you will destroy all those who speak a lie.* The parallelism works like this: you can refer *the bloodthirsty man* to "the one who works iniquity," and *deceitful* to "lying." For a definition of deceit is that someone does one thing while pretending to do another. What is more, the psalmist uses an appropriate word in saying, *loathsome,* for the disinherited are usually referred to like this. But this psalm is *for her who receives her inheritance,* and to her hope

she adds rejoicing, saying, *In the abundance of your mercy I shall enter your house.* Perhaps by these words the Church is speaking of the abundance of men and women, perfect and blessed, of whom that city[9] will consist. Here and now the Church is in labor with that multitude and is bringing them to birth little by little. But who can deny that the abundance of God's mercy refers to those many men and women who are regenerate and perfect, when it is very correctly asked, *What is a human being that you remember him, a mere mortal that you visit him?* (Ps 8:5(4)). The psalm continues, *I shall enter your house.* This means, I suppose, like a stone into a building. For what is God's house other than God's temple, of which it is said, *God's temple is holy and that temple is yourselves* (1 Cor 3:17)? The cornerstone of this building is the one whom the power and wisdom of God, coeternal with the Father, took to himself.[10]

Advancing toward the temple

9. *I shall worship in the direction of your holy temple, in fear of you.* By the words, *in the direction of your temple,* we understand "near the temple"; for the psalmist does not say, "I shall worship in your holy temple," but, *I shall worship in the direction of your holy temple.* This should be understood as suggesting not perfection itself, but the advance toward perfection: the phrase, *I shall enter your house* signifies perfection. But in order that this may happen the psalmist first says, *I shall worship in the direction of your holy temple.* And perhaps he adds *in fear of you* because this is a great source of protection for those progressing toward salvation. But when each of us has arrived, the promise of scripture will be fulfilled in us, *charity made perfect casts out fear* (1 Jn 4:18). For those to whom it is said, *I call you servants no longer, but friends* (Jn 15:15), are not afraid of one who is now a friend,[11] when they have been led right through to what was promised.

Verses 9-10. How does God punish?

10. *Lord, lead me onward in your justice, because of my enemies.* Here the psalmist has made it perfectly clear that he is on a journey, that is, on the way toward perfection, but is not yet part of that perfection itself, since what he is asking for is to be led onward. But the phrase is *in your justice,* not in what people imagine to be justice. The repaying of evil by evil looks like justice, but it is not the justice of the one of whom it is said, *He causes his sun to rise over the*

---

9. The holy city, new Jerusalem, constantly present to Augustine's mind as the goal of the Church's pilgrimage.
10. See Eph 2:20-22; 1 Cor 1:24.
11. *Amicum.* A variant reading is *amici*: "being now friends they are not afraid."

good and the wicked (Mt 5:45). When God punishes sinners, he does not inflict on them his evil but abandons them to their own evils. The psalmist says, *That person has been giving birth to injustice. Just look at him! He has conceived toil and has brought forth iniquity; he made a hole and dug it out, and then he fell into the pit which he had made. His pain shall rebound onto his own head; his iniquity shall descend to crown him* (Ps 7:15-17(14-16)). Therefore when God punishes as a judge, he punishes those who break the law, not inflicting on them evil from himself, but driving them out toward that very thing they have chosen, to fill up their misfortunes to the brim. But when a human being repays evil for evil, he does so with an evil intent. That is exactly why such a one in the first instance is himself evil in wanting to punish evil.

The spiritual journey

11. *Guide my journey in your sight.* Nothing is clearer than that the psalmist is referring to the time within which we are making progress. For this is a journey which is made not by any change of geographical location on earth, but with the desires of our minds.[12] *In your sight*, the psalmist says, *guide my journey*; that is, where no one sees, for other people are not to be trusted whether they praise or blame. They are completely incapable of passing judgment on another's conscience, where someone's path is being guided to God. That is why the psalmist has added, *because the truth is not on their lips.* He is referring to those whose judgment is in no way to be trusted, and for that reason we must take flight within, to our conscience, to the place where God sees. *Their heart is empty*: how, then, can truth be on their lips, when their heart is deceived on the matter of sin and the punishment of sin? Accordingly men and women are called back by that cry, *Why love emptiness and chase falsehood?*

Verse 11. Open graves and evil speech

12. *Their throat is an open grave.* This could refer to the ravenous appetite which often prompts people to tell flattering lies.[13] *An open grave* is exactly the right phrase to use, because such ravenous appetite is always open-mouthed. It is not like ordinary graves which are closed up once the corpses have been put inside. Another interpretation is also possible: by telling lies and employing se-

---

12. Similarly in his *Confessions*, VIII,8,19, describing the struggle preceding his conversion, Augustine reflects, "It was a journey not to be undertaken by ship or carriage or on foot . . . for to travel—and more, to reach journey's end—was nothing else but to want to go there, but to want it valiantly and with all my heart."

13. The Latin *voracitas* generally means gluttony, but this seems alien to the present context. It is perhaps better to take it as an insatiable appetite for praise or flattery.

ductive flattery people draw to themselves those whom they entice to sin, and they swallow them, so to speak, when they make them turn to their own style of life. When this happens the flatterers die through their sin,[14] and so it is right to refer to those by whom they are drawn in as open graves; indeed, they themselves are somehow lifeless in that they lack the life of truth, and they gather in to themselves the dead whom they have slain by lying words and empty hearts, making their victims into copies of themselves. *They dealt deceitfully with their tongues,* that is, with evil tongues. This is what it seems to mean when the psalmist emphasizes "their own tongues," for the evil have evil tongues, that is, they say evil things when they give voice to deceit. The Lord says to them, *How can you, who are evil, utter good things?* (Mt 12:34).

Prophetic statements

13. *Judge them, Lord; let them fall by their own thoughts.* This is a prophecy, not a curse: the psalmist does not want it to happen but sees what is sure to happen. It does befall them, not because he seems to have wished it, but because they are the type to deserve that such a fate should befall them. The same holds for what he goes on to say later, *Let all who hope in you rejoice.* He says this in a prophecy because he foresees that they will rejoice. In the same way the prayer, *Stir up your power and come* (Ps 79:3(80:2)), is a prophecy, because the psalmist foresaw that he would come.

Perhaps the saying could also mean, *Let them fall away from their own thoughts,* and so be understood as something that he wished for with good intent, envisaging that they might fall away from their own thoughts in the sense of thinking evil no longer. But the words that follow, *drive them out,* preclude such an interpretation, for it is absolutely impossible for the idea of anyone being driven out by God to be interpreted positively. That is why it should be understood as spoken in a prophecy rather than out of ill will. What has been said is what will of necessity happen to such people as wish to persevere in the sins which have been mentioned. Therefore the meaning must be, "Let them fall away because of their thoughts." Let them fall by their self-accusing thoughts, for their own conscience bears witness against them, as the apostle says, *whether their thoughts accuse or defend them, when God's just judgment is revealed* (Rom 2:15.16).

---

14. A variant reading is *peccato suo consummato,* "once their own sin has been accomplished."

Expulsion from God's presence

14. *In accordance with the great number of their wrongdoings,*[15] *drive them out*; that is, drive them far away, for the point of the phrase, *in accordance with the great number of their wrongdoings,* is that they are to be driven out completely. The ungodly are driven out from that inheritance in which God is possessed by understanding and vision. It is like the way in which diseased eyes are forced to shut by the dazzling brightness of the light. What brings joy to others is punishment to them. They, therefore, will not stand by in the morning and see. And that expulsion is a punishment as great as is the reward which is described in these terms: *my good is to hold fast to God* (Ps 72(73):28). The opposite of this punishment is the invitation, *Enter into the joy of your Lord* (Mt 25:21.23). Matthew's words, *Cast him into outer darkness* (Mt 25:21.30), evoke this expulsion.

15. *Because they have found you bitter, Lord.* The Lord said, *I am the bread which has come down from heaven* (Jn 6:51), and again, *Work for the food which does not decay* (Jn 6:27); and a psalm invites us, *Taste and see that the Lord is sweet* (Ps 33:9(34:8)). To sinners, however, the bread of truth is bitter. That is why they hate the lips which speak the truth. Therefore those who have found God bitter are they who by sinning have reached such a point of sickness that they cannot bear the food of truth in which healthy souls delight. To them it is like gall which they cannot endure.

Verse 12. Enjoying the glory of God

16. *But let all who hope in you rejoice,* that is, of course, those to whose taste the Lord is sweet. *They shall exult for ever and you will dwell in them.* That, then, will be the eternal rejoicing, when the just are the temple of God, and he, dwelling in them, will be their joy. *And all who love your name shall glory in you,* having ready access to the enjoyment of what they love.[16] The phrase, *in you,* is good: it is as if they already possess the inheritance referred to in the title of the psalm, when they too are his inheritance. This is what is meant by, *you will dwell in them.* Those whom God drove out in accordance with the multitude of their ungodly acts are debarred from this supreme good.

Verse 13. Prevenient grace

17. *Because you will bless the just person.* This is what blessing is: to glory in God, and to be indwelt by God. Sanctification like this is granted to the righteous, but in order that they may become righteous, their calling comes first. It depends not on merits but on God's grace. For all have sinned, and are stripped

---

15. *Impietatum,* acts of impiety.
16. *Ad fruendum quod diligunt*: see note on *frui* at *Exposition of Psalm 4,* 8.

of the glory of God.[17] But those whom he called, he has also justified; and those whom he has justified, these he has also glorified.[18] Because, therefore, the calling does not derive from our merits but from God's kindness and mercy, the psalmist added the following statement: *Lord, you have encompassed us as with the shield of your good will.* God's good will precedes our good will, in order that he may call sinners to repentance. And these are the weapons which overcome that enemy against whom scripture demands, *Who will bring any accusation against those whom God has chosen?* and *If God is for us, who can stand against us? He did not spare even his own Son, but delivered him up for us all. If Christ died for us while we were still enemies, how much more, now reconciled, shall we be saved from wrath through him?* (Rom 8:33.31.32; 5:10) This is the most invincible shield, by which the enemy is driven back, that enemy who all the time is prompting us to despair of salvation because of the overwhelming number of tribulations and temptations.

Summary of the progression of the psalm

The whole text of the psalm, therefore, is a prayer that the Church may be heard, from the opening, *hear my words, Lord,* through to *my king and my God.* Then follows an explanation of those things which hinder our seeing God, in order to make the Church learn that it has been heard, from the phrase, *I will pray to you, Lord, and in the morning you will hear my voice,* to *a bloodthirsty and deceitful person is loathsome to the Lord.* The third section tells how the Church, which is to become the house of God, hopes now to approach him in fear, even before reaching the perfection which casts out fear, from the point, *in the abundance of your mercy,* through to *I will worship in the direction of your holy temple, in fear of you.* Fourthly, as it progresses and moves forward through the very things by which it feels it is being impeded, the Church prays for help inwardly, where nobody sees, and begs not to be turned aside by evil tongues. This is expressed from *Lord, lead me onward in your justice, because of my enemies* as far as *they dealt deceitfully with their tongues.* Fifthly, there is a prophecy of the punishment awaiting the ungodly, when even the just person will find it difficult to be saved, and of the reward the just will obtain. They were called, then came and, until they were led right through to their goal, endured all things manfully.[19] This is contained in the section from *judge them, God* right through to the end of the psalm.

---

17. See Rom 3:23.
18. See Rom 8:30.
19. *Viriliter.*

Exposition of Psalm 6

Verse 1. Reckoning the day of the Lord

1. *To the end, in the hymns about the eighth, a psalm of David.* The phrase, *about the eighth*, seems obscure, though the remainder of this title is clearer. Some have taken it as pointing to the day of judgment, that is, the time of our Lord's second coming, when he will come to judge the living and the dead. People believe that this coming, reckoning the years from Adam, will be after seven thousand years. This means that seven thousand years pass like seven days, and then that time comes like the eighth day.[1] But the Lord himself said, *It is not for you to know the times or seasons which the Father has appointed by his own authority* (Acts 1:7), and *No one knows the day, or the hour: no angel, no power, nor even the Son, but the Father alone* (Mk 13:32). There is also that other statement, that the day of the Lord comes like a thief.[2] These all show quite clearly that nobody should arrogate to himself knowledge of that time, simply by counting up the years. If that day were sure to come after seven thousand years, anyone could work out when it will come, just by counting up the years, and then what is meant by saying that the Son does not know it? The truth is expressed in this way because people like you and me do not come to know it through the Son. This is not to say that he himself does not know it, but the same principle is applicable as to that other saying: *The Lord your God tests you, in order to know* (Dt 13:3), which really means, "to make you know;" and that other saying too: *Arise, Lord* (Ps 3:7), where what is meant is "make us arise."[3] When therefore the Son is described in this way as not knowing that day, it is not that he does not know it; instead he sees to it that those for whom

---

1. The Jewish sabbath was observed on the seventh day; according to the Priestly tradition it recalled God's rest after the six days' work of creation (see Gn 2:2-3; compare Ex 20:11; 31:17). The Deuteronomic tradition associates it with Israel's deliverance from Egypt (see Dt 5:15). Although the first Christian generation continued to honor the Jewish sabbath, it was being replaced even in apostolic times by Sunday, the day of the Lord's resurrection (see Acts 20:7). But Sunday, the first day of the week, was also the eighth day, the day after the "week" of earthly time, the day of the new creation and so a symbol of eternity. Augustine alludes to this in the following paragraph. Christian baptism was often administered on Sunday, and baptisteries were built in octagonal form. Clement of Alexandria, Origen, Cyril of Alexandria, and Ambrose were all conscious of this symbolism.
2. See 1 Thes 5:2.
3. These same two examples occur in his Exposition of Psalm 5, 4.

the knowledge is not expedient do not know it. This simply means that he does not reveal it to them. What a fruitless presumption this is—to count up the years and wait for the day of the Lord as something which simply has to happen after seven thousand years!

The number eight

2. Let us, therefore, accept willingly our ignorance of what the Lord has wanted us to be ignorant about, and let us try to find out what is meant by the title as written: *about the eighth*. Even without rushing into counting up the years, it is possible to understand the day of judgment as the eighth day, because immediately after the end of this age, once eternal life has been gained, the souls of the righteous will not be subject to the ebb and flow of time. Perhaps because all time revolves around a seven-day cycle, the time which will be subject to none of that changeableness has been called the eighth day.[4]

There is another interpretation, which it would not be unreasonable to accept, explaining why judgment is called "the eighth." It will take place after two generations, one which belongs to the body, the other to the soul. For from Adam right down to Moses the human race lived by the body, that is, according to the flesh. The human race in this era is called the outer and the old person;[5] and to it was given the Old Testament in order that it might herald spiritual things yet to come by means of rites which, however religious, were nonetheless bodily. Throughout this time, when everyone lived according to the flesh, *death reigned*, as the apostle says, *even over those who did not sin* (Rom 5:14). However, it reigned *after the likeness of Adam's transgression*, in the words of the same apostle. This is because the period from Adam *as far as Moses* must be taken to mean as long as the works enjoined by the law—that is, those ritual observances carried out in carnal fashion—were obligatory (albeit in virtue of a mysterious dispensation) even upon those who were subject to the one God. But the Lord's coming has resulted in a shift from the circumcision of the flesh to the circumcision of the heart. The call has gone out that humankind should live spiritually, that is, according to the inner person, who is also called the new person because of our rebirth and the renewal which enables us to live by the spirit. However, it is clear that the number four refers to the body because of those four well-known elements in which the body consists and because of the four qualities: dry, wet, warm, and cold. As a result the body is also regulated by four seasons: spring, summer, autumn, and winter. All of this is very well known. The fourfold number which relates to the body is treated elsewhere, in a more sophisticated but at the same time more complicated way. This is something I

---

4. In Pythagorean thought, eight was the symbol of perfection, and denoted eternity and rest, but Christianity developed the idea; see preceding note.
5. See Eph 4:22.

want to avoid in the present sermon, which I want to be readily accessible to the less learned. The number three, however, can be understood to belong to the mind, because we are bidden to love God in a threefold way, with all our heart, with all our soul, with all our mind.[6] With each of these individually we must deal in our exploration not of the psalms but of the gospel; but now, as to proving that the number three refers to the mind, I think that what has been said is enough. But once we have done with the numbers of the body which refer to the old person and to the Old Testament, and also with the numbers of the mind which are related to the new person and the New Testament, the number seven will be over and done with, because everything operates within time, four being apportioned to the body, three to the mind. Then will come the number eight, the day of judgment, which assigns to each one's merits what is due. It will conduct the saints not to temporal activities but to eternal life, and the ungodly it will condemn for ever.

Verse 2. Reproof and censure

3. Standing in fear of this condemnation, the Church prays in this present psalm, saying, *Lord, do not accuse me in your anger*. The apostle also speaks of the wrath of judgment: *You are storing up against yourself anger that will be manifest on the day of God's just judgment* (Rom 2:5). Whoever longs to be healed in this life does not want to be charged in God's anger. *Do not reprove me in your fury*. The term *reprove* seems more gentle, for it implies correction, for when one is charged, that is to say, accused, of wrongdoing there is the fear that one will end by being condemned. Because fury seems to be something more extreme than anger, the reader may wonder why what is gentler, that is, "reproof," is linked with what is harsher, that is, with "fury." But I think that one and the same thing is meant by two different words. For in Greek θυμός, which is in the first verse, means the same as ὀργή, which is in the second; but when the Latins in their turn wanted to use two different words, they wondered what was close to anger, and *fury* was used. That is why there are variant readings. In some manuscripts anger is found first and then fury. In others first fury is found, then anger. In others "indignation" or "rage" is used instead of fury. But whatever it is, it is a surge of activity in the soul, prompting it to inflict punishment. Yet this surge of emotion should not be attributed to God as it might be to a soul. Of God scripture says, *You judge in tranquillity, O Lord of might* (Wis 12:18). What is tranquil is not disturbed, and disturbance has no part to play in God as judge. But what takes place in his agents is referred to as his anger, because it happens through his laws. As far as this anger is concerned, the soul which now prays wants not simply to avoid being accused; it hopes even to escape reproof, that is, being corrected or instructed (for in Greek the manuscript reads

6. See Dt 6:5; Mt 22:37.

παιδεύσης, that is, "instruct"). But in the day of judgment all those who do not have Christ as their foundation will be accused, while those who have built on this foundation in wood, hay and stubble will be corrected, that is purged, for though they will suffer loss, they will be saved as if they had passed through fire.[7] What, then, is this person praying for, who does not want either to be reproved or corrected in the Lord's anger? What else but to be healed? For where good health is, death is not to be feared, nor the hand of the doctor using either cautery or amputation.

Verses 3-4. The suffering of the soul

4. The psalmist, therefore, goes on to say, *Have mercy on me, Lord, because I am weak; heal me, Lord, because my bones are troubled.* This means the firm support of my soul, my strength; for this is what bones signify. Therefore the soul is saying that its strength is troubled, when it talks about bones, for we should not believe that the soul has bones such as those we see in the body. Accordingly the next verse, *and my soul is greatly perturbed,* makes it clear that the language of bones does not refer to the bones of the body. *And you, Lord, how long?* Here, obviously, is a soul wrestling with its own diseases, but long untreated[8] by the doctor, in order that it may be convinced how great are the evils into which it has launched itself by sinning. For you do not normally take much precaution against what is easily healed, but the more difficult something has been to heal, the greater the care you will take to preserve health once recovered. Therefore God, to whom it is said, *And you, Lord, how long?* is not to be reckoned as cruel but as a good persuader of the soul with regard to the evil it has occasioned for itself. Not yet does this soul pray so perfectly as to hear the promise, "While you are still speaking I will say, Behold, here I am."[9] At the same time the purpose is that it may realize how great is the punishment prepared for the ungodly who do not wish to turn to God, if those who do turn suffer such great difficulty; as it is written in another place, *what will become of the wicked and the sinner if the righteous will scarcely be saved?* (1 Pt 4:18).

Verse 5. God rescues the soul

5. *Turn, Lord, and rescue my soul.*[10] In the act of turning itself, the soul prays that God also may turn to it, as scripture says, *Turn to me and I shall turn to you, says the Lord* (Zec 1:3). Or perhaps *Turn, Lord* is to be understood to mean "make me turn,"

---

7. See 1 Cor 3:11-15.
8. *Dilatam,* "put off," referring to *animam,* the soul. Some manuscripts add *medicinam,* "with medicine long delayed by the doctor."
9. See Is 65:24; 52:6.
10. Some manuscripts have *et libera,* "and set free."

since the soul in the very act of turning experiences difficulty and hardship. For our conversion, once completed, finds God ready and waiting, just as the prophet says: *We shall find him ready like the dawn* (Hos 6:3, LXX). This is because we lose him by turning away, not by the absence of him who is everywhere present. *He was in this world*, says the apostle John, *a world made by him, yet the world did not know him* (Jn 1:10). If, therefore, he was in this world and the world did not recognize him, it was because our squalid state cannot endure the sight of him. But while we are turning ourselves, that is, by a change of our old life we are refashioning[11] our spirit, we find it a tough and uphill struggle to twist ourselves away from the gloom of earthbound desires, back to the serenity and tranquillity of the divine light. In a difficult situation such as this we say, *Turn, Lord,* that is, help us, so that there may be fully achieved in us the conversion which finds you ready and waiting, and offering yourself to those who love you for their enjoyment. And that is why, after saying, *Turn, Lord*, he added, *and rescue my soul*, as if enmeshed in the perplexities of this world, and suffering the thorns of the longings which tear the soul apart, even as it strives to turn. *Save me*, he says, *because of your mercy*. He understands that it is not on his own merits that he is being healed, because a righteous condemnation is most certainly due to the sinner who transgresses the commandment as laid down. Heal me, therefore, says the psalmist, not in proportion to what I in fact deserve, but in proportion to your own abundant mercy.

Verse 6. Hell

6. *Because there is no one who is mindful of you in death.* He understands also that now is the time for conversion, because when life is past, there remains only the settling of accounts in relation to what we deserve. *Who will confess to you in hell?*[12] That fellow Dives, of whom the Lord speaks,[13] confessed in hell, when he saw Lazarus at rest and felt sorry for himself, tormented as he was. He confessed to this extent, that he wanted members of his own family to be warned to refrain from sinning, because of the punishments which, contrary to popular belief, do exist in hell. Although such confession was in vain, Dives nonetheless confessed that the torments which befell him were what he deserved, since he wanted his own family to be warned against falling into the same situation. What, then, is the meaning of *Who will confess to you in hell?* Does hell mean the place into which the ungodly will be hurled after the judgment, where, because of the deeper darkness, they will see no light of the God to whom they can confess anything? For Dives by raising his eyes, however vast the gulf between them, was still able to see Lazarus firmly

---

11. *Resculpimus*, "form anew," a rare and vivid verb.
12. She'ol, the abode of the dead, a place of shadows, was for the Hebrew mind a place where no praise could be offered to God.
13. See Lk 16:23-31.

established in a restful state. By comparing Lazarus' lot with his own he was driven to a confession of what he deserved.

Another possible interpretation is that he calls "death" the sin which is committed in contempt of the divine law, in the same way as we call the sting of death by the name "death," because it causes death to happen. For the sting of death is sin.[14] In such a death to be unmindful of God is to hold in contempt his law and commandments. So by "hell" the psalmist means the blindness of the mind which captures and envelops the person who is sinning—that is, dying. *Because they did not see fit to acknowledge God, he gave them over to their own depraved way of thinking*, says the apostle Paul (Rom 1:28). It is from this death and this hell that the soul prays earnestly to be kept safe while it sets about its conversion to God and experiences all the difficulties which stand in its way.

Verse 7. The weeping of the soul

7. And so the psalmist makes the link by saying, *I have toiled in my groaning*; and as if this had been of little use, he adds the following: *I will wash my bed with tears every single night*. What in this context is called the "bed" is where the sick and feeble mind rests, that is, in the gratifications of the body and in every worldly pleasure. Whoever tries to free himself from that delight bathes such pleasure in tears, for he sees that he is already condemning carnal longings; and yet his weakness is held captive by his delight and lies down in it willingly. The mind cannot rise from it unless it is healed. What about the phrase, *every single night*? Perhaps the psalmist wanted it to be understood like this: a person whose spirit is willing is aware of some light of truth, and yet from time to time rests in the delight of this world through the weakness of the flesh.[15] As a result such a one is forced to put up with alternations of day and night, through conflicting emotions. When Paul says, *With my mind I submit to God's law*, it is as if he is experiencing the day; whereas when he says, *but with my flesh to the law of sin* (Rom 7:25), it is as if he veers toward night, until every night passes and there comes the one day about which it is said, *In the morning I will stand before you and contemplate you* (Ps 5:5(3)). Then he will stand beside God, but at present he is lying down on the bed which he will wash every single night, in order that by so many tears he may obtain the most powerful medicine dispensed by God's mercy. *With tears, I will drench my couch* is a repetition of what has already been stated; for when he says, *with tears* he is repeating *I will wash*. Here we understand *couch* to be the same as *bed* above. But *I will drench* is something more than *I will wash*, because something can be washed on the surface, whereas drenching seeps through deep within and signifies weeping

---

14. See 1 Cor 15:56.
15. Compare Mk 14:38.

right to the depths of the heart. The variety of tenses suggests what any of us should say to ourselves when we have toiled and groaned, and achieved absolutely nothing. So he uses the past tense when he says, *I have toiled in my groaning*, and the future when he says, *I will wash my bed every single night*, and the future again for *with tears I will drench my couch*. It is as if he is saying, "It did me absolutely no good to do the one thing, so I'll do the other."

Verse 8. Inner and outer darkness

8. *My eye is troubled by anger.*[16] Is this his own anger or God's? It is in God's anger that he asks not to be reproved or reproached. But if that word "anger" means the day of judgment, how can it be understood now? Or indeed, is this the first stage of it, in that here and now men and women suffer troubles and torments, and most particularly the loss of the understanding of what truth is? I have already explained that this is the meaning of the phrase: *God gave them over to their own depraved way of thinking* (Rom 1:28), for that is blindness of the mind. Whoever has been given over to it is cut off from God's inner light, but not as yet irretrievably, as long as he is in this life. There is an outer darkness, though,[17] which is better understood to refer to the day of judgment, for whoever refuses to be corrected, while time still allows, is beyond God's range completely. For what else is it to be beyond God's range than to be in deepest blindness? God inhabits light inaccessible,[18] and those to whom is addressed the invitation, *Enter into the joy of your Lord* (Mt 25:21.23), are those who will enter. The first stages of this anger, then, are what each sinner experiences in this life. Fearing the day of judgment, he struggles and weeps. His fear is that he will be brought to that very state of which he experiences the early stages here and now. And they are catastrophic enough. This is why he did not say, "My eye is completely blinded," but *my eye is troubled by anger*.

If, however, he is saying that it is by his own anger that his eye is troubled, there is nothing strange in this either. It may be why we are warned, *Do not let the sun set on your wrath* (Eph 4:26), because the mind which is not allowed by its own confusion to see the sun within, that is, the wisdom of God, thinks that it suffers within itself the setting of that sun.

Living among enemies

9. *I have grown old in all my enemies.*[19] The psalmist has spoken only of anger (if, that is, it was of his own anger that he spoke), but when he thought about the rest

---

16. *Ab ira.* The manuscripts also offer *ab indignatione* and *a furore*, perhaps derived from the use of these words in paragraph 3.
17. See Mt 25:30.
18. See 1 Tm 6:16.
19. A variant reading is *inter omnes inimicos meos*, which looks like an emendation.

of his vices, he found that he was besieged by them all. Since these vices belong to the old life and the old person which we must lay aside in order to be clothed in the new,[20] it is quite appropriate to say, *I have grown old*. But by the phrase, *in all my enemies*, the psalmist is speaking either of the vices themselves or of the men and women who refuse to turn to God. For even if these people do not know it,[21] even if they are accommodating, even if they share, on the best of terms, the same meals and households and cities, without any obvious antagonism, and enjoy frequent social contacts in apparent cordiality, nonetheless by their aspirations they are opposed to those who are turning toward God, and hence are enemies. For when one group loves and longs for this world and the other wishes to be freed from this world, who cannot see that the former is the enemy of the latter? If they could, they would be dragging them with them to their doom. And yet it is a very special gift to live in the midst of their daily conversation and at the same time not to deviate from the way of God's commandments. For often as the mind strives to press ahead toward God, it is roughly handled while on the road and loses its nerve. This why it often fails to fulfill its good intention, for fear of offending those with whom it lives, who love and pursue other things which are good, but nonetheless perishable and transient. Every sane person is separated from them, not geographically but in the mind. Bodies are contained in particular places, but the mind's place is what it loves.

Verses 9-10. Wheat and chaff

10. It is impossible that a plea fervently made, after so much hard toil, groaning, and repeated showers of tears, to God who is the fount of all mercies, should not avail. Very truly is it said, *The Lord is close to the brokenhearted* (Ps 33:19(34:18)). So now, after such terrible difficulties, the devout soul, which can legitimately be taken as the Church, knows itself to have been heard, and goes on to say, *Depart from me, all you who work iniquity, because the Lord has heard the voice of my weeping*. This is said either as a prophecy, because they will depart, that is to say, the ungodly will be separated from the just when the day of judgment comes, or with immediate reference. Even if they are all together and are included in the same social gatherings, nevertheless on the open threshing-floor the grains are already separated from the chaff, although they lie hidden in among the chaff. They may live and consort together, but they cannot be carried away by the wind together.

11. *The Lord has heard the voice of my weeping; the Lord has heard my petition; the Lord has taken up my prayer*. The frequent repetition of the same idea does

---

20. See Col 3:9.10.
21. A variant reading is *nesciuntur*, "even if we do not know them."

not denote the need the speaker feels to ram home his point, but the warmth of one who rejoices. Those who rejoice usually speak in such a way that it is not enough for them to give voice to their joy only once. This is the fruit of that laborious groaning, and of those tears by which the bed is washed and the couch drenched; because whoever sows in tears will reap in joy,[22] and those who mourn are blessed because they will receive consolation.[23]

Verse 11. Obstruction and mockery from the worldly

12. *Let all my enemies blush with shame and be thrown into confusion.* Earlier the psalmist had said, *Depart from me, all of you.* This can happen even in the present life, as has been explained. However, as to his saying, *Let them blush with shame and be thrown into confusion,* I do not see how it can come about except on the day when the rewards of the just are revealed, and the punishments of sinners too. For as things are, so far are the godless from blushing with shame that they never cease to insult us. What usually happens is that so successful are they with their mockery that they make the weak blush with shame at the name of Christ. For this reason scripture says, *If anyone is ashamed of me before his fellows, I will be ashamed of him before my Father* (Lk 9:26). Take the case of someone who wishes to fulfill the sublime expectations of the commandments, by sharing what he has, giving to the poor so that his righteousness may endure for ever,[24] selling off all his earthly possessions and distributing them to the needy so as to follow Christ, saying, *We have brought nothing into this world, and we can certainly take nothing away with us; if we have food and clothing, let us be content with that* (1 Tm 6:7.8). Such a person is a butt for the profane banter of the godless, and is called insane by those who refuse to be restored to sanity. Often, in order to avoid being called insane by those who are beyond hope, he is afraid to act and puts off what the most trustworthy and powerful of all physicians has ordered. These, then, are not the ones disposed to feel shame at the present time, the ones we wish would stop causing shame to us, calling us back, obstructing and hindering us on the journey we have already decided to make. But the time will come when they will be ashamed and say of us, in the words of scripture, *These are the people we once held in derision, as a byword and a butt for our mockery! Fools that we were, we thought their life madness and their end a disgrace. How are they now reckoned among the children of God, with their lot among the saints? No doubt of it, we strayed from the path of truth. On us the light of righteousness did not shine, nor did the sun rise for us. We have had our fill of the ways of iniquity and wantonness; we have walked in*

---

22. See Ps 125(126):5.
23. See Mt 5:5.
24. See Ps 111(112):9.

harsh deserts, but we have not known the way of the Lord. What good has our pride done us, or what benefit has come to us from our vaunted wealth? All these things have passed away like a shadow (Wis 5:3-9).

Swift judgment

13. With regard to his saying, *Let them be turned back and put to shame*, who would not reckon this to be the most proper punishment, that those who refuse the sort of turning which leads to salvation should be subject to a turning that lands them in confusion? Then he adds, *very quickly*, for when everyone has already begun to think that the day of judgment will not come, when people say, *"Now we have peace," sudden destruction will overtake them* (1 Thes 5:3). But whenever it does come, the very thing we had ceased to expect will in fact come very quickly. It is only when our hopes are fixed in this life that we can think of life as long. In fact, though, nothing seems to have gone by more quickly than the portion of our life which is already over. When, therefore, the day of judgment comes, sinners will realize how short is the whole of this transient life. The very thing they do not want, or rather do not believe will come, will seem to them not to have been at all slow in coming.

This can also be interpreted in a different way as follows: because God has taken note of the petitioner's groaning and frequent and protracted weeping, this soul should be recognized as one who is now set free from sins and has subdued all the unruly impulses of bodily desire. It truly declares, *Depart from me, all you who work iniquity, because the Lord has listened to the voice of my weeping.* Since this has been granted, it is not surprising that the soul is already so perfect as to pray for its enemies. This may also be why it begged, *May all my enemies blush with shame and be confused*, a prayer that they should repent of their sins, something which is not possible without confusion and turmoil. Nothing, therefore, prevents us from also taking in the same sense what follows: *Let them be turned back and put to shame*; that is, let them turn to God, and let them blush at having once boasted of the earlier darkness of their sins, as the apostle says, *What glory did you once have in those things, of which now you are ashamed?* (Rom 6:21). As to the addition, *very quickly*, it should be understood as referring either to the intensity of the soul's desire or to the power of Christ, who with such speed causes nations to turn to the faith of the gospel, nations that once persecuted the Church in the cause of their idols.

Exposition of Psalm 7

Verse 1. The deep silence of God's mystery

1. *A psalm of David himself, which he sang to the Lord for the words of Hushai, the son of Jemini.* The story from which this prophecy took its origin is easy to identify in the second book of Kings. For there Hushai, the friend of King David, crossed over to the camp of Abessalon, David's son, who was waging war against his father, to spy on Abessalon's tactics and to report what he was plotting against his father at the instigation of Ahithophel. Now Ahithophel had forsaken his friendship with David and was busy setting son against father, teaching him whatever dirty tricks he could. It is not the story itself[1] which is due for consideration in this psalm. The prophet has drawn back the veil of mysteries from it, and if we have crossed over to Christ, let the veil be removed.[2] But first let us examine the meaning of the names and their significance. There has been no shortage of commentators who have scrutinized these names, not in a fleshly way according to the letter, but spiritually. They have informed us that Hushai means "silence," Jemini "right hand," and Ahithophel "the destruction of a brother." The traitor Judas has, then, crossed our path once again in these interpretations. Abessalon bears his image, according to the interpretation of that name as "a father's peace," because his father was at peace with him, even though Abessalon with his crafty schemes had war in his heart, as we saw in Psalm 3.[3] And just as we find in the gospel that the disciples of our Lord Jesus Christ are called sons,[4] so also in the gospel are they called brothers, for after his resurrection the Lord said, *Go and tell my brothers* (Jn 20:17), and the apostle Paul speaks of Jesus *as the first among many brothers* (Rom 8:29). Therefore the downfall of that disciple who betrayed Jesus is rightly understood as a brother's downfall. This is what we said was the meaning of Ahithophel. However Hushai, which is interpreted as silence, is rightly understood as our Lord's having contended against those plottings and schemings by silence, that is by that deepest of mysteries whereby blindness fell on part of Israel when they were persecuting the Lord, but only so that the full complement of Gentiles might slip

---

1. See 2 Sm 15-17.
2. See 2 Cor 3:16.
3. See Exposition of Psalm 3, 1.
4. See Mt 9:15.

113

in,[5] and thus enable Israel in its entirety to be saved. When the apostle Paul had come to this profound place of deep silence, he cried out as if struck down by a fear of its very depth, *O how deep are God's wisdom and knowledge, how unfathomable his decisions and inscrutable his ways! Who has understood the mind of the Lord, or been his counsellor?* (Rom 11:33-34). He does not so much open up that great silence by explanation as commend it with a sense of wonder. By this silence the Lord has concealed the sacrament of his glorious passion. He has used his brother's willful self-destruction, that is the despicable crime of his betrayer, to serve the dispensation of his own mercy and providence, so that what Judas did with perverse intention to bring about the death of one individual person, Christ Jesus was able by his guiding providence to direct for the salvation of all men and women.

Therefore the perfect soul which is now worthy of knowing the secret of God sings this psalm to the Lord. It sings *for the words of Hushai* because it has deserved to know the words of that silence, though among the unbelieving and persecutors, there is only silence and secrecy. However it was to his own that Christ said, *I call you servants no longer, because the servant does not know what his master is doing; I call you friends because I have made known to you all that I have heard from the Father* (Jn 15:15). Among his friends, therefore, it is not silence but the words of silence, that is, a clear explanation of that silence. This silence, that is Hushai, is said to be the son of Jemini, that is, of the right-handed one. For though there was no need to conceal from the saints what was done on their behalf, Christ said, *Do not let your left hand know what your right hand is doing* (Mt 6:3). Therefore in prophecy the perfect soul, to which that secret has been made known, sings *for the words of Hushai*, that is, for the knowledge of the same secret. God on the right hand, that is favorable[6] and well-disposed to the soul, has worked this secret. That is why this silence is called the son of the right hand, which is Hushai, son of Jemini.

Verses 2-3. Being saved from the devil

2. *Lord, my God, in you I have hoped; make me safe from all my persecutors, and pluck me out.* The psalmist is speaking, it would seem, as someone already perfect, someone for whom the only remaining enemy is the devil, now that all warfare and resistance from its vices have been overcome. *Make me safe from all my persecutors, and pluck me out, lest he ever, like a lion, tear my soul.* The apostle Peter says, *Your enemy the devil stalks about like a roaring lion, seeking whom he*

---

5. See Rom 11:25.
6. In the background is the ancient and widespread belief that the right hand represented what is of good omen. This is not obvious in modern English, though the opposite in Latin is: *sinister*, the "left hand."

may devour (1 Pt 5:8). Therefore after saying, in the plural, *Save me from all my persecutors*, the psalmist went on to use the singular, saying, *lest he ever, like a lion, tear my soul*. He did not say, "In case they tear," because he knows exactly which enemy, one violently opposed to the perfect soul, stands in his way. *While there is none to rescue or to save*, that is, let him not seize me while you are not there to rescue and save. For if God does not rescue or save, the devil snatches us away.

Verses 4-5. Christ's example of forgiveness

3. In order to make clear that the already perfect soul is saying this, a soul which needs to be on guard only against the most fraudulent wiles of the devil, the psalm continues, *Lord my God, if I have done this*. What does the psalmist mean by the word "this"? Is it the case that, because he does not name a specific sin, the broad range of sin should be understood? If this interpretation is unacceptable, we might well take the following to be what is meant: it is as if we had asked, "What do you mean by the word *this*?" and he were to reply, *If there is any iniquity on my hands*. Now it is clear that the phrase, *If I have repaid those who have paid me back with evil*, is used to refer to sin in general, for this is something which only the one who is perfect can say with any degree of truth. Indeed the Lord says, *Be perfect like your Father in heaven, who causes his sun to rise on the good and the wicked, and sends rain on just and unjust alike* (Mt 5:48.45). Therefore whoever does not pay back evil to those who repay with evil is perfect.

Let us, then, see what is meant when the perfect soul prays *for the words of Hushai, the son of Jemini*. It prays for the knowledge of that secret and that silence, which the Lord, who is merciful and kindly disposed toward us, effected for our salvation, enduring the plots of his betrayer and bearing them with the utmost patience. It is as if he were to say to this perfect soul, explaining the meaning of the secret, "It was for you, ungodly sinner, that I endured my betrayer in deep silence and inexhaustible patience, so that your iniquities might be washed away by the shedding of my blood. Should you, then, not imitate me and, in your turn, refrain from rewarding evil with evil?" The psalmist, then, perceiving and understanding what the Lord has done for him, and by following his example advancing toward perfection, says, *If I have repaid those who have paid me back with evil*, that is, if I have not myself done what you, by doing it, taught me, *let me fall empty-handed before my enemies*. And he was quite right not to say, "If I recompense those who pay me evil," but instead, "those who *repay*," for whoever repays has already received something. It is a sign of greater forbearance not to repay with evil someone who has already received benefits and yet has repaid evil for good, than would be the case had he wanted to cause harm without himself having received any previous kindness. *If I have repaid* then, said the psalmist, *those who have paid me back with evil*, that is, if I have not followed your example in that silence, in that forbearance which you showed for my sake, *let me fall empty-handed before my enemies.* Empty indeed is the boast of anyone who, himself a human being, wants to be avenged on a fellow human being. While he is trying openly to overcome a fellow human being, secretly he himself is being overcome by the devil, and is made empty by that vain and overweening joy which made him think that he was invincible.

Therefore the psalmist understands where the greater victory lies and where the Father, who sees in secret, repays.[7] In order not to recompense with evil those who have repaid him with evil, he defeats his own anger rather than a fellow human. He has obviously been well grounded in those writings which say, *Better is the one who overcomes anger than the one who captures a city* (Prv 16:32, LXX). *If I have repaid those who paid me back with evil, let me fall empty-handed before my enemies.* When someone says, "If I have done x, may I suffer y," he seems to swear by solemn oath and imprecation,[8] which is the strongest form of oath. But swearing on the lips of the one who takes such an oath is one thing, and quite another is what the prophet means to convey; he is foretelling what really will happen to those who recompense with evil those who repay with evil, not what he would call down by oath upon himself or upon anyone else.

Verse 6. Pride and rebellion from God

4. *Let the enemy, then, persecute my soul and lay hold of it.* Again naming the enemy in the singular, he points more insistently to the devil, whom he referred to above as a lion. The devil persecutes the soul, and if he outwits it, he will seize hold of it. Men and women rage to the extent of killing the body, but the soul, after this visible death, they cannot have in their power. The devil, though, will have as his possession the souls which he has persecuted and caught. *And let him tread my life into the ground,*[9] that is, by trampling it down let him make my life earth, make it into his own food; for the devil was called not only a lion, but also a snake, and to him was said, *You shall eat earth* (Gn 3:14). To the human sinner also is said, *Earth you are, and back to earth you will go* (Gn 3:19). *And let him draw my glory down into the dust.* This is the dust which the wind hurls forth from the face of the earth, that is to say, the vain and silly boastings of the proud, puffed up but without substance, like a handful of dust lifted high by the wind.[10] Therefore he was correct to use in this context the word, "glory," as something which he does not want to be dragged down into the dust. He wants to have some four-square integrity to boast of in his conscience before God, where there is no scope for bragging. The apostle

---

7. See Mt 6:6.
8. A curse invoked on the one who swears, if he fails to keep the oath.
9. *In terram.* Some manuscripts have *in terra*, "my life on earth."
10. See Ps 1:4.

Paul says, *Let anyone who boasts, boast in the Lord* (1 Cor 1:31). This integrity, however, is dragged down into the dust if through bragging someone despises the secret testimony of his conscience, where God alone tests a person, and yet wants to be a somebody among his fellows. This is what lies behind what the psalmist says elsewhere, *God will grind to pieces the bones of those who curry favor with their fellows* (Ps 52:6(53:5)). The person, however, who has learned well or has in fact undertaken the steps appropriate to overcoming vices, understands that this partic- ular vice of groundless boasting is the only vice there really is, or the one most to be avoided by those who are perfect. For the soul conquers last of all the very vice by which it fell first. *The starting-point of all sin is pride* and *the starting-point of human pride is rebellion against God* (Sir 10:15.14).

Verse 7. Praying for God's anger

5. *Rise, Lord, in your anger.* Why does the one whom we have referred to as perfect still provoke God to anger? Should we not, rather, consider him to be perfect, who said while being stoned, *Lord, do not hold this sin against them* (Acts 7:60)? Or does the psalmist make this plea more against the devil and his angels than against his fellows? It is to the devil and his angels that sinners and ungodly men and women belong. Therefore it is not so much in a rage but in mercy that a person prays against the devil, in praying for such a possession to be taken away from him by the Lord who justifies the ungodly. For when an ungodly person is justified, he or she is changed from ungodly to just, and passes from the devil's sphere of influence into the temple of God. And because being deprived of some- thing you have and want to control is a punishment, the psalmist describes this punishment as the anger of God exercised against the devil to make him lose his hold on those he possesses. *Arise*, he says, using the word to mean "appear"; he employs a human and obscure expression, as though God were asleep, when really he is hidden and unrecognized in his secret plans. *Be exalted in the territory of my enemies*: by *territory* he indicates that empire in which he wants God, rather than the devil, to be exalted, honored and glorified when the ungodly are rendered just and praise God. *And arise, O Lord my God, in the commandment which you have given*, that is, because you have taught humility, please appear in humility! You must first fulfill what you have taught, in order that by your example they may overcome pride and not be in the grip of the devil, who in defiance of your commandments encouraged them to be proud by telling them, *Eat and your eyes will be opened, and you will be like gods* (Gn 3:5).

Verse 8. The humiliation and resurrection of Christ

6. *And the gathering*[11] *of peoples will surround you*. There are two interpretations, for the gathering of peoples may be taken either as those who believe or as those who persecute, for both these reactions greeted the humbling of our Lord. The crowd of persecutors scorned his humility and encircled him, and of this crowd scripture says, *Why have the nations raged, and the peoples devised futile schemes?* (Ps 2:1). But a vast crowd of those who believed because of his humility surrounded him in such a way that with the utmost truthfulness it could be said, *Blindness has fallen upon a part of Israel that the full tally of the Gentiles may come in* (Rom 11:25), and the same goes for that other saying, *Ask of me, and I will give you the nations as your heritage, and the ends of the earth for your possession* (Ps 2:8).

And for their sake return on high, that is, for the sake of this gathering return on high; this Christ is understood to have done by his resurrection and ascension into heaven. For once glorified in this way he gave the Holy Spirit, which could not be given before his glorification, as the gospel tells us, *for the Spirit had not yet been given, because Jesus was not yet glorified* (Jn 7:39). Therefore, after returning on high in order to gather the nations, he sent the Holy Spirit. Filled with the Spirit, the preachers of the gospel in their turn filled the whole earth with churches.

Christ's returning on high[12]

7. The prayer, *Arise, Lord, in your anger, be exalted*[13] *in the territory of my enemies*, can also be understood in this way: "Rise up in your anger and do not let my enemies understand you." *Arise* therefore means, "become inaccessible," so as not to be understood. This is to be referred to the silence spoken of above. Another psalm says about that exaltation, *He rose above the cherubim and flew; he made the darkness his hiding place* (Ps 17:11-12(18:10-11)). By this exaltation, that is, concealment (since those who crucify you will have failed to understand you because of their sins), the congregation of believers will surround you. For by that very humbling Christ has been exalted, that is, he has not been understood. Accordingly the prayer, *Arise, O Lord my God, in the commandment which you have given*, may mean this: when you appear in humility, be so high or so deep that my enemies do not understand you. But sinners are the enemies of the just, and the godless the enemies of the godly. *And the gathering of the peoples will surround*

---

11. *Congregatio.* A variant reading is *synagoga.*
12. *Altus*, which recurs throughout these paragraphs, can mean "high" or "deep." The former is appropriate to Augustine's present consideration of Christ's ascension, the latter to Paul's wondering exclamation quoted earlier.
13. An unconvincing variant is *et ex altare*, "and from the altar."

you. This means: through the very fact that those who crucify you do not understand you, the nations will believe in you, and so the congregation of the peoples will surround you.

The weakening of the churches' faith

But if what follows really means what I think it does, it is more painful inasmuch as it is already beginning to be felt, than joyful because understood. For the psalm continues, *And for its sake, return on high,* that is, for the sake of this gathering of the human race, by which the churches are filled, return on high. By this is meant, "become difficult to understand once more." What, then, is meant by, *for its sake?* Surely it means that this congregation will offend you, in such a way that you may with complete truthfulness foretell the future by asking, *When the Son of Man comes, do you think he will find faith on earth?* (Lk 18:8). So too Christ says about the false prophets, who are to be understood as the heretics, *Because of their iniquity, the love of many will grow cold* (Mt 24:12). Since, then, even in the churches, in that gathering of peoples and races where the name of Christ is widely revered, the abundance of sins is so great—a state of affairs of which we are well aware—can we not see this verse as predicting the famine of the word which another prophet also threatens?[14] Surely God returns on high because of this gathering too, which by its sins has distanced itself from the light of truth. Because he withdraws, sincere faith, purified from the defilement of all base opinions, is upheld and understood by hardly any, or by those very few of whom it is said, *Blessed is the one who perseveres to the end; such a one will be saved* (Mt 10:22). Scripture is not wrong to say, then, "And because of this congregation" *return on high,* that is, withdraw once more into the height[15] of your secret workings, even on account of this concourse of the peoples which bears your name, yet does not perform your deeds.

Verse 9. Judgment, and God's gift of righteousness

8. Whether the first explanation of this phrase or the second is more appropriate (or any other that may be better or equally good), what follows is eminently appropriate: *the Lord judges the peoples.* By the former explanation we take the reference to be Christ's returning on high, when after the resurrection he ascended into heaven, and that is where he will come from to judge the living and the dead; so the statement, *the Lord judges the peoples,* follows on well. But by the second explanation Christ returns on high when the proper understanding of truth abandons sinful

---

14. See Am 8:11.
15. Or "depth."

Christians, because with regard to his coming scripture said, *When the Son of Man comes, do you think he will find faith on earth?* (Lk 18:28). Accordingly *the Lord judges the peoples.* Which Lord, if not Jesus Christ? *The Father judges no one, but has entrusted all judgment to the Son* (Jn 5:22). Notice how this soul, therefore, which prays perfectly, does not fear the day of judgment and with a longing that is truly carefree says in its prayer, *Thy kingdom come* (Mt 6:10).

Judge me, Lord, it says, *according to my righteousness.* In the previous psalm a sick person was praying, calling on God's mercy rather than rehearsing any personal merit, because the Son of God came to call sinners to repentance.[16] That is why at that point the psalmist said, *Save me, Lord, according to your mercy* (Ps 6:5(4)): that is, not on the strength of any merit of mine. But now this soul has been called, and has held fast to the commandments it received, and kept them; and so it dares to say, *Judge me, Lord, according to my righteousness and my harmlessness, which are above me.* This is true harmlessness which harms[17] not even an enemy. Therefore the one who was able truly to say, *If I have repaid those who paid me back with evil,* is right to ask to be judged in accordance with his harmlessness. The addition, *above me* can be understood as referring not only to harmlessness but also to righteousness. This, then, is the sense that is meant to be conveyed, "Judge me, Lord, in accordance with my righteousness, and in accordance with my innocence. This righteousness and this innocence are above me." By such an addition the psalmist shows that the soul does not have its righteousness and innocency through itself, but through God who gives light and brightness. For of the soul he says in another psalm, *You, Lord, will light my lamp* (Ps 17:29(18:28)), and of John the Baptist it is said, *He was not himself the Light, but came to bear witness about the Light* (Jn 1:8); and again, *He was a burning, shining lamp* (Jn 5:35). That Light, from which souls are lit like lamps, shines forth with its own dazzling splendor, not with one borrowed from someone else. This Light is Truth itself. When, therefore, the psalm says, *According to my righteousness and my innocence, which are above me,* it is as though a burning, shining lamp were to say, "Judge me according to the flame which is over me, that is, not by that which I am of myself, but by that flame with which I shine when set on fire from you."

Verse 10. The direction of the just

9. *But let the wickedness of sinners be consummated.* In this context, *consummated* means "brought to completion," in tune with what is said in the Apocalypse, *Let the righteous become more righteous yet, and the filthy still wallow in their filth* (Rv 22:11). The wickedness of those who crucified the Son of God seems to be

---

16. See Lk 5:32.
17. A play on words: *innocentia, quae nec . . . nocet.*

complete, but greater still is the wickedness of those who do not wish to live uprightly and hate the commandments of truth for which the Son of God was crucified. The psalmist said, therefore, *Let the wickedness of sinners be consummated*, that is, let it come to the pinnacle of wickedness, so that the righteous judgment can come immediately. But because scripture says not only, *Let the filthy still wallow in their filth*, but also, *Let the righteous become more righteous yet*, the psalmist appends these words, *And you will direct the just, you, God, who examine the heart and the inward parts*. How, then, can the just person be directed except in secret? At the beginning of the Christian era, when the saints were still oppressed under persecutions inflicted by the lovers of this world, certain events seemed matter for wonder; yet now, when through these same events the Christian name has come to hold a place of such high dignity, there are those who, under the pretense of the Christian name, prefer to find favor with their fellows rather than with God. How, then, is the just person to be guided when caught in the thick of such great confusion and pretense, unless God examines his heart and inward parts? God sees the thoughts of everyone; this is what the word "heart" means. He also sees the things which give everyone pleasure; they are to be understood by the expression, "inward parts." Indeed, it is appropriate that delight in temporal and earthly things be attributed to the inward parts, because that is the lowest part of the human body and also the region where the pleasure of sex dwells, by which human nature is passed on from generation to generation through a succession of offspring, into this miserable life of false joy. God therefore examines our heart and explores carefully to see that it is where our treasure is, that is, in heaven.[18] He examines also our inward parts and explores carefully to see that we do not capitulate to flesh and blood but rejoice in God. Thus he guides the just person's conscience in his own presence, guides it in the place where no human being sees; he alone sees who discerns what each person thinks and what causes each person delight. For delight is the object of our efforts: each of us strives by care and thought to attain our own delight. Therefore the one who examines the heart sees the things which we really care about. But he who explores our inward parts sees also the object of our striving, and where we seek our joy, so that when he finds that our efforts do not incline toward the lust of the flesh, nor toward the craving of the eyes, nor toward worldly ambition,[19] all of which pass away like a cloud, but are raised upward to the joys of things eternal, which are disturbed by no changefulness, then God who examines the heart and the inward parts can direct the just. For our works, expressed in deeds and words, can be well known by other people, but only the God who examines the heart and the inward parts knows with what intention they are done and what we want to gain through them.

---

18. See Mt 6:21.
19. See 1 Jn 2:16.

Verse 11. Spiritual medicine

10. *My righteous help is from the Lord, who saves the upright in heart.* Medicine has two functions, one whereby infirmity is cured, the other whereby good health is maintained. In accordance with the former, it is said in the previous psalm, *Have mercy on me, Lord, because I am weak* (Ps 6:3(2)). In accordance with the latter, it is said in this psalm, *If there is any iniquity on my hands, if I have repaid those who have paid me back with evil, let me fall empty-handed before my enemies.* In the first case the psalmist prays as a weak person, asking to be set free, in the latter as one now restored to health, asking not to fall ill again. In tune with the former, there it is said, *Save me because of your mercy;* in accordance with the latter, here it is said, *Judge me, Lord, according to my righteousness.* In the former case he sought a remedy to escape from sickness, in the latter, protection to avoid falling back into sickness. In the former case it is said, *Save me, Lord, because of your mercy,* in the latter case, *My righteous help is from the Lord, who saves the upright in heart.* Both in fact save us, but while the former effects the transition from sickness to health, the latter upholds us in that state of good health. Therefore in the former case the assistance is merciful, because the sinner has no merit of his own, but still longs to be justified by believing in the one who justifies the ungodly. In the latter case, the assistance is just, because it is given to one who is already righteous. Therefore, the sinner who confessed, *I am weak,* was right to say there, *Save me, Lord, because of your mercy,* and the just person who said previously, *If I have repaid those who paid me back with evil,* can say now, *My righteous help is from the Lord, who saves the upright in heart.* For if God dispenses the medicine by which in our weakness we are healed, how much more should he provide the means by which we are preserved once we are well? If Christ died for us when we were still sinners, how much more, now that we are justified, shall we be saved from God's wrath through him?[20]

Good and bad desires

11. *My righteous help is from the Lord, who saves the upright in heart.* The God who examines the heart and inward parts directs the just person, but with his righteous help he saves the upright in heart. He does not save those who are upright in heart and in the inward parts in the same way that he scrutinizes the heart and the inward parts. Evil thoughts are found in a depraved heart and good thoughts in an upright heart; but pleasures which are not good belong to the inward parts, because they are lower and earthbound, whereas good pleasures belong to the heart itself, not to the inward parts. This is why people cannot be spoken of as upright in the

---

20. See Rom 5:8.9.

inward parts in the same way as they are said to be upright in heart , since pleasure follows thought, and so uprightness is possible only when someone's thoughts are of things divine and eternal. *You have given joy to my heart*, says a psalmist, after saying, *The light of your countenance is stamped on us, Lord* (Ps 4:7). The fantasies of temporal things which the mind conjures up for itself when it is tossed to and fro by empty, mortal ambition may often yield a crazed and foolish joy; but this plea-sure is to be ascribed not to the heart but to the lower parts, because all such imagi-native fantasies have been brought on by inferior things, by earthly and carnal stimuli. So it is that the God who examines the heart and inward parts, and who identifies in the heart right thoughts and in the inward parts no inappropriate objects of delight, offers righteous help to the upright in heart, where heavenly delights are wedded to pure thoughts. And that is why, in another psalm, after the psalmist had said, *Moreover, even into the night my inward parts rebuked me*, he added, on the subject of help, *I kept the Lord always before my eyes; he is at my right hand, and so I shall not be thrown off course* (Ps 15(16):7,8). By this the psalmist showed that he had experienced nothing more than promptings from the inward parts, not the desires themselves. Had he experienced them, he would have been thrown off course forthwith. But he said, "The Lord is on my right hand, to prevent my being thrown off course." Then he adds, *This is why my heart was delighted* (Ps 15(16):9). The point is that the inward parts may have been able to rebuke him but not delight him. True delight is not, therefore, in the inward parts, but where God has been kept in sight at our right hand, as our defence against the rebuke of our inward parts; and that means in the heart.

Verse 12. God's anger and long-suffering

12. *God is a just judge, strong and long-suffering.* What god is judge except the Lord who judges the peoples? He is just who will recompense each of us in propor-tion to our works. He is strong who, while himself most powerful, for our salvation endured even godless persecutors. He is long-suffering who did not, immediately after his resurrection, seize those who persecuted him, in order to punish them; instead, he bore with them, in order that they might eventually turn from such impiety to salvation. And still he bears with them, reserving the final punishment until the final judgment, and even today still inviting sinners to repentance. *He does not bring anger to bear* [21] *on them every single day.* Perhaps it is more significant to say *bring anger to bear* (as we find in the Greek manuscripts) than *be angry;* it means that the anger by which he punishes is not in God himself but in the minds of his ministers who obey the commandments of truth. Through them orders are given to inferior ministers also, who are called angels of wrath, for the purpose of punishing sins. They derive their pleasure from the punishment of humans on the

---

21. A variant has *numquid irascetur*, "will he be angry?"

basis of ill will, not of justice in which they have no delight. Therefore God *does not bring anger to bear every single day*, that is, he does not gather his ministers together every day to inflict punishment. For here and now God's patience invites us to repentance,[22] but at the end, when humankind through its own stubbornness and unrepentant heart has stored up for itself anger in the day of wrath, when God's righteous judgment will be revealed,[23] then he will brandish his sword.

Verse 13. The sword and judgment

13. *Unless you turn*,[24] says the psalmist, *he will brandish his sword*. It may be that the Lord-Man[25] himself should be understood as God's double-edged sword, that is, the sword which he did not brandish at his first coming, but hid in the sheath of humility.[26] But he will brandish it, when at his second coming to judge the living and the dead, in the radiant splendor of his brightness, he will dazzle the just with light, and the ungodly with terrors. For in some manuscripts we read, "he will make his spear glisten," instead of *he will brandish his sword*. I think that, in the former phrase, the final coming of the Lord's brightness is most clearly expressed, since what another psalm says is understood as referring to him, *Set my soul free from the ungodly, O Lord, your spear from the enemies of your hand* (Ps 16(17):13-14). *He has stretched his bow and made it ready*. The tenses of the verbs should not be passed over without due consideration. When speaking of the *sword* the psalmist used the future, *he will brandish*, but of the bow, the past, *he has stretched*. The verbs which follow next are in the past tense.

Verse 14. The arrows of divine love

14. *And in it he has prepared implements of death. He has fashioned his arrows for those who are burning*. That bow, then, I would happily understand as the holy scriptures, where the rigidity of the Old Testament is bent and subdued by the strength of the New Testament, as by some sort of bowstring. The apostles are launched from it like arrows, or divine proclamations are hurled from it. These arrows *he has fashioned for those who are burning*, that is, to make those who are smitten by them blaze with the love of God. For by what other arrow was the woman struck who said, *Bring me into the wine cellar, set me amidst perfumes, pack me all round with honeycombs, because I have been wounded by love* (Sg 2:4-5, LXX)? By what other arrows is that person set on fire, who wants to go back to God and to return home from his wandering, who seeks help against deceitful

---

22. See Rom 2:4.
23. See Rom 2:5.
24. Or passive, "are turned."
25. See note at Exposition of Psalm 1, 1.
26. *Vagina humilitatis*, possibly a reference to his birth from Mary.

tongues and is told, *What is to be given to you, what shall be added to you, that you may withstand the deceitful tongue? Sharp arrows of the mighty one, with all-devouring coals* (Ps 119(120):3-4). What this means is: once smitten by these and set on fire by them, you must blaze with so great a love for the kingdom of heaven that you scorn the tongues of all who block your path and want to call you back from your fixed resolve. You must also scoff at their persecutions, saying, *Who shall part me from the love of Christ? Shall tribulation, or distress, or hunger, or nakedness, or danger, or persecution, or the sword? I am certain that neither death nor life, nor angels, nor spiritual powers, nor things present, nor things to come, nor brute force, nor height, nor depth, nor any other created thing, shall separate us from the love of God, which is in Christ Jesus our Lord* (Rom 8:35.38-39). He made his arrows for those who burn like this, for this is what we find in the Greek manuscripts, *He made his arrows for those who are burning*; but the majority of Latin manuscripts[27] have "He made burning arrows." Yet either makes good sense, whether the arrows are themselves ablaze or make others blaze, something which they could not do, of course, unless they themselves were also ablaze.

The arrows as instruments of death

15. But because the Lord is said to have prepared not only arrows, but also *implements of death* in his bow, it may be asked what the implements of death are. Perhaps they are heretics? For they too, out of the same bow, that is, from the same scriptures, leap into souls who are destined not to be set alight with love, but to be destroyed by poisons, but this only because they deserve it. And so even that arrangement is to be attributed to divine providence, not because providence makes them sinners, but because it works them into an ordered framework after they have sinned.[28] For by reading the scriptures with a perverse hidden agenda because of sin, they are forced to understand them perversely. This itself is a punishment for sin. And yet by their death, the children of the Catholic Church are raised from sleep, as if pricked by thorns, and they progress to an understanding of the divine scriptures. Paul said, *Heresies there must be, so that those who are tested may be clearly identified among you* (1 Cor 11:19); identified, that is, among men and women, since they are in any case apparent to God. Or perhaps he arranged for the same arrows to be death-dealing weapons for the destruction of unbelievers, and burning missiles (or missiles aimed at those who will burn) for the instruction of the faithful? For the apostle made no mistake when he said, *We are the fragrance of Christ. For some this is the scent of life, leading to life, but for others*

---

27. That is, the African Latin psalters.
28. The providential assimilation of evil into the scheme of order is dealt with by Augustine in the dialogue *Order* I,18; II,12.

the stench of death unto death. Who is equal to this? (2 Cor 16). Small wonder, then, if the same apostles are both implements of death in the case of those from whom they have suffered persecution and also arrows on fire to kindle the hearts of those who believe.

Verse 15. Travailing with injustice

16. But after this present dispensation, just judgment will come. The psalmist speaks of this in such a way that we understand that for each person there is punishment for his sin, and his iniquity is turned into chastisement. He certainly does not want us to think that the tranquillity and ineffable light of God bring forth from themselves the punishment for sins. Rather, the sins themselves are set within an ordered framework, in such a way that those things which were once enticements to someone while sinning should be the Lord's tools when he punishes. *Look at that person* says the psalmist, *who has been in travail with injustice.* What did such a person conceive, to be travailing with injustice? *He conceived toil,* the psalm tells us. This is why we are warned, "In toil you will eat your bread."[29] From this, too, derives that other saying, *Come to me, all you who toil and are heavily burdened, for my yoke is kindly and my burden light* (Mt 11:28.30). The cycle of toil could not be brought to an end unless everybody loves what cannot be taken away against our will. For when the things we love are the sort of things we can lose against our will, we have no option but to toil for them in utmost misery. Even worse, in order to gain possession of them, we must devise wicked and unscrupulous schemes amid the bitter, restricting circumstances of this world, where everyone wants to grab those things for himself and to get in before someone else, or to snatch them away from others. Rightly, therefore, and strictly in order did he who conceived toil travail with injustice. Surely one can give birth only to that with which one has travailed, even though what one has conceived is not that with which one is in travail now. For the thing which is conceived is not what is born. The seed is conceived, what is born is what is formed out of the seed. Toil is thus the seed that grows into iniquity, but what first conceives toil is sin—the first sin, that is, rebellion against God.[30] Therefore the one who conceived toil travailed with injustice. *And he brought forth iniquity.* Iniquity is the same as injustice. Therefore he gave birth to that with which he had travailed. What follows thereafter?

Verses 16-17. Digging a pit of earthly desires

17. *He made a hole and dug it out.* To open up a pit in earthly matters is, as it were, to make ready a trap in the ground, into which someone might fall whom the unjust person wants to deceive. But this pit is opened when compliance is given to

---

29. See Gn 3:17.19.
30. See Sir 10:14.

the evil prompting of earth-bound desires. And it is dug out, when, after consenting, we press on to putting the deception into practice. But how can iniquity harm first of all the just person against whom it proceeds, and not rather the unjust heart whence it proceeds? So the embezzler of money, for example, while he wishes to cripple another with financial loss, is himself harmed by the wound of greed. Who, even a madman, does not see how great is the difference between these two, when the one suffers loss of money, the other loss of innocence? Therefore *he will fall into the pit which he has made*. As another psalm has it, *The Lord is known when he passes judgment; the sinner is caught in the works of his own hands* (Ps 9:17(16)).

18. *His toil shall rebound onto his own head; his iniquity shall descend to crown him.* Because he himself did not wish to escape sin, he has been subjected to sin like a slave, as the Lord says, *Whoever commits sin is the slave of sin* (Jn 8:34). Therefore his iniquity will be "over him," since he is subject to his own iniquity. He was unable to say to the Lord what the innocent and upright say, *My glory, who lift up my head* (Ps 3:4(3)). Therefore he will be underneath in such a way that his iniquity is above and falls upon him, because it oppresses him and weighs him down and does not allow him to fly back to rest with the saints. This happens when in a wicked person reason is enslaved and lust holds the upper hand.

Verse 18. Confession of praise

19. *I will confess to the Lord in accordance with his justice.* This is not a confession of sins, for the one who makes it is the one who earlier said with complete truthfulness, *If there is any iniquity on my hands* . . . . Rather, it is the confession of God's justice, by which we speak like this: "Truly, Lord, you are just when you protect the just in such a way that through yourself you enlighten them, and set sinners in an ordered framework in such a way that they are punished not by your malevolence but by their own." This confession praises the Lord in such a way that the slanders of the ungodly have no impact, of those, that is, who want to excuse their own wicked deeds and refuse to attribute their sinning to their own fault. The plain truth is that they do not want to attribute to their own fault what is their own fault. That is why they find either fortune or fate to blame, or the devil, even though the God who made us willed that it be in our power not to consent to the devil. They may even introduce an alien nature which is not from God.[31] What pathetic creatures they are—wavering and wandering rather than confessing to God so that he may pardon them. For he cannot pardon anyone except the one who says "I have sinned." Therefore whoever sees that what souls deserve is ordered by God in such a way that, while each is given his due, the beauty of the whole is in no sense violated, praises God in all things. This is the confession not of sinners, but of the

---

31. As the Manicheans did.

righteous. For it is no confession of sins when our Lord says, *I confess to you, Father, Lord of heaven and earth, because you have hidden these matters from the wise, and have revealed them to little ones* (Mt 11:25). So too it is said in Ecclesiasticus, *Confess to the Lord in all his works. And this is how you must confess to him: "All the Lord's works are exceedingly good"* (Sir 39:19-21).

The same thing can be understood in this psalm, if someone with devout mind and with the Lord's help distinguishes between the rewards of the just and the punishments of sinners, and also discerns how by both of these the whole creation, which God both founded and still rules, is adorned with a marvelous beauty, known only to a few. That is why the psalmist says, *I will confess to the Lord in accordance with his justice*, as if he were someone who saw that darkness was not created by God but set in a providential order nonetheless. For God said, *Let there be light, and light came to be* (Gn 1:3). He did not say, "Let there be darkness," and darkness came into being; and yet he did set that darkness in order. And that is why scripture says, *God made a division between light and darkness. He called the light "day" and the darkness he called "night"* (Gn 1:4-5). This is the distinction: the one he made and also ordered, the other he did not make but, nonetheless, he ordered it. You will again find that sins are what is meant by darkness in the prophet who said, *And your darkness will be like noonday* (Is 58:10), and in the apostle who said, *Whoever hates his brother is in darkness* (1 Jn 2:11), and above all in Paul's words, *Let us cast off the deeds of darkness and don the armor of light* (Rom 13:12). There is no such thing as a nature consisting in darkness. For all nature, insofar as it is nature, must exist. To exist, however, belongs to the light, not to exist belongs to the darkness. Therefore, whoever deserts the God by whom he was made and leans in the direction of that from which he was made, that is, toward nothing, is darkened in this sin. And yet he does not perish completely, but is given a place in the ordered hierarchy among the lowest. Therefore, after saying, *I will confess to the Lord*, the psalmist added this final passage, *And I will sing to the name of the Lord most high*, to make sure that we do not take it to mean confession of sins. Singing belongs to joy, but repentance of sins to sadness.

Another interpretation possible

20. This psalm can also be understood as spoken by the Lord-Man,[32] provided that those things which are said in it with humility are referred to our weakness, which he bore.

---

32. See note at Exposition of Psalm 1, 1.

Exposition of Psalm 8

Verse 1. First interpretation: the winepress and the Church

1. *To the end, for the presses, a psalm of David himself.* The writer does not seem to say anything about winepresses in the text of the psalm of which this is the title.[1] From this it is clear that one and the same thing is often suggested in the scriptures by many different similes. We can, therefore, take winepresses as referring to the churches, by the same line of reasoning as we understand the threshing-floor in terms of the Church, because, whether on the threshing-floor or in the winepress, what happens is that fruit is stripped of its covering. The coverings were necessary for two reasons: that the crop might come to life, and that it might reach its maturity, whether of the harvest or the vintage. The crop, therefore, is stripped bare of its covering or supports: grain is separated from the straw on the threshing-floor, grapes are stripped of their skin in the winepress. The same process takes place in our churches, so that through the work of God's ministers good people may be sifted out by spiritual love from the crowd of worldly people gathered there with them, a crowd which has, nonetheless, been necessary to bring the good to birth and prepare them to receive the divine word. Even now this is happening, so that the good may be separated from the evil, not on a geographical basis, but by their hearts' intention, even though they continue to keep company with each other in the churches so far as bodily proximity is concerned. But there will be a time in the future when the grain will be separated into granaries, the grapes, now wine, into cellars. Scripture says, *The grain he will store in granaries, but the chaff he will burn with inextinguishable fire* (Lk 3:17). The same idea can be understood by another simile: the grapes he will store in cellars, but the grapeskins he will throw to the cattle. The bellies of the cattle can be taken as a metaphor for the punishments of hell.

Second interpretation: the fermentation of the word of God

2. There is another way in which we can understand winepresses, while at the same time not losing sight of their interpretation as churches. The divine Word can also be understood as a grape. Even the Lord has been described as a cluster of

---

1. See also the Exposition of Psalm 80 for reflections on wine- and olive-presses.

grapes, which those who were sent on ahead by the people of Israel brought from the land of promise, hanging on a stick[2] like a victim of crucifixion. Therefore when the divine Word takes over the sound of the human voice in order to speak and reach the ears of his hearers, the content of the Word is encased like wine within the sound of the voice which, in turn, is like grapeskins. In this way the grape reaches our ears as if it were coming into the place where the grapes are trodden, and there it is processed in such a way that while the sound penetrates the ears, the meaning is caught in the memory of those who hear, as it were in a vat, and trickles through into a rule of behavior and habit of mind. It is like what happens to wine which goes from the vat into the cellars: if it does not go sour there through neglect, it will mature with age. It did indeed turn sour in the Jews, and it was some of this vinegar that they gave the Lord to drink.[3] But that wine which the Lord will drink with his saints in the kingdom of his Father,[4] from the produce of the vine of the New Testament, has to be the sweetest and the most mature.

Third interpretation: the harvest of martyrdom

3. The winepresses are also frequently understood to mean martyrdoms. The mortal remains of those who have been trampled underfoot by the brutality of persecution for confessing the name of Christ remain on earth like discarded grapeskins, but their souls flow out, to rest in their heavenly habitation. But we have not by such an interpretation as this deviated from the idea of fruit-bearing in the churches. The psalm is being sung, then, *for the winepresses*, for the establishment of the Church, when our Lord, after his resurrection, ascended into heaven. For it was then that he sent the Holy Spirit. Once filled by the Spirit, the disciples preached with boldness to gather the churches together.

Verse 2. The glory of the Lord

4. And so the psalm begins, *O Lord, our Lord, how wonderful is your name in the whole earth!* My question is: why is his name wonderful in the whole earth? The reply is: *Because your magnificence has been raised above the heavens.* The meaning, then, is this: Lord, you who are our Lord, how all who inhabit the earth marvel at you! This is because your magnificence has been raised up from earthly humility far above the heavens. From this it is clear who you are who came down, when some saw and others believed (without seeing) where you ascended.

---

2. See Nm 13:24.
3. See Jn 19:29.
4. See Lk 22:18.

Verse 3. Milk and solid food

5. *Out of the mouths of infants and nurslings you have perfected praise, because of your enemies.* I cannot take *infants and nurslings* to be any others than those to whom the apostle says, *As if to little children in Christ I gave you milk to drink, rather than solid food* (1 Cor 3:1-2). The children who ran before the Lord singing praises are representative of them; and of these children the Lord himself used this verse from the psalms as evidence when he replied to the Jews, who told him to rebuke them, *Have you not read, "Out of the mouths of infants and nurslings you have perfected praise"?* (Mt 21:16). He was quite right not to say, "You have evoked praise," but, *You have perfected praise*; for in the Church there are also some who are given milk to drink no longer, but are fed on solid food. To them the same apostle refers when he says, *We speak wisdom among the perfect* (1 Cor 2:6). But the churches are not made perfect by drawing only on people like this, because if they consisted of these alone, there would be scant regard for the human race as a whole. There is due regard given, however, when those too who are not yet able to understand things spiritual and eternal are nurtured by faith in the history which unfolds through time. After the period of the patriarchs and prophets, this history was carried through for our salvation by the most excellent power and wisdom of God, especially in the mystery of the humanity which God took to himself. In this lies salvation for everyone who believes. Inspired[5] by his authority, every believer must submit to his commandments, and being thereby cleansed and established in love must run with the saints. Such a person is no longer a child drinking milk but a youth eating solid food, able to comprehend the breadth, the length, the height, and the depth of the mystery, and to know the love of Christ that surpasses all knowledge.[6]

Heretics and some philosophers as enemies of faith

6. *Out of the mouths of infants and nurslings you have perfected praise, because of your enemies.* By enemies of this providential dispensation which was brought about by Jesus Christ, and him crucified, we ought in a general sense to understand all who forbid us to believe in things beyond our experience, while themselves promising certain knowledge. This is what all heretics do, and the same holds for those who among superstitious Gentiles pass for philosophers. It is not that the promise of knowledge is reprehensible in itself, but rather that they think that the step of faith can be bypassed, a step most conducive to salvation and necessary for us. Yet it is precisely by taking this step that the ascent must be made to any form of real certainty, which cannot be other than eternal. From this it is clear that they do

---

5. Variant reading *commonitus*, "warned."
6. See Eph 3:18-19.

not possess even that knowledge which they promise, while scorning faith, because they are completely unaware of the step which is useful and necessary as a means to it. Therefore *from the mouths of infants and nurslings* our Lord has *perfected praise,* first laying down through the prophet the rule, *unless you believe, you will not understand* (Is 7:9, LXX), and then later saying in his own person, *Blessed are those who have not seen, yet will believe* (Jn 20:29).

Because of your enemies: that is, those against whom this is said, *I praise you, Father, Lord of heaven and earth, because you have hidden these matters from the wise and knowing, and have revealed them to little ones* (Mt 11:25). In saying, *from the wise,* he meant not those who are truly wise, but people who think they are. *In order that you may destroy the enemy and the defender.*[7] Who is this, except the heretic? The person who gives the impression of defending the Christian faith, when in fact he is attacking it, is an enemy-cum-defender. At the same time it is also true that the philosophers of this world are rightly understood as enemies-cum-defenders, since indeed the Son of God is the power and wisdom of God,[8] by which everyone who is made wise by the truth is enlightened. They purport to be lovers of wisdom, hence their name, "philosophers." And that is why they look as if they are defending the truth, while they really are its enemies, since they never cease recommending harmful superstitions, trying to persuade people that the elements of this world are to be worshiped and venerated.[9]

Verse 4. The heavenly scriptures

7. *Because I shall see the*[10] *heavens, the works of your fingers.* We read that the law was written by the finger of God and given through Moses, his holy servant.[11] Many understand the finger of God as the Holy Spirit.[12] Therefore, if, because of the Holy Spirit at work in them, we are right in understanding God's ministers, filled with his Spirit, as the fingers of God, since through them the whole of the divine scripture was written for us, we can legitimately take *the heavens* in this context to mean the books of both Testaments. And it was said also of Moses himself by the wise men of King Pharaoh when they had been defeated by him, *This is the finger of God* (Ex 8:19). There is that other saying too, *Heaven will be*

---

7. Here Augustine was reading *defensorem,* but when quoting the same verse in his Exposition of Psalm 102, 14, he remarks that a better reading is *vindicatorem,* "avenger"; compare the Septuagint's ἐκδικητήν, Vulgate *ultorem.*
8. See 1 Cor 1:19-24.
9. Augustine had had plenty of experience of these plausible "philosophers" among Manicheans, Academics, and "astrologers," as he recounts in Books IV to VII of his *Confessions;* but Col 2:16-23 is probably also in his mind.
10. Or, with some manuscripts, "your."
11. See Ex 31:18; compare Dt 9:10.
12. As in the Latin hymn, *Veni, Creator,* where the Spirit is invoked as *dextrae Dei tu digitus.*

rolled up like a scroll (Is 34:4). Even if this refers to the sky, those other heavens which are the holy books are allegorically indicated by the same simile. *Because I will see*, says the psalmist, *the heavens, the works of your fingers*. By this is meant, "I will investigate and understand[13] the scriptures which by the operation of your Holy Spirit you have written through your ministers."

Divine condescension

8. Therefore the heavens named above can also be understood as books, when the psalmist says, *Your magnificence is raised above the heavens*. The full meaning of this phrase, *your magnificence is raised above the heavens*, is as follows: your magnificence has surpassed the words of all the scriptures. Out of the mouths of infants and suckling children you have perfected praise, in the sense that those who want to gain knowledge of your magnificence should begin from belief in the scriptures. Your magnificence is raised above the scriptures because it surpasses and stretches beyond the proclamations of all words and tongues. Therefore God has brought the scriptures right down within the range of infants and nurslings, as is sung in another psalm: *He bowed the heavens and came down* (Ps 17:10(18:9)). This he did on account of his enemies who, being enemies of the cross of Christ through their pride and talkativeness, cannot be of any use to infants and nurslings, even when they say some things that are true. This is how the enemy-cum-defender is toppled. Whether it is wisdom or the very name of Christ which he gives the impression of upholding, nonetheless it is from the step of this very faith that he mounts his attack on that truth which he is so ready to promise. It is crystal-clear that he does not have the truth, for by attacking its first step, which is faith, he proves he has not the faintest idea how to climb up to it. By this means, therefore, that rash and blind person who promises truth but who is also its enemy-cum-defender is toppled. This happens when the heavens are seen as the works of God's fingers, that is, when the scriptures, brought right down to the slowness of babies' comprehension, are understood. They raise these infants up to the very things of which they tell with such conviction; but the infants are now well nurtured and strengthened to scale the heights and understand things eternal, through the humility of faith rooted in a history which has been worked out within time. Those heavens, that is, those books, are indeed the works of God's fingers, for it was by the operation of the Holy Spirit in the saints that they were written. Those who sought their own glory rather than the salvation of humankind spoke without the Holy Spirit, in whom are the depths of the mercy of God.

---

13. Or, "Let me investigate and understand."

The Church, moon and stars

9. *Because I will see the heavens, the work of your fingers, the moon and stars which you have established.* The moon and the stars are set in heaven, because both the Church universal which is often represented by the moon, and the individual churches in specific places which are, I think, adumbrated by the word, "stars," are placed together in the same scriptures; and these scriptures, as we believe, are referred to by the term, "heavens." Why the word "moon" is rightly interpreted to mean "Church" will be considered more appropriately in another psalm, where it is said, *Sinners have bent their bows to shoot those of honest heart when the moon is darkened* (Ps 10:3(11:2)).

Verse 5. Humankind, old and new

10. *What is a mere man that you remember him, a son of man that you visit him?* What, it may be asked, is this distinction between man and the son of man? Were there no distinction, the psalm would not say, *man, or the son of man*, in this way, making an explicit distinction.[14] For if it were written like this: "What is man that you are mindful of him *and* the son of man that you come to him," it would simply look like a repetition of the word *man.* But when in fact it says, "man, *or* the son of man," a clearer distinction is suggested. This, of course, is to be kept in mind, that every son of man is a man, although not every man can be deemed a son of man. Adam was indeed a man, but not a son of man. And so from this it is now possible to examine the text and to decide what the distinction is between man and son of man. It is as follows. Those who bear the image of the earthly man,[15] who is not a son of man, can be called "men"; but those who bear the image of the heavenly man are more truly called "sons of men." For the former is also called the old man, the latter the new man; but the new is born from the old because spiritual regeneration is begun by a change of earthly and worldly life,[16] and on that account the new man is called a son of man. Therefore "man" in this context is earthly, whereas the "son of man" is heavenly. The former is separated from God at a great distance, the latter is present with God; and that is why God remembers the one, as far away from him, but the other he comes to visit; and by his presence he illuminates him with his countenance. For *salvation is far from sinners* (Ps 118(119):155), but *the light of your countenance is stamped upon us, Lord* (Ps 4:7(6)).

So another psalm associates men and women with beasts, saying that they are saved together with beasts not by the presence of inner illumination but through the

---

14. Insistence on inclusive language in this paragraph would involve an unacceptable degree of verbal contortions.
15. See 1 Cor 15:49.
16. See Eph 4:22.24.

increase of the mercy of God, whereby his goodness reaches even to the lowest things. This is because the salvation of carnal men and women is carnal, like that of cattle. But by separating "sons of men" from those whom, as "men," he has linked with cattle, the psalmist proclaims that they are blessed in a far more exalted way, by the illumination of the truth itself and by an overflowing of the fountain of life. For this is what he says: *Men and beasts you will save, Lord, as your mercy has been multiplied, O God. But the sons of men will hope under the shelter of your wings. They will be inebriated by the rich abundance of your house, and you will give them the full flow of your delights to drink, for with you is the fountain of life, and in your light we will see light. Extend your mercy to those who know you* (Ps 35:7-11(36:6-10)). God remembers "man," then, through the multiplication of his mercy, in the same way as he is mindful of beasts, because such multiplied mercy has reached even those who are far off. But he visits the "son of man" to whom he extends mercy under the protection of his wings, and gives such a person light in his own light, and offers him some of his own delights to drink, and inebriates him with the abundance of his own house, to enable him to forget the sorrows and meanderings of his former way of life. The repentance of the old man brings to birth, with pain and lamentation, this "son of man," that is, the new man. Although new, he is nonetheless referred to as carnal, since he needs to be fed with milk. *Not as spiritual persons could I speak to you*, said the apostle, *but only as carnal*; but in order to show that it is to men and women already regenerate that he is speaking, he continues, *as if to little children in Christ, I gave you milk to drink, rather than solid food*. When we fall back, as often happens, into the old life, we hear the tone of reproach reminding us that we are merely human: *Are you not carnal still, conducting yourselves in a merely human way?* (1 Cor 3:1-3).

Verses 6-7. Humiliation and exaltation of the Son

11. The "son of man" is visited in the first instance in the person of the Lord-Man[17] himself, born of the virgin Mary. On account of his fleshly weakness, which the wisdom of God condescended to bear, and on account of the humility of his suffering, scripture rightly says of him, *You have made him a little lower than the angels*. But mention is made too of his glorification, in that he rose and ascended into heaven: *with glory and honor you have crowned him; and you have set him above the works of your hands*, says the psalm. Since the angels also are the works of God's hands, we understand that the only-begotten Son is set even above the angels, the same Son whom we hear and believe to have been made a little lower than the angels through the humility of his birth in the flesh and his suffering.

---

17. See note on this expression at Exposition of Psalm 1, 1.

Verses 8-9. Sheep and oxen

12. *You have put all things under his feet,* says the psalmist. He allows for no exceptions when he says, *all things,* and to prevent its being understood in any other way, the apostle insists that it should be so believed when he says, *except for the one who subjected all things to him* (1 Cor 15:27). In writing to the Hebrews[18] he uses the same verse from this psalm, when he wants to make it clear that all things have been subjected to our Lord Jesus Christ in such a way that there are no exceptions. However the psalmist does not seem to make any significant addition by saying, *all sheep and cattle, and even the wild beasts, birds of the air, and the fishes of the sea, who roam the pathways of the deep.* It seems that, leaving aside heavenly Principalities and Powers, and all the cohorts of angels, leaving aside also mankind itself, he has made subject to him the beasts only. The alternative is to understand sheep and cattle as holy souls, inasmuch as they either yield the fruit of innocence or even work to make the earth fruitful: work, that is, so that earthly men and women may be reborn to abundant spiritual fruitfulness. We ought to understand these holy souls, then, not only as men and women, but also as all the angels, if we wish to understand from this that all things are subject to our Lord Jesus Christ. For no creature will fail to be subject to him to whom the principal spirits, so to speak, are being subjected. But how will we prove that sheep can be interpreted as the most sublimely blessed, not as mortals even but as spirits of the angelic creation? Could it be from the Lord's saying that he had left ninety-nine sheep on the mountains, that is, in lofty places, and had gone down for the sake of only one?[19] For if we understand Adam to be the one lost[20] sheep (because Eve, of course, was made from his side), we are left with the conclusion that the ninety-nine left on the mountains must be not human but angelic spirits. (This is not the time to consider and deal with these questions about Adam and Eve in a spiritual way.)

As to the oxen, the development[21] of this idea is easy: human beings themselves are called oxen for no other reason than that by proclaiming the word of God they act like the angels. Of them scripture commands, *You shall not muzzle an ox while it is threshing* (Dt 25:4; 1 Cor 9:9; 1 Tm 5:18). How much more easily, then, do we interpret oxen as referring to the angels themselves, the messengers of truth, when the evangelists by sharing their name have been called oxen? Therefore, says the psalmist, you have subjected to him *all sheep and oxen,* that is, all the holy spiritual creation. In this too we include those holy men and women who are in the Church, in those winepresses, I mean, which have been alluded to under a different simile as the moon and stars.

---

18. See Heb 2:8.
19. See Mt 18:12.
20. *Lapsam,* "fallen."
21. *Expeditio;* a variant is *expositio,* "explanation."

The comprehensiveness of the Church

13. *What is more*, says the psalmist, *the beasts of the field*. The addition of *what is more* is by no means superfluous. First, because sheep and cattle can also be called beasts of the field: if goats are the beasts of the rocky and steep places, sheep are rightly understood as the beasts of the field. Therefore even if it had been written like this: "all sheep and oxen and beasts of the field," the question could rightly be asked: "What is the meaning of beasts of the field, when sheep and oxen themselves can be understood in this way?" However the addition *what is more* pushes us further to recognize some differentiation. Under this additional phrase, *what is more*, not only are the beasts of the field alluded to, but also the birds of the air and the fish of the sea, which weave their way through the pathways of the sea. What, then, is the distinction?

Think of the winepresses with grapeskins and wine, and the threshing-floor containing chaff and grain, and the nets in which were enclosed fish both good and bad,[22] and Noah's ark in which there were animals both clean and unclean.[23] There you will see that the churches in their interim state, in this present age until the final time of judgment, contain not only sheep and cattle, that is, holy members both lay and clerical, but, *what is more, beasts of the field, birds of the air, and fishes of the sea, who roam the pathways of the deep*. For it is best to understand beasts of the field as men and women who rejoice in the pleasure of the flesh. Such a life involves climbing nothing precipitous, nothing arduous. The open plain is a broad road and it leads to death,[24] and it was in the open field that Abel was killed.[25] So we have reason to be afraid that anyone coming down from the mountains of God's justice (for *your justice is like God's mountains* (Ps 35:7(36:6), says scripture) and choosing the broad expanses and easy ways of bodily pleasure will be cut down by the devil. Now look also at the birds of the air, the proud, of whom it is said, *Their boastful talk is directed to the sky* (Ps 72:9(73:8)). Just see how high they are wafted by the wind, those who say, *We will make a great show with our eloquence; our lips are our own, and who is our master?* (Ps 11:5(12:4)).Observe also the fish of the sea, that is, the inquisitive[26] who weave their course through the pathways of the sea, by which is meant those who search in the deep for the temporal things of this world, which disappear and die as quickly as do pathways in the sea when the water flows together again and mixes, after it has made way for any who pass through, for ships or for anything that walks or swims. For the psalm did not say, "They walk the

---

22. See Mt 13:47-48.
23. See Gn 7:8.
24. See Mt 7:13.
25. See Gn 4:8.
26. *Curiosos*: for Augustine *curiositas* was a vice more serious than the English word suggests to us. He identified it with the "lust of the eyes" mentioned in 1 Jn 2:16 and saw it as the perversion of the mind that is made for truth.

pathways of the sea," but *they weave their way through,* drawing attention to the most stubborn enthusiasm of those who chase after empty things which do no more than float past. These three types of vices, that is, indulgence of the flesh, pride and inquisitiveness, embrace all sins.[27] They seem to me to be identified by the apostle John when he says, *Love not the world, because all that is in the world is the concupiscence of the flesh, and the concupiscence of the eyes, and worldly ambition* (1 Jn 2:15-16). It is through the eyes in particular that inquisitiveness prevails. As for the rest, what they involve is clear. The temptation of the Lord-Man also was threefold: (1) through food, that is, through the lust of the flesh, where Satan suggests: *Say to these stones, "Become loaves of bread"* (Mt 4:3); (2) through empty boasting, where he is set on a mountain, and all the kingdoms of this earth are shown to him and promised to him if he will worship Satan; (3) through inquisitiveness, when the suggestion is made that he cast himself down from the pinnacle of the temple, in order to test if, in fact, he is held up by the angels. This is why, after the enemy had been unable to overcome him by tempting him with any of these things, scripture says, *After the devil had completed the whole temptation* (Lk 4:13).

So, then, in accordance with the simile of the winepresses, not only the grapes but also the husks are trodden under his feet. This means, not only sheep and cattle, that is to say, the holy souls of the faithful, either in the people or among the clergy, but, what is more, beasts of pleasure also and birds of pride and fish of inquisitiveness. All these types of sinners we see here and now in the churches mixed up with the good and the holy. Let God work, then, in his churches and separate wine from grapeskins. Let us cooperate with God so that we may be wine or sheep or cattle, rather than husks or beasts of the field or fish that weave their way through the pathways of the deep. This is not to say that these words can be understood and explained only in this way, but this is what the present context dictates. Somewhere else they may have a different meaning. This rule of thumb is to be upheld in every allegory, that what is expressed through a simile should be judged in the light of its immediate context. Such is the teaching of our Lord and the apostles. Therefore let us repeat the last verse which is also set at the beginning of the psalm, and let us praise God saying, *Lord, our Lord, how wonderful is your name in all the earth!* It is quite appropriate for us after the body of the sermon to return to the heading, to which the whole sermon should be related.

---

27. This statement is expanded in the tenth book of his *Confessions.*

Exposition of Psalm 9

Part 1

Verse 1. The hidden and open judgments of God

1. The title of this psalm is, *To the end, concerning the hidden things of the son, a psalm of David himself*. One may well ask what is meant by *the hidden things of the son*; but because the psalmist did not add whose son, it must be understood as the only-begotten Son of God. When the title of Psalm 3 mentioned David's son it specified, *When he (David) was in flight from the face of Abessalon his son*. In that case his name was used and there could be no hiding the identity of the subject; yet the title had not merely, *from the face of the son Abessalon* but added *his* to the word "son." Here, on the contrary, because "his" is not added and because much is said about the Gentiles, it cannot rightly be understood as referring to Abessalon. The war which that scoundrel waged against his father did not in any way involve the Gentiles, since in that situation the people of Israel was divided against itself. Therefore this psalm is sung about the hidden things of the only-begotten Son of God. The Lord himself also uses the word, "Son," without further clarification when he wants it to be understood as himself, the only-begotten, as when he says, *If the Son shall have set you free, you will be free indeed* (Jn 8:36). He did not say, "The Son of God," but by saying no more than *the Son* he makes it sufficiently clear whose Son is meant. His pre-eminence alone allows us to use this idiom, so that we can speak of him in such a way that even though we do not name him, he can nonetheless be understood. Similarly we say, "It is raining, it is clearing up, it is thundering," and suchlike things, without adding who is doing it. The pre-eminence of the one who does this springs spontaneously to everybody's mind and has no need of words.

What, then, are the hidden things of the Son? From this phrase we must first understand that there are some clearly visible aspects of the Son, from which must be distinguished those which are referred to as hidden. So since we believe in two comings of the Lord, the one already past, which the Jews did not understand, the other future for which both Jews and Gentiles hope, and since the coming which the Jews failed to recognize was beneficial to the Gentiles, it is not inappropriate to take the phrase, *concerning the hidden things of the Son*, as referring to this first coming where blindness has fallen on part of Israel, to enable the full complement of Gentiles to come in.[1] Indeed two judgments are hinted at throughout the scriptures,

---

1. See Rom 11:25.

if anyone takes notice: the one secret, the other open. The secret judgment is taking place here and now. Of it the apostle Peter says, *It is now time for judgment to take place, beginning from the house of the Lord* (1 Pt 4:17). The hidden judgment, therefore, is the chastisement by which even now we are either put through our paces with a view to our purification, or cautioned with a view to our conversion, or, if we scorn God's invitation and instruction, blinded and eventually condemned. But the open judgment is that whereby the Lord will come and judge the living and the dead. Everyone will then acknowledge that he is the one who apportions rewards to the good, punishments to the evil. But at that time such confession will be unavailing to put right the wrongs which have been committed; indeed, it will serve only to compound condemnation. It seems to me that the Lord spoke about these two judgments, the one secret, the other open, when he said, *Whoever believes in me has passed from death to life already, and will not come to judgment* (Jn 5:24)—to the open judgment, that is. For the passage from death to life through some form of suffering, by which God scourges every son whom he takes to himself [2] is God's secret judgment. He also says, *Whoever does not believe is already judged* (Jn 3:18); this means that such a person has already been prepared by the hidden judgment for the open judgment. We read also of these two judgments in the Book of Wisdom, where it is written, *You made a mockery of them by imposing a sentence as if they were children devoid of understanding. But those who were not corrected by this sentence suffered from God the judgment that was their due* (Wis 12:25.26). Therefore those who are not made to improve by this hidden judgment of God will most deservedly be punished by the open judgment yet to come.

In this psalm, then, we should take note of the hidden things of the Son, that is, both his coming in humility, by which he greatly profited the Gentiles in the face of the blindness of the Jews, and the punishment which now is being meted out secretly. It does not as yet involve the total condemnation of sinners, but is intended to provide discipline for those who have been converted, or admonition to conversion for others, or to bring upon those who refuse to be converted a blindness which serves only to prepare them for damnation.

Verse 2. Visible and invisible works of God

2. *To you, Lord, I will confess with my whole heart.* Whoever entertains doubts about God's providence in any particular does not confess to God with a whole heart. Wholehearted confession is, rather, the mark of the person who already discerns the hidden things of the wisdom of God, and how great is his invisible reward, the person who says, *We even rejoice in our sufferings* (Rom 5:3). Such

---

2. See Heb 12:6.

people understand that all the hardships which are imposed on the body either offer training to those who have turned to God, or warn them to turn, or else prepare the stubborn for the final and just judgment; and so they see that all things which the foolish think happen somehow by chance and at random, without any divine direction, are to be referred to the guidance of divine providence. *I shall tell all your marvelous deeds.* The person who sees that all God's marvelous deeds take place not only in bodies for all to see, but also in souls invisibly, and in a much more exalted and excellent way there, is the one who tells of them. Both those who are earthbound and those who are given over to secret things[3] marvel more that the already-dead Lazarus rose in the body than that the persecutor Paul rose in the soul. But whereas the visible miracle calls the soul to enlightenment, the invisible miracle enlightens the soul which comes, once called; and so the person who believes in the visible and makes the transition to understanding the invisible tells all the marvelous deeds of God.

Verse 3. The future content of rejoicing

3. *I will rejoice and exult in you.* Not now in this age, not in the pleasure of bodily caresses, not in the flavors of the palate and the tongue, not in sweet scents, not in pleasant sounds that fade away, not in beautifully colored objects,[4] not in the vanities of human praise, not in matrimony and offspring which one day will die, not in the abundance of temporal riches, not in this world's getting, whether it extend in space, or be prolonged in the succession of time; but *in you I will rejoice and exult,* that is, in the hidden things of the Son, where the light of your face, O Lord, has been stamped on us.[5] For indeed *you will hide them,* says a psalmist, *in the hidden recess of your face* (Ps 30:21(31:20)). Therefore whoever tells all your marvelous deeds will rejoice and exult in you. But the phrase, "will tell all your marvelous deeds," is spoken prophetically, with reference to him who came to do not his own will, but the will of him who sent him.[6]

Verse 4. Turning back the devil

4. Now the person of the Lord begins to appear as the speaker in this psalm. For what follows is, *I will sing to your name, O Most High, in turning my enemy back.* When is his enemy turned back? Surely when is he told, *Get back, Satan* (Mt

---

3. Reading, with most witnesses, *et occultis dediti.* A variant is *et oculis dediti,* "and led only by their eyes." These would then be the same people as the "earthbound" just mentioned.
4. This paragraph is reminiscent of his long discussion of the senses in *The Confessions,* Book X, 30,41—35,47.
5. See Ps 4:7(6).
6. See Jn 6:38.

4:10)?[7] On that occasion the one who by temptation wanted to put himself in front was driven backward, by failing to deceive the one tempted and proving powerless against him. Earthly men and women are behind, but the heavenly man is in front even though in time he came later. The first human being was of the earth, earthly; the second was from heaven, heavenly.[8] But he came from the same stock as the man who said, *The one who comes after me ranks before me* (Jn 1:15). The apostle too forgets the things which are behind and stretches forward to those which are in front.[9] The enemy was thus turned backward when, having failed to deceive the heavenly man whom he tempted, he turned himself to earthly men and women over whom he can exercise domination. This is precisely why nobody goes before him and forces him back, except a person who sets to one side the image of the earthly man and puts on the image of the heavenly.

If, however, we prefer to understand the phrase, *my enemy*, more generally as a sinner or a pagan, that will not be out of line. What is suggested by *in turning my enemy backward* would not even be a punishment but a kindness, and such a kindness as to be beyond comparison; for what is more blessed than to lay aside pride and not to want to be in front of Christ, as though one were healthy and in no need of a doctor, and rather choose to walk behind him? When calling a disciple in order to make him perfect, Christ said, *Follow me!* (Mt 19:21).

All the same, the phrase, *in turning my enemy back*, is more fittingly understood as spoken in relation to the devil, for he is pushed to the rear when he persecutes the just, and is more useful as a persecutor[10] than if, as a leader and prince, he were to march before them. Therefore we must sing to the name of the Most High in turning back our enemy. Fleeing from him while he pursues us is better than following him as our leader, for we have somewhere to flee and to hide in the hidden things of the Son, because God has become a refuge for us.[11]

Verses 4-5. *Making God's judgment our own*

5. *They will be weakened and perish from before your face.* Who will be weakened and perish, but the unjust and the godless? *They will be weakened* when they become ineffectual; and *they will perish* because as ungodly they will cease to exist. They will cease *from before the face* of God, that is, they will no longer be ungodly as God knows them, just as the apostle Paul had "perished" when he said, *I live my own life no longer; it is Christ who lives in me* (Gal 2:20). But why will the

---

7. Compare Mk 8:33; Mt 16:23.
8. See 1 Cor 15:47.
9. See Phil 3:13.
10. The contrast is clearer in Latin, where *persecutor* is more obviously derived from *sequere*, "to follow."
11. See Ps 89(90):1.

godless *be weakened and perish from your face*? Because, says the psalmist, *you have made the judgment, and the case against me, mine*. By this he means that you have made mine the judgment in which it looked as though I was judged, and you have made mine the case in which others condemned me, just and innocent though I am. These happenings fought on Christ's side in order to secure our liberation. It is like the way in which sailors speak of "their" wind, referring to the one they use for a safe voyage.

Interpretations of "You are seated on your throne"

6. *You are seated on your throne, you who judge with equity.*[12] The possibilities are: (1) Perhaps the Son is speaking to the Father. The same Son also said, *You would have no power over me, had it not been given you from above* (Jn 19:11), attributing to the Father's fair judgment and to his own hidden workings the subjection of the Judge of men and women to judgment for the advantage of humankind. (2) Or again it could be an ordinary person like ourselves saying to God, *You are seated on your throne, you who judge with equity*, calling our own soul God's throne; and then perhaps our body could represent the earth, which is called God's footstool;[13] for God was in Christ reconciling the world to himself.[14] (3) Finally it is possible that the soul of the Church, already perfect and without spot or wrinkle,[15] worthy indeed of the hidden things of the Son, since the king has brought her into his bedchamber,[16] is here saying to her spouse, *You are seated on your throne, you who judge with equity*, because you have risen from the dead and ascended into heaven and sit on the Father's right hand.

No matter which of the above is preferred as an interpretation of this verse, none of them transgresses the rule of faith.

Verse 6. The age of this age

7. *You have rebuked the heathen, and the ungodly has perished*. We do better to understand this as said to the Lord Jesus Christ than to take it as spoken by him. Who else but Christ has rebuked the heathen, so that the ungodly has perished, who else but he who, after ascending into heaven, sent the Holy Spirit in order that the apostles, once filled by the Spirit, might with assurance of faith preach the word of God and freely reprove the sins of men and women? By this rebuke the ungodly has been destroyed, because ungodly people have been justified and have been made

---

12. Variant reading, "justice."
13. See Is 66:1.
14. See 2 Cor 5:19.
15. See Eph 5:27.
16. See Sg 1:3.

godly instead. *Their name you have blotted out for this age and for the age of this age.*[17] The name of the ungodly has been blotted out, for those who truly believe in God are not called ungodly. But their name is blotted out not only *for the age*, that is, as long as the temporal age runs, but also for *the age of the age*. What is *the age of the age*, if not that of which this age is a kind of image and shadow? The cycle of times which succeed each other, while the moon wanes and again waxes full, while the sun each year finds its height again, while the spring, or summer, or autumn, or winter passes only to return—all this is a kind of imitation of eternity. But the age of this age is that which consists in unchangeable eternity. It is like a verse which exists in the mind and a verse which is spoken. The former is understood, the latter is heard; and the former regulates the latter. That is why the former is effective in art and endures, whereas the latter sounds in the air and is gone. Likewise the mode of being of this changeable world is defined by that unchangeable world, which is spoken of as *the age of this age*. And for this reason the latter endures in the art, that is, in the wisdom and power of God; but the other is carried on through the providential administration of the created order. But if it is not simply repetition, the phrase, *and for the age of this age*, is added to prevent the phrase *for this age* being understood in terms of the passing world only. For in the Greek manuscripts it is εἰς τὸν αἰῶνα καὶ εἰς τὸν αἰῶνα τοῦ αἰῶνος. The Latins by and large have interpreted it not as meaning *for this age and for the age of this age*, but as *for ever, and for the age of this age.*[18] This means that the words, *for the age of this age*, should be understood as meaning, *for ever.* Therefore *you have wiped out the name of the ungodly for ever*, because from now on there will never be ungodly people. And if their name does not endure to the end of this world, much less does it extend into the age of this age.[19]

---

17. *In saeculum, et in saeculum saeculi*. In this and the following sentences Augustine is meditating on the phrase *in saeculum saeculi*, which could literally mean either "unto the age of [this] age" or "unto the world of [this] world." *Saeculum* means primarily a generation or a lifetime, and so a long period or an age; then, like the scriptural *'olam* or αἰών, the present world, conditioned by temporal succession. A variant reading here is *in aeternum*, but this is to anticipate Augustine's remark at the end of this paragraph.
18. *In aeternum, et in saeculum saeculi.*
19. The thought of this paragraph echoes the Neo-Platonic doctrine of hypostases: from the absolutely undifferentiated One sprang a second hypostasis, Intellect, in which were contained the Platonic "forms" or "ideas." A third hypostasis, Soul, sprang from Intellect, and cast upon formless matter a shadow of the forms; thus the material cosmos came into being. Soul originated time, and hence the restlessness characteristic of time-bound existences, which prefer succession to the eternal "now." So in the present context Augustine thinks of the duration of the present age or world as only a shadow of the "age" of eternity.

Verse 7. The state of vices

8. *The swords*[20] *of the enemy have given way at the end.* This sentence does not speak of enemies in the plural but of this particular enemy in the singular. But which enemy apart from the devil is it, whose swords have given way? These swords, then, are to be understood as various misguided opinions by which the devil destroys souls as though by cutting them down. It is to overcome these weapons and to reduce them to nothing that the great sword menaces, that one of which it is said in the seventh psalm, *Unless you turn, he will brandish his sword* (Ps 7:13(12)). And perhaps that is the *end* before which the swords of the enemy have given way, because up to that point they have some force. At present the sword works secretly, but at the last judgment it will be brandished openly. It is by this sword that cities are destroyed, for the psalm continues like this, *The swords of the enemy have given way at the end; and you have destroyed the cities*: the cities, clearly, in which the devil rules, where deceitful and fraudulent purposes have something approaching the status of government. This sovereignty is maintained by the services of various parts of the body acting as satellites and ministers, the eyes for curiosity, the ears for lewdness, or whatever else of ill repute is willingly listened to, the hand for looting or any other outrage or atrocity, and the other parts enlisted in a similar way under this tyrannical regime, that is, in the service of these evil purposes. The ordinary people, so to speak, of this city are all the self-indulgent desires and the unsettling emotions of the mind, whipping up insurrection within a person every day. Now where a king, a court, ministers, and common people are to be found, there is a state. Such characteristics would not be found in evil states unless they occurred first in individual people, who are like elements and seeds of city-states. God brought about the destruction of these states when he drove out their ruler, of whom it is said, *Now has the ruler of this world been cast out* (Jn 12:31). These kingdoms are laid waste by the word of truth, the wicked purposes are silenced, base desires are subdued, the activities of limbs and senses taken prisoner and handed over to the active service of justice and good works. This is to make sure that here and now *sin shall reign no more in our mortal body* (Rom 6:12), as the apostle says, together with other suchlike things. Then the soul is given peace and the person concerned put in proper order so as to receive serenity and blessedness. *Their memory has perished with an uproar*, that is, the memory of the ungodly. The addition, *with an uproar,* indicates either that there is uproar when impiety is overturned; for nobody passes over to the highest peace, where there is greatest silence, except the one who first has waged war with his own vices amid a

---

20. *Frameae*. A variant is *framea*, which would make the sentence mean "the enemies have fallen by the sword." The *framea* was originally a spear, used by the ancient Germans, though in later Latin the word often means a sword.

great hullabaloo; or else *with an uproar* is a prayer that the memory of the ungodly may perish even as the din itself dies away, that uproar where impiety raises a riot.

Verse 8-9. Judgment with justice

9. *And the Lord abides for ever.* Why then have the nations raged, and the peoples devised futile schemes against the Lord and against his Christ?[21] *The Lord abides for ever. He has prepared his seat in judgment, and he himself will judge the earth with equity.* He prepared his seat when he himself was judged, for through his endurance and suffering, humankind won heaven, and God in man benefited those who believe. This is the Son's hidden working. But he will also come openly and clear for all to see in order to judge the living and the dead; therefore he has prepared his seat by his secret judgment, and he will also in open fashion *judge the earth with equity*; that is, he will distribute rewards appropriate to deserts, setting sheep on his right hand, goats on his left.[22] *He will judge the peoples with justice*: this means the same thing as what was said earlier, *He will judge the earth with equity*, not in the way you or I might judge. We do not see the hearts of the accused. In our courts as a general rule those acquitted are worse than those condemned. But the Lord will judge in equity and with justice while conscience bears witness, and thoughts either accuse or defend.[23]

Verse 10. Holy poverty

10. *The Lord has become a refuge for the poor.* However comprehensively the enemy who has been turned back persecutes, what harm will he do to those for whom the Lord has become a refuge? But this is what will happen if in this world, in which the enemy holds sway, people opt for poverty by loving nothing which either deserts a living person who loves it here on earth, or else is left behind at death. To such a pauper as this the Lord has become a refuge, *a helper at times when he is needed, in tribulation.* He makes people poor, inasmuch as he scourges every son whom he receives.[24] The psalmist explains the meaning of *a helper at times when he is needed* by adding *in tribulation*, for the soul is not turned to God except while it is turning away from this world. There is no more appropriate time for it to be turning away from this world than when toils and tribulations are mixed in with its futile, harmful and dangerous pleasures.

---

21. See Ps 2:1.2.
22. See Mt 25:33.
23. See Rom 2:15.
24. See Heb 12:6.

Verse 11. Knowledge of God and the future hope of eternity

11. *Let those who know your name hope in you,* when they have ceased to hope in riches and in the other allurements of this world. When the soul which is being turned away from this world is looking for somewhere to place its hope, the knowledge of God's name welcomes it at exactly the right moment. For the name of God is by now spread far and wide, but knowledge of that name exists only when he is known, whose name it is: a name is not a name for its own sake, but for the sake of that which it signifies. Scripture says, *The Lord is his name* (Jer 33:2; Am 5:8). This means that whoever has willingly subjected himself to God as a servant has come to know this name. *And may those who know your name put their trust in you.* The Lord said to Moses, *I am who I am. Thus shall you say to the children of Israel, HE WHO IS has sent me* (Ex 3:14). *Let those,* therefore, *who know your name put their trust in you,* to avoid putting it in things which flow past in the swift flux of time, things that have no being other than "will be" and "has been." What in them is future is instantly past as soon as it has come; it is anticipated with eagerness, and let go of with sorrow. But in God's nature there will not be anything which does not yet exist, or anything that was, which is not now; there is only that which is, and that is eternity itself. Therefore those who know the name of the one who said, *I am who I am,* and of whom it was said, *The I AM has sent me,* should stop hoping for and loving temporal things, and instead should devote themselves to the eternal hope. *Because you have not abandoned[25] those who seek you, Lord.* Those who seek him do not seek things which are already passing and soon will die. For nobody can serve two masters.[26]

Verse 12. Watching and vision

12. *Sing to the Lord, who dwells in Zion.* This invitation is addressed to those whom the Lord does not abandon as they seek him. He himself lives in Zion, which means "watching," and bears the image of the Church which now is, as Jerusalem bears the image of the Church which is yet to be, that is, of the city of the saints who enjoy the angelic life. This is because Jerusalem means "vision of peace." Watching goes before seeing, as this Church precedes that other Church which is promised, the immortal and eternal city. But it has precedence in time, not in dignity, because the goal we are straining to reach is of more value than what we do to merit reaching it. We put all our efforts into watching, in order to see. But unless the Lord dwells in the Church which now is, our watching, no matter how assiduously done, will result in some sort of going astray. To this Church is said, *God's temple is holy, and that temple you are* (1 Cor 3:17), and *May Christ dwell within*

---

25. *Non dereliquisti*; a variant is *non derelinques*, "you will not abandon."
26. See Mt 6:24.

you, in your hearts through faith (Eph 3:16-17). Therefore we are bidden to sing to
the Lord, who lives in Zion, to praise with one heart the Lord who inhabits the
Church. *Proclaim among the peoples his miraculous deeds.* So it has been done,
and it will not cease to be so.

Verse 13. The martyrs' blood

13. *Because in requiring their blood he has remembered.* It is as if those who
have been sent out to preach the gospel were replying to the command, *Proclaim
among the peoples his miraculous deeds*, by objecting, *Lord, who has believed our
report?* (Is 53:1), or *For your sake we are done to death all day long!* (Ps
43(44):22). It is quite appropriate for the psalmist to go on to say that Christians will
indeed die in persecution, but not without the great reward of eternity, *because in
requiring their blood he has remembered*. But why did he choose to mention *their
blood*? Perhaps it was because he thought someone less experienced and of weaker
faith might ask the question, "How will they preach, when the faithlessness of the
heathen is sure to rage against them?" The reply to this is, *in seeking their blood he
has remembered*, that is to say, the final judgment will come, when both the glory
of those killed and the punishment of the killers are made known. But as for *he has
remembered*, nobody should think that this is said to suggest that God is prone to
forgetfulness. It is included for the sake of weak men and women who, because the
judgment will take place only after a long interval, might suppose that God has
forgotten, because he does not do something as quickly as they want. To them too is
addressed the assurance that follows, *He has not forgotten the crying of the poor*; he
has not forgotten, as you imagine. It is as if, after hearing, *He has remembered*, they
might say, "You see, he had forgotten after all!" No, says the psalmist. *He has not
forgotten the crying of the poor.*

Verses 14-15. Gates of Zion and gates of death

14. But, I ask, what is this lament of the poor which God does not forget? Is it the
cry, *Have mercy on me, Lord, see how I have been humbled by my enemies*? But
why, in that case, did the psalmist not say, "Have mercy on us, Lord, look how we
are being humbled by our enemies," to indicate that a great number of poor people
were crying, instead of expressing it as if only one were doing so, *Have mercy on
me, Lord*? Is it because one alone intercedes for the saints, the one, that is, who first
was made poor for our sakes, although he was rich?[27] And is it he himself who says,
*You who lift me up from the gates of death, that I may declare all your praises in the
gates of the daughter of Zion*? But in him it is not only the manhood he assumed that

---

27. See 2 Cor 8:9.

is exalted, not he alone who is the Head of the Church, but every one of us who are numbered among his members. And so in him humankind is lifted up away from all wayward desires, desires which are the gates of death because the route to death goes through them. But the very act of luxuriating in our pleasure when we get something we have desperately craved for—this is death already. Greed is the root of all evils,[28] and that is why it is the gate of death, just as the widow who lives surrounded by luxuries is dead.[29] The way to these luxuries is through cravings, and so cravings are the gates of death.

But there are also the gates of the daughter of Zion, all the most honorable pursuits. Through them is the road leading to the vision of peace in holy Church. Therefore within these gates all the praises of God are proclaimed properly, so that what is holy is not given to dogs, nor are pearls thrown before pigs.[30] There are those who prefer obstinately to bark rather than carefully to search, or who prefer neither to bark nor to search but to wallow in the filth of their own pleasures. But when the praises of God are proclaimed by honorable pursuits, gifts are given to those who ask, seekers are shown what they sought, and the door is opened to those who knock.[31]

Could another interpretation perhaps go like this? The gates of death are the bodily senses and particularly the eyes, which were opened for human beings when they had tasted the fruit of the forbidden tree.[32] The people who are lifted clear of these gates are they who are bidden to seek not the things that are seen but the things that are unseen, because things seen are temporal, things not seen are eternal.[33] And as for the gates of the daughter of Zion, are these the sacraments and the first steps in faith, which are opened to those who knock, to grant them access to the hidden things of the Son? For the eye does not see, nor the ear hear, nor does the human heart conceive the things which God has prepared for those who love him.[34] The cry of the poor whom the Lord has not forgotten reaches even as far as this.

Verse 16. Good and bad delights

15. Then there follows, *I will rejoice over your salvation*, that is to say, in happiness shall I be held fast by your salvation, which is our Lord Jesus Christ, God's power and wisdom.[35] It is the Church speaking, here and now hard pressed and yet saved in hope. As long as the Son's judgment is hidden, the Church says, *I will*

---

28. See 1 Tm 6:10.
29. See 1 Tm 5:6.
30. See Mt 7:6.
31. See Mt 7:7.
32. See Gn 3:7.
33. See 2 Cor 4:18.
34. See 1 Cor 2:9.
35. See 1 Cor 1:24.

rejoice over your salvation, but says it in hope, because now it is being worn away by the might of the nations roaring round about, or their capacity to lead astray. *The nations are deeply rooted in the corruption*[36] *which they have wrought.* Notice how the punishment is reserved for the sinner from out of his own deeds, and how those who have wanted to persecute the Church are rooted in the corruption which they thought they were inflicting. They wanted to kill bodies while they themselves were dying in their own souls. *Their own foot has been caught in the very mouse-trap which they set.*[37] This hidden mousetrap is deceitful scheming. The foot of the soul is properly understood as love. When it is misshapen it is called concupiscence or lust; when it is well formed it is called love or charity. Love moves a thing in the direction toward which it tends.[38] But the dwelling-place of the soul is not in any physical space which the form of the body occupies, but in delight, where it rejoices to have arrived through love. Destructive pleasure follows greed, fruitful delight follows love. This is why greed is called a root.[39] Now the root can be regarded as the foot of the tree. Love too is spoken of as a root, when the Lord speaks of the seeds which shrivel up in stony places in the scorching heat of the sun[40] because they have no deep root.[41] It means, then, those who rejoice at receiving the word of truth, but yield to persecutions which can be resisted by love alone. The apostle prays, *that rooted in charity and built up on charity, you may understand . . .* (Eph 3:17). The foot of sinners, that is, their love, is caught in the trap which they themselves hide. This is because when pleasure has followed deceitful action, when God has handed them over into the lusts of their heart,[42] the pleasure already binds them in such a way that they do not dare to tear their love from it and apply it to useful objects. When they try to do so they will suffer great inner pain, longing to pull their foot from the snare. Conquered by this pain, they refuse to withdraw from the harmful things they love. In the *mousetrap which they* have *set,* therefore, that is, in deceitful plotting, *their foot has been caught,* for their love has led them to empty pleasure, from which pain results.

---

36. Variant: "in the destruction."

37. *Muscipula,* "mousetrap"; but a variant reading has *in laqueo,* "in the snare."

38. A key idea with Augustine. In his *Confessions* XIII,9,10 he speaks of all things being drawn to their proper places by a natural love comparable to "weight," a stone downward, fire upward. Only when rightly ordered can they find their places, and therein also find rest. "Love is my weight," he concludes.

39. See 1 Tm 6:10.

40. *Exurente sole,* "when the sun is scorching"; some variants are *exeunte sole,* when the sun comes out; *exeunt, et sole veniente,* "they spring up, and when the sun comes."

41. See Mt 13:5.

42. See Rom 1:24.

Verse 17. The torture of sinners

16. *The Lord is known*[43] *as he passes judgment.* These are God's judgments. Not from the tranquillity of his blessedness, nor from the secret places of wisdom, in which blessed souls are received, is there brought forth a sword or fire or a wild beast or any such thing by which sinners may be afflicted. How then are they afflicted? And how does God pass judgment? The psalmist tells us, *The sinner is caught in the works of his own hands.*

Verse 18. The hidden separation

17. Here is interjected the phrase, *A song of the diapsalma.* As far as we can judge, it is like a secret joy at the separation which already exists, not in terms of place but in the affections of the heart, between sinners and those who are just, as wheat is separated from the chaff still on the threshing-floor. The psalm continues, *Let sinners be turned toward hell,* that is, let them be delivered into their own hands when they are spared, and let them be ensnared by the delight which brings death in its wake. *All peoples who forget God:* because they did not see fit to acknowledge God, he gave them over to their own depraved way of thinking.[44]

Verse 19. Long-suffering

18. *Because the poor will not be forgotten for ever.* By this is meant the person who seems to be forgotten here and now, when to all appearances sinners flourish in the happiness of this world, and the just are struggling. But the psalmist promises, *the long-suffering of the poor will not be wasted for ever.* That is why people need the virtue of long-suffering so as to put up with the evil ones who are already separated in their wills, until they are also separated by the last judgment.

Verses 20-21. Servitude

19. *Arise, Lord, do not let humankind prevail.* This is a plea for the future judgment, but before it comes, *let the nations be judged in your sight,* prays the psalmist; this means in secret, in God's presence, with only a few holy and righteous people knowing what is happening. *Establish, Lord, a lawgiver over them.* I think the psalmist is alluding to Antichrist, of whom the apostle says, *The man of sin will be exposed* (2 Thes 2:3). *Let the nations know that they are mere mortals.* This is to ensure that those who refuse to be set free by the Son of God and to belong to the Son of Man, and to be sons of men themselves, that is, new men, should serve a man, that is, the old man, the sinner, *because they are but men.*

---

43. Variant: "will be known."
44. See Rom 1:28.

Part 2

Verses 1-4. The tribulation of the little ones fires their goodness

20. It is believed that Satan will come to such a pinnacle of empty glory and will be allowed to do such terrible things against all men and women, and against the saints of God in particular, that some of the weak will then indeed think God does neglect human affairs. This is why a diapsalma has been introduced and why the psalmist adds what seems to be the voice of those who groan and ask why judgment is being delayed: *Why, Lord, have you withdrawn so far away?* Then, as if suddenly understanding, or as if he knew already, but asked questions only in order to teach others, he goes on to say, *You look away at critical moments, in times of trouble.* This means that you look away at seasonable times and cause trouble in order to fire the minds of men and women with longing for your coming. For the fountain of life is even sweeter to those who have been very thirsty. Accordingly he hints at the purpose of the delay by saying, *While the ungodly is proud, the poor is on fire.* It is amazing and yet true that little ones are kindled with intense and hopeful enthusiasm to live upright lives, by the negative example of sinners. As part of the same mystery it happens that even heresies are allowed to exist, not because heretics themselves intend it so but because divine providence brings this result from their sins. It is providence which both makes and orders the light, but does no more than order the darkness.[45] When compared with darkness light is more pleasant, in the same way that the discovery of truth is sweeter when compared with what heretics have to offer. For it is by a comparison such as this that the upright who are known to God are recognized as such among their fellows.

Sinners, flattered and deceived, provoke the Lord

21. *They are caught*[46] *in the thoughts they think,* that is, their evil thoughts become like chains to them. But why do they become chains? *Because,* says the psalmist, *the sinner is praised in the longings of his own soul.* The tongues of sycophants tie souls up in sins, for it is delightful to do those things in which not only is there no need to fear rebuke from anyone, but one may even hear oneself praised. *And whoever does evil deeds is blessed.* This is how they are caught in the thoughts they think.

22. *The sinner has provoked the Lord.* Nobody should congratulate the person who prospers in his own way, whose sins go unavenged and who has someone to praise him. This is the Lord's anger, an anger all the greater. The sinner has

---

45. See Gn 1:3-4.
46. Variant: "Let them be caught."

provoked the Lord, and deserved to suffer precisely this absence of any lashes of reproach. *The sinner has provoked the Lord, but the Lord is too angry to demand an account.* He is seething with anger all the time he does not conduct his search, and seems to forget and not give heed to sins, and so through deceit and acts of skulduggery someone may get riches and public honors. This is what will happen particularly with the Antichrist, who will seem to everyone so happy as even to be thought of as God. But how great God's anger really is will be clear from what follows.

Verse 5. The delusion of Antichrist

23. *God is not in his sight, his ways are defiled all the time.* Whoever knows what gives joy or delight in the soul knows how great an evil it is to be abandoned by the light of truth.[47] People consider physical blindness, which means the withdrawal of daylight, a great evil. Just imagine, then, how great the punishment people suffer who, while their sins are a roaring success, are led to the point where God is no longer in their field of vision, and where their ways are defiled all the time, which means that their thoughts and machinations are absolutely filthy! *Your judgments are removed [48] from before his face.* People with bad consciences may believe that God does not judge; in this way God's judgments have been removed from before their face, and though they imagine that they are suffering no punishment whatsoever, this itself is in fact the greatest condemnation. *And he shall have dominion over all his enemies.* Scripture says that the Enemy will overcome all kings and will rule alone as king. This is in line with the words of the apostle who says of him, *He will seat himself in God's temple, exalting himself above anything claiming to be God, everything that people worship* (2 Thes 2:4).

Verse 6. Infamy and magical arts

24. Because he is now handed over to the lusts of his own heart and destined for final condemnation, and because he will come through evil designs to that vain and empty pinnacle of power, the psalm continues, *For he has said in his heart: I will not survive from generation to generation without evil.* This means, "My reputation and my name will not pass from this generation to the generation of those who come after me unless by unscrupulous means I attain to a position so high that posterity cannot keep silent about it." For the soul which is lost, devoid of honorable intentions and a stranger to the light of justice, carves out for itself by evil designs a path to fame so everlasting that even among subsequent generations it will be noised abroad. Those who cannot be known for what is good crave even a

---

47. *Luce deseri veritatis:* Two variants are: *lucem deserere veritatis*, "to abandon the light of truth"; and *lucem deseri*, "for the light of truth to be abandoned."
48. Variant: "will be removed."

bad reputation among their fellows, provided that their name is widely noised abroad. This is what I think is the meaning of the words being used here, *I will not survive from generation to generation without evil.*

There is also another possible interpretation. Perhaps a soul, vacuous and full of error, thinks that it cannot proceed from this mortal generation to the generation of eternity, except by evil designs. This indeed was widely reported about Simon Magus,[49] who thought that he would win heaven by wicked designs and that he would pass from this human generation to a divine generation by using magic. What wonder, then, if that *man of sin*, who will, as scripture foretells, carry to completion every form of villainy and ungodliness which the false prophets began, and will perform signs so great as to deceive, if possible, even the elect,[50] should say in his heart, *I will not survive from generation to generation without evil?*

Verse 7. Toil, grief and deception

25. *His mouth is full of cursing and bitterness and deceit.* It is a terrible curse to seek heaven by such abominable means and to get together such resources to storm the eternal throne. But his mouth is full of such cursing. Greed like this will achieve nothing, but in his mouth will serve only to destroy the one who was rash enough to promise these things to himself with bitterness and deceit. By this I mean, with anger and scheming, by which he means to draw a vast number to his side. *Under his tongue are toil and grief.* Nothing is more fraught with toil than iniquity and godlessness. Grief follows this toil, because all the effort is not only fruitless but also ends in destruction. This toil and grief relate to what he said in his heart, *I shall not survive from generation to generation without evil.* This is why the phrase used is, *under his tongue*, not "on his tongue," because he will hatch these plots in silence and to his fellows he will say quite different things, to make himself appear good and righteous and a son of God.

Verse 8. Satan's ambush

26. *He lies in ambush with the rich.* Who are these rich people? Surely those whom he will pile high with the gifts of this world? And he is described as sitting in ambush with them precisely because he will make a show of their false happiness in order to deceive others. It is because of their perverted will that they want to be like this, and do not seek the good things which will last, and so they will fall into his snares. *That he may kill the innocent in the dark.* I presume that *in the dark* refers to some situation where it is not easy to determine what you should pursue and what

---

49. See Acts 8:9-24.
50. See Mt 24:24.

you should run away from. To kill the innocent is to turn the innocent into the guilty.[51]

Verse 9. The three persecutions

27. *His eyes look toward the poor*, for he will persecute most of all those righteous people about whom the Lord said, *Blessed are the poor in spirit, because the kingdom of heaven is theirs* (Mt 5:3). *He lies in ambush in secret, like a lion in his den.* The psalmist describes as a lion in his den someone in whom both violence and deceit will work. The first persecution of the Church was violent,[52] for it attempted by the confiscation of property, by torture and murders, to force the Christians to sacrifice. A second phase of persecution works rather by guile; it is carried on in our day by heretics and false brethren of any and every sort. There remains a further and third persecution yet to come through the Antichrist. Nothing is more dangerous than this because it will be both violent and deceitful. He will be violent in the exercise of power, deceitful in the miracles he performs. The simile, *lion*, refers to his violence, *den* to his guile. These points are then repeated in inverse order: *he lies in ambush*, says the psalmist, *so that he may ensnare the poor person* (this refers to deceit); but what follows, *to seize the poor person while he drags him in*, refers to violence. For *he drags them in* means "he brings them into his clutches by striking them with whatever torments he can."

Verse 10. Satan's dominion over the poor

28. The two statements which follow are just the same. *In his snare* [53] *he will lay him low* refers to deceit; but *he will bow down and fall, while he exercises dominion over the poor* refers to violence; for the word "mousetrap" well describes ambush, while "dominion" most clearly indicates terror. The psalmist was right to say, *He will lay him low in his snare*, for when the Antichrist begins to perform those signs, the more wonderful they seem to people in general, the more will the saints of that time be scorned and counted as nothing. The one they resist by their righteousness and innocence will look as if he is overcoming them by doing quite amazing things.

---

51. *Ex innocente facere nocentem.*
52. Persecution of Christians was sporadic during the first and second centuries, and was usually set in motion more by local decisions than by imperial policy. It became systematic in the mid-third century under the Emperor Decius, and it is this persecution (in A.D. 250), with its insistence on the cult of the emperor, that Augustine seems to be describing here, especially because his great predecessor Saint Cyprian had to deal with its consequences. Systematic and imperially-directed persecution using similar methods characterized a further period early in the fourth century under Diocletian.
53. Literally "mousetrap" as in verse 16 above.

But *he will bow down and fall while he exercises dominion over the poor*, that is, while he inflicts unspeakable punishments on the servants of God who resist him.

Verses 11-12. Arise, Lord!

29. But how will he bow down and fall? *He said in his heart, God has forgotten, he has turned his face away so as not to see to the end.* This is a change for the worse and the most miserable of falls. The human mind seems to prosper in the midst of its iniquities and thinks that it is being spared, whereas it is instead being blinded and kept on hold for the final and timely punishment, in view of which the psalm prays even now, *Arise, Lord God, let your hand be lifted up*; that is, may your power be clearly seen. Earlier the psalmist had said, *Arise, Lord, do not let humankind prevail, let the nations be judged in your sight* (Ps 9:20-21(19-20)); he was praying then that it would happen in secret, where God alone sees. And happen it did when the ungodly reached what people imagine to be great happiness. A lawgiver[54] is set over them, such as they have deserved. He it is of whom the psalm prayed, *Establish, Lord, a lawgiver over them, and let the heathen know that they are mere mortals.* But now he is not concerned with that hidden punishment and vengeance; instead he says, *Arise, Lord God, let your hand be lifted up*, and obviously he does not mean in secret, but now in brightest glory, *lest you forget the poor to the end.* This is what the ungodly imagine to have happened, those who say, *God has forgotten, he has turned away his face so as not to see to the end.* The people who maintain that God does not see them to the very end are those who assert that he does not concern himself with human and earthly affairs. This earth is like the end, in that it is the last element in which men and women work according to a very definite order, though they are unable to see the ordered pattern of their labors, for this belongs particularly to the hidden things of the Son. Therefore the Church which labors in such times, like a ship in great waves and storms, wakens the Lord as if he were asleep, in the hope that he will command the waves and that calm may return.[55] That is why the psalmist says, *Arise, Lord God, let your hand be lifted up, lest you forget the poor to the end.*

Verses 13-14. God's toil and anger

30. Seeing the prospect of open judgment, and rejoicing at it, the righteous ask, *Why has the ungodly angered God? What was the point in doing such terrible things? The wicked has said in his heart, God will not settle the account.* The next line is *You see that you face toil and anger, to deliver them into your own hands.*

---

54. That is, the Antichrist.
55. See Mt 8:26; Mk 4:39; Lk 8:24.

This sentence needs careful elucidation, because its meaning is obscured if there is any misunderstanding. The ungodly said in his heart, "God will not settle the account," as if God might think it a laborious undertaking, and one that would arouse anger, to get them into his own hands. It is as if he might be afraid of suffering discomfort and experiencing anger, and for that reason would spare them in case punishing them might sit heavily on him; or maybe that he would want to avoid being churned up by a storm of anger, as people often are, and therefore suppress their desire for revenge in case it might make them uncomfortable or angry.[56]

Spiritual orphans

31. *The poor person has been abandoned to you*, for the poor are precisely those who have despised all the temporal goods of this world, in order that you alone may be their hope. *To the orphan you will be a helper*, that is, to the one whose father, by which is meant this world, dies. Through this world he was born according to the flesh, but now such a person can say, *The world has been crucified to me, and I to the world* (Gal 6:14). God becomes a Father to orphans like this. Indeed the Lord teaches that his disciples are orphans, for to them he says, *Call no one on earth your father* (Mt 23:9). He was the first to give an example in the matter, by saying, *Who is my mother? Who are my brothers?* (Mt 12:48). On the basis of this, some very dangerous heretics[57] wish to assert that he had no mother. They do not see that it follows, if they heed these words, that his disciples would have no fathers; because, just as he said of himself, *Who is my mother?* he taught them a similar lesson by commanding them, *Call no one on earth your father.*

Verses 15-17. The power and the powers of God

32. *Break the arm of the sinner and the wicked*, his arm, that is, about whom it was said above, *He shall have dominion over all his enemies* (v. 5). By speaking of his arm the psalm means his power, but to this Christ's power stands opposed, and so the psalmist prays, *Arise, Lord God, let your arm be lifted up*. It continues, *His fault will be sought out, and he will not be found because of it*: that is, he will be judged for his sin and he himself will perish because of his sin. What wonder, then, if the next line is *The Lord will reign for ever and to the end of time. You nations will perish from his earth*? By *nations* he means sinners and ungodly persons.

---

56. A variant reading is *qui dissimulata vindicta elaborant ne irascantur*, "who, concealing their thirst for revenge, work hard not to show their anger."
57. Manicheans, whose radically dualistic doctrine made belief in a real incarnation of the Word impossible, and more generally any who held a docetist or Gnostic view of the incompatibility between matter and the holiness of God.

33. *God has heard the longing of the poor.* This is the longing with which they were set on fire when amid the hardships and tribulations of this world they longed for the day of the Lord. *Your ear has heard the preparation of their heart,* that same preparation of which another psalm sings, *My heart is ready, O God, my heart is ready* (Ps 56:8(57:7)). The apostle Paul says of it, *If we hope for what we do not see, we wait for it in patience* (Rom 8:25). Now as a general rule of interpretation we ought to understand the ear of God not as a part of his body but as the power by which he hears. So whatever parts of God that are spoken of by name as parts of the body which you and I can see ought to be understood as God's various capacities for doing things. I do not want to keep repeating this. It is not right to think of it as something bodily, because the Lord God does not so much hear the voice speaking as attend to the preparation of the heart.

Verse 18. Judging for the orphan

34. *Judge for the orphan and the humble,*[58] that is to say, not for the person who is conformed to this age nor for the proud. For it is one thing to judge the orphan, another to judge for the orphan. The one who condemns judges the orphan, but whoever gives a verdict in the orphan's cause judges for the orphan. *So that humankind may no longer vaunt itself on earth.* For they of whom is said, *Establish, Lord, a lawgiver over them, let the nations know that they are mere mortals,* are men and women just like you and me; and even the person who in that same text is understood to be placed over them will be an ordinary mortal too. So this prayer is made with him in view: let *humankind no longer vaunt itself on earth* when the Son of Man comes to judge for the orphan, who in divesting himself of the old nature has in a sense buried his father.

David's son and Lord

35. Therefore after the hidden things of the Son, of which in this psalm much is said, there will be the clearly visible things of the Son, about which a few things have now been said at the end of the psalm. The title is derived from the hidden things which here occupy the greater part. The very day of the Lord's coming can also rightly be numbered among the hidden things of the Son, even though the presence of the Lord will be clear to see; for of that day it was said that nobody knows it, neither angels, nor heavenly powers, nor the Son of man.[59] What, then, is so hidden as that which is said to be hidden even from the judge himself, not as far as his knowing it is concerned, but as regards his revealing it? However, with regard to

---

58. *Humili,* but a variant reading is *egeno,* "the needy."
59. See Mk 13:32; Mt 24:36.

the hidden things of the Son, if anyone prefers to understand this as not as the Son of God, but as the son of David (to whom the whole psalter is attributed, for the psalms are commonly called the psalms of David), such a person should listen to those words addressed to the Lord, *Take pity on us, son of David* (Mt 20:30); in this way we may still take the psalm as referring to the Lord Christ, whose hidden things give this psalm its title. The angel too announced that *God will give him the throne of his father, David* (Lk 1:32). There is no conflict between this interpretation and the Lord's question to the Jews, "If Christ is the son of David, *how is it that David in the Spirit calls him Lord, saying, The Lord said to my Lord, Sit at my right hand, until I make your enemies into your footstool?"* (Mt 22:43-44). This question was put to the untutored, for although they hoped that Christ would come, they nonetheless expected him as a human being, not as the power and wisdom of God. He is therefore teaching the most true and genuine faith: that because he is the Word in the beginning, God with God, through whom are made all things,[60] he is Lord of King David, but at the same time he is David's son, inasmuch as he was made for him[61] from the seed of David according to the flesh. For he does not say, "Christ is not David's son," but rather, "If you already hold that he is his son, learn how he is also David's Lord. In Christ's regard you should not hold on to the fact that he is a son of man (which is how he is David's son) and let go of his being Son of God (which is how he is David's Lord)."

---

60. See Jn 1:1-3.
61. God; see Rom 1:3.

Exposition of Psalm 10

1. *To the end, a psalm of David himself.* This title does not need to be explained again, for we have adequately covered already what is meant by *to the end.*[1] Therefore let us look at the text of the psalm itself. It seems to me that it should be sung against the heretics.[2] By rehearsing and exaggerating the sins of many in the Church, as if either all or the majority of the just were with them, they struggle to turn us aside and tear us away from the breasts of the one Church, the true mother, asserting that Christ is with them. With a show of piety and concern they suggest to us that by transferring our allegiance to them we would be making the move to be with Christ, whom they pretend to possess. Now it is well known that in prophecy Christ, while he is alluded to allegorically by many names, is also called a mountain. We must, then, respond to them and say, *I trust in the Lord. How can you say to my soul, Migrate to the mountains*[3] *like a sparrow?* There is one mountain I hold to, in which I put my trust. How can you tell me to cross over to you,[4] as if there were many Christs? Or if you say out of pride that you are the mountains, then I would need to be a sparrow with virtues and God's commandments for wings; yet these

---

1. See his Exposition of Psalm 4, 1.
2. The Donatist schism, which rent the Church during the fourth century and preoccupied Augustine for much of his episcopal ministry, is in view throughout this Exposition. Superficially, the origin of the schism was as follows. During the persecution under the Emperor Diocletian in A.D. 303 and the following years some Christians had yielded to pressure and given up their sacred books. They were later denounced by zealots among the Christians as *traditores.* In 312 Caecilian became Bishop of Carthage, but some of his personal enemies declared his consecration invalid, because one of the consecrating bishops had been a *traditor.* A rival bishop was set up, whom Donatus succeeded in 313. From then onward there were two opposing "churches," and great bitterness. African national pride played a part, for the Donatists thought of themselves as purely African, while the Catholics looked to Rome. Deeper theological questions were at issue, however, notably divergence about the nature of the Church. The Donatists claimed that they were the pure wheat in the field, while the Catholics were the weeds. Augustine fought vehemently against the doctrine that the Church is, or is intended to be, a communion of the perfect. The controversy became even more embroiled because of the Donatists' contention that the validity of a sacrament depended on the state of grace of the minister, an idea that Augustine opposed, and to which he refers in the present Exposition. His polemical writings against the Donatists enriched the Catholic Church, particularly with regard to the theology of the sacraments and ecclesiology.
3. Plural here and in Augustine's *Homilies on the Gospel of John* 4,11.
4. Plural.

are the very things which prevent me from flying into those mountains and from placing my hope in proud fellow-humans. I have a house to rest in, because I trust in the Lord. For even the sparrow has found herself a house.[5] And the Lord has become a refuge for the poor.[6] Therefore let us speak with complete assurance in case, while looking for Christ among the heretics, we lose him. *I trust in the Lord. How can you say to my soul, Migrate to the mountains like a sparrow?*[7]

Verse 3. The arrows of the wicked

2. *For see, sinners have bent their bows; they have their arrows ready in the quiver, to shoot those of honest heart when the moon is darkened.*These are the terrors brought to bear on us by those who threaten us about sinners, to make us cross over to them as if we were crossing over to the just. Look, they say, *sinners have bent their bows*, but I believe that the bows are the scriptures which they themselves interpret in carnal fashion, so as to hurl forth poisonous opinions from them. *They have their arrows ready in the quiver*, for they have made ready in the secret recesses of their hearts the words which they will shoot forth on the authority of scripture. *To shoot those of honest heart when the moon is darkened*: this means that once they have realized that they cannot be challenged, since the light of the Church is obscured by the great number of the ill-educated and the carnal-minded, they corrupt good character with wicked conversation.[8] But against all those threats must be said, *I trust in the Lord.*

The moon, an allegory of the Church

3. I remember that I promised to consider how in this psalm it might be appropriate for the moon to signify the Church.[9] There are two plausible theories about the moon, but as to which of them is true, I think it is quite impossible, or at least very difficult, for anyone to know. For when the question is asked, "Where does the moon get her light from?" some say that she has her own light, but one half of her sphere shines and the other half is dark. While she revolves in her orbit, the part which shines is gradually turned toward the earth so that it can be seen by us, and for that reason it seems at first to be horned. Suppose you make a ball, half white and half black. If you hold in front of your eyes the part which is black, you see no brightness, but when you begin to turn the white part toward your eyes, if you do so gradually, first you will see the horns of the white part, then gradually it grows until

---

5. See Ps 83:4(84:3).
6. See Ps 9:10(9).
7. The imagery of this psalm evokes the story of Lot's flight, Gn 19:12-26.
8. Scc 1 Cor 15:33.
9. Compare Exposition of Psalm 8, 9.

the whole of the white part is in front of your eyes and none of that other part, the black, is visible. But if you continue to turn it a little further, the blackness begins to appear and the whiteness to diminish until it is horns once more, and finally the whole of the white area is turned away from the eyes and once again only the black part can be seen. They say this is what is happening when the light of the moon looks as if it is waxing until the fifteenth day of the lunar month, and then gives the impression of waning and becoming horns again toward the thirtieth day, until no light at all can be seen in her. According to this theory, the moon allegorically represents the Church, because on the spiritual side the Church is bright, but on the carnal side it is dark. Sometimes the spiritual part shows itself to men and women in good works, but sometimes it is hidden in the conscience and is known only to God, because it is only when it takes bodily form that people can recognize it. This is what happens when we pray in the heart and seem to be doing nothing, since it is not to the earth but to the Lord that we are ordered to have our hearts raised.[10]

Others say that the moon does not have her own light, but is illuminated by the sun. When she is with the sun, she turns toward us the side on which she is not lit up, and that is the reason no light is seen in her. But when she begins to draw away from the sun, she is lit up also on that part which is turned toward the earth; this process necessarily begins with the horns, until on the fifteenth day she is directly opposite the sun. On this day, as the sun sets, the moon rises, and so, if you watch the sun setting, and at the moment when it becomes invisible turn to the east, you see the moon rising. Conversely, as the moon begins to draw near to the sun again, her other side, which is not lit up, is turned toward us, until the light is reduced to horns and then disappears altogether, because the illuminated portion is directed upward toward the sky, and only the part which the sun's rays cannot reach is turned toward the earth. According to this theory too, therefore, the moon is understood as the Church, because she does not have her own light but is lit up by the only-begotten Son of God, who in many places in the sacred scriptures is allegorically called the sun. Certain heretics,[11] not knowing him and not being able to see him, try to turn away the minds of the simple to this ordinary material sun which everyone can see, the light of which is common to the bodily life of human beings and even flies. Some they do mislead, those who, as long as they are unable to discern the inner light of truth with the mind, refuse to be satisfied with the simple Catholic faith, which is the one salvation to little ones and the one milk by which progress is strongly and confidently made to the stable nourishment of more solid food.

---

10. *Sursum corda habere iubemur ad Dominum*: this sounds like an allusion to the ancient liturgical invitation, "Lift up your hearts," known to have been in use from the third century; see Cyprian, *On the Lord's Prayer*, 31.

11. The Manicheans. Compare his remarks on their worship of the sun in *A Refutation of the Manicheans*, I,3,6; II,25,38; *The Catholic Way of Life and the Manichean Way of Life*, VIII,13; and *Heresies*, XLVI,18 (given in Vol. I/18 of this series).

Whichever of these two theories is true, then, it is appropriate to understand the moon allegorically as the Church. If you have neither the inclination nor the time to flex your intellectual muscles, or if the mind is not strong enough to exercise itself in these obscure corners of knowledge, more troublesome than fruitful, it is sufficient to look at the moon with ordinary eyes, and not to seek recondite explanations but simply, like everyone else, to be aware of her waxing, her fullness and her waning. If she wanes in order to be renewed, then she shows even to the ill-educated multitude itself a figure of the Church, in which we believe in the resurrection of the dead.

The darkened moon

4. Next it must be asked what is meant in this psalm by *the darkened moon*, at which sinners have prepared to shoot those of honest heart. There is more than one way in which the moon can be described as darkened, for when she completes her monthly cycle, when her brightness is interrupted by a cloud, and when she is eclipsed at the full, the moon can be called dark. The intention to shoot people of honest heart in the dark time of the moon can therefore be understood to refer to those who persecuted the martyrs, perhaps at the youthful age of the Church, when it had not yet shone forth as something great on the earth, and overcome the darkness of Gentile superstition. Or again it could refer to times when the Church could not be seen clearly because of blasphemous attacks and slanders against the Christian name, as though the moon was obscured by clouds that covered the earth. Another possibility is that the deaths of the martyrs themselves and so great a shedding of blood are like an eclipse by which the moon is darkened and seems to be showing a bloodstained face. This has resulted in the weak being frightened off the name of Christian. In such a reign of terror sinners were hurling such treacherous and profane words about that they undermined even those of honest heart. The verse can also be understood of those sinners included within the Church, because at that time they took the opportunity afforded by this darkened moon and committed many crimes with which we are now taunted and reproached by the heretics,[12] even though their own leaders are reported to have committed them.

But whatever the nature of what was done at the darkness of the moon, now that the Catholic name has been spread abroad and proclaimed the world over, why should I be troubled by things which cannot now be known for certain? For *I trust*

---

12. The reference is to the Donatist accusation against Catholics who were in earlier days *traditores* (see note 2 on paragraph 1, above). See also Augustine's Letters 76,2 ; 105,2. In the latter place he says, addressing a Donatist opponent, "You call us *traditores*, yet your forebears could not establish the charge against ours, any more than you will be able to make it stick against us. . . . I wish that we could rather demonstrate to you that the people who condemned Caecilian and his companions as traitors were more truly traitors themselves."

in the Lord. I do not listen to those who say to my soul, *Migrate to the mountains like a sparrow. For see, sinners have bent their bows; they have their arrows ready in the quiver, to shoot those of honest heart when the moon is darkened.* Or if the moon seems dark to them now because they want to make it uncertain which is the Catholic Church, and try to charge it with the sins of carnal men and women, whom it contains in large numbers, why should this concern anyone who with utter sincerity says, *I trust in the Lord?* All who say this prove that they are grain, and tolerate the chaff with great patience until the time of winnowing.

Donatist exclusivity

5. *Trust in the Lord,* then. Those who put their trust in a fellow-human have good cause for alarm, and people who swear by a man's grey hairs cannot deny that they belong to a man's sect.[13] And when in conversation they are asked to whose communion they belong, unless they say they are of the party of Donatus, they cannot be identified. Tell me, what do they do when the countless daily sins and crimes of those with whom their community is full are recounted to them? Can they possibly say, *In the Lord I trust. How can you say to my soul, Go off into the mountains like a sparrow?* No, for those who say that sacraments are valid only when administered by holy persons fail to trust in the Lord. When they are asked who these holy people are, they are embarrassed to say, "We are." Or even if they are not embarrassed to say it, those who hear are embarrassed for them. Therefore these Donatists force those who receive the sacraments to place their hope in a mere human whose heart they are unable to see. And cursed is everyone who places his hope in someone human.[14] For what does it mean to say, "What I give is holy," except "Place your hope in me"? But what if you are not holy? Show me your heart instead. If you cannot do that, how am I to see that you are holy? Or perhaps you will say that it is written, *By their works you will know them* (Mt 7:16)? Well then, I see some amazing works, the daily acts of violence perpetrated by the Circumcellions under the leadership of bishops and priests, how their gangs roam around and call their terrifying cudgels Israels.[15] These are things which the men and women who are alive now see and feel daily. As to the Macarian era, about which they are so outraged, the vast majority has not seen that era, and nobody does

---

13. The Donatists swore by the grey hairs of Donatus.
14. See Jr 17:5.
15. The Circumcellions were fanatical bands of warlike peasants who roamed Numidia and other parts of North Africa in the fourth century. Originally they seem to have been fighting for the redress of social injustices, but they became linked to the Donatist cause and helped to bring it into disrepute. They called themselves *Agonistici* (fighters for Christ), but they were nicknamed "Circumcellions" because they surrounded the homes of Catholics (*circum cellas*).

now.[16] And any Catholic who did see it could say, if he wanted to be God's servant, *In the Lord I trust.* This is what all those say now who see in the Church many things they do not like, and feel that they are still swimming inside nets full of good and bad fish, until they reach the seashore, where the bad are sorted from the good.[17] But what do the Donatists reply if the person whom they are baptizing says to any one of them, "Why do you suggest such presumption to me? If there is any credit due to giver and recipient, let it redound to God, who gives, and my conscience, that receives. Two things there are that hold no uncertainty for me: God's goodness and my faith. Why thrust yourself in between, you, of whom I can know nothing with certainty? Allow me rather to say, *In the Lord I trust.* What ground for confidence in you is this, that you did no wrong on this particular night? And anyway, if you persuade me to trust you, will I be able to extend my trust any further? Can I place any confidence in those with whom you had to do yesterday, and have to do today, and will have to do tomorrow? How can I be sure that they have done no evil during these three days? On the other hand, if events of which we are ignorant have contaminated neither you nor me, what justification have you for rebaptizing those who know nothing of the days of betrayal or the bitterness of Macarius' time? Why do you presume to rebaptize Christians coming from Mesopotamia who have not so much as heard the names of Caecilian and Donatus, and to deny that they are Christians? If the sins of other people about which they know nothing defile them, you yourself are condemned by whatever is committed every day by members of your party without your knowledge. You vainly hurl imperial edicts at Catholics when in your own camp the cudgels and firebrands of private citizens wreak such savagery."

Look how far they have fallen, those who, seeing sinners in the Catholic Church, have been unable to say, *I trust in the Lord*, and instead have placed their hope in a fellow human being. This is what they would say were not they themselves (or rather they too) just what they thought other people were— those others from whom, in their sacrilegious pride, they pretended to seek separation.

Verse 4. What heretics have in common

6. Therefore let the Catholic soul say, *In the Lord I trust. How can you say to my soul, Off you go to the mountains like a sparrow? For see, sinners have bent their bows; they have their arrows ready in the quiver, to shoot those of honest heart when the moon is darkened*; and let this soul turn from the Donatists and address the

---

16. Optatus, Bishop of Milevis, in his treatise *Against Parmenian the Donatist*, III, explains that Macarius and Paul had been sent by the Emperor Constans to Africa in about A.D. 348, to bring schismatics back into unity with the Church. The Donatists claimed to have been persecuted by them. Augustine refers to it also in his Letter 44,5.

17. See Mt 13:47-48.

Lord, saying, *They have destroyed what you made perfect.* And let the Catholic soul say this not against them alone but against all heretics. For all, as much as in them lies, have destroyed the praise which God has made perfect from out of the mouths of babies and nurslings,[18] disturbing little children with pointless and over-ingenious questions and refusing to allow them to be nourished on the milk of faith. It is as though such a soul were asked, "Why do they say to you, Go off into the mountains like a sparrow? Why do they frighten you with sinners who have bent their bow to shoot at those of honest heart when the moon is darkened?" It replies, "This is why they terrify me: *because they have destroyed what God made perfect.*" Where have they done that, if not in their conventicles, where instead of feeding milk to little children and those who do not know the inner light, they kill them instead with poison? *But what did the just person do?* If Macarius did you harm, if Caecilian did you harm, what did Christ do to you? He said, *My peace I give to you, my peace I leave with you* (Jn 14:27), but you have besmirched that peace with your unspeakable schism. What did Christ do to you? It was Christ who endured his own betrayer with such patience that he gave him the first Eucharist consecrated with his own hands and blessed with words from his own lips, as he gave it to the other apostles. What did Christ do to you? It was Christ who sent his own betrayer with the other disciples to preach the kingdom of heaven, that same betrayer whom he called a devil,[19] who even before his treason could not be trusted with the Lord's purse.[20] And he sent him out to preach in order to show that the gifts of God come to those who receive with faith, even if those through whom they receive are like Judas.

Verse 5. The Lord's holy temple

7. *The Lord is in his holy temple.* It is just as the apostle says: *God's temple is holy, and that temple is yourselves. If anyone violates God's temple, God will destroy that person* (1 Cor 3:17). Whoever violates unity violates God's temple, for he does not keep hold of the Head, from whom the whole body is united and consolidated through every kind of mutual service, so that as each constituent joint plays its due part, the whole body grows and builds itself up in love.[21] The Lord is in this holy temple. It consists of many members, each carrying out its own duties and functions, built together by love into one structure. Any who separate themselves from this Catholic fellowship for the sake of their own pre-eminence violate its unity. *The Lord is in his holy temple, the Lord is enthroned in heaven.* If you understand heaven as the just person, in the same way as you understand earth as the

---

18. See Ps 8:3(2).
19. See Jn 6:71.
20. See Jn 12:6.
21. See Eph 4:16; Col 2:19.

sinner, to whom is said, *Earth you are and back to earth you shall go* (Gn 3:19), you will understand that *the Lord is in his holy temple* is repeated in the phrase, *the Lord is enthroned in heaven.*

The eyes of God look on the poor

8. *His eyes look kindly on the poor.* It is to him that the poor are left, he it is who has become a refuge for the poor.[22] And that is why all seditions and uprisings which occur within those nets before they are hauled to shore are caused by those who refuse to be the poor of Christ. The heretics taunt us about them, but only to their own ruination, and to put us back on the right track. Yet they do not really turn God's eyes away from those who want to be his poor, for *his eyes look kindly on the poor.* Is there any need to fear that in a crowd of rich people God will not be able to see a few paupers to nurture, as they are kept safe in the bosom of the Catholic Church? *His eyelids question the sons of men.* Here I would be inclined to interpret *the sons of men* by a well-known principle[23] as those who have been born anew by faith, having previously been old. They are tested by abstruse passages of scripture to prompt them to ask questions, and then it is as if God's eyes are closed. And again, they are enlightened by some easily interpreted passages, and this gives them joy; then it is as if God's eyes are open. This frequent opening and closing of passages in the sacred books is what is referred to as the eyelids of God, which interrogate, that is, test, *the sons of men,* who are not worn out, but instead made fitter by the obscurity of such things; nor are they puffed up when they discover the meaning, but strengthened.

Verse 6. Hating one's own soul

9. *The Lord questions the righteous and the ungodly.* Why, then, are we afraid that the ungodly may do us harm if they happen to share with us in the sacraments with an insincere heart? The Lord questions the just and the ungodly. *But whoever loves iniquity hates his own soul*: that is, the lover of iniquity harms only his own soul, not the person who believes in God and refuses to trust in a fellow human being.

Verses 7-8. The rain which falls on good and bad alike

10. *He will rain snares upon sinners.* If the clouds are understood as prophets in general, whether good or bad (the bad are also called false prophets), then the false

---

22. See Ps 9:10(9).
23. See his elaboration of this in his Exposition of Psalm 8, 10.

prophets are contained within an ordered providential framework by the Lord God in such a way that from them he rains snares down on sinners. For only sinners fall into the trap of following them, whether as a preparation for the final punishment, if they really choose to persevere in sinning, or in order to discourage pride,[24] so that they may sooner or later seek God with more sincere conviction. But if clouds are understood as only good and true prophets, it is clear that from them too God rains snares down on sinners, although he also waters the godly from them to make them fruitful. *For some*, says the apostle, *we are the scent of life, leading to life, but for others the stench of death unto death* (2 Cor 2:16), for not only prophets but all who water souls with the word of God can be described as clouds. When they are incorrectly understood, God rains snares on sinners. But when they are correctly understood he makes fruitful the hearts of the Godfearing and the faithful. Take, for example, the saying, *They will be two in one flesh* (Gn 2:24). If someone interprets this as an encouragement to lust, God rains a snare down on the sinner. But if you understand it along the same lines as the one who says, *I am referring it to Christ and the Church* (Eph 5:32), God rains a shower on fertile ground. But it is by the same cloud, that is, divine scripture, that both are done. Likewise the Lord says, *It is not what enters into your mouth that defiles you but what comes out* (Mt 15:11). Sinners hear this and get their palates ready for gluttony. The just hear it and are safeguarded from superstition in the matter of distinguishing between foods. Here also, then, from the same scriptural cloud rain falls on each as he deserves, on the sinner a rain of snares, on the just the rain of plenty.

The portion of their cup

11. *Fire and brimstone and the blast of the tempest are the portion of their cup.* This is the punishment and the death of those through whom the name of God is blasphemed. It means that, to begin with, they are ruined by the fire of their own lusts. Next they are cast out from the company of the blessed because of the stench of their evil works. Finally they are whisked away and overwhelmed and they suffer unspeakable punishments. This is the portion of their cup, unlike the cup of the righteous, which is called "your brimming cup, intoxicating and lovely,"[25] for they will be inebriated by the rich abundance of your house.[26] I think it is called a cup so that we should not think that anything is done beyond moderation and measure, even with regard to the punishment of sinners within the operation of divine providence. And that is why, as if offering an explanation, the psalmist has added, *Because the Lord is just and loves justices*. The plural is not as redundant as

---

24. *Ad desuadendam superbiam*, an unusual verbal form. Variants are the more common *dissuadendum*, and *desudandam* "to make pride sweat."
25. See Ps 22(23):5.
26. See Ps 35:9(36:8).

it sounds. It is used only because the psalmist is speaking about human beings: the word *justices* should be understood as meaning just persons, for in many just individuals there seem to be a multitude of justices, so to speak, yet God's justice, in which all participate, is one.[27] It is as if one face looks into several mirrors. What in that particular face is only one in number is reflected as many from those many mirrors. This is why he again returns to the singular, saying, *His face has looked on equity.* Perhaps the phrase, *his face has looked on equity*, really means that equity has been seen in his face, that is, in knowing him, for God's face is the power by which he is known to those who are worthy of it. Or maybe the phrase, *his face has looked on equity*, is used because he does not offer himself to be known to the evil but to the good. And this is equity.

Interpretation of the Jews and Christ

12. But if anyone wants to understand the moon as the synagogue he should interpret the psalm in the light of the Lord's passion and say of the Jews, *They have destroyed what you made perfect*, and say of the Lord himself, *But what did the just person do?* They accused him of being a destroyer of the law. But it was they who had destroyed his commandments by living corruptly, by condemning those commandments, and by setting up their own instead. Accordingly, we may hear the Lord himself speaking from a human angle, as he often does, and saying, *I trust in the Lord. How can you say to my soul, Go over into the mountains like a sparrow?* in face of the terrifying threats of those who wanted to arrest and crucify him. It is quite appropriate to understand it also as referring to sinners who want to shoot their arrows at *people of honest heart*, that is, those who had believed in Christ, *when the moon was darkened*, which means when the synagogue was full of sinners. To what then does *the Lord is in his holy temple, the Lord is enthroned in heaven* refer? I think it is the Word-in-man or the Son of man himself who is in heaven. *His eyes look kindly on the poor*, either upon the poor man whom he, as God, assumed, or the poor for whose sake he suffered as man. *His eyelids question the sons of men.* The closing and the opening of his eyes, which is probably what is meant by the word eyelids, can suitably be understood as his death and resurrection, in which he tested the sons of men, his disciples, who were both terrified by his suffering and overjoyed by his resurrection. *The Lord questions the righteous and the ungodly,* for he is now steering the Church from heaven. *But whoever loves iniquity hates his own soul.* What follows shows why this is so. For the statement, *he will rain snares upon sinners*, should be understood in accordance with the explanation above. The same holds for everything else right to the end of the psalm.

---

27. A Platonist reflection: individual instances are derived from the one Form of Justice.

Exposition of Psalm 11

Verse 1. The eighth day

1. *To the end, for the eighth, a psalm of David.* It was said in the sixth psalm that the eighth day can be understood as the day of judgment. The phrase, *for the eighth*, can also be understood as meaning for the eternal age, because after this time which revolves in a seven-day cycle eternity will be given to the saints.[1]

Verses 2-5. Shortage of saints, widespread deceit and pride

2. *Make me safe, Lord,*[2] *because holy people have failed*, or, in other words, are nowhere to be found. This is the sort of phrase we use when we say, "The corn has failed," or "The money has failed." *Because all expressions of the truth have vanished from humankind.* The truth by which the souls of the saints are enlightened is one in number, but because there are many souls, it is possible to speak of many expressions of the truth in them, just as there are many images of the one face in a hall of mirrors.[3]

3. *They all lie to their neighbors.* The word *neighbor* ought to be understood as embracing everyone, because there is nobody to whom we should do evil, and love of one's neighbor does no evil.[4] *They speak evil things*[5] *with guileful lips and a double heart.* This phrase, *double heart,* clearly indicates duplicity.

4. *May the Lord destroy all guileful lips.* The psalmist uses the word *all* to prevent anyone from imagining that he or she is exempt. It is like the apostle Paul's stricture against *every human soul whose deeds are evil, the Jew first, but also the Greek* (Rom 2:9). The psalmist continues, *and every boasting tongue*, which means a proud tongue, clearly.

5. *They have claimed, "We will make a great show with our eloquence; our lips are our own, and who is our master?"* Proud hypocrites are what is meant,

---

1. See Exposition of Psalm 6, 1-2.
2. A variant has "God."
3. Compare his remarks on this in his Exposition of Psalm 10, 11.
4. See Rom 13:10.
5. Variant: "vain things."

those who place their hope in what they say in order to deceive their fellows. They refuse to submit themselves to God.

Verse 6. *God comes to the help of the poor*

6. *Now I will arise because the needy are in wretched straits and the poor are groaning, says the Lord.* Just so did the Lord himself in the gospel take pity on his people, because they had none to guide them when they could well have obeyed. On the same grounds it is also said in the gospel, *the harvest is great, but the workers are few* (Mt 9:37). This, however, should be taken as spoken in the person of God the Father who deigned to send his Son for the sake of the poor and needy, that is, those who suffered need and poverty in lacking spiritual good things. It is also the point of departure for the Sermon on the Mount in Matthew's Gospel, when the Lord says, *Blessed are the poor in spirit, for the kingdom of heaven is theirs* (Mt 5:3). *I will set in salvation.* The psalmist does not say what he will set, but *in salvation* is to be understood as in Christ, in accordance with the phrase, *My eyes have seen your salvation* (Lk 2:30). And this is why he is understood to have put into Christ whatever relates to the taking away of the wretchedness of the poor and the relief of the destitute who are groaning. *In him I will deal confidently*, and with good reason in view of the gospel word, *He was teaching them as one with authority, not like their own scribes* (Mt 7:29).

Verse 7. *The fire-proved words of God*

7. *The words of the Lord are pure words.* This is spoken in the person of the prophet himself. *The words of the Lord are pure words.* By *pure* he means without any alloy of deceit. For there are many who preach the truth impurely, because they sell it for the advantages this world can pay. Of such as these the apostle Paul says that they preach Christ, but not purely.[6] *Silver tried by fire for the earth.*[7] For sinners these words of the Lord are words tested and proved through hardships, *purified seven times*: by fear of God, by devotion, by knowledge, by fortitude, by deliberation, by understanding, by wisdom.[8] The steps of blessedness are also seven in number as the Lord rehearses in the same sermon which he delivered on the mountain, according to Matthew's account: *Blessed are the poor in spirit, blessed are the gentle, blessed are the mourners, blessed are those who are hungry and thirsty for righteousness, blessed are the merciful,*

---

6. See Phil 1:15.17.
7. *Argentum igne examinatum terrae*: probably "for the earth," meaning "for sinners," as the next sentence explains; but it would be possible to translate "tried by fire of the earth."
8. See Is 11:2-3, a passage on which the traditional list of "seven gifts of the Holy Spirit" is based.

blessed are the pure of heart, blessed are the peacemakers (Mt 5:3-9). You should notice that the whole of that extensive sermon is delivered on the theme of those seven beatitudes. For the eighth, in which he says, *Blessed are those who suffer persecution for the sake of righteousness*, signifies the very fire by which the silver is tried seven times. At the end of the sermon the evangelist relates, *He was teaching them as one with authority, not like their own scribes* (Mt 7:29), which accords with the assertion in this psalm, *In him I will deal confidently.*

Verses 8-9. The increase of the children of God

8. *You, Lord, will preserve us, you will keep us safe from this generation and for ever*: here as the poor and destitute, there as the rich and wealthy.

9. *The wicked walk*[9] *round in a circle*, that is, in their greed for temporal things. Such desire revolves in a sevenfold cycle of days, like a wheel. For this reason they do not reach the eighth, that is, eternity, which gives this psalm its title. So too it is said by Solomon, *A wise king is a winnower of the ungodly, and he sends against them the wheel of the wicked* (Prv 20:26, LXX). The psalm continues, *In your high wisdom*[10] *you have increased humankind*. There is also an increase of temporal things, which turn people away from the unity of God. That is why the corruptible body weighs down the soul, and this earthly dwelling oppresses a mind that considers many things.[11] But the just are increased in accordance with the high wisdom of God when they walk from many powers to one single power.[12]

---

9. Variant: "will walk."

10. *Altitudinem tuam*; a variant has *multitudinem*, "in great numbers."

11. See Wis 9:15.

12. See Ps 83:8(84:7). The more usual translation is "will walk from strength to strength," but here and in his Exposition of Psalm 83 Augustine is thinking of the contrast between earthly multiplicity and the simplicity of God. See Exposition of Psalm 83, 11, where Christ is the "single power," and note there.

Exposition of Psalm 12

1. *To the end, a psalm of David.* This title is given because *Christ is the end of the law, bringing justification to everyone who believes* (Rom 10:4). The psalm begins, *How long will you forget me, Lord? Even to the end?* "How long," he complains, "will you put me off from spiritually understanding Christ, who is the Wisdom of God[1] and the true end of every intention of the soul?" *How long will you turn your face away from me?* God no more turns away his face than he forgets, but scripture adopts our human idiom. God is said to turn away his face as long as he refuses knowledge of himself to a soul whose spiritual eyes are not yet pure.

2. *How long shall I take counsel in my mind?* There is need for seeking counsel only in adverse circumstances, so his question, *How long shall I take counsel in my mind?* is equivalent to asking, "How long will things go badly for me?" Or else it is a reply to his previous query, and the meaning is, "You will go on forgetting me, Lord, even to the end, and you will go on turning your face away from me, until I take counsel in my mind." We may infer that unless we take counsel within ourselves with a view to exercising perfect mercy, God does not steer us toward our end,[2] nor does he grant us full, face-to-face knowledge of himself. *Grief in my heart all day long?* We should understand this to mean, "How long must I go on harboring it?" But the words, *all day long*, imply continuity, for "day" means "a period of time;" so that a person who longs to be delivered from this temporal existence harbors interior grief of spirit, begging to ascend to eternal life and endure this human day no more.

Verses 3-5. The righteous under pressure

3-5. *How long will my enemy rise up against me?* The enemy could be either the devil or habitual weakness of the flesh. *Look upon me, Lord my God, and hear me.* The plea, *look upon me*, harks back to his lament, *How long will you*

---

1. See 1 Cor 1:24.
2. Christ.

turn your face away from me? and his petition, *hear me*, recalls his further question, *How long will you forget me—even to the end?* He continues, *Enlighten my eyes, lest I ever fall into the sleep of death*. We must understand the eyes of the heart here: he is praying that they may not be closed by the pleasurable myopia of sin. *And lest my enemy claim, I have beaten him*: we have good reason to fear the devil's taunt-song. *Those who harass me will make merry if I am shaken*. These are the devil and his angels, who harassed the righteous man, Job, but had no opportunity to make merry over him, because he was never shaken: he did not shift away from the stability of his faith.[3]

Verse 6. Thanksgiving

6. *But I have trusted in your mercy*. When a righteous person has not been shaken, but has stood firm in the Lord, he or she must not claim the credit for it; pride itself may shake such persons loose, even while they are boasting of not being shaken. *My heart will rejoice in your salvation*, which obviously means in Christ, the Wisdom of God.[4] *I will sing to the Lord, who has granted good things to me*: spiritual goods, that is, which have nothing to do with this human day. *And I will play on the harp to the name of the Lord Most High*. This is tantamount to declaring, "I give thanks to you joyfully, and conduct my bodily life with careful temperance,"[5] for this is the spiritual song of the soul. It may be, however, that we should make a distinction here: *I will sing* in my heart and *play the harp* by my actions to the Lord, inasmuch as he alone sees; but I will do so *to the name of the Lord* as well, that name which is made known to human beings not to his advantage, but to ours.

---

3. See Jb 1:20-22.
4. See 1 Cor 1:24.
5. *Ordinatissime utor corpore*: the phrase recalls Augustine's famous distinction between what is to be enjoyed (*frui*) for its own sake, and what is to be used (*uti*) as a means to an end. See note at Exposition of Psalm 4, 8.

Exposition of Psalm 13

Verse 1. Christ the end

1. *To the end, a psalm of David himself.* There is no need to repeat again and again what is meant by *to the end*, for *Christ is the end of the law, bringing justification to everyone who believes*, as the apostle Paul says (Rom 10:4). We believe in him when we begin to walk on the good road, and we shall see him when we have arrived. That is why he is the end.

Denying God

2. *The ignorant[1] person has said in his heart, There is no God.[2]* Ignorant indeed, for not even profane and abominable philosophers, who hold perverse and false opinions about him, have dared to say, "There is no God." This, therefore, is the reason why the phrase, *has said in his heart*, is used, because no one dares to say this out loud, even if he has dared to think it. *They are corrupt and have become detestable in their desires*, that is, in loving this world, and not loving God. These are the desires which corrupt the soul, and blind it so completely that the ignorant can go so far as to say in their hearts, *There is no God.* When such people are not content to acknowledge God, he gives them over to their own depraved way of thinking.[3] *There is no one who does anything good, no, not even to the very last one.* This expression, *not even to the very last one*, can either be understood as including that particular one, which would mean nobody at all, or it can be taken to mean "with the exception of one," indicating the Lord Christ. When we say something like "that field stretches right down to the sea," we do not, of course, count the sea in with the field. This latter interpretation is the better one, for nobody is deemed to have done anything good right down to Christ, because nobody can unless Christ himself has shown how. And

---

1. *Imprudens*, a variant is *insipiens*, foolish.
2. The text of this psalm is almost the same as that of Ps 52(53), but Augustine's Exposition of Psalm 52 is considerably different.
3. See Rom 1:28.

175

this judgment is quite true, because no human beings can act rightly until they know the one God.

Verse 2. The sons of men: the Jews

3. *The Lord has looked out from heaven on the sons of men, to see if there is anyone who understands or is seeking God.* This can be taken to mean that he looked out upon the Jews, since we may suppose that the psalm has given them the more honorific title, "sons of men," on the grounds of their worship of the one true God, by contrast with the Gentiles, of whom it was said in the preceding verse, *The ignorant has said in his heart, There is no God,* and so on. But if God "looks out" it is in order to see things through the souls of his saints. This is the meaning of *from heaven,* for in his own person nothing escapes his notice.

Verse 3. Gluttony and flattery

4. *All have fallen away and become useless.*[4] This suggests that the Jews have become as bad as the Gentiles who are referred to above. *There is no one who does good, no, not even to the very last one*: the earlier thought is here reiterated.[5] *Their throat is an open grave.* Either this is a description of the greediness of a gaping throat, or the phrase is used figuratively to indicate those who kill and seem to devour their victims by persuading them to adopt their own perverse habits. On similar lines, but with the opposite meaning, Peter received the instruction, *Slay and eat* (Acts 10:13), urging him to convert the Gentiles to his faith and his good way of life. *They have used their tongues for guileful speech,* for flattery is the companion of gluttons and of all who are wicked. *Snakes' poison is on their lips.* By *poison* the psalmist means guile, and he calls it *snakes' poison* because they refuse to hear the precepts of the law, just like snakes which pay no heed to the words of the snake-charmer. This point is examined in more detail in another psalm.[6] *Their mouths are full of cursing and bitterness*—snakes' poison, surely. *Their feet are swift to shed blood*: swift because so practiced in evildoing. *Chagrin and unhappiness beset their ways,* for all the paths of evil men and women are full of struggle and misery. So the Lord cries out, *Come to me, all you who struggle and are heavily burdened, and I will give you relief. Shoulder my yoke, and learn from me, for I am gentle and humble of heart. My*

---

4. A variant adds, "in their pursuits."
5. The lines from here to the end of verse 3 are absent from the Hebrew, but found their way from certain Greek manuscripts into Augustine's Latin version. The passage is quoted from the Septuagint with the extra lines by Paul in Rom 3:10-18.
6. See Ps 57:5-6(58:4-5).

yoke is kindly, and my burden light (Mt 11:28-30). The psalm continues, *They know not the path to peace.* This is the path which the Lord describes, as I said, when he speaks of his gentle yoke and light burden. *There is no fear of God before their eyes.* These people do not say, "There is no God," yet neither do they fear him.

Verse 4. Devouring God's people

5. *Will they not realize[7] it, all those who commit iniquity, those who consume my people as if eating bread?* The psalmist is threatening them with judgment, and he means that they devour his people every day, for bread is an everyday food. Those who gobble up the people are those who feather their own nests at the people's expense. They do not direct their service to the glory of God or to the salvation of those over whom they hold authority.

Verse 5. Fear of loss

6. *They have not invoked the Lord.* Anyone who longs for those things which displease the Lord does not truly call on him. *They quaked with fear where there was nothing to fear,* that is, over the loss of temporal things. So the Jews said, *If we leave him alone like this, everyone will believe in him, and then the Romans will come, and sweep away our land and our nation* (Jn 11:48). They were afraid of losing the earthly kingdom, where there was nothing really worth being afraid about, and they lost the kingdom of heaven, something of which they ought to have been afraid. And this is to be understood as referring to all good things which belong only to this passing age. When people fear to lose them, they do not reach the good things which are eternal.

Verse 6. The coming of the Son of God in humility

7. *Because God is among the kindred of the righteous,* rather than among those who love the world; for it is no righteous thing to abandon the Creator of worlds, and to love the world, and to serve the creature rather than the Creator.[8] *You have frustrated the plans of the poor person because the Lord is his hope;[9]* that is, you have despised the coming of the Son of God in humility, because you did not see in him the grandeur of the world. This was to ensure that those whom

---

7. Variant: "Do they not realize."
8. See Rom 1:25.
9. Variant: "because God will despise them."

he came to call should place their hope in God alone, not in the things which must pass away.

Verse 7. The gathering in of Israel

8. *Who will give Israel salvation out of Zion?* We must supply, "other than the one whose humility you have despised?" For he himself will come in glory to judge the living and the dead and to usher in the kingdom of the just. This would mean that, as by his coming in humility blindness fell upon part of Israel until the full tally of the Gentiles should come in, so, by that glorious coming, the rest of the prophecy may come true, and all Israel be saved.[10] For the apostle takes as a reference to the Jews that testimony of Isaiah where it is said, *From Zion shall come the one who will turn away ungodliness from Jacob* (Rom 11:26),[11] as though it were an answer to the question in this psalm, *Who will give Israel salvation out of Zion?* The psalm ends with a repetition, as so often, for in the verse, *when the Lord turns away the captivity of his people, Jacob will rejoice and Israel will be glad*, I think that *Israel will be glad* is the same as saying, *Jacob will rejoice*.

---

10. See Rom 11:25-26.
11. Compare Is 59:20.

Exposition of Psalm 14

Verse 1. Tents

1. *A psalm of David himself.* There is no dispute about this title. The psalm begins, *Lord, who will sojourn¹ in your tent?* Although the word tent² is used sometimes to denote an everlasting habitation, strictly speaking a tent is something associated with war. Hence soldiers are referred to as tent-companions,³ because their tents are grouped together. This interpretation receives further backing from the words, *who will sojourn?* For we do battle with the devil for a time, and we need a tent in which to regain our strength. This points in particular to faith under this temporal dispensation established for us within time by our Lord's incarnation. *And who will take rest on your holy mountain?* Perhaps the psalmist is now referring to our eternal habitation,⁴ and if so we should understand by the word *mountain* the towering greatness of Christ's love in eternal life.

Verses 2-3. Walking unstained: truth in heart and mouth

2. *Whoever walks without stain and acts justly.* This is a general statement. In what follows the psalmist expounds it in detail.

3. *Whoever speaks the truth in his heart.* Some have the truth on their lips and yet do not have it in their heart. Suppose someone were to give false directions

---

1. *Peregrinabitur*: the word implies pilgrimage, temporary abode, impermanence. In the original Hebrew of this psalm the verb is used of a newcomer or one without established rights. It was applied to the patriarchs who wandered in Canaan without title to the land, and to the Israelites as sojourners in Egypt; see especially the profession of faith in Dt 26:5.
2. *Tabernaculum.*
3. *Contaubernales*, derived from *con-* + *taberna* + *-alis*.
4. In the desert the Lord had been a wanderer with his wandering people, and his abode was mobile like theirs, the Tent of Meeting (see Ex 26; 33:7-11; 36:8-34; 40:18-38; Nm 11:16; 12:4-10). After their settlement in Canaan and the eventual building of the temple by Solomon, the Lord's house was still poetically referred to as a "tent," and in the original perspective of this psalm the "tent" is almost certainly the temple and the "mountain" the temple mount in Jerusalem. So the question with which the psalm opens is spoken by a would-be guest in the Lord's temple. But Augustine is thinking rather of the believer's earthly campaigning, and there is support for this alternative imagery in the New Testament; see 2 Cor 5:1.2; 2 Pt 1:13.14.

deliberately, knowing full well that on the road in question there were brigands, and were to say, "If you go this way you will be safe from brigands;" and then it turned out that in fact there were no brigands to be found there. Our imaginary person would have spoken the truth, but not in his heart. He was thinking otherwise, and he spoke the truth unwittingly. Therefore it is insufficient to utter the truth unless it also exists in the heart. *Who has not practiced deceit with his tongue*. Deceit is practiced with the tongue when one thing is professed with the lips and another is concealed in the breast. *And has done no evil to his neighbor*. It is well known that by "neighbor" everyone is to be understood. *And has not entertained slander against his neighbor*: that is, has not too willingly or hastily believed a slanderer.

Verse 4. Walking unstained: perfection

4. *The spiteful person has been reduced to nothing in his sight*. This is perfection, that the spiteful should achieve nothing against such a one, and that this be proved true *in his sight*. What this means is that the righteous one knows without a shadow of doubt that there is no such thing as a spiteful person except when the mind turns itself away from the eternal changeless beauty of its Creator toward the beauty of the creature which was made out of nothing. *He glorifies those who fear the Lord*. The subject now is the Lord himself, for the fear of the Lord is the beginning of wisdom.[5] Therefore as the preceding verses described those already perfect, so what he is about to say now relates to beginners.

Verses 4-5. Stability

5. *Who swears an oath to his neighbor, and does not deceive him, who has not put his money out to usury or accepted bribes to harm the innocent*. These are no great achievements! But people who are incapable of even these are much less able to speak the truth in their hearts, to refrain from practicing deceit with their tongues, to profess the truth outwardly just as it is in their hearts, to have on their lips *a Yes that is yes, and a No that is no* (Mt 5:37), to avoid harming their neighbors (that is, anyone), or to reject a slanderous accusation against a neighbor. Such are the qualities of the perfect, in whose sight the spiteful has been reduced to nothing. Yet the psalmist concludes his enumeration of even these small-scale acts by declaring, *Whoever acts so will not be moved for ever*, suggesting that such persons will proceed to those greater things in which powerful and unshakable stability may be gained. Even the tenses of the verbs seem to be varied for a

---

5. See Ps 110(111):10 ; Sir 1:16.

good reason: the past tense occurs in the conclusion to verse four, whereas in this conclusion to verse five the future is used. At the earlier point we read, *The spiteful person has been reduced to nothing in his sight*, whereas here the psalm says, *Whoever acts so will not be moved for ever.*

Exposition of Psalm 15

Verses 1-2. Christ the King

1. The title inscribed is: *of David himself.* In this psalm our king speaks from the standpoint of the human nature he assumed.[1] At the time of his crucifixion the royal title written above him stood out clearly.[2]

2. He begins, *Preserve me, Lord, for I have hoped in you; I said to the Lord, You are my God, because you have no need of any good things from me.* No, you are not looking to be blessed by any good things I can give.

Verse 3. The land of the living

3. *For the saints who are in his land*: he gives thanks for the saints who, though they still live in the flesh on this earth, have placed their hope in the land of the living, the citizens of the heavenly Jerusalem whose spiritual way of life is fixed securely by the anchor of hope[3] in that country which is rightly called the land of God; for *he has wonderfully fulfilled all my wishes in them.* For these saints he has brought[4] to wonderful fruition all I could have wished for in their advancement. Accordingly they have realized how much to their advantage has been the humanity which my godhead assumed, so that I might die, and the divinity in my manhood, which enabled me to rise again.[5]

Verse 4. The illness which leads to healing

4. *Their infirmities have been multiplied*, not to bring them to ruin but to make them long for a doctor. *But thereafter they made haste.* As their infirmities increased, they made haste to seek healing. *I will not gather them into assemblies*

---

1. Augustine is constantly aware that Christ speaks in the psalms, sometimes in his own person, sometimes in our name, often as the Head who associates his members with his own prayer. The present Exposition assumes this throughout. See the *Introduction.*
2. *Eminuit*; a variant is *emicuit*, "shone out."
3. See Heb 6:19.
4. Variant: "I have brought."
5. Literally "the humanity of my divinity, so that I might die, and the divinity of my manhood, which. . . ."

by blood-offerings. Gathered they will be, but not in carnal assemblies, nor will I draw them together as if I were a god appeased by the blood of cattle.[6] *Nor shall I perpetuate their names upon my lips.* By means of a spiritual transformation they will forget what they once were. Then I shall not call them sinners, or enemies, or mortals, but rather the righteous, my brothers and sisters, and children of God through my peace.

Verses 5-6. Christ's inheritance

5. *The Lord is my allotted inheritance and my cup,* for together with me they will possess as their inheritance the Lord himself. Let others choose earthly and temporal portions to enjoy; the share of the saints is the Lord eternal. Let others drink deep of death-dealing pleasures; the Lord is the cup allotted to me. When I say, *my,* I include the Church, because where the Head is, there the body is too. I will gather together their assemblies to be my inheritance, and as I drink deep of the cup I will forget their old names. *You are he who will restore[7] to me my inheritance,* that the glory I had with you before the existence of the world may be known to these also whom I set free.[8] You will not restore to me what I never lost, but you will restore to those who have lost it the knowledge[9] of that bright glory. Yet because I am among them, *you will restore it to me.*

6. *The measuring-lines have fallen for me in bright, glorious places.* The territory marked out for me is within your radiance; this is my lot, as God is the possession of the priests and the Levites.[10] *Indeed my inheritance is glorious to me.* Glorious it is indeed, but not to everyone—only to those who can see. Because I am among them, I can say, *to me.*

---

6. See Is 1:11.12.

7. Variant: "are restoring."

8. See Jn 17:5.

9. Plato's theory of ἀνάμνησις suggested that learning is simply remembering, a recalling of knowledge the soul had before entering the body (see *Meno* 81 D). Plotinus, whose writings influenced Augustine, taught that the soul could recognize beauty from some ancient knowledge (see *Enn.* 1,6,2). There may be echoes of these doctrines here, but the biblical idea of "knowing God" predominates: an intimate relationship made possible by God's gracious self-revelation and a human response of faith and obedience. The gift of eternal life by Jesus, identified by him with knowledge of the one true God (Jn 17:3), is the principal background here.

10. In the apportioning of territory in the promised land, the Levites have no inheritance, scripture reiterates, because "the Lord himself is their inheritance, as he told them." See Nm 18:20; Dt 10:9; Sir 45:22; Lm 3:24.

Verses 7-9. Understanding, suffering and hope

7. *I will bless the Lord, who has granted me understanding*, by which that inheritance may be seen and possessed. *Moreover, even into the night my inward parts rebuked me.* Yes, and more than understanding, for my lower part too, this flesh which I have taken on, instructed me even to the point of death, that I might experience the darkness proper to mortality, a darkness which the understanding does not know.

8. *I kept the Lord always before my eyes.* Confronted by the things which pass away, I did not take my eye off him who abides always, for I looked forward to speeding back to him when my passage through temporal things should be over. *He is at my right hand, and so I shall not be thrown off course*, because his favor rests upon me, and holds me steadfastly in him.

9. *And so my heart was delighted and my tongue rejoiced.*[11] For this reason there is both happiness in my thoughts and rejoicing in my words. *And even my flesh shall rest in hope.* My very flesh will not fail and decay, but will sleep sound in the hope of the resurrection.

Verse 10. The joy of seeing God face to face

10. *For you will not leave my soul in hell*—will not hand it over as a prey to the underworld, that is—*nor allow your holy one to suffer corruption*: you will not allow the sanctified body, through which others also are to be sanctified, to undergo decay.[12] *You have made known to me the ways of life*: rather have you made known through me the ways of humility, so that men and women may return to the life from which they fell through pride; but I can say, *You have made known to me*, because of my union with them. *You will fill me with joy in beholding your face.* You will fill them to the brim with gladness, so that they will look for nothing further when they see you face to face. Again, because I am among them, *you will fill me* can be the words I use. *Your right hand will be full of delights for ever.* Delight is to be found in your favor and mercy while we are on the journey of this life, which leads to the goal of beholding your face in glory.[13]

---

11. Variant: "will rejoice."

12. This verse is cited by Paul in his sermon at Pisidian Antioch (Acts 13:35) as a testimony to Christ's resurrection; and the whole of verses 8-10 in Peter's Pentecost sermon (Acts 2:25-28) to the same effect.

13. Here and in Ps 48:16(49:15) a vague, inchoate hope of eternal life is expressed, born of a conviction that a friendship with God which has become so real in this life cannot be extinguished by death. The belief was to come into sharper focus in the second century B.C. under the persecution of Antiochus Epiphanes—see 2 Mc 7:9; Dn 12:2—and would be clearly vindicated by the teaching and the resurrection of Jesus. Augustine reads the psalm in the light of Christian faith; see *Introduction*.

Exposition of Psalm 16

Verses 1-2. True judgment

1. *A prayer of David himself.* This psalm is to be assigned to the Lord in person, together with the Church, which is his body.

2. *Give ear to my righteous appeal, O God, give heed to my supplication. Let your ears hearken to my prayer, one not made with deceitful lips.* No, not from deceitful lips is it addressed to you. *May my judgment proceed from your face*; in virtue of the enlightenment brought by knowledge of you, may I judge truthfully. Or perhaps we should understand it like this: Let the judgment I pronounce proceed from your face, but be expressed without deceit on my lips, so that when I am judging I may say nothing other than what I understand in you. *And my eyes look upon what is fair*: the eyes of the heart, evidently.

Verses 3-4. Testing by night and by fire

3. *You have tested my heart and visited me by night*, for my very heart has been proved by the visitation of distress; *you have tried me by fire, and no iniquity has been found in me.* This distress by which I have been tried and found to be just is not to be called *night* merely, night being associated with restlessness, but *fire* too, because it burns.

4. *So that my mouth speak not of human deeds.* I pray that nothing may come out of my mouth but what redounds to your glory and praise, rather than what relates to the works of men and women, the things they do contrary to your will. *Because of the words of your lips*—the words of your peace, perhaps, or of your prophets—*I have kept to difficult ways*, the troublesome paths of human mortality and suffering.

Verse 5. The path to peace

5. *To make my steps perfect in your pathways.* This is a prayer that the Church's love may grow to perfection through those narrow paths by which it attains your rest. *And that my footprints may not be obliterated.* May the signs of my journey not be removed, those signs which have been impressed like footprints on the sacraments and the apostolic writings, so that people who want to

follow me may discern and observe them. Alternatively we may interpret the verse like this: May I abide steadfastly in eternity after I have finished these arduous journeys, and made my steps perfect within the narrow limits of your pathways.

Verses 6-7. God's mercy

6. *I have cried out, for you have heard me, O God.* With free and fervent intent I have directed my pleas to you, for you heard me when in a weaker state I prayed to have strength like this. *Incline your ear to me, and listen to my words.* Do not let your willingness to listen abandon me in my humble state.

7. *Reveal the wonder of your mercies*: he prays that your mercies be not accounted cheap, lest people do not love them as much as they should.

Verses 7-9. Christ's humanity is like a lens

8. *You who save those who hope in you from the opponents of your right hand*, from those, that is, who oppose the favor[1] you rest upon me. *Guard me, Lord, like the apple of your eye*, a thing that seems very small and unimportant; yet through it the gaze is directed and we differentiate light from darkness. The same is true of divine judgment, which through Christ's humanity distinguishes between the just and sinners. *Cover me with your wings and protect me,*[2] protect me in the shelter of your love and mercy *from the menace of the ungodly who have persecuted me.*

Verses 9-12. The wicked attack Christ

9. *My enemies have ringed me round, they have choked on their excesses*, for they have been buried under their own gross joy after sating their greed with evildoing, and they did so *mouthing pride*: they certainly did mouth pride when they said, *Hail, King of the Jews!* (Mt 27:29) and uttered similar taunts.

10. *They cast me out and now they surround me.* Casting me outside the city, they now surround me on the cross. *They have resolved to keep their eyes on the ground*, to lower the aspirations of their hearts to earthly things, supposing that the one who was being killed suffered a great evil when the ones who were killing him suffered no such thing.

---

1. The right hand was regarded by many ancient peoples as the sign of what was favorable or propitious.
2. Variant: "you will protect me."

11. *They captured me like a lion ready for its prey*, seizing me like that adversary who roams about seeking whom he may devour.[3] *Or like a lion-cub lurking in its lair*, for the people to whom it was said, *You are children of your father, the devil* (Jn 8:44) is aptly called the devil's cub as it devises the ambush with which it means to trap and destroy a just man.

Verses 13-14. Deliverance from the enemies of God

12. *Arise, Lord, outwit and overthrow them.* Wake up, Lord! They thought you were asleep and heedless of the iniquities of men and women. Let them be blinded instantly by their own wickedness so that punishment may get in ahead of their doing anything. Yes, topple them!

13. *Deliver my soul from the ungodly* by raising me from the death inflicted on me by the ungodly, *and your sword from the enemies of your hand*, for my soul is your sword. Your hand, that is, your eternal power, has grasped it to subdue the kingdoms of iniquity, and to separate the just from the ungodly. *Deliver* it, then, *from the enemies of your hand*. Your hand is your power, and the enemies in question are my enemies. *Lord, destroy them from the face of the earth, scatter them*[4] *while yet they live.* Destroy them, Lord, from the face of this earth they inhabit, and scatter them throughout the world in this life, which those who lose hope imagine to be their one and only life. *You have secretly filled their bellies*, for not only will they be overtaken by this punishment, clear for all to see; but, even worse, their memory is so filled with sins as to make them forget God, because sins are like darkness which hides from the light of your truth. *They are stuffed with pork*, because they are filled with uncleanness, and have trampled underfoot the pearls of God's words.[5] *And they have left the consequences to their children* by shouting, "May this sin be upon us and our children!"[6]

Verse 15. Christ's revelation in glory

14. *As for me, in your justice I shall appear before you*: I, who have not appeared to those who with their filthy and darkened heart are unable to see the light of wisdom, will appear in your justice before you. *I shall be satisfied when your glory is revealed*: when they have been so sated with their own squalor that they cannot understand me, I shall be fully satisfied when your glory is revealed in those who do understand me.

---

3. See 1 Pt 5:8.
4. A variant adds, "and trip them up."
5. See Mt 7:6.
6. See Mt 27:25.

We should note that in the verse which says, *They are stuffed with pork*, some copies have *They are full-fed with children*. From an ambiguity in the Greek two possible interpretations have arisen.[7] But by *children* we understand works: as good children stand for good works, so bad children symbolize evil deeds.

---

7. Some Greek codices had υἱῶν (sons), others had ὑῶν (pigs) or ὑείων (pork). In his letter to Paulinus (Letter 149,5) Augustine says that he now thinks the translation "sons" or "children" better suited to the context than "pork" which he had dictated long ago in his Exposition of the psalm. Since this letter to Paulinus is dated 414, the present Exposition must be considerably earlier.

Exposition of Psalm 17

Verse 1. Saul and David

1. *To the end, for the Lord's servant, David himself.* This means for Christ, strong of hand in his humanity. *The words of this psalm were spoken by David on the day when the Lord whisked him to safety from the hand of all his enemies, and from the hand of Saul.* Saul was the king whom the Jews had demanded for themselves.[1] For as "David" is said to mean "strong of hand," so "Saul" means "demand." It is well known how the Jewish people sought and received a king for itself, in accordance with its own will, not God's.

Verses 2-4. The horn of salvation: refuge in God

2. Accordingly Christ and the Church, the whole Christ, Head and body, are speaking here when the psalm begins, *I will love you, Lord, my strength.* I will love you, Lord, through whom I am strong.

3. *O Lord, my firm support, my refuge and my liberator.* Lord, you have supported me because I sought refuge with you; and I sought refuge because you have set me free. *God is my helper, and I will hope in him.* You, my God, first granted me the help of your calling so that I might hope in you.[2] *My protector, the horn of my salvation, my redeemer.* You are my protector because I have not relied upon myself, as though tossing proud horns against you; rather have I found you to be my horn, my unshakable heavenly savior, and you redeemed me that I might find it.

4. *I will call upon the Lord in praise, and I shall be saved from my enemies.* When I seek not my own glory, but the Lord's, and call upon him, the errors of ungodliness will have no means of harming me.

Verses 5-7. Mortal peril

5. *The sorrows of death encircled me*, that is, the sorrows of the flesh; *and the torrents of iniquity have thrown me into confusion.* Wicked crowds that were

---

1. See 1 Sm 8:5.
2. A clearly Augustinian reference to prevenient grace.

189

whipped up for a time, like rivers swollen by rain but soon to subside, have contrived to throw me into confusion.

6. *The pains of hell encompassed me.* Among the surrounding enemies bent on my destruction were the pangs of envy, which are death-dealing and can plunge people into the hell of sin. *The snares of death beset me before their time,* assailed me because they sought to harm in advance what would be delivered to them later.[3] But they do indeed fatally capture any whom they have wickedly persuaded by a boastful show of righteousness, glorying against the heathen in a reputation which has no reality underlying it.

7. *In my anguish I called on the Lord, crying to my God, and he heard my voice from his holy temple.* He heard my voice from my heart, which is where he lives.[4] *And my crying is done in his presence.* Yes, and this crying of mine, done not in the hearing of others but before God himself within, *will reach his ears.*[5]

Verses 8-9. *Cosmic convulsions*

8. *The earth was moved and shook,* because when the Son of Man was glorified, sinners were moved and shaken. *And the foundations of the mountains were unsettled,* for the hopes of the proud, grounded in this world, were upset. *They were moved because God was angry with them,* obviously to ensure that hope in purely temporal things should no longer have a firm footing in the hearts of men and women.

9. *Up went the smoke in his anger,* the tearful prayer for pardon from repentant sinners when they realized what God was threatening against the ungodly. *Fire flared*[6] *from his face,* for glowing love begins to kindle from that knowledge of him which follows repentance. *Leaping flames from glowing coals were lit by him.* Those who were already dead, abandoned by the fire of good desire and the light of justice, people who remained in cold and darkness, have come to life again, rekindled and brightly lit.

Verse 10. *Incarnation*

10. *He bowed*[7] *the heavens and came down.* God *bowed the heavens* in making the Just One so humble as to come down to the weakness of men and women.

---

3. Or "in advance, for which they would later be requited."
4. An echo of Augustine's habitual awareness of God's indwelling, articulated especially in *The Confessions*: people "pursue outside themselves what they are making, but forsake the One within by whom they are made, and so destroy what they were made to be by driving it out of doors . . . . Late have I loved you, Beauty so ancient and so new, late have I loved you! Lo, you were within, but I outside, seeking there for you . . ." (*Confessions* X,34,53; X,27,38).
5. Variant: "has reached."
6. Variant: "will flare."
7. Variant: "will bow."

A dark cloud was beneath his feet, for the ungodly who think earthbound thoughts did not know him because of the gloomy blackness of their malice. The earth is beneath his feet, serving as his footstool.

Verses 11-12. The hidden God

11. *He rose above the cherubim and flew.*[8] He was raised above the full range of knowledge, so that no one should come to him by any means other than love, for the fulfillment of the law is love.[9] And without delay he showed those who love him that he is ultimately unknowable, to prevent them from thinking that he is to be understood by the sort of thoughts[10] we have in our bodily state. *He flew upon the wings of the wind.* The speed with which he showed himself to be incomprehensible is above the spiritual capabilities by which souls lift themselves up from their earthbound fears, as though on wings, into the upper atmosphere of freedom.

12. *He made the darkness his hiding-place.* He shrouded his sacraments in mystery, willing them to be a hidden hope in the hearts of believers, to make a place where he might hide himself without in any way abandoning them, for in this darkness, where we still walk by faith, not by sight,[11] we wait patiently in hope for what we do not see.[12] *Like a tent round about him.* Those who believe in him turn to him and surround him, because he is in their midst, since he befriends all equally, and dwells in them at the present time as though in a tent. *Dark water in the clouds.* Let none imagine that because they understand the scriptures properly they are therefore already in that light which we shall enjoy in the future, when we have passed from faith to sight, for in the prophets and in all the preachers of the divine word there is obscure teaching.

Verses 13-15. Divine thunderstorms

13. *In advance of the lightning of his presence*, in preparation, that is, for the brightness of his manifestation, *his clouds have passed over*, for the preachers of his word[13] are no longer confined within the borders of Judea, but have crossed over to the nations. *Hailstones and fiery coals.* By this figure of speech we should understands reproofs, which batter hard hearts like hail. But if the well-cultivated and receptive soil of a godly mind receives reproofs, the hard-

---

8. Variant: "will fly."
9. See Rom 13:10.
10. Variant: "images."
11. See 2 Cor 5:7.
12. See Rom 8:25.
13. As often, Augustine sees clouds as symbolic of preachers, who shower down the life-giving water of the word.

ness of the hail is dissolved into water, because the terror of a reproof, charged with lightning and frozen hard, is dissolved into nourishing doctrine, while hearts come back to life when kindled by the fire of love. All these benefits have passed over to the gentiles in his clouds.

14. *The Lord thundered from heaven*; in the full assurance of the gospel the Lord has spoken from the heart of the Just One. *The Most High raised his voice* so that we should receive it, and in the depths of human affairs hear heavenly things.

15. *He shot his arrows and scattered his enemies.* He sent out his evangelists to fly on straight courses, on wings of strength, using not their own powers but those of the One by whom they were sent; and he scattered those to whom they were sent, that to some among them the evangelists might be the savor of life leading to life, but to others the stench of death leading to death.[14] *He intensified his lightning-flashes and dismayed them*, for he has increased miraculous happenings and thrown[15] his enemies into disarray.

Verse 16. Fountains and foundations

16. *Springs of water appeared.* Springs of water appeared, opened up in the preachers, leaping up to eternal life.[16] *And the foundations of the world were revealed*, for the prophets were a revelation, and though they were not understood, yet on them was to be built the world which believes in the Lord, *at your rebuke, Lord*, as you cry out, *The kingdom of God has come upon you* (Lk 10:9), *at the blast of your angry breath* as you warn us, *Unless you repent, you will all die likewise* (Lk 13:5).

Verses 17-20. God welcomes the Church

17. *He sent from above and took me up* by calling me from the Gentiles into my inheritance, to be a glorious Church, with neither spot nor wrinkle.[17] *He drew me to himself from the vast tract of waters*,[18] for he drew me to himself from the great crowd of the peoples.

18. *He rescued[19] me from my strongest enemies*: from those enemies he rescued me who had succeeded in ruining and overthrowing this temporal life of

---

14. See 2 Cor 2:16.
15. Variant: future tense in both verbs.
16. See Jn 4:14.
17. See Eph 5:27.
18. Some manuscripts add here, "He will deliver me because he wanted me," anticipating verse 20.
19. Variant: "will rescue."

mine; *and from those who hate me, because they were too strong for me*, too strong as long as I am subject to them and living in ignorance of God.[20]

19. *They forestalled me on my day of adversity*, they were the first to harm me, while I still bear a mortal body prone to pain. *But the Lord became my foundation*: since the foundation of earthly pleasure has been shaken and disrupted by bitter miseries, the Lord has become my foundation.

20. *He led me forth into open ground.* Because I was suffering the constrictions of the flesh, he led me forth into the wide spiritual plains of faith. *He rescued me*[21] *because he wanted me.* Before I wanted God *he rescued me from my most powerful enemies* who bore a grudge against me when I began to want him, *and from those who hate me* because I want him now.

Verses 21-25. Purity of heart

21. *The Lord will repay me in accordance with my righteousness.* The Lord will requite me in accordance with the righteousness of my good will, he who first showed mercy before I had a good will.[22] *And in accordance with the purity of my hands he will repay me*, for he will repay me for the purity of my deeds, who by leading me into the open plains of faith enabled me to act rightly.

22. *Because I have kept to the pathways of the Lord*, so that there may be for me a broad expanse of good works, resulting from faith, and long-suffering perseverance.

23-24. *I have not strayed in wickedness from my God, for all his judgments are before me.* All his judgments: that is, the rewards of the just, the punishments of the ungodly, the scourges of those under correction and the temptations of those who are being tested. All these I examine with untiring scrutiny. *And I have not cast his just decrees away from me*: this is what they do who are flagging under the burden of his just decrees, and they return to their own vomit.[23] *And so I shall be spotless before him, and shall guard myself against wrongdoing.*

25. *The Lord will repay me in accordance with my righteousness.* The Lord will therefore repay me in accordance with my righteousness not only for wide-reaching faith which works through love,[24] but also for sustained perseverance. *And in accordance with the purity of my hands in his sight*, not as men and women see, but in God's eyes; for things which are seen are temporal, but things unseen are eternal,[25] and to them our hope stretches upward.

---

20. A variant has *qui ignorant*: "as long as I was subject to those who know not God."
21. *Eruit.* Variants are *eruet*: "will rescue" and *liberabit*: "will deliver."
22. See note on paragraph 3 above.
23. See Prv 26:11; 2 Pt 2:22.
24. See Gal 5:6.
25. See 2 Cor 4:18.

Verses 26-30. God, holy and blameless, enlightener and savior

26. *With a holy person you will be holy.* There is a deeply hidden sense in which you are known as holy with the holy, because you make them holy. *And with the innocent you will be innocent,* because you harm no one,[26] whereas each and every one of us is bound by the strands of our own sins.[27]

27. *With the chosen you will be chosen,* for you are chosen by the person whom you choose. *And with the perverse you will deal perversely,* because to perversely-minded people you seem to be perverse too; they allege, *The Lord's way is not straight* (Ez 18:25).

28. *Because you will save a humble people.* That you should save those who confess their sins seems perverse to those who themselves are perverse; *but you will bring proud looks down to earth,* for you will humiliate those who do not know God's righteousness and seek to set up their own instead.[28]

29. *You, Lord, will light[29] my lamp.* Since our light does not come from ourselves, it is you, Lord, who will light my lamp. *My God, you will enlighten my darkness.* Of ourselves we are darkness by reason of our sins, but you, my God, *will enlighten my darkness.*

30. *By you I shall be delivered[30] from temptation*: not by my own efforts shall I be delivered, but by you. *And in my God I shall leap over the wall.* Again, it is not by my own strength but in my God that I shall leap over the wall which sins have built between humankind and the heavenly Jerusalem.

Verses 31-32. The pure way of God

31. *As for my God, his way is spotless.* My God does not come to men and women unless they cleanse the way of faith by which he may come to them, for his way is spotless. *The utterances of God are tried in fire,* because his words are proved by the fire of tribulation. *He is the protector of all who hope in him,* for that tribulation does not destroy those who trust not in themselves but in him, for hope follows upon faith.

32. *Who is God apart from the Lord* whom we serve? *And who is God except our God?* Who indeed is God other than the Lord whom we will possess after a period of faithful service, like children coming into a longed-for inheritance?

---

26. *Tu nulli noces*: the antithesis between "innocent" and "harm" is clearer in Latin.
27. *Criniculis*: "fine hairs." Prv 5:22 speaks of the ropes of sin.
28. See Rom 10:3.
29. Variant: "are lighting."
30. Variant "plucked away."

Verses 33-37. God has equipped me

33. *God who girded*[31] *me with strength*, who girded me that I might be strong, and that the loosely-flowing folds of concupiscence might not impede my actions or my steps, he *has made my path immaculate*. He has laid down the spotless road of love so that by it I may come to him, as spotless too is the road of faith by which he came to me.

34. *He who made my feet perfect like a deer's*, who has made my love perfect, to leap over the thorny, dark entanglements of this world, *he will set me on the high places*. He will direct my gaze to my heavenly habitation, that I may be filled with all the fullness of God.[32]

35. *He trains my hands for battle*, teaching me how to conduct myself to overcome the enemies who try to bar our access to the heavenly kingdom. *You have made my arms like a bronze bow*, for you have given me a zeal for good works that is untiring.

36. *You have protected me with your saving help, and your right hand has upheld me*: this means that I have been upheld by your gracious favor.[33] *Your instruction has steered me to the end*, for your reproof, by not allowing me to deviate, has guided me to relate whatever I do to the goal of union with you. *Your instruction itself will teach me*, for that same reproof of yours will teach me how to arrive at the place toward which it pointed me.

37. *You have made room for my steps under me*. The constraints of the flesh will not hold me back, for you have enlarged the scope of my love, enabling it to work with joy even in dealing with things which are beneath me, things that perish and my own body. *And my footsteps have not grown faint*, for neither have my pathways been blotted out, nor have the footprints I left that my followers might imitate me.

Verses 38-43. Victory

38. *I shall pursue my enemies and catch them*, for I shall hound down my carnal affections; I shall not be seized by them, but rather take hold of them and rob them of their strength, *not turning away until they fall to the ground defeated*. I shall not turn aside from my purpose or seek rest until those who make an uproar against me collapse into defeat.

39. *I shall dash them to pieces*[34] *and they will have no strength to stand*, nor will they hold out against me. *They will fall beneath my feet*, and then, having rid

---

31. Variant: "girds."
32. See Eph 3:19.
33. See note on Exposition of Psalm 16, 8.
34. *Confringam*; a variant is *confligam*, "I shall set them at each other's throats."

myself of them, I will set before me those ways of love on which I walk for ever.[35]

40. *You have girded me with strength for war.* Tightly and strongly you have bound up the loosely-flowing desires of my flesh, that I may not be hindered by them in the battle. *You have subdued my assailants under me*, for you have caused those who pressed upon me to be outwitted, so that those who sought to dominate me are under my feet.

41. *You have thrust my enemies behind me*, turning them round and pushing them behind me so that they have to follow me. *But you have destroyed those who hate me*, for others there were among them who persisted in hatred, and those you destroyed.

42. *They cried but there was no one to save them*, for who could save those you would not save? *They cried to the Lord, but he did not listen to them.* Not to anyone at random did they cry, but to the Lord, yet he did not consider them worth listening to, since they did not forsake their wickedness.

43. *I will crush and scatter them like dust before the wind*: I will crush them, for they are bone-dry, deprived of the shower of God's mercy. Lifted high and inflated with pride, may they be swept away from any firm and secure reliance, as though from the solid, immovable earth. *I will brush them off like mud from the streets*. As they meander and slide along the broad paths of perdition, where many walk, I will brush them off.

Verses 44-46. Sovereignty over the Gentiles

44. *You will lift me clear*[36] *of hostile allegations*, like the protests of those who complained, "If we let him alone, the whole world will go after him."[37]

45. *You will establish me at the head of the nations. A people I never knew has come to serve me*, for the Gentile peoples, whom I did not visit by bodily presence, have given me their allegiance. *As soon as they heard of me they obeyed me*; though they did not see me with their own eyes, by receiving my preachers they have heard me and obeyed me.

46. *But my own sons are estranged and have lied to me*. These children who have no right to be called mine, misbegotten children to whom it was rightly said, *You are children of your father, the devil* (Jn 8:44), they have lied to me. *My sons are estranged, they have hardened with age*: these base-born children, to whom I brought the New Testament to make them new, have persisted in their

---

35. Compare Exposition of Psalm 9, 15, where he says, "The foot of the soul is love."
36. Or imperative, with variant readings, "Lift me clear."
37. See Jn 11:48; 12:19.

old ways,[38] *and have hobbled away from their paths*. They were like people crippled in one foot, because they held on to the Old Testament while spurning the New. They had a spiritual limp, preferring to follow their own teachings in relation even to the old law, rather than God's teaching; for they were in the habit of finding fault with hands that had not been washed[39] because such were the paths they had beaten and were accustomed to tramping on themselves, wandering from the ways of God's commandments.

Verses 47-50. Praise and thanksgiving to God

47. *The Lord lives, and blessed be my God*. It is death to judge by the standards of the flesh,[40] for the Lord is alive, and may he, my God, be blessed. *May the God of my salvation be highly exalted*, and may I not think in an earthly way about the God of my salvation, nor hope for any salvation from this earth, but set my sights high and hope in him.

48. *O God, you who vindicate me and have subdued whole peoples under me*, you it is who avenge me by subjecting them to me, *you who set me free from my enraged enemies*, from the Jews, that is, who cried, *Crucify! Crucify!* (Jn 19:6).

49. *You will lift me to safety from those who rise against me*. From the clutches of the Jews who rose against me in my passion, you will lift me up in my resurrection. *From the unjust man you will tear me away*, freeing me from their iniquitous rule.

50. *Therefore I will confess to you among the Gentiles,*[41] *Lord*, for it is through me, Lord, that the gentiles will confess to you, *and I will sing psalms to your name*, for you will become more widely known through my good works.

Verse 51. Christ, Head and body

51. *Glorifying the saving exploits of his king*. It is God who glorifies them, who makes wonderful in our eyes the deeds of deliverance his Son grants to believers. *And showing mercy to his Anointed*: it is God, clearly, who shows mercy to his Anointed, *to David and to his descendants for ever*. To the strong-armed liberator who overcame the world,[42] and to those who believe in the gospel, whom he has begotten for life eternal, he shows mercy.

---

38. Literally "have remained in the old person," an allusion to the doctrine of the "new man" in Christ; see Eph 4:13; Gal 6:15, etc.
39. See Mk 7:2-5.
40. See Rom 8:6.
41. Variant: "peoples."
42. See Jn 16:33.

Now whatever is said in this psalm and cannot apply in strict terms to the Lord himself, the Head, should be referred to the Church; for here the whole Christ is speaking, and all his members are contained in him.

Exposition 1 of Psalm 18

Verse 1

1. *To the end, a psalm of David himself.* This title is by now familiar. The Lord Jesus Christ does not say these words, but they are said about him.

Verses 2-3. The heavens' proclamation, day and night speak

2. *The heavens proclaim God's glory.* The righteous evangelists, in whom God dwells as though in the heavens, tell out the glory of our Lord Jesus Christ, or the glory with which the Son glorified the Father on earth.[1] *And the firmament tells of his handiwork*, for it proclaims the deeds the Lord wrought in strength. It was previously earth by reason of its fear, but has become heaven through trust in the Holy Spirit.

3. *Day speaks the message to succeeding day.* To spiritual persons the Spirit brings forth the fullness of the unchangeable wisdom of God, the Word who was God with God in the beginning;[2] but *night imparts knowledge to night,* for to those whose outlook is carnal, who are still far off, the very mortality of their flesh proclaims knowledge to come later, by suggesting the possibility of faith.

Verses 4-5. Hearing the voice

4-5. *No speech, no utterance goes unheard,* for there is no mode of speech through which the voices of the evangelists have not been heard, since the gospel was preached in every language. *Their sound echoed*[3] *throughout the world, and their words to the ends of the earth.*

Verse 6. God's tent

6. *He has pitched his tent in the sun.* The Lord came to wage war against the kingdoms founded on the falsehoods of this temporal world, and he meant to

---

1. See Jn 17:4.
2. See Jn 1:1.
3. Variant: "will echo."

199

bring not peace on earth but a sword.[4] Accordingly he set up his military head-quarters (that is to say, the economy of his incarnation) in time, in broad daylight, in the sun. *And he was like a bridegroom coming forth from his bridal chamber* as he proceeded from a virgin's womb where God was joined with human nature as a bridegroom is united with his bride. *He leapt up like a giant to run his course with joy*, for he rejoiced like a very strong man, head and shoulders above all others in his incomparable strength. The racecourse is for running on, not for living in! And so he did not dally in the way of sinners.[5]

Verse 7. The heat of the Son

7. *From highest heaven he set out*. His going forth was from the Father, not by temporal procession but eternal; of the Father he is born eternally. *He speeds back again even to heaven's height*, for in the fullness of his divinity he reaches even to equality with the Father. *There is no one who can hide from his heat*. When the Word was made flesh and lived among us, taking our mortality on himself, he did not allow any mortal to evade death's shadow, but the heat of the Word penetrated even death.

Verse 8. The Lord is the undefiled law

8. *The Lord's law is undefiled, and converts the soul*, but the Lord's law is the Lord himself, for he came to bring the law to its fullness, not to dismantle it;[6] and he is himself the undefiled law, because he committed no sin, nor was deceit found on his lips.[7] He did not burden souls with the yoke of slavery but turned them round so that they would imitate him freely. *The Lord's witness is trustworthy, and imparts wisdom to little children*.[8] Trustworthy it is, because no one knows the Father except the Son, and those to whom the Son wishes to reveal him.[9] Such things are hidden from the wise and revealed to little children, because God thwarts the proud but gives his grace to the humble.[10]

Verses 9-10. Purity and fear

9. *The Lord's ordinances are honorable; they make the heart[11] rejoice*. In him who taught nothing that he did not practice himself, all the statutes of the Lord are honorable; and so those who imitated him had cause for joy of heart in

---

4. See Mt 10:34.
5. See Ps 1:1.
6. See Mt 5:17.
7. See Is 53:9; 1 Pt 2:22.
8. Variant: "it is Wisdom, imparting itself. . . ."
9. See Mt 11:27.
10. See Mt 11:25; Jas 4:6; 1 Pt 5:5.
11. Or "hearts" as a variant here and as in his second Exposition of this psalm.

what they did freely with love, not slavishly out of fear. *The Lord's command-ment shines brightly, giving light to the eyes.* It shines because it is not obscured by the veil of carnal observances,[12] but illumines the vision of the innermost heart.

10. *The fear of the Lord is pure, enduring for ever and ever.* This does not re-fer to the fear which has to do with punishment and works in the sphere of law, living in terror of having its temporal goods taken away, the fear which prompts the soul to fornication. No, this fear is pure, and it is the fear of the Church: the more ardently she loves her Bridegroom, the more fearful she is of offending him. That is why perfect love does not cast out fear of this kind;[13] rather it abides for ever.

Verses 10-11. God's sweet judgments

11. *The judgments of the Lord are true, and altogether righteous.* The judg-ments of him who himself judges no one, but has committed all judgment to the Son,[14] are unchangeably righteous. When God utters either threats or promises he does not mislead anyone, nor can anyone deflect God's punishment from the ungodly or his reward from the faithful. *They are more desirable than gold and the most precious gem.*[15] Whether this means that the gold and gems are plenti-ful, or that the gem is very precious, or that the judgments are very desirable, it is certain that the judgments of God are more to be desired than the pomp and wealth of this age. If we set our hearts on such empty display, the judgments of God are not longed for, but either feared, or scorned and not believed in. But we may think of persons who are themselves gold, and made of such precious stones that they are not consumed by fire, but stored in God's treasury; these people love and long for God's judgments more than they love themselves, and prefer his will to their own. *Sweeter than honey and the honeycomb.* Some people are already honey, perhaps: people, I mean, who are already freed from the entan-glements of this life and are waiting for the day when they will arrive at the Lord's banquet. Others, perhaps, are still in the honeycomb, wrapped round by this life as if by wax, not stuck to it but rather filling it. They need some pressure from God's hand, a squeezing that does not crush them but presses them out so that they may trickle from temporal into eternal life. For all such persons the

---

12. He is probably thinking of the rituals of the Old Law, now obsolete, and of Paul's imagery of the veil over the minds of those Jews who could not see whither they pointed; see 2 Cor 3:14-15.
13. See 1 Jn 4:18.
14. See Jn 5:22.
15. Variant: "than gold set with the most precious gem." The Latin of the text he used, *lapidem pretiosum multum*, is slightly ambiguous, as he goes on to point out.

judgments of God are sweeter than they are to themselves, being sweeter than honey and the honeycomb.

Verses 12-13. Keeping the commandments

12. *Indeed, your servant keeps them,* for the day of the Lord is bitter to anyone who does not keep his commandments. *In keeping them there is great reward,* not a reward found in some advantage outside oneself, but a magnificent reward in simply observing God's judgments because we find joy in them.

13. *But who understands his transgressions?* What sort of pleasure, then, can be found in committing transgressions, if there is no understanding to be had in them? And how can anyone understand transgressions that close the very eye to which truth is attractive, the eye to which God's judgments are desirable and sweet? Just as darkness blinds the eyes, so transgressions close the mind and do not allow it to see either the light or itself.

Verses 13-14. The first and last transgression

14. *Cleanse me from my secret sins, Lord;* from the lusts that lie hidden in me, Lord, cleanse me. *And spare your servant from the faults of others;* let me not be led astray by others, for anyone cleansed from his own sins is not ensnared by other people's. Against such evil desires protect not a proud person, not one who wants to be his own master, but me, your servant. *If they do not get the better of me, I shall be spotless.* If neither my own secret sins nor those of other people have power over me, I shall be spotless indeed, for there is no third[16] source of sin; only one's own, by which the devil fell, and the sin of another, by which humankind was seduced when by compliance mortals made it their own. *And I shall be cleansed from the great transgression.* What else can this be, but the sin of pride? For there is no greater transgression than apostasy from God, and that is the point of departure for all the pride of humanity. The person who is free even from this transgression is truly spotless, because this is the last sin lying in wait for those who are returning to God, as it was the first for those who were departing from him.

Verse 15. Pleasing the Lord

15. *Then will the words of my mouth be such as to please you, and the meditation of my heart will always be in your sight.* My heart's meditation is not directed to a boastful display designed to curry favor with other people, because

---

16. Variant: "more certain."

now there is no pride left; it is always in your presence, for your gaze pierces a pure conscience. *Lord, my helper and my redeemer:* you are my helper, Lord, as I stretch out toward you, for you were first my redeemer that I might begin to stretch out to you. Keep us in this mind, lest anyone attribute to his own wisdom his act of turning toward you, or to his own strength his attaining to you, and so rather be driven back by you who thwart the proud. Such persons are not yet cleansed from the great transgression, nor pleasing in your sight, for you redeem us that we may turn to you, and help us that we may reach you.

Exposition 2 of Psalm 18

A Sermon to the People[1]

Singing with mind and voice

1. We have just been imploring the Lord to cleanse us from our secret sins and to preserve his servants from the sins of others. We ought to try to find out what this means, because we want to use our human reason as we sing, not merely to sing like parrots. Blackbirds and parrots and crows and magpies and other species are sometimes taught by people to give voice to words they do not understand; but God has willed to grant human beings the ability to sing with understanding. And just think how many prima donnas there are who do sing in this way: what they sing is all of a piece with their minds and hearts. Well we know it, and doesn't it make us wince! They are all the worse for it in that they cannot possibly be ignorant of what they are singing. They know that their ditty is about disgraceful actions, and yet the filthier the theme, the more they enjoy singing about it, because the more squalid they are, the luckier they consider themselves. But we who have learned to sing the words of God in church ought to bend our efforts to be like those of whom scripture says, *Blessed the people that understands the reason for its joy* (Ps 88:16(89:15)). In the same way, my very dear friends, we ought to know and perceive with clear hearts what we have sung together with harmonious voices. Each of us has begged a grace from the Lord in the words of this psalm; we have said to God, *Cleanse me from my secret sins, Lord, and spare your servant from the faults of others. If they do not get the better of me, I shall be spotless, and I shall be cleansed from the great transgression.*[2] So let us briefly run through the psalm in order to understand what this verse means and what are its implications, insofar as the Lord enables us.

Verse 1. God's glory is proclaimed in the forgiveness of sins

2. The psalm is sung about Christ, as is abundantly clear from a line in it: *He is like a bridegroom coming forth from his tent.* Who is this bridegroom? Surely he

---

1. This heading was assigned by the Maurist editors to distinguish preached sermons in the series from dictated expositions. See Introduction.
2. Apparently they had sung only verses 13 and 14. He comments on the whole psalm until he catches up with the verses in question; see paragraph 13 below.

to whom a virgin was betrothed by the apostle, a virgin on whose behalf the groom's chaste friend is anxious with a chaste fear lest, as once the serpent deceived Eve by his wiles, so too the mind of this virgin bride may be seduced from the chastity which is in Christ.[3] The bridegroom, our Lord and Savior Jesus Christ, has been endowed with great and abundant grace, of which the apostle John says, *We beheld his glory, as the glory of the Father's only-begotten Son, full of grace and truth* (Jn 1:14). This glory *the heavens proclaim.* By the heavens the psalm here means the saints, who are raised high above the earth and carry the Lord, though the sky too proclaimed in its own way the glory of Christ. When was that? When a new star, never seen before, appeared at the Lord's birth. But more real, more sublime, are the heavens of which the psalm goes on to say, *No speech, no utterance goes unheard; their sound went forth throughout the world, their words to the ends of the earth.* Whose words would that be? The words of the apostles, of course. They proclaim the glory of God to us, which is the grace set in Christ Jesus for the remission of our sins. For all have sinned and are deprived of God's glory, and all are justified freely through Christ's blood.[4] It is because it is free that it is called grace, for it would not be grace were it not given gratis. But gratis it is, because we had previously done nothing to entitle us to such benefits. Rather, because punishment would have been imposed deservedly, kindness was granted undeservedly. Our previous conduct entitled us to nothing but damnation. Yet Christ saved us through the water of rebirth, not on account of any righteousness of our own but because of his mercy.[5] This, I tell you, is God's glory, this is what the heavens have proclaimed. Yes, I repeat, this is God's glory, not yours; for you have done no good at all, yet you have received so much good. If, then, you share in this glory which the heavens have proclaimed, say to the Lord your God, *You are my God, for your mercy will forestall me* (Ps 58:11(59:10)). Forestall you it did; yes, of course it did, because it found no good in you. You forestalled his punishment by being proud, but he forestalled your undergoing of that punishment by wiping out your sins. You are a justified sinner, an ungodly person made godly, one formerly condemned but now welcomed into the kingdom; so say to the Lord your God, *Not to us, Lord, not to us, but to your name give the glory* (Ps 113B:1(115:1)). Yes, let us say, *Not to us,* for think who would be receiving glory if it were given to us! But, I tell you, we must say, *Not to us,* because if God were to act toward us as we deserve, he could do nothing but inflict punishment on us. Not to us, but to his own name may he give glory, because he has not treated us as our iniquities deserve.[6] *Not to us,* then, *not to us:* the repetition reinforces the truth. *Not to us, Lord, but to your*

---

3. See 2 Cor 11:3.
4. See Rom 3:23-24.
5. See Ti 3:5.
6. See Ps 102(103):10.

name give the glory. This is the truth the heavens knew when they told forth
God's glory.

Verse 2. God's word and hand

3. *The firmament tells of his handiwork.* What was first called *the glory of God*
reappears now as the works of his hands. What are these? It is not true that God
made all things by his word, and then created humankind, his noblest work, with
his own hands, as some people mistakenly suppose. No one should take this
view; it is a weak and unsophisticated doctrine, for he made all things by his
word. Although many and various works of God are enumerated, and among
them the creation of humanity in God's image and likeness, nevertheless all
things were made through his Word and without him nothing was made.[7] As to
God's hands, scripture also declares that *the heavens are the work of your hands;*
and to make sure that you do not take "heavens" in that context to mean the
saints, the psalmist adds, *They will perish, but you yourself abide* (Ps
101:26-27(102:25-26)). Clearly, then, God made with his hands not only people
but the heavens too, which one day will perish; and that is why scripture says to
him, *the heavens are the work of your hands.* The same thing is said of the earth,
for another psalm declares, *The sea is his, for he made it, and his hands laid
down the dry land* (Ps 94(95):5). So if he made both the heavens and the earth
with his hands, it was not people only that he made by hand; and if he made the
heavens by his word, and the earth by his word, then he made people with his
word as well. To make by word is to make by hand; to make with his hand is the
same thing as to make with his word. The being of God is not diversified into
members, like the human body. He is everywhere in his totality and is not confined within any particular space. What he made by word he made by wisdom,
and what he made by hand he made by his strength,[8] but the strength and wisdom
of God is Christ.[9] All things were made through him, and without him nothing
was made.[10] The heavens have told, are telling and will tell the glory of God. The
heavens will proclaim it, I say, for the saints are the heavens; they have been
raised up from the earth, bearing God, thundering with his commandments,

---

7. See Jn 1:3.
8. Clearly and confidently stated here, this doctrine of God's simplicity and immateriality was
   attained through a long philosophical struggle in Augustine's earlier years. He had wrestled
   with the difficulty of conceiving a substance at once real and immaterial; and had for some time
   been deterred from acceptance of Catholic teaching by the apparent incompatibility between a
   God immaterial and unchangeable, and the belief that human beings are made in his image and
   likeness. See *Confessions* VII,1,1-VII,2,3; VI,3,4-VI,4,5.
9. See 1 Cor 1:24.
10. See Jn 1:3.

sending forth the lightning-flashes of his wisdom,[11] and what they proclaim is God's glorious grace, by which we have been saved despite our unworthiness.

The younger son in the parable recognized this unworthiness of ours, this absence of any merit. Trapped in poverty, far away from his father in a strange country, he recognized it. As a swineherd he was much the same as a demon-worshiper, yet trapped as he was in penury he recognized God's glory. And because by that glory we have been made what we did not deserve to be, he confessed to his father, *I am not worthy to be called your son.*[12] Poor wretch! Through this humility he wins happiness, showing himself worthy by the very confession of his unworthiness. This glory of God *the heavens proclaim, and the firmament tells of his handiwork.* Heaven, the firmament—these suggest firmness of heart, not timidity. These things have been proclaimed among the ungodly, among God's enemies, among those who love this world and persecute the just. Right in the middle of a hostile world they have been proclaimed; but then what power had a hostile world, when the firmament was telling forth things like this? *The firmament tells. . . .* Tells what? The works of his hands. And what are they? The glorious grace of God by which we have been saved, by which we have been created in good works; for we are his handiwork, created in Christ Jesus in good works.[13] We did not make ourselves; he made us,[14] and made us not only men and women, but also righteous, if that is what we are.

Verse 3. Day and night

4. *Day speaks the message to succeeding day, and night imparts knowledge to night.* What is all this about? Maybe it is just plain and simple: *day speaks the message to succeeding day*—plain and simple as daylight itself. But as for *night imparts knowledge to night,* well, this is obscure, like night-time. *Day to day,* saints telling saints, apostles telling the faithful, Christ himself telling the apostles. After all, he told them, *You are the light of the world* (Mt 5:14). This seems straightforward and easy to understand. But what about *night imparts knowledge to night?* Some have understood these words in their obvious meaning, and perhaps this is the right way. They reckon that the meaning is this: what the apostles heard in the time of our Lord Jesus Christ, while he walked on earth, was passed on to succeeding generations, from age to age, "day to day, night to night," the previous day to the next day, the previous night to the night that fol-

---

11. Perhaps an allusion to Ezekiel's vision; see Ez 1.
12. Lk 15:21. This passage echoes Augustine's own experience. In his *Confessions* he frequently sees in the story of the prodigal son a reflection of his own wandering and his journey back to God. To be distant from God by sin and rebellion is to find oneself in a "land of unlikeness" where the filial image is obscured and lost.
13. See Eph 2:10.
14. See Ps 99:2(100:3).

lows, because this doctrine is preached day and night. If this simple interpretation satisfies anyone, well and good. But some words of scripture by their very obscurity give rise to a variety of interpretations. So if this phrase had been perfectly clear, you would have heard one thing and nothing more; but because it is obscure, you will hear a good deal more! There is another interpretation of "day to day, night to night." It could mean spirit to spirit, flesh to flesh. Or again, "day to day" could mean spiritual people to spiritual people, and "night to night" carnal people to carnal people; for both groups hear, but they do not understand in the same way. The one group hears something like a word blurted out, the other hears knowledge proclaimed. What is blurted out is belched at persons present, but what is proclaimed is proclaimed to those far off. Various different interpretations of "heaven" can also be found, but we must call a halt now because our time is limited. Let us just air one further possibility which some have opened up as a conjecture only: when the Lord Christ spoke to the apostles, it is suggested, day was blurting out the word to day, but when Judas betrayed the Lord Christ to the Jews, night was proclaiming knowledge to night.

Verses 4-5. Everyone has heard

5. *No speech, no utterance, goes unheard.* Whose speech is this, if not the utterance of the heavens which proclaim the glory of God? *No speech, no utterance, goes unheard.* Read the Acts of the Apostles, and see how, when the Holy Spirit descended upon them, all were filled with the Spirit and began to speak in the tongues of all nations, as the Spirit empowered their proclamation.[15] Listen to what the psalm says: *No speech, no utterance, goes unheard.* But it was not only in that place where they were filled with the Spirit that they spoke, for *their sound went forth throughout the world, their words to the ends of the earth.* That is why we too are speaking about it here. The sound which has gone out into every land has reached as far as us, yet still the heretic does not come into the Church. That sound has gone out into every land precisely so that you may enter heaven. You pernicious, quarrelsome, mischievous creature, still obstinately wayward, you proud son, listen to what your Father tells you.[16] What is clearer, what more obvious? Their sound has gone forth into every land, their words to the ends of the earth. Surely there is no need of an interpreter? Why struggle against your own best interests? Do you want to be left contentiously clutching a part, when you could have the whole lot by being reconciled to us?[17]

---

15. See Acts 2:4.
16. Aimed at the Donatists, clearly, with overtones of the prodigal son evoked earlier in the sermon, a prodigal not repentant this time, as emerges from the following paragraph.
17. The Donatists maintained that the true Church was to be found only in Africa, in their own sect. See note at Exposition of Psalm 10, 1.

Verse 6. The prodigal heretic

6. *He has pitched his tent in the sun*, set his Church in the open, not hidden away. It is not something invisible or clandestine, something that could for the hordes of heretics be out of sight. It was said to someone in holy scripture, *You acted in secret, but you will be punished in open sunlight* (2 Sm 12:12), and this means, "You sinned secretly, but you will suffer punishment in full view of everyone." *In the sun*, then, *he has pitched his tent*. Why do you flee into the dark, you heretic? Are you a Christian? Then listen to Christ. Are you a servant? Then listen to your master. Are you a son? Listen to your Father. Mend your ways, come back to life. Give us the chance to say of you also, *He was dead, but has come back to life, he was lost, but is found* (Lk 15:24,32). Don't say to me, "Stop looking for me then, if I am lost." It is precisely because you are lost that I am looking for you. "Well, don't look for me," he retorts. This doubtless would be the wish of the iniquity that divides us, but not of the charity that makes us brothers and sisters. Were I to go looking for my servant,[18] no one would find fault with me, so why am I denounced when it is my brother that I am seeking? Whoever is devoid of fraternal love may take that line; but I am looking for my brother. Let him be angry, provided only that he is being sought, and will be pleased about it once he is found. I am looking for my brother, I say, and I am appealing to my Lord not against him but on his behalf. I am not going to say as part of my plea, "Lord, tell my brother to divide the inheritance with me,"[19] but "Tell my brother to keep the inheritance with me." Why, then, brother, are you wandering off? Why go scurrying off through nooks and crannies? Why are you trying so desperately to hide? *He has pitched his tent in the sun, and he is like a bridegroom coming forth from his bridal-chamber.* You recognize him, don't you? Like a bridegroom coming out of his marriage-chamber, he *leaps up like a giant to run his course with joy*; he *pitched his tent in the sun*. When the Word was made flesh he was like a bridegroom who found himself a bridal-chamber in a virgin's womb. Once wedded to human nature he came forth from that purest of all rooms, humbler in mercy than all others, stronger than all in majesty. What is meant by *he leaps up like a giant to run his course* is that he was born, he grew, he taught, he suffered, he rose, he ascended; he ran his course, he did not tarry on the way. This bridegroom thus pitched his tent, his holy Church, *in the sun*, that is, in the open, plain to see.

---

18. Or "slave."
19. See Lk 12:13.

Verses 7-9. The sending of the Spirit

7. Do you want to hear what road he has taken, as he runs so fast? *From highest heaven he sets out; he speeds back again even to heaven's height.* After running out from there and speeding right round and back again, he sent his Spirit. To those on whom the Spirit came there appeared tongues branching like fire.[20] The Holy Spirit came like fire for he was to consume the hay of the flesh, and to refine the gold as in a crucible. And so the psalm warns, *No one can hide from his heat.*

8. *The Lord's law is undefiled, and converts the soul*: this is the Holy Spirit. *The Lord's witness is trustworthy, and imparts wisdom to little children*, not to the proud. This too is the Holy Spirit.

9.*The Lord's ordinances are honorable*, not terrifying; *they make hearts rejoice*, and this is the Holy Spirit. *The Lord's commandment shines brightly, giving light to the eyes*, not dulling them. This refers not to the eyes of the flesh but to the eyes of the heart, not to the outer person's eyes but to our inner sight. This is the Holy Spirit.

Verse 10. The language of unity

10. *The fear of the Lord* is not something servile, but *pure*. It loves freely and fears not punishment from the one at whom it trembles, but separation from the one it loves. Pure fear is not driven out by love made perfect;[21] it *endures for ever and ever.* This is the Holy Spirit, for the fear I am talking about is the fear which the Holy Spirit grants, confers, implants. *The judgments of the Lord are true, and altogether righteous*; they lead not to squabbling divisions but to our coming together in unity, for this is what *altogether*[22] means, in the selfsame Holy Spirit. This is why he made those to whom he first came speak in the languages of all sorts of different peoples, to show that he was going to gather the languages of all peoples into a unity. At that time a single person by receiving the Holy Spirit spoke in the tongues of all; today it is our unity which achieves the same thing—it speaks in all languages. And today it is still one person who speaks in all nations and all tongues, one man, Head and body, one person who is Christ and the Church, a perfect man, he the bridegroom, she the bride.[23] But, says

---

20. See Acts 2:3.
21. See 1 Jn 4:18.
22. *In idipsum.* In the original psalm the meaning is probably "in themselves" or "altogether," but Augustine sometimes takes the phrase as a mystical name for God, Being-Itself, evoking the revelation of the divine name in Ex 3:14. See note at Exposition of Psalm 4, 9. In the present context both meanings are suggested.
23. The key idea in Augustine's understanding of the psalms.

scripture, *they will be two in one flesh* (Gn 2:24).[24] *The judgments of the Lord are true, and altogether righteous* in view of this unity.

Verse 11. Gold, gems and honey

11. *They are more desirable than gold and the most precious gem.*[25] This may mean much gold, or exceedingly costly gold, or exceedingly desirable gold and gems; but anyway exceedingly something, though little enough for the heretics. They do not love this "selfsame" together with us,[26] and yet together with us they confess Christ. I beg you, love with me the same Christ you confess with me. Whoever does not want this communion[27] rejects it, kicks against it, spits it out. Not for them is this a treasure more to be desired than gold or the most precious gem. Listen to the rest: *sweeter than honey or the honeycomb*, but quite the opposite to those wandering in error. Honey is bitter to someone with a fever, but sweet and acceptable once the patient has recovered, because only healthy persons fancy it. So God's judgments are *more desirable than gold or the most precious gem, and sweeter than honey or the honeycomb.*

Verse 12. The sweetness of the commandments

12. *Indeed your servant keeps them.* Your servant tests their sweetness by keeping them, not merely by talking about it, and keeps them because they are sweet even now, and will bring him everlasting health in the future; for *in keeping them there is great reward.* Heretics are so attached to their rancor that they cannot see this brilliance, nor taste the sweetness.

Verses 13-14. Sin and temptation

13. *Who understands his transgressions?* Father, forgive them, for they do not know what they are doing.[28] Accordingly, says the psalmist, that person is a servant of God who conserves the sweetness, the savor of charity, the love of unity; but this servant prays, "I, yes, even I who do keep these things, beg you to *cleanse me from my secret sins*, lest any of them creep up on me, weak mortal that I am, or any of them take me by surprise, for *who understands his transgressions?*" This is what we sang, and here we are at last, our sermon has caught up

---

24. Evidently a further shot at the Donatists' disruption of the unity God intended.
25. *Pretiosum multum* can be variously translated; here as in his first *Exposition* of the psalm he plays on the differences.
26. *Idipsum:* see note on preceding paragraph.
27. *Idipsum.*
28. See Lk 23:24.

with this verse. Let us say it , and sing it intelligently, and pray as we sing it, and may our prayer be heard: *Cleanse me from my secret sins, Lord.* For which of us understands our transgressions? They are no more comprehensible than darkness is visible. When we eventually repent of what we have done wrong, we are in the light. But as long as we are caught up in the sin, we are incapable of seeing it, because it is as if our eyes are wrapped in darkness and closed, just as when your bodily eye is covered you cannot see anything, not even the blindfold itself. So then, let us say to God, who is well able to see what he needs to purge and to examine what he needs to heal, yes, to him let us say, *Cleanse me from my secret sins, Lord, and spare your servant from the faults of others.* My own transgressions defile me, says the psalmist, and the faults of others cause me trouble. Cleanse me from the one, and spare me from the other. Remove evil thoughts from my heart, and drive the evil counselor away from me: this is what is meant by *Cleanse me from my secret sins, and spare your servant from the faults of others.* This twofold liability to sin, one's own and other people's, has been unmistakably obvious from the very beginning of things. The devil fell by his own sin, but Adam's fall was occasioned by the sin of another. So here we have God's servant, keeping the commandments and finding great reward in doing so, but in another psalm he prays, *Let not the foot of pride come near me, nor the hands of sinners disturb me* (Ps 35:12(36:11)). To pray, *Let not the foot of pride come near me* is equivalent to asking, *Cleanse me from my secret sins, Lord*; and to ask, *Let not the hands of sinners disturb me*, is the same as begging, *Spare your servant from the faults of others.*

14. *If they*—this includes my secret sins and the transgressions of other people—*do not get the better of me, I shall be spotless.* The psalmist does not venture to promise this as though his own strength could achieve it, but prays to God to bring it about, as also he prays in another psalm, *Guide my steps according to your word, and let no iniquity get the better of me* (Ps 118(119):133). If you are a Christian, do not be afraid of any human tyrant outside yourself, but fear the Lord your God always. Fear the evil within you, your own unruly desires, not what God created in you, but what you have made of yourself. God made you a good servant, but you have set up an evil master for yourself in your own heart. You deserve to be subjected to iniquity, you deserve to be subjected to a master you have made for yourself, because you refused to be subject to him who made you.

Pride, the great transgression

15. *If they do not get the better of me, I shall be spotless, and I shall be cleansed from the great transgression,* he says. From what transgression? What are we to think it is? It may perhaps be something quite different from what I am about to suggest; all the same, I shall not keep quiet about what I think. It seems

to me that the great transgression must be pride. A hint of this lies in the statement, *I shall be cleansed from the great transgression*, because you may ask,
"What could be as great as the sin of pride, which overthrew an angel, turned an
angel into a devil, and debarred him from the kingdom of heaven for evermore?"
Yes, this is a great transgression, the fountainhead and source of all transgressions; as it is written, *The starting-point of all sin is pride*, and, lest you dismiss
this as something insignificant, *The starting-point of human pride is rebellion
against God* (Sir 10:15.14). This vice is no slight evil, my brothers and sisters.
Christian humility makes no headway in those whom you see as persons of substance who are infected with this vice. It makes them refuse to bow their necks to
the yoke of Christ, yet they harness themselves all the more tightly to the yoke of
sin. They will not get away without being bound in service to someone or other.
They do not want to serve, yet serving is to their advantage, for by refusing to
serve the only thing they achieve is that they do not serve the good God; it is not
as though they succeeded in not being servants at all. Anyone who is unwilling to
serve love must of necessity serve iniquity. From this vice, which is the capital of
all vices because from it all the others are born, spiritual rebellion against God
begins, as the soul wanders off into darkness and abuses its free will, and so other
sins follow. Hence the soul squanders its substance with harlots and lives waste-
fully, until the one-time companion of angels is reduced to minding pigs.[29] It was
because of this vice, this great sin of pride, that the Lord came in humility. This
great sin, this devastating disease in the souls of men and women, brought down
from heaven the all-powerful doctor, humbled him to take the form of a
servant,[30] loaded him with insults and hung him on a cross, and all this so that
through the healing properties of such powerful medicine our swelling might be
cured.[31] Now at long last let men and women be ashamed to be proud, since for
them God became humble. Only then, says the psalmist, shall I be *cleansed from
the great transgression*, because God thwarts the proud, but gives grace to the
humble.[32]

Verse 15. Pleasing God rather than human beings

16. *Then will the words of my mouth be such as to please you, and the meditation of my heart will always be in your sight.* If I am not cleansed from this great
transgression, what I say may give pleasure in the presence of other people, but
not in yours. A proud soul wants to be pleasing to the public, but a humble soul

---

29. See Lk 13:15.
30. See Phil 2:7.
31. *Tumor*, swelling, suggesting both malignancy and pride.
32. See Jas 4:6; 1 Pt 5:5.

wants to give pleasure in secret, where God sees.[33] If the soul pleases others by doing something good, it should rejoice with those whom the good work pleases, but not congratulate itself, for it ought to be content simply to have done the good thing. *Our boast is this,* said Paul, *the witness of our own conscience* (2 Cor 1:12). With this in mind let us say the next verse too: *Lord, my helper and my redeemer:* helper in the performance of good works, redeemer from all that is bad; helper so that I may live in your love, redeemer that you may free me from my iniquity.

---

33. See Mt 6:4.6.18.

Exposition of Psalm 19

Verses 1-4. May Christ's offering be accepted

1. *To the end, a psalm of David.* This superscription is by now well known. It is not Christ who speaks here, but the prophet who addresses Christ, singing in the guise of one who longs for what is to come.

2. *May the Lord hear you in the day of trouble.* On that day may he hear you, when you pray, *Father, glorify your Son* (Jn 17:1). *May the name of Jacob's God protect you,* for the later-born people belongs to you, since scripture says that the elder will serve the younger.[1]

3. *May he send you help from his holy place, and protect you from Zion,* fashioning for you a sanctified body, the Church, which by reason of its vigilance is safe, and eagerly awaits your arrival from the wedding-feast.[2]

4. *May he remember all you sacrificed,* and make us mindful of all the tortures and insults you bore for our sake. *May your holocaust be richly full*: may he turn into resurrection-joy that cross on which you were offered up in your entirety to God.

Pause

Verse 5. Its usefulness

5. *May the Lord grant your desire according to your own heart.* May the Lord grant it to you, not in accord with the hearts of those who thought they could destroy you by their persecution, but according to your own heart, which told you how profitable your suffering would be. *And may he fulfill your every intention.* Yes, may he fulfill not only your intention to lay down your life for your friends, so that the seed, by dying, might spring again more abundantly, but also your intention that by the partial blinding of Israel the entry of the whole Gentile world should be facilitated, and thus the salvation of all Israel be assured.[3]

---

1. See Gn 25:23.
2. See Mt 25:1-13. The Latin editors suggest "at the wedding-feast."
3. See Jn 15:13; 12:25; Rom 11:25.

Verse 6. Rejoicing in God's salvation

6. *We shall rejoice in your salvation*, rejoice that death will not harm you, for so you will show us that it will not harm us either. *And by the name of the Lord our God we shall be honored*, for not only will confessing your name bring us to no disaster; it will even redound to our glory.

Verse 7. Christ prays for us

7. *May the Lord grant all your requests*—all of them, not only the petitions you offered on earth, but those also by which you intercede for us in heaven. *Now I know that the Lord has saved his Anointed.*[4] Now, says the psalmist, it has been prophetically revealed to me that the Lord will raise up his Christ again. *He will hear him from his holy heaven*, not only from the earth, where he prayed to be glorified,[5] but also from heaven, where he now intercedes for us at the right hand of the Father,[6] and whence he has poured the Holy Spirit down on those who believe in him. *Our victory is the salvation wrought by his right hand*, for our strength is to be found in the salvation he graciously confers when he helps us out of trouble, so that when we are weak, we may be strong.[7] For vain is the help of men and women;[8] it is the help not of the right hand but of the left;[9] for sinners who have attained temporal prosperity are exalted to lofty arrogance by this kind of help.

Verse 8. Good and bad rejoicing

8. *Some find joy in chariots and some in horses*, for some people are drawn by the revolving succession of temporal good things, others are elevated to high office and so made proud, and both sorts rejoice in their good fortune. *But as for us, we will exult*[10] *in the name of the Lord our God*. Fixing our hope on eternal things and not seeking our own glory, we will rejoice in the name of the Lord our God.

---

4. *Christum suum*. At the level of the original psalm this expression referred to any anointed descendant of David, heir to the promises made to David's house. But after the exile, when the Jews were subject to foreign powers and had no king of their own, psalms celebrating the Davidic hope continued to be used, focused now more upon the future, and the coming of One in whom the promise would be fulfilled (see Lk 1:32-33). Augustine takes it in this plenary sense.

5. See Jn 17:1.

6. See Rom 8:34.

7. See 2 Cor 12:10.

8. See Ps 59:13(60:11).

9. See Exposition of Psalm 16, 8, note 1, on the significance of the right hand.

10. This is Augustine's reading, and that of the Codex Sinaiticus; a variant is *magnificabimur* (as in verse 6): "we shall be honored."

Verse 9. Providential stumbling and blinding

9. *They were shackled and they fell.* The Jews were shackled by greed for temporal advantages, and feared to spare the Lord lest they be dispossessed by the Romans.[11] Running headlong onto the stumbling-stone, the rock set to trip them, they fell[12] away from their hope of heaven. On them the partial blindness of Israel descended; they did not recognize God's justice and they sought to establish their own.[13] *But we have arisen and we stand upright*: so that the Gentile peoples might come in, we were raised up from the stones as children of Abraham;[14] we who did not previously seek righteousness have embraced it now, and so we have arisen, but not by our own strength. Justified through faith, we stand upright.

Verse 10. Christ offers sacrifice for us

10. *Lord, save the king*, that he who by his suffering gave us an example of how to do battle may offer our sacrifices as well, as our priest risen from the dead and established in heaven. *And hear us on the day we call upon you.* As Christ now offers sacrifice on our behalf,[15] hear us on the day we call upon you.

---

11. See Jn 11:48.
12. See Rom 9:32-33.
13. See Rom 10:3.
14. See Mt 3:9.
15. A variant addresses this verse to Christ: "As you offer yourself on our behalf."

Exposition of Psalm 20

Verses 1-4. Christ's joy

1. *To the end, a psalm of David himself.* The title is familiar; the psalm is sung about Christ.

2. *O Lord, the king will rejoice in your strength.* In your strength, Lord, by which the Word became flesh, the man Christ Jesus will rejoice, *and over your salvation he will be exceedingly glad*, for he will exult over that saving deed by which you give life to all things.

3. *You have given him what his soul longed for.* He longed to eat the passover, to lay down his life when he willed, and to take it up again when he willed; and all these you have granted to him.[1] *You did not deny his express desire*; for he said, *My peace I leave with you* (Jn 14:27), and so it was.

4. *Because you came to meet him with sweet blessings.* Because he had already drunk the blessing of your sweetness, the bitter poison of our sins did not harm him.

Pause

You have set on his head a crown of precious stones. As he began his sermon,[2] precious stones gathered to him and ringed him round; these were his disciples, from whom preaching about him would begin.

Verses 5-7. Resurrection, time and eternity

5. *He asked for life, and you gave it to him*: he prayed for his resurrection, saying, *Father, glorify your Son* (Jn 17:1), and you answered his prayer. *He asked for length of days, stretching to eternity.* Long endurance for the Church he asked, throughout this present age, and then eternity for evermore.

6. *Great is his glory in your salvation*: great indeed the glory he receives in that saving act by which you raised him from the dead; yet *you will set glory and great beauty upon him*, for you will continue to heap magnificent glory and beauty upon him when you place him at your right hand in heaven.

---

1. See Lk 22:15; Jn 10:18.
2. See Mt 5:1.

7. *Because you will give him blessing for evermore.* This is the blessing which you will give him for ever and ever: *you will gladden him and fill him with the joy of your face,* for with the vision of your face you will delight his human nature, which he has lifted up to you.

Verse 8. Christ's humility

8. *For the king puts his trust in the Lord.* This king is not proud, but humble of heart, so he puts his trust in the Lord; *and by the mercy of the Most High he will not be displaced,* for by the mercy of the Most High his obedience, which took him even to the point of dying on the cross, will not shake his humility.

Verses 9-14. The king will judge his enemies

9. *May your hand make itself felt³ upon your enemies.* When you come to judge, O king, may your power make itself felt by all your enemies, who failed to discern it in your humility. *May your right hand find all those who hate you:* let that splendor in which you reign at the Father's right hand find out on the day of judgment all who hate you, and punish them because they have not found it now.

10. *You will make them like a red-hot oven,* for you will set them on fire within, as consciousness of their impiety burns them, and this *at the time you show your face,* the time, that is, when you manifest yourself. *The Lord will harass them in his anger, and fire will engulf them.* After being convicted by their own consciences and thrown into confusion by the Lord's vengeance, they will be given over to eternal fire to be devoured.

11. *You will destroy their fruit from the earth.* Whatever fruit they have borne is but earthly, and so you will destroy it from the earth, *and their seed from among the children of men,* because their works, along with any people they may have led astray, you will not reckon among the children of men whom you have called to an everlasting inheritance.

12. *Because they diverted evils onto you.* This punishment will be visited upon them because they turned upon you, to compass your death, those calamities which they supposed would threaten them from your reign. *They devised a scheme which they were unable to carry through,* for they plotted, saying, It is expedient that one should die for all (Jn 11:50), but they could not prevail, for they did not know what they said.

13. *You will set them behind you,* for you will range them with those on whom you will turn your back, those you have rejected and condemned. *With what you*

---

3. Variant: "Your hand will make itself felt."

left behind you will prepare their face,[4] for though you put ambition for an earthly kingdom behind you, you will use their indecent eagerness for it to bring about your passion.[5]

14. *Be lifted up, Lord, in your strength.* They did not acknowledge you, Lord, when you were humble, so now be lifted up in that strength of yours which they mistook for weakness. *We will sing of your powerful deeds and celebrate them with psalms,* for with heart and action we will celebrate and make known your mighty exploits.

---

4. *In reliquiis tuis praeparabis vultum eorum*: almost unintelligible in Augustine's Latin version, and his explanation of the phrase is scarcely more luminous.
5. *Praeparabis tibi ad passionem impudentiam eorum.* An alternative interpretation would take *passionem* to refer to their punishment.

Exposition 1 of Psalm 21

Verse 1. Death and resurrection

1. *To the end, for his taking up in the morning, a psalm of David.* To the end, because the Lord Jesus Christ speaks here, praying for his own resurrection, for he was raised in the morning, on the first day of the week. On that day Jesus Christ was taken up into eternal life, and death will never hold sway over him again;[1] but the words of this psalm are spoken in the person of the crucified one, for here at its beginning is the cry he uttered while he hung upon the cross. He speaks consistently in the character of our old self, whose mortality he bore and which was nailed to the cross with him.[2]

Verse 2. Abandonment

2. *O God, my God, why have you forsaken me, and left me far from my salvation?* Far indeed from my salvation, because salvation is far away from sinners.[3] *The tale of my sins,* for this is no tale of righteousness, but the tale of my sins. Our old self, nailed to the cross with Christ, is speaking here, ignorant even of the reason why God has abandoned it. Or perhaps we should punctuate the verse like this: *The tale of my sins leaves me far from salvation.*

Verse 3. Crying to God for the wrong things

3. *O my God, I will cry to you all day, and you will not listen to me.* My God, I will cry to you when things are going well in this life, to ask that my prosperity may not change; but you will not listen to me, because these cries are part of the tale of my sins. *And in the night, but you will not collude with my foolishness,* for in this life's misfortunes I will cry to you to make things prosper for me, and likewise you will not listen. You refuse, not to drive me to further folly, but that I may have wisdom to know what you truly want me to pray for: not to ask in

---

1. See Rom 6:9.
2. See Rom 6:6.
3. See Ps 118(119):155.

sinful words prompted by longing for temporal life, but in the words of one
converted to you and tending to eternal life.

Verse 4. Inner and outer eyes

4. *But you, the praise of Israel, dwell in holiness.* You live in a holy place,[4]
and so you pay no heed to unclean, sinful words. You are the praise of one who
sees you,[5] not of the one who sought his own praise by tasting the forbidden fruit,
and then, once his bodily eyes were opened, tried to hide from your sight.

Verses 5-6. The just hope in God

5. *Our fathers hoped in you*: all the just, that is, those who sought not their
own praise, but yours, *they hoped in you, and you delivered them.*

6. *To you they cried, and they were saved*, saved because they cried to you,
but not with words that belonged to the tale of their sins, from which salvation is
far away. *In you they hoped, and they were not disappointed.* They hoped in you,
and their hope did not deceive them, because they did not place it in themselves.

Verse 7. Christ's humiliation

7. *But I am a worm and no man.* I speak now not in the guise of Adam, but in
my own person as Jesus Christ. I was virginally born in the flesh to be a human
being though beyond all humans, for I thought that human pride would then
deign to imitate my own humility. Yet *scorned by all and cast out by the people*, I
became an object of public contempt, so much so that they could insult someone
with the sneer, *You be his disciple* (Jn 9:28), and the people could despise me.

Verses 8-9. Mocking lips

8. *All those who watched me sniggered at me*: they laughed at me, all those
onlookers. *They mouthed at me and wagged their heads.* They spoke not in their
hearts, but only with the lips.

9. They wagged their heads in mockery, saying, *He put his hope in the Lord,
so let the Lord rescue him; let him save him, since he holds him dear!* These were
words, yet only mouthings.

---

4. Or "in a person who is holy;" Augustine alludes to this sense in verse 26 below.
5. The aspiration of the true "Israel" is to see God; compare Jn 1:46-51.

Verse 10. The womb of the Jewish people

10. *It was you who drew me out of the womb*, you who pulled me out not simply from the virgin's womb, as the common lot of human birth is to be pulled so out of the maternal womb, but also from the womb of the Jewish people; for anyone who trusts for salvation in the material observance of the sabbath and circumcision and the like is still enclosed in Jewish darkness, and not yet born into the light of Christ. You are *my hope from my mother's breasts*. My hope is God, but this does not mean from the time when I began to be nourished by milk from the virgin's breasts, for God was certainly my hope before that. Rather does it mean that just as you drew me forth from the womb of the synagogue, so too you plucked me away from the synagogue's breasts, lest I drink in their carnal attitudes.

Verses 11-12. Closeness to God

11. *In you I was strengthened⁶ from the womb*: from the womb of the synagogue, which did not support me but threw me out; yet I did not fall, because you grasped me firmly. *From before my birth you have been my God*, for my mother's womb did not make me forget you, even as a tiny baby.

12. *You are my God, do not leave me, for anguish is very near*. Since then you are my God, do not leave me; anguish is very close to me, it is even in my body, and *there is no one to help*, for who can help, if you do not?

Verses 13-14. The raging mob

13. *Bull-calves throng round me*, because the wanton mob has surrounded me in great numbers; and *fat bulls besiege me*, for the leaders of this people, glad about my affliction, have hemmed me in.

14. *They opened their mouths at me*, not quoting from your scriptures, but speaking from their own greedy desires, *like a ravening, roaring lion*. This lion's ravening was my being arrested and led away, and its roar is *Crucify! Crucify!* (Jn 19:6).

Verse 15. Melting wax

15. *I was poured out⁷ like water, and all my bones were scattered*. I was poured out like water in that place where my persecutors fell back,⁸ and the

---

6. *Confirmatus*; but the editors suggest that this is a contamination from Ps 70(71):6, and we should read here *iactatus*, "I was cast . . . " as Augustine does in his second Exposition of this psalm. This latter reading agrees with his comment in the following line.

7. *Effusus sum*; a variant is *effusa sunt*, "they were poured out," meaning his bones.

8. This last clause seems to refer to Jn 18:6, where those sent to arrest Jesus fall to the ground. It would be possible to understand *lapsi sunt* as "they fell upon me," but this is an unusual meaning for the verb. The whole sentence clearly envisages Christ's agony in Gethsemane.

supportive skeleton of my body, my Church, deserted me when my disciples scattered through fear. *My heart has become like melting wax in my belly*, for my wisdom, written in what the holy books had to tell of me, had not hitherto been understood, but seemed hard and tightly packed; but when the fire of my passion was brought to bear upon it, it seemed to melt, it grew clear, and was stored up in the memory of my Church.

Verse 16. The potsherd

16. *My strength dried up like an earthenware pot.* My strength was fired by my passion, not consumed like hay, but made stronger like earthenware. *My tongue stuck to my jaws*, for those through whom I was to speak to others kept my teaching within themselves. *You brought me down into the dust of death*, down among the ungodly condemned to die, whom the wind sweeps away from the face of the earth.[9]

Verses 17-19. Crucifixion

17. *Many dogs surrounded me*, ringing me round in their hordes and barking, not seeking truth but out of inveterate custom. *A band of ruffians beset me. They dug holes in my hands and my feet*, dug into my hands and feet with nails.

18-19. *They numbered all my bones*: as my bones were stretched out on the wood of the cross the onlookers could count them all. *These same people looked on and watched me*, yes, these same, for in no way were they changed. They looked on and watched. *They shared out my garments among them, and cast lots for my tunic.*

Verses 20-22. Prayer for deliverance

20. *But you, Lord, do not keep your help far from me.* You, Lord, I beg, raise me up, not at the end of time like all others; raise me up at once. *Look to my defense*, see that they do not hurt me.

21. *Deliver my life from the sword*, save it from discordant tongues, *and my only one*[10] *from the power of the dog*, from the violence, that is, of people accustomed to bark at my Church.

22. *Save me from the lion's mouth*: save me from the clutches of the kingdom of this world, *and my humility from the horns of unicorns*: keep me safe in my

---

9. See Ps 1:4.
10. That is, in the perspective of the psalm, " the only life (or soul) I have," but Augustine takes *unicam meam* to be a reference to the Church, in line with Sg 6:8(9).

humility from the pride of those who lift themselves up, lofty and unrivaled, unwilling to have anyone else alongside them.

Verses 23- 24. Joy and praise at the good news

23. *I will tell of your name to my brothers and sisters.* I will tell of your name to my humble brothers and sisters, who love each other as they are loved by me.[11] *In the full assembly I will sing your praise*: with joy I will proclaim you in the midst of the Church.

24. *All you who fear the Lord, praise him.* Do not seek to be praised yourselves, all you who fear the Lord, but rather praise him. *You whole progeny of Jacob, extol him*: all you descendants of him whom his elder brother must serve, extol him.[12]

Verse 25. God hears the prayer of the poor

25. *Let all the seed of Israel fear him.* Let all who are born to the new life fear him, all those restored to the vision of God.[13] *For he has not rejected or scorned the poor person's prayer.* The prayer God did not disdain is not the prayer of those who cry to him in sinful words,[14] hoping that their empty life may not pass away, but the prayer of a poor person, one not swollen with transient ostentation. *Nor did he turn his face away from me,* as he did from one who said, *I will cry to you, but you will not listen to me* (v.3). No, for *when I cried to him, he heard me.*

Verse 26. The worldwide Church

26. *My praise is for you,* for I do not seek praise for myself;[15] you are my praise, you who dwell in what is holy, and hearken to this holy one now pleading with you, who are the praise of Israel. *In the great assembly I will confess you*: in the worldwide Church I will confess you. *I will fulfill my vows in the presence of those who fear him,* for I will offer the mysteries of my body and blood in the presence of those who fear him.

---

11. See Jn 15:12.
12. See Gn 25:23.
13. Israel, who aspires to see God: see note on verse 4 above.
14. See verse 2 above.
15. See Jn 8:50.

Verse 27. The banquet of the poor

27. *The poor shall eat and be satisfied.* The humble, those who despise this world, will eat, and they will imitate me, for being so nourished they will neither strive for this world's plenty, nor fear its want. *And those who seek the Lord will praise him*, for the praise of the Lord is the belching out of that fullness. *Their hearts will live for ever and ever*, for that food nourishes the heart.

Verses 28-30. God's reign among the Gentiles

28. *All the ends of the earth will be reminded, and will turn to the Lord.* They will be reminded, for God had slipped out of the minds of the Gentiles who were born only for mortality and bent on external pursuits, but then all the ends of the earth will be converted to the Lord. *And all the families of the Gentiles will worship in his presence*, for all those Gentile nations will pay him homage in their consciences.

29. *For the kingship is the Lord's, and he will hold sway over the nations.* Sovereignty belongs to the Lord, not to the proud, and lordship over the nations is his.

30. *All the rich of the world have eaten, and worshiped*, for even the rich of this world have eaten the body of their Lord's humility; but unlike the poor they were not satisfied to the point of imitating him. Nonetheless they did worship. *All who go down into the earth will fall prostrate in his sight*, for the Lord alone sees how they all fall, those people who abandon a heavenly way of life and choose rather to appear happy on earth in the sight of others, who cannot see their ruin.

Verses 31- 32. "He shall see his heirs"

31. *And my soul will live to him.* In its contempt for this world my soul seems to many to be dying,[16] yet it will live, not to itself but to him. *My posterity will serve him*: for my works, or those who through me will believe, will serve him.

32. *A generation yet to come will be proclaimed for the Lord*, for the generation of the New Covenant will be proclaimed in his honor. *And they will proclaim[17] his righteousness*; this proclamation of his righteousness will be made by the evangelists *to people still to be born, whom the Lord has created*: the people to be born to the Lord by faith.

---

16. Or "my soul seems to many to be dying, for it is the object of this world's contempt."
17. A variant has "the heavens will proclaim. . . ."

Exposition 2 of Psalm 21

A Sermon to the People[1]

Annual commemoration of the Lord's passion

1. What God did not want kept quiet in his scriptures, I must not keep quiet about either, and you must listen. The Lord's passion happened only once, as we know, for Christ died only once, a just man for the unjust.[2] And we know, we hold as certain, we maintain with unshakable faith, that, *rising from the dead, Christ will never die again, nor will death ever again have the mastery over him.* Those are the words of the apostle Paul. Yet to ensure that we do not forget what was done once, it is re-enacted every year in our liturgical commemoration of it. Does Christ die every time his passover is celebrated? No, yet the yearly remembrance in a sense makes present what took place in time past, and in this way it moves us as if we were actually watching our Lord hanging on the cross, but watching as believers, not mockers. Hanging on the wooden cross he was mocked; enthroned in heaven he is worshiped. Or perhaps he is still being mocked? Yes, and today it is not with the Jews that we should be angry, for they at least jeered only at a dying man, not a reigning King.[3] Who is it who still tries to mock Christ? I wish there were only one of them, or only two, or at any rate a countable group! But no, all the chaff on his threshing-floor mocks him, and the wheat groans to hear its Lord derided. This is what I mean to groan over now, together with you, for this is the time to lament. The Lord's passion is being commemorated: it is a time for groaning, a time for weeping, a time for confessing and imploring God's help. Who among us is capable of shedding tears worthy of a pain so great? What did the prophet pray for just now?[4] *Who will give water to my head, and to my eyes a fount of tears?* (Jer 9:1). Truly, if there were a fountain of tears in the eyes of each of us, it would not be enough. To think of Christ being mocked openly, in a situation where no one can make the excuse, "I did not understand!" To one who possesses the whole earth, only a

---

1. Preached on a Good Friday.
2. See 1 Pt 3:18.
3. The reference here is to the Donatists, who are Augustine's target more explicitly later in the sermon. See note on verse 1 of his Exposition of Psalm 10.
4. *Quid modo ait propheta?* Evidently a reading or chant from the day's liturgy. A variant reading opens the phrase with *quomodo*, which could yield the following meaning: ". . . a pain so great, even had we what the prophet prays for. . . ."

part is being offered; he who sits at the right hand of God is told, "Here you are, here is your domain." Instead of the whole earth, they merely offer him Africa![5]

The woman and the ointment

2. What are we to do with the words we have just heard, brothers and sisters? If only they could be written in tears! Who was this woman who came in bringing ointment?[6] Whom did she symbolize? Surely the Church? And the ointment, what did that represent? The goodly aroma of Christ, I think, of which the apostle Paul spoke: *We are the fragrance of Christ in every place* (2 Cor 2:14-15). The apostle too represented the Church, and when he said, *We are*, he said it to the faithful. And what was it he said? That we are Christ's sweet fragrance everywhere. So while Paul said that all the faithful are Christ's good scent in every place, he is flatly contradicted. "No," say the Donatists, "Africa alone smells good; the rest of the world stinks." We are the fragrance of Christ in every place: who says so? The Church. The vial of ointment in which the Lord was drenched stood for that sweet fragrance. Let us see if the Lord himself does not corroborate this. Some there were, greedy fellows, rascals, feathering their own nests—Judas, I mean—who had this to say about the ointment: *What is the point of this waste? A valuable thing like that could have been sold[7] to help the poor.* He wanted to sell the sweet fragrance of Christ! What did the Lord say to this? *Why do you all interfere with this woman? She has done me a beautiful service.* And what can I add to that, when the Lord himself said, *Wherever this gospel is preached in the whole world, what this woman has done will also be told* (Mt 26:8-10.13)? Is there anything to add to it? Or can we subtract anything? Is there any reason to give ear to slanderers? Did the Lord tell a lie, or was he deceived? Objectors can decide which they want to say: either that Truth lied, or that Truth was deceived. *Wherever this gospel is preached . . . .* And if you should ask him, "Where will it be preached, then?" *In the whole world*, he will say.

Let us listen now to the psalm, and see if it agrees. Let us listen to a song sung as a lament; and, I tell you, there is all the more matter for lament when it is sung to the deaf. It is amazing, brothers and sisters, to think that this psalm is also being sung today by the Donatists. Well, I ask you, brothers and sisters, what do they make of it? I confess I don't know, but Christ in his mercy knows that I am astonished that they are no more capable of hearing it than if they were stone-deaf. Could anything be put more plainly to such deaf people? The passion

---

5. Where alone, according to the Donatists, the true Church survived.
6. See Mt 26:7; Mk 14:3; Jn 12:3. One of these passages must also have formed part of the day's liturgy.
7. A Louvain manuscript adds "at a high price."

of Christ is recounted in this psalm as clearly as in the gospel, yet the psalm was composed goodness knows how many years before the Lord was born of the virgin Mary. It was a herald, giving advance notice of the coming of the Judge. Let us read it insofar as the constraints of time allow. Not as the depth of our sorrow might wish but, as I said, as far as the constraints of time allow.

Verse 2. The first word from the cross

3. *O God, my God, look upon me, why have you forsaken me?* This opening verse we heard from the Lord on the cross, when he cried, *Eli, Eli,* which means, *My God, my God*; and *Lama sabachthani?*, which means, *Why have you forsaken me?* (Mt 27:46). The evangelist interpreted it, explaining that he had said in Hebrew, *My God, my God, why have you forsaken me?* What did the Lord mean? God had not abandoned him, since he himself was God. Listen to the evangelist John, who at the beginning of his gospel poured out what he had deeply drunk from the Lord's breast;[8] let us see if Christ is God. *In the beginning was the Word, and the Word was with God; he was God.* And then this Word who was God *was made flesh, and dwelt among us* (Jn 1:1,14). And yet when this God-Word had become flesh, he hung on the cross and cried, *My God, my God, look upon me, why have you forsaken me?* For what other reason was this said than that we were there, for what other reason than that Christ's body is the Church? Why did he say, *My God, my God, look upon me, why have you forsaken me?* unless he was somehow trying to catch our attention, to make us understand, "This psalm is written about me"? *The tale of my sins leaves me far from salvation.* What sins could these be, when it was said of Christ, *He committed no sin, nor was any guile found on his lips* (1 Pt 2:22)? How, then, could he say, *the tale of my sins*, except because he himself intercedes for our sins,[9] and has made our sins his own, in order to make his righteousness ours?[10]

Verse 3. Fear

4. *O my God, I will cry to you all day, and you will not listen to me, and in the night, but you will not collude with my foolishness.* Beyond doubt, he was speaking of me, of you, of him over there, of her, for he was acting as his own body, the Church. Do you suppose, brothers and sisters, that when the Lord said, *Father, if it is possible, let this cup pass from me* (Mt 26:39), he was afraid to die? A soldier is not braver than the commander-in-chief; it is enough for a servant to

8. See Jn 13:23.
9. See Is 53:12.
10. See 2 Cor 5:21.

be like his master.[11] Yet Paul, a soldier enlisted in the army of Christ the King, says, *I am hard pressed on both sides. I long to die and to be with Christ* (Phil 1:23). If Paul craves death in order to be with Christ, can Christ himself fear it? Why did he make that prayer, then, except because he was bearing our weakness, and made it for those members of his body who still fear death? That was where the words came from; this was the voice of his members, not of the Head, as also are these words of the psalm: *I have cried by day and by night, and you will not listen.* Many people cry aloud in distress, and are not heard, but this is for their ultimate salvation, not to convict them of foolishness. Paul cried to God to have the thorn in his flesh removed, and he was not heard; it was not removed. And he was told, *My grace is sufficient for you, for my power finds complete scope in weakness* (2 Cor 12:9). He was not heard, then, but this was to make him wiser, not reduce him to foolishness, and so we were all helped to understand that God is a doctor, and that our troubles are a medicine bringing us to salvation, not a punishment leading to damnation. Under medical treatment you undergo cautery, or the knife, and you scream with pain. The doctor does not listen when you beg him to stop, but he does listen to your need for healing.

Verse 4. Fiery trials

5. *But you, the praise of Israel, dwell in holiness.* You live in those whom you have sanctified, and with your help they understand that there are some to whom you do not listen, but to their advantage, while others you do heed and it leads to their damnation. Paul was not listened to, and this turned to his profit. The devil was heeded, but to his damnation. He asked for Job, to tempt him, and his request was granted.[12] The demons asked to go into the pigs, and they were listened to.[13] The demons are heard, the apostle is not! But they are listened to with damnation as the outcome; the apostle is not listened to, but his salvation is in view, because the principle in his case is *you will not collude with my foolishness.* But you, the psalm continues, *you, the praise of Israel, dwell in holiness.* Why do you not listen even to your own children?

Why am I saying things like this? Remember, there is a phrase which should always be on your lips: "Thanks be to God." There is a large crowd here, and those who don't usually come have come. I am telling all of you alike: Christians are tested by suffering, and they prove their worth, if they do not abandon their God. When the time is right for him or her, a Christian is left alone. The fire is set going in the furnace; yes, indeed, the goldsmith's furnace is a mysterious and wonderful symbol. Inside it there is gold, inside it there is chaff, inside it the fire

---

11. See Mt 10:25.
12. See Jb 1:9-12.
13. See Mt 8:31-32.

works in a confined space. That fire is not of differing intensities, yet it produces different effects: it turns the chaff to ashes, but removes impurities from the gold. Those in whom God dwells are certainly improved by suffering, refined like gold. If our enemy the devil has begged for someone to put to the test, and his request has been granted, and he tests us whether by some bodily pain, or by financial loss, or by loss of family members, then we must keep our hearts fixed on God, who does not withdraw from us. If God seems to turn his ear away from our weeping, he nonetheless bestows mercy on us when we beg for it. He who made us knows what to do, he knows even how to remake us. A good mason has built the house, and he is well able to repair it.

Verses 5-6. God's deliverance

6. See what the psalm says: *Our fathers hoped in you; they hoped in you and you delivered them.* We know how many of our forefathers who hoped in God were rescued by him; we have read about them. He delivered the people of Israel from the land of Egypt; he delivered the three young men from the furnace;[14] Daniel he delivered from the lions' den, and Susanna from false accusation.[15] All of them called on him, and they were delivered. How could he fail with regard to his only Son, and not hear him as he hung on the cross? But why is he not delivered immediately, he who prayed, *Our fathers hoped in you, and you delivered them?*

Verse 7. "A worm and no man"

7. *I am a worm, and no man.* A worm, and yet no man; for though a human being too is a worm, he says, *I am a worm, and no man.* In what sense "no man"? Because he is God. Why then did he so demean himself as to say "worm"? Perhaps because a worm is born from flesh without intercourse, as Christ was from the virgin Mary? A worm, and yet no man. Why a worm? Because he was mortal, because he was born from flesh, because he was born without intercourse. Why "no man"? Because *In the beginning was the Word, and the Word was with God; he was God* (Jn 1:1).

Christ's humiliation

8. *Scorned by all and outcast by the people.* See how much he suffered! So that we may speak of the passion and approach it with deeper groaning,[16] let us

---

14. See Dn 3:19-23, 91-93, LXX.
15. See Dn 14:30-40; 13:1-60.
16. Variant: "that we may approach that deeper groaning."

see how much he is suffering now, and then see why. What was the purpose of it? Our fathers put their hope in him, and were delivered from the land of Egypt; and, as I have said, very many others who called on him were freed immediately, instantly, not just in the life to come but straightaway. Job was indeed handed over when the devil asked for him, and rotted with maggots, yet even in this life Job regained his health and received in double measure all he had lost,[17] while the Lord was flogged, and nobody came to his aid; he was disfigured by spittle, and nobody came to his aid; he was beaten and punched, and nobody came to his aid; he was crowned with thorns, and nobody came to his aid; he was hoisted onto a wooden cross, yet nobody rescued him; he shouted out, *My God, my God, why have you forsaken me?*, and no help was forthcoming. Why, my brothers and sisters, why? What did he gain by suffering so terribly? He endured it all because it was the price of something. What it was that cost him all that pain, we must spell out; let us see what he says. Let us ask first what he suffered, then why. And let us see how hostile to Christ are those who admit that he did suffer so terribly, and yet defraud him of what he bought. Hold onto both of these, the what and the why. Let me explain the "what" first, but not take too long over it, because the words of the psalm tell you the story better than I could. Think what the Lord suffers, give heed, fellow Christians: he is *scorned by all and outcast by the people.*

Verses 8-9. Mocking Christ

9. *All those who watched me sniggered at me; they mouthed at me and wagged their heads. "He put his hope in the Lord, so let the Lord rescue him; let him deliver him, since he holds him dear!"* Why did they say those things? Because he had become human, they reviled him as they might an ordinary human being.

Verses 10-11. The Word and the womb

10. *It was you who drew me out of the womb.* Surely they would not have hurled their insults against that Word who was in the beginning, the Word who is God? The Word through whom all things were made was not drawn out of the womb, except when he was made flesh and lived among us. *It was you who drew me out of the womb, you who are my God[18] from my mother's breasts*, for while you are my Father before all ages, from my mother's breasts you are my God.

---

17. See Jb 42:10.
18. In his first Exposition of this psalm Augustine read "my hope" here, not "my God."

11. *Upon you I was cast from the womb*, that you might be my sole hope. I speak now as a human being, as a weakling, as Word made flesh. *From my mother's womb you have been my God.* Not from my birth from you are you my God, for from my eternal birth you are my Father. But from the womb of my mother you are my God.

Verses 12-14. Abandonment to savagery

12. *Do not leave me, for anguish is very near, and there is no one to help.* Contemplate him, abandoned. Woe betide us if he abandons us, for there is no one else to help.

13. *Bull-calves throng round me, and fat bulls besiege me.* These are the people and its leaders: the throng of calves are the people, and the fat bulls their rulers.

14. *They opened their mouths at me like a ravening, roaring lion.* Listen to their roaring in the gospel: *Crucify! Crucify!* (Jn 19:6).

Verse 15. Free-flowing scripture

15. *I was poured out like water, and all my bones were scattered.* By his bones he means his strong supporters, for bones are the strong parts of the body. When did he scatter his bones? When he said to them, *See, I am sending you out like sheep among wolves* (Mt 10:16; Lk 10:3). When he scattered his strong supporters he was poured out like water, which when poured out either washes us or irrigates our crops. Christ was poured out like water, the filthy were washed clean, minds were irrigated.[19] *My heart has become like melting wax in my belly.* By his belly he means the weak in his Church. How did his heart become like wax? His heart is his scripture, or rather his wisdom in the scriptures. But scripture was closed; nobody understood it. When the Lord was crucified, it began to flow freely like wax, so that all the weak could understand scripture. As a result of the crucifixion even the veil of the temple was torn, because what had previously been veiled was now revealed.

Verse 16. Fired by suffering

16. *My strength was dried up like an earthenware pot.* What a wonderful thing to say: my name has been made stronger as a result of my suffering. Just as clay is soft before it goes into the kiln and hard afterwards, so the name of the Lord was always being scorned before his passion, but ever since then it has been

---

19. *Rigatae sunt mentes*; a variant has *rigati sitientes*, "the thirsty given drink."

held in honor. *My tongue stuck to my jaws.* As that member has no function except to speak, so Christ described his preachers as his tongue; they stuck to his jaws, in order to draw wisdom from deep within him. *And you brought me down into the dust of death.*

Verses 17-18. Touching the wounds

17. *Many dogs surrounded me, a band of ruffians beset me*: yes, that is what the gospel says. *They dug holes in my hands and my feet*: then were made those wounds of which the doubting disciple later handled the scars, the disciple who declared, *Unless I put my finger into the scars of his wounds, I will not believe.* When Christ said to him, *Come, bring your hand here, unbeliever*, he put his hand in and cried, *My Lord and my God!* Then Christ replied, *Because you have seen, you believe; blessed are they who do not see, and believe* (Jn 20:25.27-29). *They dug holes in my hands and my feet.*

18. *They numbered all my bones*: this was when Christ was hanging spread out on the tree. The stretching out of his body could not be more aptly described than by saying, *They numbered all my bones.*

Verse 19. Dividing Christ's garments

19. *They looked on and watched me.* They looked on, but did not understand; they watched, but did not see. They had eyes to see his body, but no discerning heart to reach the Word. *They shared out my garments among them.* His garments are his sacraments. Now pay close attention, brothers and sisters. His garments, his sacraments, could be torn apart by heresies, but there was one garment that no one tore: *they cast lots for my tunic.* The evangelist tells us that *there was a tunic woven from the top* (Jn 19:23) — down from heaven, then, from the Father, from the Holy Spirit. What is this tunic, which no one can tear apart? Charity. What is this tunic? Unity. Dice are thrown for it, but nobody tears it. The heretics have been able to tear apart the sacraments for their own use, but love they could not tear. And because they were not able to, they have taken themselves off, but love remains whole. Love falls to the lot of some people, and whoever has love is safe. Nobody ousts such a person from the Catholic Church, and if any begin to take hold of love from without, they are brought inside, as the olive branch was by the dove.[20]

---

20. Augustine always hoped and worked for the reintegration of Donatists into the Catholic Church; here he likens the process to the entrance of the dove into the ark; see Gn 8:11.

Verses 20-22. Prayer for help

20. *But you, Lord, do not keep your help far from me.* And he did not, for after three days Christ rose again. *Look to my defense.*

21. *Deliver my life from the sword,*[21] that is, from death, for the *framea* is the same thing as the *gladius,*[22] and by "sword" the psalmist meant to indicate death; *and my only one from the power of the dog.* By "my life, and my only one" he means "myself and my Church," head and body, for *my only one* is the Church.[23] He says, literally, "from the dog's paw," meaning *from the power of the dog.* Who are the dogs? Those who bark like dogs[24] without understanding whom they are barking at. No one is annoying them, yet still they bark. What harm has any passer-by done to the dog? Yet it barks. So those who bark blindly, with no idea against whom or for whom they are barking, are dogs.

22. *Save me from the lion's mouth.* You know who this lion is, my friends, the roaring lion that prowls around seeking someone to devour.[25] *And my humility from the horns of unicorns.* By *unicorns* the psalm simply means the proud, which is why it speaks of *my humility.*

Verse 23. The reason why: the fruit of the passion

23. You have heard the sufferings he endured, and how he prayed to be delivered from them. Now let us turn our attention to why. You must ask yourselves, brothers and sisters, whether anyone has a right to be called a Christian who has no stake in the cause for which Christ suffered. Consider now: we understand what he suffered. His bones were counted, he was mocked, his garments were shared out, and lots were cast for one special tunic. Mad and raging, they surrounded him, and all his bones were scattered. We hear about all this in the psalm and we read it too in the gospel. Now let us see why. O Christ, Son of God, had you not wished it, you would not have suffered. Show us the fruit of your passion. "I will tell you what the fruit is," he replies. "I am not keeping it quiet, but people are deaf. Listen, then, and I will tell you the profit I had in view when I suffered all those things." *I will tell of your name to my brothers and sisters.* Does he tell of God's name in a sect? No, *I will tell of your name to my brothers and sisters, in the full assembly I will sing your praise.* This is happening now. But let us examine what the assembly is, for he said, *In the full assembly I will*

---

21. *Framea.*

22. In classical Latin *framea* is used for a spear or javelin, in later Latin for a sword. Augustine seems to feel that some explanation is still needed.

23. See note on this verse in Augustine's first Exposition of the present psalm.

24. *Canino more*; a variant has *caeco*, "blindly," anticipating the end of this paragraph.

25. See 1 Pt 5:8.

sing your praise. Let us have a look at this assembly, this Church, for which he suffered.

Verse 24. Christ and the whole earth

24. *All you who fear the Lord, praise him*. Wherever God is feared and praised, there is the Church of Christ. Judge for yourselves, brothers and sisters, whether it is without good reason that "Amen" and "Alleluia" are sung today the world over. Isn't God feared just as widely? Is he not praised everywhere too? Yet Donatus has emerged and declared, "No, certainly not; the whole world is damned." You are quite wrong to say, "The whole world is damned." Is it conceivable that only a little piece has survived, in Africa? Does Christ say nothing to gag such people? Does he say nothing to cut out by the roots the tongues of those who say such things? Let us look hard; we may find something. We are still hearing from the heretics, "When the psalm says, *In the full assembly*, it is our church that is meant." Well, what about the next line: *All you who fear the Lord, praise him*? Let us inquire whether the Donatists praise the Lord, whether the psalm is speaking of them, and whether Christ is praised in the middle of their assembly. They have a strange way of praising Christ, those people who say, "He has lost the whole world, the devil has taken it all away from him, and he himself survives only in one part." But let us look further, let the psalm say it more plainly, let there be no ambiguity in what it says, nothing that needs explanation, and no room for conjecture. *You whole progeny of Jacob, extol him*. Perhaps they still say, "Ah, but we are the progeny of Jacob." Well, let's see.

Verse 25. The prayer of the poor

25. *Let all the seed of Israel fear him*. Perhaps they still persist, "We are the seed of Israel." All right, let them say so. *For he has not rejected or scorned the prayer of the poor*.[26] Who are these poor? Those who do not presume on their own virtue. We must ask ourselves if people who say, "We are the righteous," are really poor? Christ cries aloud, *The tale of my sins leaves me far from salvation*. But let them go on saying what they like. *He did not turn his face away from me, but when I cried to him, he heard me*. Why did he hear? To what purpose?

---

26. Plural here; singular in the corresponding place in the first Exposition of this psalm.

Verse 26. The great Church

26. *My praise is for you.* To God has he directed his praise; he has taught us not to set our hopes on mortals. Let them keep on saying what they like, though in truth they have already begun to burn; the fire is getting close, and no one can hide from its heat.[27] But let them still protest, "We too have directed our praise to him; we do not presume on ourselves either." All right, let them say so. *In the great assembly I will confess you.* I think the psalmist has now begun to get to the heart of the matter. What is this great assembly, brothers and sisters? How could a tiny part of the world be the great assembly? The great assembly is the whole world. Now suppose someone wanted to argue with Christ, such a one might say, "You have prophesied, *In the great assembly I will confess you*, so tell us, where is the great assembly? You have been confined to a scrap of Africa, you have lost the rest of the world. You shed your blood for the whole of it, but you have been robbed by an invader." We have put this question to the Lord in an inquiring spirit; we know what we would answer to that; but suppose we do not know what he will reply? Surely he will answer us? "Keep quiet now, I am still speaking, and no one will be left in any doubt." Let us be alert then, to hear what he has to say. For some time now I have been wanting to settle the matter, and exclude any other interpretation of Christ's words, *in the great assembly.* You, a Donatist, say that he has confined himself to one remote region. And they still have the audacity to pretend, "Our church is the great assembly too." What, Bagai and Thamugadi?[28] If Christ says nothing to silence them, let them go on claiming that Numidia on its own is the great assembly, the great Church.

Verses 27-28. The truly poor imitate Christ

27. But let us investigate, let us go on listening to the Lord. *I will fulfill my vows in the presence of those who fear him.* What are his vows? The sacrifice which he offered to God. Do you know what sort of sacrifice that is? The faithful know what vows he fulfilled in the presence of those who fear him, for he continues, *The poor shall eat and be satisfied.* Blessed are the poor, because they eat seeking to be satisfied, they eat because they are poor; but the rich are not satisfied because they are not really hungry. The poor will eat heartily. From their number came Peter the fisherman, and another fisherman, John, and his brother James, and so did Matthew the tax collector. They were from the poor who ate heartily and were satisfied. And they suffered like him on whom they fed.[29] He gave his supper, he gave his passion; it is the one who imitates him who

---

27. See Ps 18:7(19:6).
28. Towns in the interior, southwest of Hippo, strongholds of the Donatist sect.
29. The eucharistic overtones are clear throughout this paragraph.

is filled. The poor have imitated him, for they have so suffered as to follow in Christ's footsteps. *The poor shall eat.* But in what sense are they poor? *Those who seek the Lord will praise him.* The rich praise themselves, the poor praise the Lord. In what sense are they poor? Because they praise the Lord, they seek the Lord; for the Lord himself is the wealth of the poor. This is why their houses are empty, so that their hearts may be full of riches. Let the wealthy strive to fill their treasure chests, but the poor look for what can fill their hearts; and when their hearts are full they who seek the Lord praise him. Take a good look, brothers and sisters, at what kind of wealth they have, these people who are truly poor. Their riches are not in any treasure chest, nor in a granary, nor in a store-house; but *their hearts will live for ever and ever.*

28. So now take heed. The Lord suffered: all those things you have heard about, the Lord suffered. We are asking why he suffered, and he has begun to tell us: *I will tell of your name to my brothers and sisters, in the full assembly I will sing your praise.* But they are still claiming, "That means our assembly." *Let all the seed of Israel fear him.* They say, "But we are the seed of Israel." *He has not rejected or scorned the prayer of the poor.* They still say, "That means us!" *Nor did he turn his face away from me*: Christ the Lord, that is; he did not turn his face away from himself, from the Church which is his body. *My praise is for you.* But what you Donatists want is to praise yourselves. "Not at all," they retort. "We too praise the Lord." *I will fulfill my vows in the presence of those who fear him.* The sacrifice of peace, the sacrifice of love, the sacrifice of his body—this is what his faithful know; but we can't discuss it now. *I will fulfill my vows in the presence of those who fear him.* Well may the tax collectors eat, well may the fishermen eat, let them chew on it, let them imitate the Lord, let them suffer, let them be filled. The Lord himself died, the poor too are dying. The death of the disciples is being added to the death of their Master. Why? Tell me the purpose of it. *All the ends of the earth will be reminded and will turn to the Lord.* In view of that, brothers and sisters, why ask me how we may reply to the Donatists? Look at the psalm, this same psalm that is read here today and is being read among them as well. Let us write it on our foreheads! Forward march, everyone! Let not our tongues fall silent, let us shout, "Look, Christ suffered, the merchant offered his price. The money he handed over was his blood, the blood he shed. He carried our ransom-money in a purse; he was pierced with a spear, the purse spilled out, and the price of the whole world gushed out." What have you to say to me, you heretic? That it was not the ransom-price of the whole world? That Africa alone was redeemed? You dare not say, "The whole world was redeemed, but perished later." Who attacked Christ, and robbed him of what was his own? Look what the psalm says: *All the ends of the earth will be reminded and will turn to the Lord.* Let this satisfy you, and let the psalmist have the last word. Had he said, "The ends of the earth," rather than *all the ends of the earth*, they might have

said, "Fine; as far as we are concerned, the earth ends at Morocco." But *all the ends of the earth* is what he said, you heretic; *all* is the word he used. Where are you off to, to hide from further questioning? You have no way out, only a way in.[30]

Verses 28-29. All the ends of the earth

29. Please, please, I don't want any argument, nor do I want anyone to say that it is my sermon that is important. Concentrate on the psalm, read the psalm. Christ has suffered; his blood has been shed. Look at our Redeemer, look at the price of our ransom. Then let someone tell me what he purchased. Why are we asking? Someone could well say to me, "You idiot, why are you asking? You are holding the text. You can find out from that where he bought it and what he bought." See, there you have it: *all the ends of the earth will be reminded, and will turn to the Lord.* So the ends of the earth will be reminded, but the heretics have forgotten, and that is why they have it read to them every year. Do you imagine they take it in when their reader says, *All the ends of the earth will be reminded and will turn to the Lord*? Oh well, maybe it is only one verse. Your thoughts were elsewhere, or you were chatting with your neighbor, when the reader came to that bit. Well then, go on listening, because it is repeated; it continues to hammer at the ears of the inattentive, saying, *All the families of the nations will worship in his presence.* Our Donatist friend is still deaf, he's not listening. Let's have another go! *For the kingship is the Lord's, and he will hold sway over the nations.* Keep a firm hold on these three verses, brothers and sisters. Today they have been sung in Donatist assemblies also, or maybe they have struck them out. Believe me, brothers and sisters, I am so angry, so worked up, so astounded at their deafness and hardness of heart that sometimes I doubt whether they have this passage in their texts. They are all running to church today, all listening to this psalm and concentrating hard, all listening with their hearts in their mouths. What if they do have a distraction? This is only one verse—*all the ends of the earth will be reminded and will turn to the Lord.* You are just waking up now, but still rubbing your eyes: *and all the families of the nations will worship in his sight.* Shake off your slumber, you are still drowsy; listen to the next verse: *the kingship is the Lord's, and he will hold sway over the nations.*

---

30. To the Catholic Church.

Verse 30. The terms of the will

30. I do not know whether they have anything further to say. Let them file a suit with the scriptures, not with us. Look, here is the text, let them dispute with that. What has become of their slogan, "We preserved the scriptures, to save them from being burnt"?[31] Preserved they were, yes, but only to hand you over to the flames. Think what you saved! Open them and read; you preserved them, yet now you are attacking them. Did you preserve them from the fire only to destroy them now with your tongues? I do not believe it; I do not believe that you preserved them. I absolutely do not believe it. You did not save them. Our side unquestionably speaks the truth by saying that it was you who treacherously handed them over.[32] Anyone who refuses to accept the terms of a will once it has been read is a traitor. It is being read now, and I am following it; it is being read now, and you reject it. Whose hand cast it into the flame—that of the person who believes, and observes it, or that of one who deplores the fact that there is something to be read? I am not interested in who kept it safe. The codex[33] was found somewhere or other, the testament of our father came out of some pigeon-hole. Some scoundrels wanted to steal it, some persecutor or other wanted to set it alight. But it was produced from somewhere, so let it be read. Why are you quarreling? We are brothers and sisters, why are we embroiled in legal dispute? Father did not die intestate. He made a will, and died; he died and rose again. Contention arises about the legacy of those who have died only until the will is proved, but once it is brought out in public everyone falls silent, so that the document may be opened and read aloud. The judge listens intently, the advocates are silent, the criers keep order, the whole group is on tenterhooks waiting for the words of the deceased to be read, the words of someone lifeless in the grave. He lies there in his tomb, devoid of sensation, yet his words are valid. Christ is enthroned in heaven, and is his will being challenged? Open it up, let's read. We are brothers and sisters, why are we locked in conflict? Let's all calm down and stop being so angry. Father did not leave us without making a will. He who made the will lives for ever; he hears our voices and recognizes his own. Let's read on; what are we arguing about? Once the inheritance itself is found, let us hold onto it. Open the will, and read on the first page of this same psalter, *Ask of me.* But who is speaking? Perhaps not Christ? You have it there in front of you: *The Lord said to me, You are my Son, today I have begotten you.* It is God's Son who is

---

31. The claim at the origins of the schism: Catholics had been *traditores*, "handers-over" of the sacred books to the persecutors. See note at Exposition of Psalm 10, verse 1.

32. Augustine is playing on different meanings of the verb *trado*: hand over, deliver, betray, and its cognate noun *traditor*: one who hands over, betrays.

33. A *codex* or *caudex* was a book, originally made of wooden tablets, often used for public records or accounts, and alone recognized as having legal validity. Augustine alludes to this idea in the present vivid passage, though the *codex* referred to is here, of course, the scriptures.

speaking then, or the Father addressing his Son. And what does he say to his Son? *Ask of me, and I will give you the nations as your heritage, and the ends[34] of the earth for your possession* (Ps 2:7-8). It is usually the case, brothers and sisters, that when ownership is in question, the next of kin[35] are sought. Between kinsfolk A and B they look for the heir, either the one to whom the inheritance can be given or the one who can effect a buy-out.[36] In the case we are discussing, between what sort of kinsfolk is the question of ownership being raised? Between A and B who both have possession. He who has swept away all boundaries[37] has excluded none of his kinsfolk.[38] Wherever you turn, Christ is there. You have the ends of the earth for your inheritance, come here and possess the whole lot with me. Why are you locked in dispute, why foment sectarian rivalry? Come this way; you will lose the case, but for your own good, for you will have everything. Are you still accusing us? I have read the will, yet you continue to misrepresent us. Are you trying to prolong the argument on the grounds that the psalmist spoke of the ends of the earth, but did not say *all* the ends of the earth? Let us read it, then. How did it sound when it was read? *All the ends of the earth will be reminded and will turn to the Lord, and all the families of the nations will worship in his presence. For the kingship is the Lord's, and he will hold sway over the nations*. It is his kingship, not yours. Acknowledge the Lord; acknowledge the Lord's possession.

All the baptized are Christ's property

31. But your possession is your own homes, you who want to hug what you have in private rather than holding it in our common unity with Christ, because your ambition is to be dominant on earth, not to reign with him in heaven. Whenever we approach them, and say, Let us seek the truth, let us try to sort it out, they reply, "You lot keep what you have. You[39] have your sheep, I have mine. Don't annoy my sheep, and I won't annoy yours." Well, God bless us: my sheep, his sheep—didn't Christ buy any? That is all wrong; there should not be any which are mine, or yours, they should all belong to him who bought them, him who put his brand on them. *The planter is nothing, and the one who waters is nothing; only God matters, who grants the increase* (1 Cor 3:7). Why should I have mine, and you yours? If Christ is there with you, let mine go to him, because they are not mine; if Christ is here, let yours come to us, because they are not yours. Are

---

34. *Fines.*
35. *Affines.*
36. Language of purchase and redemption by Christ, but also of the buying-out of a co-heir.
37. *Fines.*
38. *Affines.*
39. Singular.

we to let them lick our faces and hands because they are our property, only to perish because they are aliens to Christ's family?[40] "But they are not my property," he protests. What do you mean? Let us check whether or not they are your possession, let us see whether you do not lay claim to it yourself. I work under Christ's name, you under the name of Donatus. If you have eyes to see, Christ is everywhere. You say, "Look, this is where Christ is." I say, He is in every place. *Praise the Lord, you children, praise the name of the Lord.* From where do they praise him, and how far does their praise reach? *From the rising of the sun to its setting, praise the name of the Lord* (Ps 112(113):1.3). That is the Church I am showing you, the Church Christ bought, that he redeemed, for whom he shed his blood. What is your response? "I too gather for him." But he said, *Whoever does not gather with me scatters.* You are tearing apart our unity, you are looking for what you can possess.

Why are those sheep called by the name of Christ? Because you have put up Christ's name-plate,[41] but only to protect your own property. Do not some people do this on their own house? In order to deter some powerful crook from seizing his house, the householder puts up the name-plate of a powerful person, even though it is a lie. Hoping to hold onto what is his own, he wants the frontage of his house to be safeguarded by someone else's name-plate, so that when it is read an intruder may be frightened off by the great name written on it and think twice about breaking in. This is just what the Donatists did when they condemned the Maximianists. They contested before judges, and recounted the decisions of their council,[42] as though they were putting up name-plates to make themselves look like bishops. The judge inquired, "Who is this other bishop from the Donatist party?" The official representative answered, "We know no other than Aurelius, the Catholic bishop." They were afraid of the law, and therefore named one bishop only. But in order to gain a hearing from the judge, they stuck the name of Christ over their own; they put his name-plate over what was theirs.

The Lord is good; may he be lenient to them. Wherever he finds his own name, may he claim that thing for his own possession. In his mighty mercy may he do so for whomsoever he may find bearing the name of Christ, and gather them in. After all, brothers and sisters, isn't this what any important person does when he finds something with his name on it? Does he not claim it as his by right? He says, "They would not have put my name on it unless this belonged to

---

40. Conjectural translation of an obscure sentence: *propter possessiones osculentur nobis caput et manus, et pereant filli alieni.*

41. *Titulus*, a placard; but it could be understood as "title-deeds" in the present argument.

42. The Council of Bagai met on 24 April 394 to rehabilitate Primian of Carthage, the violent Donatist bishop condemned by the Maximianist Council of Cebarsussa held in June 393. See Augustine's Exposition 2 of Psalm 36.

me. Someone put up my name-plate, so this is mine; wherever I find my name, I claim what is there." He does not change the name-plate, does he? The name-plate that was there remains unaltered; the owner changes, but the title to ownership does not. So too if people who have received Christ's baptism come into unity, we do not change the name-plate or efface the name;[43] we acknowledge the name-plate of our King, the name-plate of our commander-in-chief. But what are we to say? O you sad, sad house, if only he whose name-plate you bear could possess you! You bear Christ's name, do not consent to be the possession of Donatus.

Final warning

32. We have spoken at great length, brothers and sisters, but do not let what is read today ebb away from your memory. I repeat, for it needs to be said often: by this day, by the sacred mysteries of this day, I insist that you do not let these verses slip out of your hearts. *All the ends of the earth will be reminded and will turn to the Lord, and all the families of the nations will worship in his presence. For the kingship is the Lord's, and he will hold sway over the nations.* In the face of Christ's rightful ownership, so open and so clearly demonstrated, you must not listen to what the detractor says. Whatever the Donatists allege, they are only men and women talking; but what you have just heard is spoken by God.

---

43. That is, converts from the Donatist sect were not rebaptized when reconciled with the Catholic Church.

Exposition of Psalm 22

1-2. *A psalm of David himself.* The Church is speaking to Christ, and says, *The Lord shepherds me, and I shall want for nothing*; since my shepherd is the Lord Jesus Christ, I shall not lack anything. *In a place of fresh, green pasture he has set me*, for he has led me to faith in a field of fresh grass, and placed me there to feed me. *He has nurtured me beside regenerating water*: this means that he nurtured me beside the water of baptism, where those who have lost their soundness and strength are made new.

Verses 3-4. Guidance

3. *He has turned my soul round; he has led me in paths of righteousness for the honor of his name.* He has guided me along the narrow paths of his righteousness, where few people walk; and this not for any merit of mine, but for the sake of his own name.

4. *Though I walk in the shadow of death*: even though still amid this life, which is shadowed by death, *I will fear no evil, because you are with me*. I shall not be afraid of evil happenings, because you live in my heart through faith; you are with me now, to ensure that when this shadow of death has passed away, I may be with you. *As for your rod and your staff, they are my encouragement.* Your discipline is like a rod used on a flock of sheep, and like a staff used to support older children as they grow from sensuous to spiritual life. They have done me no harm; rather they have encouraged me, because you are mindful of me.

Verse 5. The banquet

5. *You have prepared a table before me, despite those who oppress me.* The time for the rod has passed, that time when I was small and animal-like, and was instructed amid the flocks in the pasture; now after that era of the rod I have begun to be guided under your staff, and now you have prepared a table before

me, so that I may be no longer fed on milk like a baby, but as an adult eat solid food,[1] and be strengthened against those who oppress me. *With oil you have richly anointed my head*, because you have gladdened my soul with spiritual joy. *And how excellent is your intoxicating chalice,* how excellent the chalice you give us to drink, which blots out the memory of earlier empty delights!

Verse 6. God's mercy now and for ever

6. *Your mercy will follow me closely, all the days of my life*, as long, that is, as I live in this mortal existence, which is not your life but mine, *that I may dwell in the Lord's house for days without end.* The mercy of the Lord will not only follow me closely in this world, but will bring me to dwell in his house for ever.

---

1. See 1 Cor 3:2. Variant: "may eat a greater food."

Exposition of Psalm 23

Verses 1-2. Christ's glory, the Church's victory

1. *A psalm of David himself, on the first day of the week.* This is a psalm for David, dealing with the glorification and resurrection of our Lord, which took place early in the morning on the first day of the week, now called the Lord's day.

2. *The earth is the Lord's, and all that fills it, the round world and all who live in it.* This is true, for the Lord, now glorified, is preached to all nations to bring them to faith, and the whole world thus becomes his Church. *He founded it on the seas*: he himself established it most securely above all the stormy waves of this world, so that they might be subdued by the Church, and do it no harm. *And he prepared it above the rivers.* Rivers flow into the sea, and greedy men and women glide into this world; but the Church overcomes even these. With earthly cravings conquered through God's grace, the Church has been made ready by love to receive immortality.[1]

Verses 3-4. Integrity

3. *Who will climb the mountain of the Lord?* Who will ascend to the towering heights of the Lord's righteousness? *Or who will stand in his holy place?* In that place to which a person may climb,[2] that place founded on the seas and prepared above the rivers, will anyone stand fast?

4. *One with clean hands and a pure heart.* Who, then, will climb up there and stay there? Only a person innocent in action and pure in thought. *One who has not received his soul in vain*, that is, a person who has not consigned his or her soul to the things that pass away, but realizes that it is immortal and longs for a settled and changeless eternity. *Or sworn deceitfully to a neighbor:*[3] such a person's dealings with others are free from deceit, just as the things of eternity are simple and straightforward.

---

1. *Ad recipiendam immortalitatem caritate*; the editors emend to *ad recipiendam immortalitatis clarit:* "to receive the brightness of immortality."
2. Or "that place to which he [the Lord] has ascended."
3. A variant has "in grief to a neighbor."

Verses 5-6. The blessing on God-seekers

5. *Such a person will receive a blessing from the Lord, and mercy from the God who saves him.*

6. *This is the generation of those who seek the Lord.* It speaks of them as a "generation" because those who seek him are born like this.[4] *Of those who seek the face of the God of Jacob.* They are seeking the face of the God who gave first place to the one born later.[5]

Pause.

Verse 7. The everlasting gates

7. *Away with your gates, you princes!:*[6] whoever you are who seek pride of place in human affairs, get rid of the barriers of greed and fear you have put up, that they may not block the way. *But you, everlasting gates, lift yourselves up!* You gates to eternal life, gates of renunciation of this world and conversion to God, open up, *and the King of glory will enter.* The King will make his entrance; let us boast of him without fear of pride, for he overthrew the gates of mortality and flung open before him the gates of heaven, making good his claim, *Be glad, for I have overcome the world* (Jn 16:33).

Verse 8. The Lord mighty in battle

8. *Who is this King of glory?* Mortal nature quakes in wonder, and asks, *Who is this King of glory?* The answer is given, *The strong and mighty Lord,* whom you thought to be weak and vanquished, *the Lord mighty in war.*[7] Handle his scars and you will find them healed, see his human weakness restored to immortal strength. This glorification of the Lord was owed to the earth, where he did battle with death, and it has been paid in full.

Verse 9. The open way to heaven

9. *Away with your gates, you princes!* The way lies open now from earth to heaven. Let the prophet's trumpet sound again: get rid of your gates, yes, even you heavenly princes, you who have erected gates in the minds of people who

---

4. A possible allusion to rebirth in baptism, not developed here, as it was in the preceding Exposition.
5. See Gn 25:23; Rom 9:12.
6. The text has *vestri,* which makes little sense. The editors, with the Vulgate, amend to *vestras.*
7. Variant: "in battle."

worship the host of heaven.[8] *But you, everlasting gates, lift yourselves up,* gates of everlasting righteousness, love and purity, through which a soul loves the one true God, and refuses to prostitute itself to many so-called gods. *And the King of glory will enter.* The King of glory will make his way in, to intercede for us at the Father's right hand.[9]

Verse 10. Christ, the King of all powers

10. *Who is this King of glory?* What? Do even you, commander of the spiritual powers of the air,[10] marvel and ask, *Who is this King of glory?* Know then that *The Lord of hosts, he is the King of glory.* In his body now brought back to life he who once was tempted marches far above you; he who once was tempted by an apostate angel makes his progress beyond all the angels. Let none among you thrust himself in our way, attempting to close it and have us worshiping him as though he were God; for no principality or angel or spiritual potentate separates us from the love of Christ.[11] It is better to trust in the Lord than in any prince,[12] and so anyone who boasts must boast only in the Lord.[13] There are indeed spiritual beings who share in the ordering of this world, but *the Lord of hosts, he is the King of glory.*

---

8. Compare 2 Kgs 17:16; 22:4. Astral cults were a powerful temptation to both Israel and Judah in the last years of both monarchies, and invaded even the temple precincts in Jerusalem.
9. See Rom 8:34.
10. See Eph 2:2.
11. See Rom 8:38-39.
12. See Ps 117(118):9.
13. See 1 Cor 1:31; compare Jer 9:23-24.

Exposition of Psalm 24

Verses 1-3. Christ speaks in the person of the Church

1. *To the end, a psalm of David himself.* Christ is speaking here, but in the person of the Church, for the things said in this psalm are more relevant to the Christian people who have turned to God.

2. *To you, Lord, have I lifted up my soul*, with spiritual desire, because formerly my soul was trampled on the ground by carnal desires. *O my God, I trust in you, let me not be put to shame.* O my God, I have been brought to this point of bodily weakness because I trusted in myself. Having abandoned God, I aspired to be Godlike, only to find myself afraid of being killed by the most insignificant little animal. A laughing-stock by reason of my pride, I was totally ashamed. But now I trust in you, so let me be shamed no longer.

3. *Do not let my enemies mock me.* No, do not let them mock me, those who lie in wait, and with their insidious, serpentine suggestions and wily flattery have brought me to this pass. *Truly, none of those who hope in you will be confounded.*

Verses 4-5. Teach me your ways

4. *But let them be confounded, the unjust whose actions are worthless.* Yes, may they be the ones who are confounded, the people who act unjustly to acquire things that pass away. *Make your ways known to me, Lord, and train me in your paths.* They are not the wide paths that lead many to perdition; train me in your narrow ways that are known to few.[1]

5. *Guide me in your truth*, let me shun errors, *and teach me*, for of myself I know nothing but falsehood; *for you, O God, are my salvation, and I have been waiting for you all day long.* Turned out of paradise by you, and wandering to a far-off country, I cannot return by my own strength unless you come to meet me in my wandering, for my return has been waiting upon your mercy throughout the whole stretch of earthly time.[2]

---

1. See Mt 7:13-14.
2. Familiar Augustinian imagery: the prodigal son (see Lk 15:11-32) departs for a far country, the "land of unlikeness," but on his return is welcomed home by his merciful father and restored to his dignity. Augustine identifies with him throughout his *Confessions*; but the prodigal is an archetypal figure, the human race, restored in Christ to its lost likeness to God. This drama occupies "the whole stretch of earthly time." See note on Exposition 2 of Psalm 18, 3.

Verses 6-7. Please forgive and forget

6. *Remember your mercies, Lord,* remember the deeds your mercy has wrought, because people are thinking that you have forgotten. *And that your mercies are from eternity:* remember this, that your mercies are from eternity, because you have never been without them. You did indeed subject sinful humans to frustration, but you subjected them in hope;[3] you did not abandon them, but supported them with the many great comforts of your creation.

7. *Do not remember the transgressions of my youth, when I was ignorant.* Do not store up the memory of the transgressions I committed in my brash confidence and my ignorance to punish me for them, but let them slip out of your memory. *Remember me in the light of your mercy,* O God. Please do remember me, not in the anger of which I am worthy, but in your mercy, which is worthy of you, and this *because of your goodness, O Lord,* not because of what is due to me, Lord, but because of your own goodness.

Verses 8-9. God, the merciful and just educator

8. *The Lord is gracious and upright:* gracious, because he has shown such mercy to sinners and the ungodly as to forgive them all their earlier sins; but upright too, because after exercising mercy by inviting and forgiving, and conferring grace independently of any merits, he will look for properly meritorious acts at the last judgment. *Therefore he will appoint a law for those who falter on the way.* This is said because he graciously showed mercy in advance to lead them into the way.

9. *He will guide the meek in judgment.* He will guide the meek, and at the time of judgment will not frighten those who follow his will, and do not stand out against him by preferring their own. *He will teach his ways to the gentle.* He will teach his ways not to those who want to run on ahead, as if they could rule themselves better than he can, but to those who do not strut about with their heads in the air, or dig in their heels, when his easy yoke and light burden are set upon them.[4]

Verse 10. God's mercy and judgment

10. *All the Lord's ways are steadfast love and truth.* What *ways* will he teach them, other than the *steadfast love* which makes him ready to be appeased, and the *truth* which renders him incorrupt? The first of these he has demonstrated by forgiving sins, the second by judging merits. This is why the psalm speaks of *all*

---

3. See Rom 8:20.
4. See Mt 11:30.

the Lord's ways, meaning the two comings of the Son of God, one in mercy, the other in judgment. Those who reach him by holding fast to his ways, knowing themselves to have been set free through no merits of their own, cast off their pride and are henceforth wary of the severity of the judge, whom they have hitherto experienced as a gentle, kindly helper. *For those who seek his testament and his testimonies*. The gentle and mild seek that *testament* whereby he redeemed us and gave us new life through his own blood; they know him as a merciful Lord at his first coming, and a judge when he comes again. They seek his *testimonies* in the prophets and the evangelists.[5]

Verse 11. Continuing sinfulness

11. *For your name's sake, Lord, you will deal mercifully with my sin; for it is great*. Not only have you forgiven the sins I committed before I came to believe, but in response to the sacrifice I bring you of a deeply troubled spirit[6] you will deal mercifully with my present sinning. There is a great deal of it, since even for those on the way there is no shortage of stumbling-blocks.

Verses 12-15. Fear and wisdom

12. *Who is there who fears the Lord?* Fear is the beginning of an approach to wisdom.[7] *He will appoint a law for them in the way they have chosen*. On the way they have freely chosen he will appoint a law for them, lest they sin again and go unpunished.

13. *Their soul will linger in good things, and their progeny will inherit the earth and possess it*. The work of those who fear the Lord will gain them the stable inheritance of a body raised to new life.

14. *The Lord is the strong support of those who fear him*.[8] Fear looks like a characteristic of the weak, but the Lord is a strong support to those who fear him. And they are strengthened by the name of the Lord, which has been glorified throughout the world. *And he ensures that his testament is revealed to them*; he makes sure of this, because the nations are Christ's inheritance, and so are the ends of the earth.

15. *My eyes are on the Lord continually, for he will pluck my feet from the snare*. Let me not be afraid of dangers on the ground, when I am not looking

---

5. Sacrament and word, the channels of the Church's life.
6. See Ps 50:19(51:17).
7. See Ps 110(111):10; Prv 1:7; 9:10; Sir 1:16.
8. Some manuscripts add, "and those who fear/call upon the name of the Lord," which may be authentic, in view of the mention of the name in the following lines.

earthward, because he upon whom my gaze is fixed will pull my feet clear of the snare.

Verses 16-18. The one Church, laboring and humble

16. Look upon me and have mercy on me, for I am alone[9] and poor. I am one single[10] people, maintaining the humility of your one[11] Church. No heresy, no schism preserves this.

17. *The tribulations of my heart have multiplied.* The tribulations my heart suffers have been increased by mounting iniquity and the cooling down of love.[12] *Lead me out from my grievous necessity.* It is necessary for me to endure these things, so that by persevering to the end I may be saved,[13] but lead me out from my grievous necessity.

18. *Look upon my humility and my toil,* that humility which prevents me from ever tearing away from unity by any boast of righteousness, and the toil I have in enduring the unruly who are intermingled with my members. *And forgive all my sins.* I ask you to forgive me not only the sins of my youth and ignorance, committed before I believed, but also those which I commit even now when I am living by faith, whether through weakness or the dark clouds which obscure this life.

Verses 19-21. Enemies without and within

19. *Consider my enemies, and how they have increased.* Not only outside, but within, at the very heart of the Church, enemies are not lacking. *With wicked hatred they hate me,* hating me even though I love them.

20. *Guard my soul and deliver me.* Guard my soul from sliding into imitation of them; and deliver me from this confused situation where they are mixed in with me. *Do not let me be put to shame, because I have hoped in you.* If they chance to rise up against me, let me not be shamed, because I have put my trust not in myself, but in you.

21. *The innocent and the upright have clung to me, because I have waited for you, Lord.* The innocent and the upright are mixed in with me not only by physical proximity, like the wicked, but also by clinging to me in agreement of heart, by their very innocence and rectitude, because I have not fallen away into

---

9. *Unicus.*
10. *Unicus.*
11. *Unicae.*
12. See Mt 24:12.
13. See Mt 10:22.

imitating the wicked, but have steadfastly waited for you, in expectation of the winnowing that will accompany your final harvest.

Verse 22. Deliverance from distress

22. *Redeem Israel, O God, from all its troubles.*[14] Redeem your people, O God, whom you have prepared for the vision of yourself.[15] Redeem it from all the troubles it endures, not only from without but also from within.

---

14. Variants: "Redeem me, God of Israel, from all my troubles/iniquities."
15. Israel, the name associated with the vision of God. See note at Exposition 1 of Psalm 21, 4.

Exposition 1 of Psalm 25

Verse 1. The Church, stable in Christ

1. *Of David himself.* This psalm is to be ascribed to David himself, not to the mediator, the man Christ Jesus,[1] but to the whole Church,[2] now perfectly grounded in Christ.

2. *Judge me, O Lord, for I have walked in my innocence.* Judge me, Lord, because, thanks to the mercy with which you forestalled me, I have some entitlement from my innocence, and have kept to that path. *With my hope set on the Lord*[3] *I shall not be moved.*[4] But I do not on that score hope in myself; rather it is by trusting in the Lord that I shall abide in him.

Verses 2-3. God purges

3. *Examine me, Lord, and try me.* Lest even one of my secret sins elude my scrutiny, examine me, Lord, and try me. Reveal me not to yourself, from whom nothing lies hidden, but to myself and others. *Sear my affections*[5] *and my heart.* Apply a remedial purge, like fire, to my desires and my thoughts, *because your mercy is before my eyes.* It is your mercy, not my own merits, that has led me to such a life; let me keep your mercy before my eyes, that I may not be consumed in your purging fire. *And in your truth I have become pleasing to you*, for though my own falsehood displeased me, your truth has given me pleasure, and so with it and in it I have myself become acceptable and pleasing to you.

Verses 4-5. Avoiding wicked company

4. *I have not sat down in the assembly of fools*, for I have not chosen to give my allegiance to those who try to contrive what is impossible to be happy

---

1. See Mt 10:22.
2. *Omni ecclesiae*; a variant supported by many witnesses is *homini ecclesiae*, "the man/person of the Church," to balance the "man/person Christ," above.
3. Variant: "my God."
4. Variant: "I shall not be weakened."
5. *Renes*: literally "kidneys" or "loins," the seat of the emotions in Hebrew idiom, as "heart" is of thought.

through the perfect enjoyment of transitory things.[6] *Neither will I go in with those who act unjustly*, nor will I keep my conscience out of sight as they do, for this is the root cause of all unjust actions.

5. *I hate the gatherings of rogues.* Those gangs of rogues I hate, for it is only a step from there into the assembly of fools. *And I will not sit with the ungodly.* That is why I will have no truck with any such assembly, or sit with the ungodly, by which I mean that I will give no consent to their plans. *I will not sit with the ungodly.*

Verses 6-7. Purity and praise

6. *I will wash my hands among the innocent*: in the company of innocent people I will see that all I do is clean; among the innocent I will wash these hands of mine with which I shall embrace your sublime truths.[7] *And I will take my place around your altar, O Lord.*[8]

7. *That I may hear the sound of your praise*, and so learn how to praise you; *and tell of all your wonderful deeds*, that having learned myself, I may relate your wonderful deeds.

Verses 8-9. The Lord's house

8. *Lord, I have loved the beauty of your house*, of your Church, that is, *and the place where your glory dwells*,[9] the place where you live and are glorified.

9. *Do not destroy*[10] *my soul with the ungodly*: I beg you not to destroy along with the ungodly this soul of mine which has loved the beauty of your house. *Nor my life with those who shed blood*, those who hate their neighbors. With these two commandments your house is adorned.[11]

Verse 10. Mercenary piety

10. *They in whose hands are wicked deeds.* I implore you, then, not to destroy me with the ungodly and the violent, whose deeds are wicked. *Their right hands are full of bribes*, for by imagining that religion should yield dividends[12] they

---

6. Variant: "by doing transient things."
7. *Sublimia tua*, "your sublime things," unspecified.
8. In his second Exposition of this psalm, Augustine reads "the altar of the Lord" in this verse.
9. Variant: "the tent of your dazzling brightness."
10. *Perdas.* A well-supported variant is *comperdas*, "destroy together with," which Augustine reads here in his second Exposition of this psalm.
11. See Mt 22:40.
12. See 1 Tm 6:5.

have misused what was given them to obtain eternal life, diverting it to acquire what this world can offer.

Verses 11-12. Walking in innocence and love

11. *But I have walked in my innocence; redeem me, and have mercy on me.* May the immense ransom-price of my Lord's blood purchase perfect freedom for me, and amid the perils of this life may your mercy not forsake me.

12. *My foot is planted in rectitude,*[13] for my loving choice has not swerved from your righteousness. *In the churches I will bless you, Lord,* for I will not hide your blessing, Lord, from those you have called,[14] because next to love of you I will add love of my neighbor.

---

13. Variant: "on the straight road."
14. Allusion to the Greek root of the word *ecclesia*, those who are "called out."

Exposition 2 of Psalm 25

A Sermon to the People

The old and the new natures

1. When Paul the apostle was being read, holy brethren,[1] we heard him say, *The truth, as it is in Jesus, demands that you lay aside the old self[2] that corresponded to your former way of life, the self which through its delusory lusts is sinking into death. Be renewed spiritually in your minds, and clothe yourselves in the new self who is created in the likeness of God, in the righteousness and holiness of truth.*[3] Now no one should suppose that some material object is to be laid aside, as you might take off your tunic, or that you must put on something from outside like a garment, as though you were laying aside one tunic and picking up another. A carnal interpretation like this would hinder people from applying Paul's instruction spiritually within themselves. He goes on to explain what it means to shed the old self and be clothed in the new, for the rest of this reading develops the same idea. He is speaking to some imaginary questioner who objects, "How can I take off the old and put on the new? Can it be that I am some third individual who is to set aside the old self which I had, and put on a new self I didn't have before? That would mean that there are three of us! There would have to be one in the middle who discards the old self and picks up the new one." But Paul goes on to spell it out, in case anyone who is hampered by so crude and literal an interpretation should fail to do what is being asked, and make the obscurity of the passage an excuse for doing nothing about it. He continues, *So then, set aside falsehood, and speak the truth.* This is what it means to take off the old self and be clothed in the new: *set aside falsehood, and speak the truth, each of you with your neighbor, for we are members of one another* (Eph 4:25).

---

1. *Sanctitas vestra*, literally "your holiness." Augustine often uses a similar idiom, especially *caritas vestra*, "your charity"; both phrases connote the dignity he recognized in the Christian people.
2. Literally "the old man," antithesis of the "new man" who is the whole human person regenerated in Christ. Augustine says this directly at the end of paragraph 4.
3. Eph 4:21-24, part of a reading for the day.

Pagan and Christian neighbor

2. None of you, dear brothers and sisters, should conclude that "speaking with your neighbor" means that you must tell the truth to a Christian, but are allowed to lie to a pagan. No, your neighbor is anyone descended like yourself from Adam and Eve. We are all neighbors by the fact of our earthly birth, but in quite another sense we are brothers and sisters by the hope of our heavenly inheritance. You should think of everyone as your neighbor, even before he or she is a Christian, for you do not know what that person is in God's sight, or what God's foreknowledge of him or her may be. It sometimes happens that the very people at whom you sneer because they are worshiping stone deities will turn and worship God, and perhaps more fervently than you, who were just now making fun of them. It is our neighbors who lie hidden in these people who are not yet in the Church. Come to think of it, there are others hiding in the Church who are far away from us. Since we do not know the future we should regard everyone as our neighbor, not only because of the condition of human mortality, by which we arrive in this world to share the common lot, but also on account of our hope of that inheritance, for we do not know what someone who just now was nothing may turn out to be.

Sunset

3. Concentrate now on the rest of this passage about putting on the new self and discarding the old. It goes on to tell us, *Set aside falsehood and speak the truth, each of you with your neighbor, for we are members of one another. Be angry, but do not sin.* If you are angry with your servant because he has done something wrong, you had better be angry with yourself too, lest you do wrong yourself. *Do not let the sun set on your wrath* (Eph 4:26). This can be understood to refer to time, brothers and sisters, for although anger creeps up on you in consequence of the human condition and the weakness of this mortal state we endure, it ought not to be nursed for a long time, nor should yesterday's anger last into today. Rid your heart of it before the fading of the daylight you can see, lest the invisible light desert you. But there is an alternative and equally good interpretation. Our sun is Christ, the sun of righteousness,[4] Christ the Truth. He is not the sun which is worshiped by pagans and Manicheans, and is plain for even sinners to see; he is that other sun by whose truth human nature is enlightened, and angels are gladdened. The eyes of our hearts are dazzled by the brightness of its rays because of our human weakness, but they are purified by keeping the commandments until they are able to contemplate it. When this sun begins to live in you through faith, the anger which wells up inside you should not be so

---

4. See Mal 4:2; Lk 1:78.

strong as to let *the sun set on your wrath*, so strong, that is, as to drive Christ out of your soul because he does not want to live with your anger. It looks as though he is setting on you, but really you are sinking down away from him, because anger, once it becomes entrenched, turns into hatred, and once you are hating, you are already a murderer. *Everyone who hates a brother or sister is a murderer*, says the apostle John, and he also warns that *anyone who hates a brother or sister remains in darkness* (1 Jn 3:15; 2:9). It is hardly surprising that anyone on whom the sun has set remains in the dark.

Riding the storm by faith

4. Something you heard in the gospel perhaps also has a bearing on this: *the boat was in peril on the lake, yet Jesus was asleep* (Lk 8:23). We are sailing across what you might call a lake, and there are plenty of gales and storms. Our craft is almost swamped by the daily temptations of this world. Why is this? It can only be because Jesus is asleep. If Jesus were not asleep in you, you would not be battered by such storms; you would enjoy inner calm, Jesus and you keeping watch together. What does this mean: "Jesus is asleep"? Your faith, which derives from Jesus, has nodded off. Storms are blowing up on your lake: you see the wicked flourishing, the good people struggling; this is temptation, a great swell. Your soul says,[5] "O God, is this your justice, that the bad people should do well and the good have such a struggle?" You cry out to God, "Is this your justice?" And God says to you, "Is this your faith? Was this what I promised you, and did you become a Christian for this prosperity in this world? Are you tormented because the people who flourish here are the wicked, who will be tormented with the devil hereafter?[6] How can you ask such questions? Why are you tossed about by the billowing waves of the lake and the storm? Because Jesus is asleep; that is, because the faith that derives from Jesus has gone to sleep in your heart."

What are you to do? Wake Jesus up, and say, *"Master, we are perishing!* (Lk 8:24). The currents in the lake are treacherous, and we are sinking." He will wake up, your faith will come back to you, and with his help you will reflect that the things that are given to bad people now will not stay with them. Good things either desert them while they are still alive, or are left behind when they die. But what is promised to you will last for ever. What is granted to them within time is suddenly snatched away. It has flowered like grass. For all flesh is grass; the grass withers and its flower wilts, but the word of the Lord abides for ever.[7] So

---

5. Variant: "expresses doubt."
6. A variant has: "Was this why you became a Christian, in order to prosper in this world, and hereafter, in the world to come, be tormented in the utmost misery?"
7. See Is 40:6, 8.

put behind you what fades, and set your face toward what endures. Now that Christ is already waking up, the storm will not shake your heart, the waves will not sink your boat, because your faith dominates the winds and the waves, and the danger will pass. Everything the apostle says about taking off the old nature teaches the same lesson: *be angry, but do not sin; do not let the sun set on your wrath, and do not give the devil an opportunity.* The old self did; the new must not. *Let anyone who was a thief steal no more* (Eph 4:26-28). The old self did steal, but the new must not. It is the same person; it is one person: one who was Adam, but must now be Christ. What was old must now be new.

The threshing-floor

5. But let us look a little more closely at the psalm, because when anyone makes progress in the Church, putting up with the wicked in the Church is unavoidable. Such a person may not notice them much, even though many of the wicked complain about the wicked: it is like the way a healthy person can more easily put up with two invalids than two invalids can tolerate each other. Still, my brothers and sisters, I want to warn you about this. The Church in the present age is a threshing-floor. We have said often, and continue to repeat it, that there are both husks and wheat in it. Nobody must expect all the chaff to disappear before winnowing-time. Nor should anyone abandon the threshing-floor before the time for winnowing, tired of putting up with sinners. Anyone who does that should be careful not to be caught outside the threshing-floor and snapped up by birds before ever reaching the granary. Pay attention, brothers and sisters, to my reasons for saying this. At the beginning of the threshing process the grains can't even touch each other, because the husks get in the way. It is as though they don't know each other, because of the intervening chaff. And anyone who looks at the threshing-floor from a distance thinks that there is nothing there but chaff. Unless we look more carefully, and stretch out a hand, and blow on it so that our breath separates them, it is difficult to distinguish the grains.

It can happen, then, that the grains seem to be separated from each other, and not touching, and so each one who is making progress imagines that he or she is alone. It was this thought that tempted Elijah, great man though he was, and, as the apostle Paul relates, Elijah said to God, *"They have slain your prophets and overthrown your altars. I alone remain, and they are after my life too."* And what is God's reply to him? *"I have kept for myself seven thousand men who have not bent their knees to Baal"* (Rom 11:3-4; compare 1 Kgs 19:10,18). Notice that God did not say to him, "You have two or three others like yourself." What he did say was, "Do not imagine that you are alone. There are seven thousand others, and you think you are the only one!"

This, then, is the brief warning I want to give you, and began to give you just now. Please give me your complete attention, holy brethren,[8] and may God's mercy be in our hearts, so that you may understand what I have to say and it may bear fruit and work in you. Listen, it will only take a moment. Whoever is still bad must not think that there is no one who is good; and anyone who is good must not think he or she is the only one. Have you grasped that? Look, I'll say it again. Can't you see what I'm getting at? Any who are still bad, who examine their consciences and can only bring back an unfavorable report, must not think that there is nobody who is good; and anyone who is good should not think that he or she alone is good; and anyone who is good should not be afraid to be mixed in with the bad, because the time for sorting out will come. This is the very thing we have sung about today: *Do not destroy my soul with the ungodly, nor my life with those who shed blood.* What does that mean *Do not destroy my soul with the ungodly*? "Do not destroy it at the same time." I presume that the psalmist is saying to God, "As things are, you bear with all of us together, but do not destroy us all together, all of us whom you tolerate together now." This is the whole thrust of the psalm, and I want to examine it briefly with you, holy brethren, because it is only a short one.

Verse 1. Spiritual staggers

6. *Judge me, Lord.* The psalmist makes a risky, even a dangerous prayer for himself: that he be judged. What is this judgment he desires? He wants to be separated from the wicked. In another place he speaks openly about a discriminating judgment: *Judge me, O God, and distinguish my cause from that of an unholy people* (Ps 42(43):1). This clarifies what he means by *judge*. He is afraid that good and bad may go into eternal fire together, with no sorting out, seeing that at present both good and bad crowd into the Church together. *Judge me, Lord.* Why? Because *I have walked in my innocence, and with my hope set on the Lord, I shall not be moved.* What is meant by *with my hope set on the Lord*? Whoever does not hope in the Lord staggers unsteadily among the wicked; this is how schisms came about. Some were alarmed at finding themselves among bad people,[9] although they were still worse themselves; they decided they did not want to be good among the bad. If only they were genuine wheat! If they were, they would put up with the chaff on the threshing-floor right through to the time of winnowing. But because they were chaff, the wind blew too soon, before the time for winnowing, and whisked the chaff away and threw it among thorns. The chaff was blown away from there, certainly; but does that mean that only wheat

---

8. See note on paragraph 1.
9. The Donatists, who believed that they were the pure; see note at Exposition of Psalm 10, 1.

was left? The only thing that flies away in advance of winnowing-time is chaff, but what is left is both wheat and chaff. The chaff will be winnowed away when the time for winnowing comes. This is what the psalmist says: *I have walked in my innocence, and with my hope set on the Lord I shall not be moved.* If I set my hope on a human being, perhaps I shall from time to time see that person living sinfully, not keeping to the good ways he has learned or taught in the Church but drifting into those he has picked up under the devil's tutelage. And then, because my hope is set on a human being like myself, once that person totters my hope will totter too, and when he falls I shall fall. But because my hope is fixed in the Lord, I shall not be moved.

Verse 2. God's purgative fire

7. The psalm continues, *Examine me, Lord, and try me; sear my affections and my heart.* What does that mean, *sear my affections*[10] *and my heart*? Burn my pleasures, burn my thoughts (he put "heart" for his thoughts, and "affections" for his pleasures), and so prevent me from thinking evil, and let no evil thing give me pleasure. But how are you going to burn my affections? With the fire of your Word.[11] And how will you burn my heart? With the heat of your Spirit, of which scripture says elsewhere, *No one can hide from his heat* (Ps 18:7(19:6)). And of this same fire the Lord says, *I have come to set fire to the earth* (Lk 12:49).

Verse 3. Pleasing God within

8. And so it continues, *Because your mercy is before my eyes, and in your truth I have become pleasing to you,* which is to say, I have not sought human approbation, but only to please you within myself, where you see; I have no fear of incurring disapproval where human beings see. So too the apostle Paul says, *Let each of us examine his own work, and then it is only within ourselves that we will have credit, not in the eyes of others* (Gal 6:4).

Verses 4-5. Real and apparent participation

9. *I have not sat down in the assembly of fools,* he says. You must all listen carefully, holy brethren, to what this phrase means, *I have not sat down.* He means, "As God sees it, I have not sat down." There are times when, although you are not actually in an assembly, you are sitting there. For instance, you are not seated in the theatre, but you are thinking about the theatre, and it is against

---

10. Literally "kidneys."
11. Or "your word"; but the immediate parallel with "Spirit" suggests that the passage has a Trinitarian reference.

such thoughts that the psalm prays, *Sear my affections*, for you are sitting there in your heart, even though you are not there in body. On the other hand it may happen that someone takes hold of you[12] and you are hustled along willy-nilly; or again some honorable duty has you sitting there. How could that happen? Well, perhaps a servant of God has to sit in the amphitheatre to do an act of kindness, wishing to set free some gladiator or other, and obliged to sit there and wait until the one to be freed comes out. There you have it! A person like that has not sat down in the assembly of fools, even when sitting there in body as far as outward appearances go. What is sitting down? Compliance and collusion with those who are sitting down there. If you have not complied, even though you were present, you have not sat down there; if you have complied, even though absent, you have sat down there. *Neither will I go in with those who act unjustly.*[13] *I hate the gatherings of rogues* (so, you see, it means inward participation), *and I will not sit with the ungodly.*

Verse 6. Hand-washing

10. *I will wash my hands among the innocent*, but not with ordinary, everyday water. You wash your hands when in the sight of God you think responsibly and innocently about your activities, because there is another altar in God's presence, to which that priest who first offered himself for us made his entrance.[14] There is a heavenly altar, and none take their places around it except those who wash their hands among the innocent. Many who are unworthy touch this altar here, and God allows his sacraments to be profaned for the time being. But do you really think, brothers and sisters, that the heavenly Jerusalem will be like this building here? You will certainly not be gathered into Abraham's embrace with the wicked, in the same way that you are received in the company of the wicked by the walls of this church. Do not be afraid then; just wash your hands. *And I will take my place around the Lord's altar,*[15] where you make your vows to

---

12. Perhaps as Alypius was drawn to the circus against his will, as Augustine relates in his *Confessions*, VI,8,13.

13. According to a note by the Maurists, reproduced here by the CCL editors, Augustine's omission of any mention of an episode at the Council of Carthage suggests that the present sermon was preached before June 411, when that Council was convened. As Augustine relates in his book addressed to the Donatist laity, *To the Donatists after the Council*, 5, the Donatist delegates refused to sit down with the Catholics, claiming that this psalm forbade sitting down with the ungodly. It was pointed out to them that on that reading they had sinned already by entering the chamber with the Catholics, since the psalm also says, *Neither will I go in with those who act unjustly*, and that both entering and sitting down together must be understood spiritually.

14. See Heb 6:20; 9:12.

15. In this place in his first Exposition of the psalm he reads *altare tuum, Domine*: "your altar, O Lord."

the Lord, where you pour out your prayers, where your conscience is pure, where you tell God who you are. And if when you are there you find anything within you that displeases God, the one to whom you make your confession puts it right. Wash your hands among the innocent, then, and take your place around the Lord's altar, so that you may hear the sound of his praise.

Verse 7. Hearing the voice of praise

11. For this is how the psalm continues: *that I may hear the sound of your praise, and tell of all your wonderful deeds*. What is meant by *that I may hear the sound of your praise*? It means, "that I may understand," for this is what hearing is, in God's presence, not as it is with the kind of sounds that many hear and many others do not. How many there are who listen to me, yet are deaf to God! And how many there are who have ears, but not the kind of ears Jesus spoke of when he said, *Let anyone who has ears for hearing listen!* (Mt 13:9). What is it, then, to hear the sound of praise? I will tell you if I can, with the help of the Lord's mercy and your prayers. To hear the sound of praise is to understand deep within yourself that whatever evil there is in you in consequence of your sins belongs to you, and whatever good there is in the setting right of those sins belongs to God. Hear the sound of praise in such a way that you do not praise yourself, even when you are good; for by praising yourself you become bad. Humility had made you good, pride makes you bad. You turned to God to be enlightened, and by turning you became full of light; you were made luminous by that act of turning. But which way did you turn? Surely not toward yourself? If you had had the possibility of being enlightened by turning toward yourself[16] it would have been impossible for you ever to have been in darkness, because you would always have been with yourself. Why have you been enlightened? Because you have turned toward something else, something that was not you. What is that something that is not you? God is light. You were not light, because you were a sinner. The apostle says to people he wanted to hear the sound of praise, *You were darkness once, but now you are light* (Eph 5:8). What does he mean by *you were darkness once*? He is referring to our old selves, of course. *But now you are light*, he continues, and not without good reason are you light, you who were darkness for so long; you are light only because you have been enlightened. Do not think that you yourself are the light; no, he is the Light, who enlightens everyone who comes into this world.[17] You of yourself, through your sinful will, through your turning away, were shrouded in darkness; but now you

---

16. *Sed quo? Numquid ad te? Si ad te conversus posses illuminari*. . . . The editors amend to *Sed a quo? Numquid a te? Si a te conversus*. . . : "But whose doing was that? Surely not your own? If you could have been converted by yourself. . . . "

17. See Jn 1:9.

are shining. But the apostle immediately added *in the Lord*, to protect them against pride, those people to whom he had just said, *Now you are light.* These are his words: *You were darkness once, but now you are light in the Lord.* So apart from the Lord, no light. But if you are light only because you are in the Lord, *what have you that you did not receive? And if you did receive it, why boast as though you had not?* (1 Cor 4:7). This is the question put by the same apostle in another letter to proud people who wanted to take credit to themselves for what was God's, and to boast of what good they had as though it were their own. *What have you that you did not receive?* he demanded. *And if you did receive it, why boast as though you had not?* He who has given to the humble takes away from the proud; being the giver, he has power to retract his gifts.

Brothers and sisters, the words of the psalm bear directly on this point I wonder if I have explained what I intended to: I have explained it as best I could, even if not as fully as I might have wished the psalm bears directly on the same point when it says, *I will wash my hands among the innocent, and I will take my place around your altar, O Lord, that I may hear the sound of your praise.* This is what it means: I shall not presume on myself, not even on any good I may have; I shall presume only on you who have given it to me. Let me not seek praise for it in myself, or as though it derived from me, but only as from you and in you. That is why he continues, *That I may hear the sound of your praise, and tell of all your wonderful deeds*: not mine, but yours.

Verses 8-9. Where God's glory dwells

12. Now, brothers and sisters, take a good look at this lover of God who presumes on God, set as he is amid the wicked, and begging God not to let him be destroyed along with them, since God does not err in his judgment. When you see a lot of people gathered in one place, you are apt to think they all deserve the same; but never fear, God is not deceived. Using the wind as your means of discernment, you separate chaff from wheat. You want the wind to blow for you; you yourself are not the wind, but you need the wind to blow for your purposes. Once you have shaken both together in your winnowing-shovel, the wind lifts the lightweight stuff and the heavy wheat remains. So you use the wind to effect the judgment on your threshing-floor. But does God[18] look for someone else to judge with him, to make sure that he does not destroy the good with the bad? Have no fear, then; if you are good, be at peace, even amid rogues. Say the words of the psalm: *Lord, I have loved the beauty of your house.* The Church is God's

---

18. *Quaeris ergo ventum ad iudicandam aream. Numquid Deus.* The editors amend to *Quando ergo venitur ad iudicandum aream, numquid Deus*: "But when the time comes for judgment to be exercised on the threshing-floor, does God . . . ?"

house. It still contains the wicked, but the beauty of God's house is in those who
are good, in the saints, and this is *the beauty of your house* which I have loved.
And the place where your glory dwells. What is this? I will try to show you that it
means the same thing as *the beauty of your house*, though it is somewhat
obscurely expressed. May the Lord help me, and may he at the same time sustain
the concentration of your hearts, inspired as it is by the same Lord. So what is
meant by *the place where your glory dwells*? First the psalmist spoke of *the
beauty of your house*, and now he explains what that beauty is by saying, *the
place where your glory dwells*. It is not enough to say, "The place where God
dwells"; he says, "The place where God's glory dwells." What is the glory of
God? I was speaking about it just now when I said that even people who are good
should boast not in themselves, but in the Lord.[19] For all have sinned, and need
the glory of God.[20] There are people in whom the Lord dwells in such a way that
even for the good things they have the Lord is glorified, and they have no wish to
attribute the good to themselves, or lay claim to what they have received as if it
were their own property. These people are part of the beauty of God's house.
Scripture would not trouble to mention them particularly for any other reason
than that there are also people who have a gift from God, yet want to boast not in
God but in themselves. They do indeed have a gift from God, but they do not
form part of the beauty of God's house. For those who do belong to the beauty of
his house, those in whom God's glory makes its home, they are the place where
his glory dwells. But in whom does the glory of God dwell? Only in those who so
boast as to glorify not themselves, but the Lord.

So then, because I have loved the beauty of your house, that is, all those who
are within it and seek your glory, and because I have not put my trust in any
human being, and have not conspired with the ungodly, and will not enter their
assembly or sit down with them; because this is how I have conducted myself in
God's Church, how will you reward me? The psalm suggests what we should
pray for: *Do not destroy my soul with the ungodly, nor my life with those who
shed blood.*

Verses 10-12. Bribing a judge

13. *They in whose hands are wicked deeds, their right hands are full of bribes.*
It is not only money that constitutes bribes, not only gold and silver, not only
presents. Nor is it the case that all who accept such things are taking bribes. It
sometimes happens that they are accepted by the Church. I mean, Peter accepted
them, our Lord accepted them, he even had a purse; and Judas helped himself to

---

19. See 1 Cor 1:31.
20. See Rom 3:23.

what was put into it.[21] What does it mean, then, to take bribes? It means to praise someone for the sake of what you can get out of him, to fawn upon him, to curry favor with him by flattery, or to pronounce unjust judgment for the sake of bribes. But what sort of bribes? Not only gold and silver and similar things. If a person who pronounces unjust judgment does so to win praise, he is doing it for a bribe, and one which is as worthless as could be imagined. His hand was wide open to receive commendation from another person's tongue, and he has forfeited the commendation of his own conscience. Clearly then, *they in whose hands are wicked deeds, their right hands are full of bribes.* You see, brothers and sisters, such people stand under God's judgment; and others who have no wicked deeds on their hands, whose right hands are not full of bribes, they stand under God's judgment too, and they can only say to God, "You know." They can only say to God, *Do not destroy my soul with the ungodly, nor my life with those who shed blood,* for God alone can see that they do not accept bribes. Take an example: it so happens that two people have filed a law suit before a servant of God.[22] No one would admit that any cause other than his own was just, for were he to think his own cause unjust he would not be looking for a judge. One party thinks he has a just cause, and so does the other. They come before the judge. Before any verdict is given, both of them say, "We accept your judgment; whatever you decide, we will in no circumstances reject it." You, then, what do you say? "Pass whatever judgment you like, but simply pass judgment. If I resist it in any way, a curse be on me." Both are friendly toward the judge before he gives his decision. But when judgment is pronounced, it will be against one party, and neither of them knows against which. If, however, he tries to please both, what he gets as his bribe is the praise of others; and once he has accepted that gift, look what a gift he is losing! He receives something that makes a noise and then fades away; he loses what is spoken and never passes away. The word of God is always being uttered, and never passes away; the word of someone like you or me passes away as soon as it has been uttered. So the judge grasps at what is empty and loses what is enduring. But if he attends to God, he will pronounce against one party or the other, keeping God in mind, for God is the judge under whom he pronounces it.

Now it may be that this judgment cannot be overturned, because it is upheld by the law, not Church law perhaps, but that of secular rulers who have conceded to the Church that anything decided in an ecclesiastical court cannot be undone.[23] If the judge's decision cannot be overturned, then, the unsuccessful party is now unwilling to look honestly at himself; instead he regards the judge

---

21. See Jn 12:6.
22. The bishop, as appears from the following. Hearing judicial suits was a heavy burden for a Christian bishop in Augustine's day.
23. So The Code of Theodosius, XVI, section *On episcopal judgment.*

with a jaundiced eye and does his best to slander him. "He wanted to please the other fellow," he alleges. "He was prejudiced in favor of a rich man, or he received something from him, or he was afraid to antagonize him." So he accuses the judge of taking bribes. But suppose a poor person had a case against a rich person, and judgment was given in the poor person's favor, the rich party would still say, "The judge was bribed." What bribe could a poor person offer? "Well," replies the aggrieved party, "he saw that the person in question was poor, and to avoid getting a bad name for deciding against a poor defendant he suppressed justice, and gave his decision in contravention of the truth." One way or another, this is bound to be alleged, so you see that it is only in the presence of God, who alone sees who is accepting bribes, and who is not, that anyone who does not take them can say, *"I have walked in my innocence; redeem me, and have mercy on me. My foot is planted in rectitude.* I am battered on every side by the opposition and hostility of those who in their human arrogance find fault with my judgment, but *my foot is planted in rectitude."* In what sense, *in rectitude*? Because earlier the psalmist had said, *With my hope set on the Lord, I shall not be moved.*

Deeds and words

14. How does the psalm end? *In the churches I will bless you, Lord.* I will not bless myself in the churches, as though placing my confidence in people like myself; it is you I shall bless by everything I do. This is what it means to bless God in the churches, brothers and sisters: to live in such a way that through the behavior of each one of us God may be blessed, for those who bless the Lord verbally, but curse him by their deeds, do not bless God in the churches. Nearly all bless him with their lips, but not all with their deeds. Some bless with their voices, some by their behavior. But people whose behavior is inconsistent with what they say cause God to be blasphemed, with the result that those who do not yet enter the Church use their immoral Christian acquaintances as an excuse for not doing so, although their real reason is that they are attached to their sins and do not want to be Christians. They flatter and delude themselves, saying, "Why are you trying to persuade me to become a Christian? I have been cheated by a Christian, and I've never done that to anyone myself. It was a Christian who broke his word to me, and I've never done that to anyone either." And when they talk like this they are held back from salvation, and so the fact that they are only moderately bad (not really good, of course) is of no advantage to them. For just as it is of no advantage to anyone to open his eyes if he is in darkness, so it is of no advantage to be in daylight if his eyes are shut. Similarly with pagans (I speak only of those pagans who seem to lead upright lives): their eyes may be open but they are in darkness, because they do not acknowledge the Lord as their light, whereas Christians who live evil lives are certainly in the light, and no other light

than God's, but their eyes are closed. Signed with God's name and placed in his light,[24] they are no better than blind men, because by their sinful way of life they refuse to see him, and so no vision of the true light brings them life.

---

24. A baptismal allusion.

Exposition 1 of Psalm 26

Verse 1. God the protector

1. *For David himself, before he was anointed.*[1] Christ's raw recruit, approaching faith, speaks these words: *The Lord is my light and my salvation; whom shall I fear?* The Lord will give me both knowledge of himself and salvation; who will take me from him? *The Lord is the protector of my life; from whom shall I shrink?* The Lord will fend off all the onslaughts of my enemy, and every insidious attack, and I shall shrink in fear from no one.

Verse 2. Enemies try to deter me

2. *While the malevolent approach me, to eat my flesh*: with harmful intent they come close, to identify me and insult me, to assert their superiority even while I am changing for the better;[2] may their malicious teeth devour not me but my carnal desires instead. *My enemies, who afflict me*: not those only who trouble me by rebuking me in a friendly spirit, to make me pull back from what I have decided to do, but my real enemies as well, *have themselves weakened and fallen*, for while they act so, bent on upholding their own opinions, they have become too weak to believe in better things; and they have begun to hate the message of salvation, in accordance with which I am taking this course that displeases them.

Verse 3. Enemies encamped

3. *Though their camp make a stand against me, my heart will not fear.* Though a crowd of them speak and conspire against me, my heart will not be so fearful as to flee over to their side. *Even if war is declared against me, my hope will be in this*[3] petition which I am framing, for on it I will fix my hope, even though the world's persecution break out against me.

---

1. Literally "smeared." See Augustine's explanation at the beginning of his second Exposition of this psalm.
2. The editors suggest, " . . . superiority, but you have changed me for the better."
3. *In hac*, i.e. in the petition he is about make; but a variant is *in hoc*: "even in this circumstance I will hope."

Verse 4. Longing for the vision of God

4. *One thing have I begged of the Lord, and that will I seek after,* for one single petition I have made to the Lord, and that one I shall pursue: *to live in the Lord's house all the days of my life,* so that as long as I am in this life, no adversity may estrange me from the company of those who uphold the unity and truth of faith in the Lord, all the world over.[4] *That I may contemplate the Lord's delight,* to this end: as I continue steadfast in faith may the delightful vision appear to me, that I may see God face to face, *and I, his temple, may be protected.*[5] When death has been swallowed up in victory[6] I shall be clothed in immortality, being made his temple.

Verses 5-6. Firm faith, joy in God's protection

5. *For he has hidden me in his tent*[7] *on the day of my troubles.* He has hidden me under the dispensation of his incarnate Word at the time when temptations abound, these trials that beset my mortal life. *He has protected me in the hidden recesses of his tabernacle:* he has protected me, for I believe in my heart, and that will be reckoned to me as righteousness.[8]

6. *He has set me up on a rock.* That my believing may be manifest, and lead to my salvation, he has set it high up on his own unshakable strength. *See now, he has raised my head above my enemies.* What can he be reserving for me to the end, if even now when my body is dead because of sin,[9] yes, even now I feel that my mind is obedient to the law of God, and is not captive under the rebellious law of sin?[10] *I have traveled round, and now I have offered*[11] *in his tent a sacrifice of great joy,* for I have looked all round the world that is faithful to Christ; and with great rejoicing I have praised God for humbling himself for our sake within time, knowing that with such a sacrifice he is well pleased. *I will sing and play the lyre to the Lord,* rejoicing in the Lord with both heart and deed.

---

4. Typically, he thinks of "the Lord's house" not as a building, but as the company of those united with the Lord by faith and charity.
5. Variants: "may be protected by his temple / by his holy temple."
6. See 1 Cor 15:54.
7. *Tabernaculo,* a tent for augury, or for campaigning in war, but also the tent where God camped with his people during their desert march, and ordered to be pitched for him when the temple was built by Solomon. The following mention of "his incarnate Word" suggests that Jn 1:14 is in mind: "The Word was made flesh, and pitched his tent among us."
8. See Rom 10:10.
9. See Rom 8:10.
10. See Rom 7:22-23.
11. Variant: "I will travel round and offer."

Verses 7-8. Heartfelt plea: "Let me see your face"

7. *Hearken, Lord, to the voice with which I have cried*[12] *to you*: hearken, Lord, to the inner cry which I have addressed to your ears with full force. *Have mercy on me, and hearken to me*: have mercy on me, and hearken to me in this entreaty.

8. *To you my heart has spoken: I have sought your face, O Lord.* I have not paraded myself before other men and women, but in a secret place, where you alone can hear, my heart said to you, "I have asked you for no reward other than yourself, but have sought only your face. *I will look for your face, Lord.*" I will press on with determination in this quest, for it is not any worthless thing I look for, Lord, but your countenance only, that I may love you freely. Nothing more precious than that can I find.

Verse 9. Do not turn your face away, O God

9. *Do not turn your face away from me*, but let me find what I am seeking. *Do not turn away in anger from your servant*, lest while looking for you I fall in with something else, for what punishment could be heavier to bear for one who loves you, and seeks the reality of your face, than your turning away? *Be my helper, I beg.* If you do not help me, when will I find it? *Do not forsake me or despise me, O God, my salvation.* Do not scorn a mortal's search for what is eternal, for you, O God, heal the wound of my sin.

Verse 10. Being abandoned by the world

10. *My father and mother have abandoned me.* The kingdom of this world, the city of this world,[13] from which I was born in time and in this mortal state, have abandoned me as I search for you; I disdain the things they were promising because they could not give what I am seeking, and so they want nothing to do with me. *But the Lord has taken me up*, the Lord who himself can give himself to me; he has adopted me.

Verse 11. Directions for the way

11. *Appoint for me a law in your way, Lord.* As I strive to reach you, as I begin to make this great declaration of intent, that I will attain to wisdom and leave fear

---

12. Variant: "shall cry."
13. A theme he was to develop later in *The City of God.* The city of this world is pitted against God's reign, God's city.

behind,[14] appoint a law for me in your pathway, Lord, and do not let me go astray, do not leave me untaught. *Guide me along a straight path, because of my enemies.* Guide me along those straight and narrow ways; it is not enough merely to set out, for my foes will not relent until I reach journey's end.

Verse 12. Enemies try to throw me off course

12. *Do not deliver me to the will of those who harass me,* do not allow them to feast on my misfortunes. *Unjust witnesses have come forward against me;* they have risen up against me with their false allegations, to deflect me and call me back away from you, as though I were seeking human commendation. *And iniquity has lied to itself,* taking pleasure in its own falsehood. But it has not thrown me off course; a yet greater reward in heaven has been promised to me as a result.

Verse 13. The land of the living

13. *I believe that I shall see the good things of the Lord in the land of the living.* Because my Lord suffered these trials first, I believe that if I too despise the tongues of these dying[15] people—dying, because *a lie in the mouth kills the soul* (Wis 1:11)—then *I shall see the good things of the Lord in the land of the living,* where there is no room for falsity.

Verse 14. Holding out courageously

14. *Hold out for the Lord; act manfully; let your heart be strong, and hold out[16] for the Lord.* But when will he come? How long must the endurance last? It is a hard thing to ask of a mortal, and too slow for a lover to bear. But listen to a voice that cannot deceive, a voice that says, *Hold out for the Lord.* Endure the searing of your affections bravely, bear with courage the searing of your heart.[17] Do not suppose your desire has been denied you, because you do not possess it yet. If you are tempted to give up in despair, look what the psalm says: *Hold out for the Lord.*

---

14. Several codices have the variant, ". . . to reach you, as I attain to this great declaration of intent, and begin to progress toward wisdom, leaving fear behind. . . . "

15. *Morientium,* "dying;" a variant is *mentientium,* "lying."

16. *Sustine,* a much stronger verb than the English "wait for." *Sustinere* means "hold out, hold on, endure, support, maintain, withstand." The translation "manfully" has been retained here for *viriliter* because of Augustine's comment on the point in his second *Exposition* of this psalm, paragraph 23, where his view on inclusive language is made clear.

17. See Exposition 2 of Psalm 25,7.

Exposition 2 of Psalm 26

A Sermon to the People

Our voice and God's

1. The Lord our God is here speaking to us in a comforting way, because he sees that by his just judgment it is only in the sweat of our brows that we eat our bread;[1] and so he has deigned to speak to us from our own situation, to show us that he not only created us but also dwells in us. With regard to the words of this psalm which we have just heard, and partly sung, we cannot say simply that they are our words, because then we would need to be concerned whether we were telling the truth, for they are more properly the words of the Spirit of God than our own. On the other hand, if we deny that they are ours, we are lying, for there is no groaning unless from those who toil; and we would be forced to say that this whole psalm, full of grief and tears as it is, could be uttered by him who is never capable of being miserable. The Lord is merciful; we are miserable. But the merciful Lord has deigned to speak to the miserable, and he deigns also to use the voice of the miserable. In this sense both statements are true: that it is our voice here and not our voice, that it is the voice of the Spirit of God and not his voice. It is the voice of the Spirit of God, because we would not be speaking these words if he did not inspire us; but it is not his, because he is not wretched, nor is he toiling. Yet these are the groans of people who are wretched and do toil. On the other hand, they are ours, because these words give expression to our misery; yet not ours, because our entitlement even to groan is the gift of God.

Verse 1. Anointing the body of Christ

2. *A psalm of David, before he was smeared*. This is what the title of the psalm says, *a psalm of David before he was smeared*, that is, before he was anointed; for he was anointed as king. In his days only kings and priests were anointed; at that time they only were anointed persons. In these two was prefigured the one future king and priest, the one Christ with both functions; and he was given the title "Christ" in virtue of his anointing.[2] But not only was our Head anointed; his body

---

1. See Gn 3:19.
2. The Hebrew *mašiah*, anointed one, was translated into Greek as Χριστός, whence the name "Christ."

was too, we ourselves. He is king because he reigns over us and leads us; priest because he intercedes on our behalf.[3] What is more, he alone is priest in such a way as to be also the sacrifice. He offered to God a sacrifice that was nothing other than himself. He could not find a totally pure victim, endowed with reason, apart from himself. He is like a spotless lamb who redeemed us by his own spilt blood, uniting us into one body with himself and making us his members, so that in him we too are Christ. This is why anointing is proper to all Christians, even though in earlier times under the Old Covenant it was given to two kinds of persons only. From this it is obvious that we are the body of Christ, being all anointed. In him all of us belong to Christ, but we are Christ too, because in some sense the whole Christ is Head and body. This anointing will make us spiritually perfect in the life which is promised to us.

This psalm is the cry of one who longs for that life, who longs for that grace of God which will be perfected in us at the end. That is why it is entitled, *before he was smeared.* We are anointed now in the sacrament,[4] and by the sacrament what we will be in the future is prefigured. We must long for that ineffable and indefinable future blessing, and groan while we receive it sacramentally, so that we may rejoice in the very reality of which the sacrament gives us a foretaste.

The Lord is light and salvation

3. See now what the psalmist has to say. *The Lord is my light and my salvation; whom shall I fear?* He enlightens me, let the darkness roll back; he saves me, let all infirmity be banished. Now that I walk firmly in the light, whom shall I fear? God does not give the sort of salvation that could be snatched away by anyone else, nor is the light such that anyone else could overshadow it. It is the Lord who enlightens, we are enlightened; it is the Lord who saves, we are the saved. So then, if he enlightens and we are enlightened, if he saves and we are saved, it follows that without him we are darkness and weakness. But when we have a hope in him that is sure and fixed and true, whom shall we fear? The Lord is your illumination, the Lord is your salvation. Go on! Find someone more powerful, and be afraid! I belong so thoroughly to the most powerful one of all, to him who is all-powerful, that he both enlightens me and saves me; I shall fear no one except him. *The Lord is the protector of my life; from whom shall I shrink?*

---

3. See Rom 8:34.

4. From the earliest Christian times anointing was part of the rites of initiation at baptism. By the fourth century a separate rite of confirmation was common, consisting of the laying on of hands or anointing, or both, and was usually reserved to the bishop.

Verse 2. Even our flesh will be safe

4. *While the malevolent approach me to eat my flesh, my enemies who afflict me have themselves weakened and fallen.* What have I to fear, then; of whom shall I be afraid? From whom or what shall I shrink? My pursuers themselves are weakened and falling. But why are they pursuing me? *To eat my flesh.* What is my flesh? My carnal sensibilities. Let them rage and pursue me to their hearts' content; nothing in me dies except what is mortal. There will be some part of me to which my persecutor cannot penetrate, that place where God dwells. Let them eat my flesh if they want to! Once it is consumed, I shall be spirit, and spiritual. Indeed, so great a salvation does my Lord promise me that even this mortal flesh, which is apparently delivered[5] into the hands of my persecutors, will not perish for ever. What has been clearly shown in the resurrection of my Head is what all the members of his body must hope for. Whom should my soul fear, when already God dwells in it? Whom should my flesh fear, when the corruptible body is destined to put on incorruption?[6] Do you want to be assured that although our persecutors eat flesh, there is yet nothing for even our flesh itself to fear? *It is sown an animal body; it will rise a spiritual body* (1 Cor 15:44). How great must be the faith of one who is able to say, *The Lord is my light and my salvation, whom shall I fear? The Lord is the protector of my life, from whom shall I shrink?* An emperor is protected by shield-bearing troops, and he has no fear—a mortal by mortals, yet he feels safe. Can a mortal protected by the Immortal be afraid, then, and shrink from danger?

Verse 3. What can be taken away?

5. Listen, all of you, and mark how great his confidence must be, who can say, *Though their camp make a stand against me, my heart will not fear.* A camp is well fortified, but what is better fortified than God? *Even if war is declared against me. . .* , well what does war do to me? Can it deprive me of my hope? Can it deprive me of what the Almighty gives? Just as the one who gives cannot be defeated, so what he gives cannot be taken away. If what is given can be taken away, the donor is defeated. Therefore, my brothers and sisters, not even the gifts we receive in the temporal sphere can be taken away from us by anyone except the One who gave them. The spiritual gifts he grants he does not take away, unless you throw them away. Carnal and temporal things he does take away, because whoever else takes them away does so because God delegates to him or her the power to do so. We know this, and we have read in the Book of

---

5. A variant has "is apparently destroyed."
6. See 1 Cor 15:53.

Job[7] that not even that being who seems to exercise the greatest power for a while, the devil, can do anything except with God's permission. He received power over insignificant things, and lost the greatest and most important. What he has is not the power of an angry tyrant, but only the punishment of one who is condemned. Not even Satan can have any power, then, except by God's permission. We have this both in the Book of Job, which I mentioned, and in the gospel, where the Lord says, *This very night Satan has asked to sift[8] all of you like wheat; but I have prayed for you,[9] Peter, that your[10] faith may not fail* (Lk 22:31-32). Permission is granted to him, then, either for our punishment or for our testing. Since nobody can take away from us what God gives, let us not be afraid of anyone other than God. Whatever other rumblings there are, whatever other proud force rears up against us, let our hearts not be afraid.

Verse 4. Tent and home

6. *Even if war is declared against me, my hope will be in this.*[11] In what? *One thing[12] have I begged of the Lord.* He has referred to one thing in the feminine gender, as if to say, "one petition."[13] This is an idiomatic way of speaking. *One thing*, he says, *have I begged of the Lord, and that will I seek after.* Let us see what he asks for, this person who has nothing to fear. Great security of heart. Do you want to have nothing to fear? Then seek this one thing, the one thing which he who fears nothing seeks, or which he seeks in order to have nothing to fear. *One thing have I begged of the Lord, and that will I seek after.* Evidently we are concerned here with people well on the way. What is it, what is this one thing? *To live in the Lord's house all the days of my life.* This is the one thing, for the place where we will abide for ever is called a house or a home. Our dwelling while we are on pilgrimage is sometimes referred to as a house, but is more correctly called a tent. A tent is where people live who are on the move, those who are engaged in some kind of military service and fighting against an enemy. When, therefore, there is a tent in this life, there must clearly be an enemy. Having tents together is called being tent-companions,[14] and you know that is the name given to active soldiers. Here in the present, then, we have a tent, but hereafter a home. But even this tent is occasionally called a house by incorrect usage based on their similarity, and a house is

---

7. See Jb 1.
8. *Cribraret,* "sift"; some codices have *vexaret,* "shake."
9. Singular.
10. Singular.
11. Feminine singular.
12. Feminine singular.
13. Feminine.
14. *Contubernales.*

sometimes in the same way called a tent. However, correctly speaking, the one we look forward to is our home, the one we live in now is a tent.

Felicity

7. If you wonder what we may be doing in that house, you find another psalm expressing it clearly: *Blessed are they who dwell in your house; they will praise you for ever and ever* (Ps 83:5(84:4)). The psalmist here is aflame with greed, one might almost say. Burning with love, he longs to live all the days of his life in the house of the Lord, to spend all those days in the Lord's house not as days which must come to an end, but as eternal days. "Days" are spoken of in the same way as "years," and of them scripture says, *Your years will not fail* (Ps 101:28(102:27)). The days of eternal life are one day, on which the sun never sets. So this is what the psalmist is saying to the Lord: "I have longed for this, I have asked for this one thing, this I will seek." Now suppose we were to ask him, "What will you be doing there? What will your joy be? What diversion will there be for the heart? How will you amuse yourself? Where will your joy come from? You will not last long there if you are not happy, but what will provide you with happiness?" Here on earth we find happiness in various things, all sorts of human happiness, and people are called unhappy when what they love is taken away from them. People love a wide variety of things, and when they are seen to have what they love, they are deemed happy. But the person who is truly happy is not so much the one who has what he or she loves, but the one who loves what is worthy of love; for there are many who are made more unhappy by having what they love than by being without it. They are made unhappy by loving harmful things, and more unhappy still by possessing them. When our love is of the wrong sort, God is doing us a kindness by refusing us what we love; but when he gives to those who love wrongfully it is a mark of his anger. Paul states this clearly: *God has delivered them to the lusts of their own hearts* (Rom 1:24). So God gave them what they set their hearts on, but to their condemnation. Then again you find God refusing a request: *Three times I begged the Lord to take it away from me*, Paul says, referring to the sting of the flesh, *but he said to me, "My grace is sufficient for you, for my power finds complete scope in weakness"* (2 Cor 12:8-9). Clearly, then, he gave the former over to the lusts of their hearts, but denied the apostle Paul what he prayed for. To the one he gave, but only to condemn them; to Paul he refused what he wanted, to his ultimate good health. When we love what God wants us to love, without a shadow of doubt he will give it to us. This is that one thing which should be loved, that we may dwell in the Lord's house all the days of our life.

The Good from which all good derives

8. In our earthly dwellings men and women like to have different sorts of luxuries and comforts, and each one wants to live in a house where the mind will find nothing to offend it, and many things to give it pleasure. If the things that once gave pleasure are taken away, the inhabitants want to move elsewhere. Let us ask more probing questions, and let the psalmist tell us what he, and we ourselves, will be doing in that house, where he desires, longs, yearns and prays to dwell all the days of his life, as the one petition he makes to the Lord. Excuse me, but what do you intend to do there? What is it that you so long for? Listen to the answer: *"To contemplate the Lord's delight.* Now you can see what I love, now you can see why I want to dwell in the Lord's house all my days." It offers something wonderful, the chance to contemplate the Lord's own joy. Once their own night is over, mortal lovers long to be immovably established in God's light. Then will be our morning, when night has passed; this is why a psalmist says elsewhere, *In the morning I will stand before you and contemplate* (Ps 5:5(3)). At present I do not contemplate you, because I have fallen over; in the time to come I shall stand up and gaze. This is the human cry. The human race has fallen, but had we not fallen the one who was to raise us up would not have been sent. We fell, he came down. He ascended, we are lifted up, because nobody has gone up to heaven except the one who descended.[15] We who came crashing down are lifted up, because he who came down is raised on high. We should not lose hope because he ascended alone, for he raises us up, even us, to whom he descended as we were falling. We shall stand before him and contemplate, and the greatest delight will be ours to enjoy, delight beyond measure.

Now as I said all this you cried out in longing for a beauty not seen as yet. Let your heart stretch beyond all familiar things, let its gaze go beyond all the things you are accustomed to think about which are derived from the flesh, all the thoughts drawn out from the fleshly senses and any kind of fantasies. Drive the whole lot out of your mind; whatever presents itself to your thoughts, turn it down. Recognize the weakness of your heart, and whatever occurs to you, say of it, "That is not the real thing, for if it had been, I could not even have imagined it." In this way you will be desiring something good. What sort of good? The Good of all good, from which all good derives, the Good to which nothing can be added to explain what goodness is.[16] For a person is described as good, and a field as good, and a house as good, and an animal as good, and a tree as good, and a body as good, and a soul as good; and every time you said "good," you added something. But there is a simple good, sheer Goodness-Itself, in virtue of which all things are good, the Good itself from which all good things derive their goodness. This is the delight of the Lord, this is what we shall contemplate. Now, brothers and sisters, if the things which are called good

---

15. See Jn 3:13.
16. In Platonic terms, the Form of the Good.

delight us, if we are delighted with things not intrinsically good (for no changeable things are intrinsically good), what will the contemplation of the unchangeable good be like, the good which is eternal and abides the same for ever? Indeed, those things which are called good would in no way delight us unless they were good, and they could not possibly be good unless they derived from him who is intrinsically good.

Contemplation in safety

9. Surely, then, says the psalmist, you can see why I want to live in the house of the Lord all the days of my life. He has told you why: *to contemplate the Lord's delight*, to contemplate him always, with no misfortune to threaten me as I do so, no temptation to distract me, no one's power to sweep me away, no enemy to suffer from as I contemplate him, so that I may enjoy that bliss to the full with no worries, the bliss that is the Lord my God himself. What must happen to me if this is to be? He himself will protect me. Not only do I wish to see the delight of the Lord; I also want "his temple to be protected." I will be his temple, so that he may protect his temple, may protect me. Do you really think that the temple of God is like the temple of idols? The idols of the pagans need protection from their temples, but the Lord our God will protect his own temple, and I shall be free from anxiety. I shall contemplate him and find delight in him, and I shall be protected for my salvation. The protection he gives will be as perfect as the contemplation; and as the joy of contemplation will be perfect, so too will be the health he grants, which is perfect incorruption. To these two aspects correspond the two assertions with which the psalm began: *The Lord is my light and my salvation, whom shall I fear?* I shall contemplate the Lord's joy, and so he is my light; he will protect me, his temple, and so he is my salvation.

Verse 5. The hidden sanctuary

10. Why does God keep this for us until the end? Because *he has hidden me in his tent on the day of my troubles*. There will be a home for me, where I may live all the days of my life, where I may look on the delight of the Lord, and be protected as his temple. But on what grounds can I promise myself that I will reach it? Because *he has hidden me in his tent on the day of my troubles*. At that time there will be no such thing as days of troubles, but God does take notice of me now in my present days of troubles. How then can he, who looked on me in mercy when I was far off, not enlighten me when I reach home? I am not being presumptuous in making that one petition. My heart did not say to me, "What do you seek, and from whom do you seek it?"[17] Do you, an unjust sinner, dare to ask God for anything? Do you dare to hope that you will enjoy some contemplation of God, you weakling, you with your unclean heart?" "Yes, I do so dare," I answer, "because it isn't just for me, it is

the Lord's own delight that I want. I don't rely on myself, but on his pledge. Will he who gave so great an assurance while I was on my journey abandon me on my arrival? *He has hidden me in his tent on the day of my troubles."*

The day of our troubles, you see, is this present life. The ungodly experience days of trouble in one way, the faithful in another. Even those who believe, and yet are still journeying and far from the Lord (for, as the apostle Paul says, *As long as we are in the body we are on pilgrimage and away from the Lord* (2 Cor 5:6), even they endure days of trouble, for if they did not, why would the Lord's prayer say, *Deliver us from evil*? It must mean that we are amid days of trouble. In a very different way do those who still have not believed experience days of trouble, yet for all that God has not scorned them. No, Christ died for the ungodly.[18] Let the human soul make bold, then, to seek that one thing; it will have it without anxiety, possess it without anxiety. To think that the soul is so much loved when squalid! Imagine how radiant it will be when it is beautiful!

He has hidden me in his tent on the day of my troubles; he has protected me in the hidden recesses of his tabernacle. What is the hidden recesses of that tabernacle, what does the phrase mean? Many parts, limbs of the tabernacle if you prefer, are seen on the outside; but there is also a sanctuary inside, a secret inner room at the heart of the temple. And what is that? The place where the high priest alone used to enter.[19] But perhaps our high priest is himself this hidden part of God's tabernacle. He received flesh from this tabernacle, and made an inner recess of the tabernacle for us.[20] This was so that others of his members, by believing in him, might be the tabernacle, and he himself be its inner recess. As the apostle says, *You are dead, and your life is hidden with Christ in God* (Col 3:3).

Verse 6. Our Head is raised above our enemies

11. Perhaps you want to make sure that this is what he is talking about? Well now, Christ is certainly a rock.[21] Listen to what follows: *He has hidden me in his tent on the day of my troubles; he has protected me in the hidden recesses of his tabernacle.* You were asking what the inner recess of the tent is; listen, then, to the next line: *He has set me up on a rock.* This means that he has raised me up in Christ. Because you have humbled yourself in the dust, he has set you up on a rock. But Christ is up above, you are still below. So what comes next? *See now, he has raised my head above my enemies.* He says *now*, now before I arrive at that house where I want to live all the days of my life, before I come to that vision of the Lord, *even now he has raised my head above my enemies.* I still endure the enemies of the body

---

18. See Rom 5:6.
19. See Heb 9:3.7.
20. Variants: "made us an inner recess;" "made for us his inner tabernacle."
21. See 1 Cor 10:4.

of Christ, I have not yet been raised up above my enemies, but *he has raised my head above my enemies.* Our Head, Christ, is already in heaven, but our enemies can still rage against us; we have not yet been raised above them, but our Head is already there. Why did Christ say, *Saul, Saul, why are you persecuting me?* (Acts 9:4). He said that he was here below in us; therefore we are also there above in him, because *even now he has raised my head above my enemies.* Look how wonderful a pledge we have, assuring us that we too are in heaven for ever with our Head, in faith and hope and love, because our Head is with us on earth in divinity, in goodness, in unity, even to the consummation of this age.[22]

The wonders of creation

12. *I have traveled round, and now I have offered in his tent a sacrifice[23] of great joy.* We offer a sacrifice of joy, a sacrifice of gladness, a sacrifice of thanksgiving which cannot be expressed in words. Yes, we sacrifice, but where? In that same tabernacle of his, in holy Church. What then do we sacrifice? Superabundant and inexpressible gladness, not with words, but with wordless cries of rejoicing. This is our *offering of great joy.* Where was it sought, where was it found? By walking round. *I have traveled round,* he says, *and now I have offered in his tent a sacrifice of great joy.* Let your mind roam round the whole creation: from all sides creation will cry to you, "God made me." Whatever delights you in art points you to the artist, and all the more so if you go round the whole created order: gazing on it fills you with longing to praise its maker. You see the heavens: they are the mighty works of God. You see the earth: God made the numbers of different seeds, the different species of plants, the great multitude of animals. Keep going round the heavens, right around back to the earth, leaving nothing out. Everything everywhere shouts back to you the name of the Creator, and the varied beauties of created things are a chorus of praise to him. But who can unravel all the secrets of creation? Who can turn it all into words of praise? Who can praise heaven and earth, the sea, and all things in them as they deserve? And these are only the visible things. Who could worthily praise Angels, Thrones, Dominions, Principalities and Powers? Who could praise as it deserves this force which pulses in us, enlivening the body, moving the limbs, activating the senses, embracing so many things in the memory, sifting out so many by the understanding: who can worthily praise that? And if human speech has such a struggle with these creatures of God, what is it to say of the Creator, unless rejoicing alone remains when speech has fallen silent? *I have traveled round, and now I have offered in his tent a sacrifice of great joy.*

---

22. See Mt 28:20.
23. *Hostia,* a sacrificial victim.

The Church, already victorious, praises God

13. There is also another interpretation, which seems to me more appropriate to the pattern of the psalm. The psalmist said that he had been set up on the rock, the rock that is Christ; and his head, that is, Christ, had been raised above his enemies. He wanted to make it clear that he himself had also been raised in that same Head above his enemies, since he was set up on Christ, the rock. This is an allusion to the honor of the Church, now that its persecuting enemies have yielded to it. And because this state of affairs has been brought about by the faith of the whole world, *I have traveled round*, he says, *and now I have offered in his tent a sacrifice of great joy*. This means: I have taken stock of the faith of the whole world, and in this faith my Head has been lifted up over those who used to persecute me; and so in this very tabernacle of his, the Church spread over the whole earth, I have praised God with a joy that cannot be put into words.

Verse 7. The end of all longings

14. *I will sing and play the lyre to the Lord.* We shall be free from anxiety, and carefree we shall sing, and carefree we shall play the lyre when we contemplate the delight of the Lord and are protected as his temple, in that incorruptibility where death is swallowed up in victory.[24] But what of the present? Already we have spoken of the joys that will be ours when that one petition is granted to us. But what of the present? *Hearken, Lord, to my voice.* Let us groan now, let us pray now. Groaning is proper only to people in misery, prayer only to those in need. Prayer will pass away, praise will take over; weeping will pass away, joy will take its place. In the meantime, when we are in the days of our troubles, let our prayer to God not cease, and let us go on asking him for that one thing. Let us not interrupt that petition until it is answered, by God's gift and through God's goodness. *Hearken, Lord, to my voice, with which I have cried to you; have mercy on me, and hearken to me.* He made that one petition; through his long begging, weeping, groaning, he asked only that. He has made an end of all desires; that one plea alone is left.

Verse 8. Seeing the light

15. Listen, then, to what this one thing is, that he asks. *To you my heart has spoken: I have sought your face.* This is what he said a little earlier: *that I may contemplate the Lord's delight.* Now he says, *To you my heart has spoken: I have sought your face.* If our joy were in the sun up there, it would be not our heart, but

---

24. See 1 Cor 15:54.

the eyes of our bodies that would be saying, *I have sought your face*. To whom does our heart say, *I have sought your face*? Only to him who offers himself to the eyes of the heart. One kind of light is what the eyes of our flesh seek, the other is sought by the eyes of the heart. But you want to behold the light which is seen by the eyes of the heart, because God is that light itself. *God is light*, says John, *and in him there is no darkness at all* (1 Jn 1:5). Do you aspire to see that light? Make your eye clean, so that you can see it, because *blessed are the clean of heart, for they shall see God* (Mt 5:8).

Verse 9. Seeking God's face

16. *To you my heart has spoken: I have sought your face, O Lord, for your face will I seek.* One thing I have sought from the Lord, and this I will seek: your countenance. *Do not turn your face away from me.* How the psalmist has stuck to that one petition! Do you want to get what you ask for? Ask for nothing else; be satisfied with that single one, for that one will satisfy you. *To you my heart has spoken: I have sought your face, O Lord, for your face will I seek. Do not turn your face away from me, nor turn away in anger from your servant.* How wonderful that is; nothing more consonant with God's being can be said. Those who are truly in love experience this. Other people may yearn to be blessed and find a sort of immortality in the pleasures they enjoy by satisfying their earthly desires. And perhaps that is their motive for worshiping God, and praying that they may live on here a long time in the midst of what they enjoy, and that nothing which earthbound desire possesses may be lost to them. They would not want to lose gold, or silver, or some estate which caught their eye; they would not want their friends to die, or their children, or their wives, or their dependents. Their wish would be to live forever amid these pleasures. But because it is not possible to do so for ever, and they know they are mortal, perhaps they love God, and pray to God, and groan to God, to ensure that all these good things may be available to them well into old age. And if God were to say to them, "Look, I am making you immortal in your enjoyment of these things," they would receive it as a great blessing, and be so pleased and happy that they would hardly be able to contain themselves. But this is not what the psalmist wants, he who asked for the one thing from God. What does he want? To contemplate the Lord's joy all the days of his life. And again, those other people, who worshiped God in that way and for that reason, would not be afraid of God's anger as long as they had all those temporal benefits to hand; their only fear would be that God might take it all away. But our psalmist does not fear an angry God for that reason, since indeed he has even said of his enemies, "Let them eat my flesh." Why does he fear God's anger, then? He is afraid that God might take away what he has loved. And what has he loved? *Your face.* So he reckons it to be God's anger if he turns his face away: "Lord," he prays, *do not turn away in anger from your servant.* A possible challenge to him might go like this: "Why are you afraid of his turning

away from you in anger? Surely if in his anger he does turn away from you, he will not punish you, whereas if you run into him while he is angry, he will punish you. You would be better advised, then, to hope that he will turn away from you when he is angry." No, he replies. He knows what he wants.[25] God's anger is nothing other than the turning away of his face. "What if he were to make you immortal in the pleasures and the enjoyment of earthly satisfactions?" Such a lover replies, "That is not what I want. Whatever is not God holds no sweetness for me. Whatever my Lord may want to give me, let him take away the whole lot, if he will give me himself." *Do not turn away in anger from your servant.* Perhaps he does turn away from some, but not in anger, as from those who say to him, *Turn your face away from my sins* (Ps 50:11(51:9)). When he turns his face away from your sins, he is not turning away from you in anger. By all means, then, let him turn his face away from your sins, but let him not turn his face away from you.

Grace and free will

17. *Be my helper, I beg; do not forsake me.* Look at me, I am on the way. I have put one request to you, that I may dwell in your house all the days of my life, to contemplate your delight, to be protected as your temple. This has been my one petition, but in order to reach it, I am on my journey. Perhaps you will say to me, "Make an effort! Keep walking! I have given you free will, so it is within your power. Follow the path, seek peace and pursue it.[26] Do not deviate from the way, do not remain static, do not look back. Keep on walking, for the one who perseveres to the end will be saved."[27] Yes, you have received free will, but it looks as if you are over-confident in your walking ability.[28] Do not trust yourself. If God abandons you, you will stumble on the road, you will fall, you will wander off it, you will get stuck in it. Say to him, then, *Be my helper, I beg; do not forsake me or despise me, O God, my salvation.* You who have made us, also help us; you who have created us, do not leave us in the lurch.

Verse 10. God, our father and mother

18. *My father and mother have abandoned me.* The psalmist has made himself a little child in relation to God. He has made God both his father and his mother. God

---

25. Some codices, instead of *Non, inquit. Novit enim . . .* , have *Non in ira. Quid novit . . .* : "Not in anger. For what does he know, what does he want?" Others have *In ira non accedat. Quid novit . . .* : "Let him not approach in anger. For he knows. . . ." Others again: *Non accedat. Quid . . .* : "Let him not approach. For what does. . . ."

26. See Ps 33:15(34:14).

27. See Mt 10:22; 24:13.

28. This sounds like an attack on Pelagian doctrine, which found its way into Africa in A.D. 411. A possible indication of the date of this sermon.

is our father because he created us, because he calls us, gives orders and rules us; he is our mother because he cherishes us, nourishes us, feeds us with milk, and holds us in his arms. *My father and mother have abandoned me; but the Lord has taken me up*, both to guide and to feed. Mortal parents procreate, children succeed them in the next generation, mortals following mortals; those who form the next generation are born in order that those who brought them into the world may die. He who created me will not die, nor shall I depart from him. *My father and mother have abandoned me; but the Lord has taken me up*. Disregarding those two parents from whom we were born according to the flesh: our father, the male partner, our mother, the female, like Adam and Eve; disregarding these, I say, we have here another father and another mother, or rather, we have had. Our father according to this world is the devil. He was a father to us when we were devoid of faith, for it is to the faithless that the Lord says, *You are children of your father, the devil* (Jn 8:44). If he who is at work in the children of unbelief [29] is the father of all the ungodly, who is their mother? She is a city called Babylon. That city is the community of all those who have been lost, from east to west. She controls the kingdom of this world. A certain state is called after the city, Babylon, a state which you now see growing old and shrinking.[30] She was our first mother, for in her we were born. But we know another Father—God. We have left the devil behind; for when does the devil dare to approach those whom God, who is stronger than all, has taken to himself? And we know another mother, the heavenly Jerusalem, holy Church, a part of which is on pilgrimage on earth; we have left Babylon behind. *My father and mother have abandoned me*. They no longer have anything to give me, and when they did seem to be giving me something, it was you who were giving it, though I attributed it to them.

Can the false gods give anything?

19. Even if we think only of this world's benefits, is anything given to human beings except by God? Or what is taken from anyone, unless God, who gave it in the first instance, allows it to be? Foolish people think their gifts are given by the demons they worship; indeed they sometimes say to themselves, "God is necessary for eternal life, for spiritual life, but we need to worship those other powers to make sure of temporal things." Oh, the empty-headedness of the human race! You set greater store by those advantages for the sake of which you want to worship demons; in fact you think it more important to pay cult to them—well, perhaps I should not say more important, but at any rate equally important. But God does not

---

29. See Eph 2:2.
30. A reference to barbarian encroachments throughout the empire, perhaps especially the Visigothic invasion of Italy, and the sack of Rome in A.D. 410. In Rv 18 the pagan, persecuting Rome of an earlier age is called Babylon.

want to be worshiped along with them, not even if he gets much more worship and they much less. "What," you will say, "aren't those gods necessary too, if we are to secure everyday things?" Absolutely not. "But we should still be afraid that they may do us harm if they are angered." They will do no harm unless God allows it. They will always have the will to do harm; they never stop wanting to, even if they are appeased or appealed to, for this is characteristic of their ill-will. What will you achieve, then, by worshiping them, except to displease God? And if he is offended you will be handed over[31] into their power, with the result that those who could do nothing to you when God was well disposed will be able to do whatever they like once he is angry. If any one of you thinks that this sort of worship is necessary to secure temporal well-being, the following example will help you to see the futility of it. Take all those who worship Neptune: are they immune to shipwreck? What about all those who scoff at Neptune: does that mean they never reach harbor? And all those women who worship Juno: do they all give birth successfully? Or do all those who scoff at Juno miscarry? You must understand, beloved,[32] that the men and women bent on worshiping these gods are empty-headed, for if it were necessary to pay cult to them for earthly things, only people who worship them would have these earthly things in plentiful supply. Even if that were the case, we should nonetheless shun such gifts and seek from God only the one thing, and all the more so because the God who is slighted when such gods are worshiped gives us earthly things too. So let our father leave us, and our mother too; let the devil leave us and the city of Babylon leave us. And let the Lord take us into his arms to console us with temporal things, and bless us with the gifts of eternity. *My father and mother have abandoned me; but the Lord has taken me up.*

Verse 11. Law and mercy

20. So the psalmist has been taken up by the Lord, and has abandoned that city which is ruled by the devil; for the devil is the ruler of the ungodly, the ruler of this world of darkness.[33] What darkness is this? Sinners and unbelievers. That is why Paul says to those who do now believe, *You were darkness once, but now you are light in the Lord* (Eph 5:8). Now that we have been taken up by God, what are we to say? *Appoint for me a law in your way, Lord.* What a daring request, to ask for a law! What if the Lord were to say to you, "But will you keep a law? If I give you a law, will you keep it?" The psalmist would not have dared to ask for it unless he had first been able to say, *The Lord has taken me up.* So then, Lord, if you will give me help, if you will take charge of me, give me a law: *appoint for me a law in your way,*

---

31. *Daberis*, "you will be handed over." Variants are *haberis*, "you will be held," and *laberis*, "you will slip."
32. *Caritas vestra*: see note at Exposition 2 of Psalm 25, paragraph 1.
33. See Eph 6:12.

Lord. That means, appoint for me a law in your Christ, for the Way himself has spoken to us, and told us, *I am the way, the truth, and the life* (Jn 14:6). A law rooted in Christ is a law tempered with mercy. That law is Wisdom, of whom it has been written, *She carries law and mercy on her tongue* (Prv 31:26). And if you falter in any way in regard to the law, he who shed his blood for you forgives you when you confess it. All you must do is decide not to abandon the way. Say to him, "Take me to yourself. *Guide me along a straight path, because of my enemies*. Give me a law, but do not take away your mercy." He said in another psalm, *He who gave the law will give a blessing too* (Ps 83:8(84:7)). When he says, *Appoint for me a law in your way, Lord*, he envisages a commandment. What about mercy? *And guide me along a straight path, because of my enemies*.

Verse 12. The iniquity that lies to itself

21. *Do not deliver me to the will of those who harass me*; that is, do not let me collude with my oppressors. If you collude with the mind and intention of your oppressor, somehow it is not your flesh that he will devour; in his malevolence he will eat up your soul. *Do not deliver me to the will of those who harass me*. Give me over, if such is your will, to the hands of those who harass me, but only their hands. This is what the martyrs said to God, and he delivered his own into the hands of persecutors. But what was it that he handed over? Not them, just their flesh. As the Book of Job puts it, *Earth has been given over into the hands of the ungodly* (Jb 9:24); similarly, flesh was given over into the hands of the persecutors. *Do not deliver me*, the psalmist prays—not my flesh, I mean, but me. I am speaking to you as a soul, I am speaking to you as a mind; I am not asking, "Do not give over my flesh into the hands of those who harass me," but *Do not deliver me to the will of those who harass me*. How are men and women given over to the will of those who harass them? *Unjust witnesses have come forward against me*. Yes, it is because they are unjust witnesses, and make many wicked allegations about me, and in so many ways undermine me, that if I am given over to their will, I too shall be a liar, and I will be their ally. Instead of being a sharer in your truth, I would then be an accomplice in their lies against you. *Unjust witnesses have come forward against me, and iniquity has lied to itself*. To itself, not to me. Let it always lie to itself, but let it not lie to me. If you give me over to the will of those who harass me, that is, if I comply with their will, iniquity will no longer have lied to itself, but to me too. But if they rampage as much as they wish, and try to hamper my progress, I pray that you will not give me over to their will. By not complying, I will abide; I will abide steadfastly in your truth. Then iniquity will lie not to me, but to itself.

Verse 13. The land of the living

22. After all his dangers, tribulations and difficulties, the psalmist returns to that one request he made to God; in turmoil, gasping, toiling in the hands of his persecutors and oppressors, yet resolute and confident because God has taken him to himself, and he is under God's guidance and rule, he returns to it. After all that traveling around, and rejoicing, and elation, and groaning in his labors, at last he heaves a sigh: *I believe that I shall see the good things of the Lord in the land of the living.* Ah, the good things of the Lord, how sweet they are, undying, beyond compare, everlasting, unchangeable! When shall I see you, good things of the Lord? I believe that I shall see you, but not in the land of those who are dying. *I believe that I shall see the good things of the Lord in the land of the living.* The Lord will rescue me from the land of those who die, he who for my sake deigned to take upon himself the clay of those who die, and to die at the hands of people who were themselves dying. The Lord will rescue me from the land of the dying, and *I believe that I shall see the good things of the Lord in the land of the living.* The psalmist says it panting, struggling; he says it while in danger in the midst of a great throng of temptations, but at the same time hoping unreservedly in the mercy of him to whom he said, *Appoint for me a law, O Lord.*

Verse 14. Holding out until the Lord comes

23. And what does God, who appoints the law for him, have to say? Let us listen to the voice of the Lord encouraging us from on high and comforting us. Let us hear the voice of him whom we have in place of the father and mother who have abandoned us; yes, let us hear his voice. He has heard our groanings, he has seen our yearnings, he has taken notice of our desire, and he has willingly accepted that one petition of ours, that one plea that reaches him through Christ our advocate. While we are still plodding along and have not yet finished our pilgrimage, he defers what he has promised, but not to deprive us of it. He urges us, *Hold out*[34] *for the Lord.* You will not be holding out for a liar, nor for one who could himself be deceived, nor for one who will be unable to find anything to give us. The all-powerful God has promised, the sure God has promised, the true God has promised. *Hold out for the Lord, act manfully!* Do not collapse, or you may end among those of whom it was said, *Woe betide those who have lost the will to hold out* (Sir 2:16). This command, *hold out for the Lord*, is addressed to all of us, but it is addressed also to one single individual. We are one in Christ, we are the body of Christ, we who want that one thing, we who ask for that one thing, we who groan in these days of our troubles, we who believe that we shall see the good things of the Lord in the land of

---

34. Singular.

the living. To all of us who are one in the One is said, *Hold out for the Lord, act manfully; let your heart be strengthened, and hold out for the Lord.* What else can he say to you? He can only repeat what you have just heard. *Hold out for the Lord, act manfully.* It implies that whoever has lost the power of endurance has become effeminate and lost strength. Men and women alike must listen to this, because in the one Man are comprised both male and female.[35] When someone is in Christ there is neither male nor female.[36] *Hold out for the Lord, act manfully; let your heart be strengthened, and hold out for the Lord.* By holding out for the Lord you will come to possess him; the one for whom you are holding out will be yours for ever. Long for something else, if you can find something greater, better or more lovely!

---

35. *In uno viro vir et femina*: Augustine's view on inclusive language.
36. See Gal 3:28.

Exposition of Psalm 27

The Mediator speaks

1. *Of David himself.* The speaker here is the Mediator himself, strong of hand in the conflict of his passion. When he seems to be praying for calamities to fall upon his enemies, it is not to be thought that he does so out of malevolence. Similarly when in the gospel he invokes woes upon the towns where he had performed miracles, the towns which in spite of that had not believed in him,[1] he does not pray out of malice, but foretells the disasters that will fall upon them.

Verses 1-2. The man Christ is united to the eternal Word

2. *I cry to you, O Lord; O my God, do not refuse to speak a word to me.* To you, Lord, have I cried; O my God, do not sever from my humanity that unity which binds your Word to me. *Do not ever be silent toward me, or I shall be like those who go down into the pit.* It is because the eternity of your Word never ceases to unite itself to me that I am not like the rest of humankind. They are born into the deepest misery of this world, where because your word is not known, it is as if you are silent. *Hear the sound of my plea as I pray to you, as I stretch out my hands toward your holy temple.* I stretch them out as I am crucified, for the salvation of those who by believing become your holy temple.

Verses 3-5. Deceivers deceived

3. *Do not drag my soul away with sinners, nor destroy me with those who work iniquity, who speak peaceably with their neighbors,* like those who say to me, *We know that you have come as a teacher from God* (Jn 3:2). *But wickedly in their hearts,* for they are all the while speaking evil in their hearts.

4. *Recompense them according to their deeds.* Repay them in accordance with what they have done, for this is just. *And according to the wickedness of their endeavors,*[2] for through striving after evil things they have become unable to find

---

1. See Mt 11:20ff.
2. *Affectationum,* "strivings," "endeavors," in the best manuscripts; but some have *affectionum,* "dispositions."

what is good. *Give them what their deeds deserve.* No matter how effective for the salvation of others their actions may be, repay them nonetheless according to their intentions. *Pay them their recompense:* since they wanted to repay with falsehood the truth they were hearing, may their own deceit deceive them.

5. *Because they have not understood the deeds of the Lord.* How is it evident that such a punishment has fallen upon them? From the fact that *they have not understood the works of the Lord.* Clearly this was already a punishment for them, that they were unable to recognize God incarnate in the one whom they maliciously baited as a man, nor to understand why the Father sent him. *Nor the works of his hands:* they were not moved either by those visible works of God presented to their very eyes. *You will overthrow them, and not build them up.* Do not allow them to harm me in any way, nor to achieve anything by their repeated attempts to mount their offensive weaponry against my Church.

Verses 6-7. Triumph

6-7. *Blessed be the Lord, because he has heard the voice of my entreaty. The Lord is my helper and my protector.* Amid such grievous suffering the Lord helps me, and with immortality he protects me when I rise again. *My heart has hoped in him, and I have been helped. My flesh has blossomed anew:* that is, my body has risen from the dead. *And of my own free will I shall confess to him.* Now that the fear of death has been done away with, those who believe in me will confess to him, not constrained by fear under the law, but freely and in harmony with the law. And since I am in them, I shall confess to him.

Verse 8. The Lord strengthens and protects

8. *The Lord is the courage of his people.* This does not refer to the people that was ignorant of God's righteousness and sought to establish its own (see Rom 10:3); rather it looks to another people that has not believed it could be brave of itself, but knows the Lord to be its fortitude as it contends with the devil in the difficulties of this life. *And the protector of those healed by his Christ,* so that when the time is past for that warlike fortitude which has been brought to victory by his Christ, he may protect it at last with peaceful immortality.

Verse 9. God's lordship now and hereafter

9. *Save your people, Lord, and bless your heritage.* Now that my flesh has blossomed anew I am interceding on their behalf, for you have promised, *Ask of me, and I will give you the nations as your heritage* (Ps 2:8). *Save your people, and*

bless your heritage, yours, because everything that is mine is yours.[3] *Rule over them and lift them up for ever:* rule them in this temporal life, and lift them up from here to life eternal.

---

3. See Jn 17:10.

Exposition of Psalm 28

Verse 1

1. *A psalm of David himself, of the completion of the tabernacle.* This is a psalm of the strong-armed Mediator concerning the perfection of the Church in this world, where it wages war within time against the devil.

Verse 2. The heart as the court of the Lord

2. The prophet is speaking: *Bring to the Lord, you children of God, bring the offspring of rams to the Lord,* bring yourselves as the offering, you whom the apostles as leaders of the flock have brought to birth through the gospel.[1] *Bring to the Lord glory and honor:* may he be glorified and honored through your deeds. *Bring glory to the Lord and to his name:* may it[2] be known throughout the world and highly honored. *Worship the Lord in his holy court.*[3] Worship the Lord in your heart, a heart widened and sanctified; for you are his regal and holy habitation.

Verse 3. Thunderous preaching

3. *The Lord's voice over the waters:* this means the voice of Christ over the nations. *The God of majesty has thundered.* From the cloud of his flesh the God of majesty has struck fear by his preaching of repentance. *The Lord is over many waters,* for this same Lord Jesus, having made his pronouncement over the peoples and greatly terrified them, converted them to himself and made them his dwelling.

Verses 4-5. God speaks in strength

4. *The Lord's voice in strength,* for the Lord's voice is in them now, and renders them powerful. *The Lord's voice in splendor,* for the voice of the Lord achieves splendid results in them.

---

1. See 1 Cor 4:15.
2. Or "he."
3. *In aula sancta eius.* Variants are *in atrio sancto,* "in his holy room/hall"; *in regia sancta,* "in his holy palace."

294

5. The Lord's voice shattering[4] *the cedars:* this refers to the voice of the Lord that humbles the proud to contrition of heart. *The Lord will shatter the cedars of Lebanon*, for the Lord will grind down in repentance those who lift themselves high in the brilliant distinction of earthly rank, since to their confusion he has chosen to reveal his godhead to the most insignificant of this world.[5]

Verse 6. Noble birth and humility

6. *He will break them in pieces like a calf of Lebanon.* Once he has lopped off their pride and haughtiness he will cut them down to the shape of his own humility, for he was led like a calf to slaughter by the nobility of this world: *The kings of the earth arose, and the rulers conspired together against the Lord and against his Christ* (Ps 2:2). But *the beloved is like the foal of a unicorn*, for though he was the dearly-loved and only Son of the Father, he emptied himself of his nobility, and being made human[6] he became like a child of the Jewish race, who knew nothing of God's righteousness and proudly flaunted their own righteousness as a single horn, unrivaled.

Verse 7. Cutting through the frenzy of the people

7. *The Lord's voice cuts across fierce flames.* This is the voice of the Lord who passed through the fiercely burning hatred of those who jostled him, without any harm to himself,[7] or cut through the raging anger of his persecutors, some of whom said, "Perhaps this really is the Messiah?" while others said, "No, it couldn't possibly be. He is leading the people astray";[8] in this way he cut through their mad uproar, so as to bring some over within the reach of his love, and leave others in their malice.

Verse 8. The word in the world's desert

8. *The Lord's voice shaking the wilderness.* This is the voice that stirred to faith the peoples who were once without hope and without God in the world,[9] where no prophet, no preacher of the word of God was to be found, so that it was as though no

---

4. *Conterens*, from *contero*, meaning "pound, crush, grind down"; from this verb derives the idea of "contrition." A variant here and again in the next sentence has the appropriate parts of *confringo*: "break, destroy, break down, ruin."
5. See 1 Cor 1:28.
6. See Phil 2:7.
7. See Lk 4:30.
8. See Jn 7:12.41.26.
9. See Eph 2:12.

humans lived there. *The Lord will shake the desert of Kadesh,* for the Lord will cause the holy word of his scriptures to be proclaimed there, the word deserted by the Jews, who did not understand it.

Verse 9. *God reveals the mysteries of the scriptures*

9. *The Lord's voice making the deer[10] perfect,* for the voice of the Lord has made perfect those who overcome and repel venomous tongues.[11] *And he will strip the forest,* opening up for them the obscurities of the sacred books and the shadowy depths of the mysteries hidden in them, so that they may freely feed there.[12] *And in his temple each one cries out "Glory!"* for in his Church every one born again to an eternal hope praises God for the gift that he or she has received from the Holy Spirit.

Verse 10. *The Church, an ark*

10. *The Lord dwells in the flood.* Therefore the Lord at first dwells in the flood of this world in the persons of his holy ones, who are kept safe in the Church as in an ark. *The Lord will be enthroned as king for ever,* for over them he will reign eternally.

Verse 11. *The peace of the Lord*

11. *The Lord will give strength to his people.* This is said because he will endow his people with strength as they contend against the world's storms and squalls; for he did not promise them peace in this world. *The Lord will bless his people with peace.* However, this same Lord will bless his people by granting them peace in himself, for he said, *My peace I give to you, my peace I leave with you* (Jn 14:27).

---

10. *Cervos*; some codices have *cedros*, "cedars."
11. In his Exposition of Psalm 41, 3, Augustine makes use of a popular belief, derived from Pliny, that deer killed snakes, and after doing so suffered intense thirst, which furnishes him with an allegory for baptism.
12. In his prayer for an understanding of the scriptures at the beginning of Book XI of his *Confessions*, Augustine prayed, "Not in vain have you willed so many pages to be written, pages deep in shadow, obscure in their secrets; not in vain do harts and hinds seek shelter in those woods, to hide and venture forth, roam and browse, lie down and ruminate. Perfect me too, Lord, and reveal those woods to me. Lo, your voice is joy to me, your voice that rings out above a flood of joys" (*Confessions* XI,2,3).

Exposition 1 of Psalm 29

Verse 1. The dedication of the temple

1. *To the end, a psalm sung for the dedication of the house, for David himself.* To the end, a psalm of the joy of the resurrection, of transition to the state of immortality, and of the renewing of the body; and this as concerning not only the Lord's body, but that of the whole Church too. In the previous psalm[1] the completion of that tent in which we live in our time of warfare was celebrated, but now we have the dedication of the house which will abide in everlasting peace.[2]

Verse 2. No joy for the Church's oppressors

2. So now it is the whole Christ who speaks: *I will exalt you, Lord, because you have taken me up.* Yes, Lord, I will praise you who are so eminent, because you have taken me up, *and have not let my enemies gloat over me.* You have given them no joy at my expense, those who throughout the world have constantly attempted to crush me with every kind of persecution.

Verses 3-4. Healing and rescue

3. *O Lord my God, I cried to you, and you healed me.* I cried out to you, Lord, my God, and now no longer do I bear a sick body, wounded by its mortality.

4. *Lord, you have brought my soul back[3] from the depths, you have saved me from those who go down into the pit.* You have rescued me from the condition of profound blindness and the lowest slime of corruptible flesh.

Verse 5. The time between

5. *Sing to the Lord, you who are his saints.* Foreseeing what will happen, let the prophet exult and bid us, *Sing to the Lord, you who are his saints, and make the*

---

1. See Exposition of Psalm 28, 1.
2. The contrast between tent-dwelling and being finally at home was expounded in Exposition 2 of Psalm 26, 6.
3. *Reduxisti.* A variant is *eduxisti,* "you have led out."

297

remembrance of his holiness your confession. Confess to him because he has not forgotten that holiness by which he made you his saints, even though all this in-between time would seem long to your desire.

Verse 6. Evening and morning

6. *Because he is provoked, there is anger.* He has punished you for that first sin, for which you paid the penalty of death, *but in his will there is life,* for he has willed to give you the eternal life to which you could not have found your way back by any power of your own. *Weeping will linger in the evening:* the time of weeping began in the evening, when the light of wisdom faded away from sinful humanity and we were condemned to death. From that evening there will be a prolonged period of weeping, while God's people labors amid temptations, awaiting the day of the Lord; but *toward morning there will be rejoicing,* for we weep only until that morning of resurrection gladness, looking to the joy which blossomed in advance in the early-morning resurrection of the Lord.

Verses 7-8. Security is only from God

7. *I said in the midst of my plenty, "I shall be unmoved for ever."* I am that people which has been speaking from the outset, and I have spoken amid my plenty, for no longer do I suffer any want: *I shall be unmoved for ever.*

8. *Lord, in your kindly will you have added strength to my beauty.* I have learned, Lord, that the abundance I have is not mine in the sense of deriving from me; rather it is you who have willed to endow my beauty with strength. I learned this because *you turned your face away from me, and I became distraught.* When from time to time you averted your face from me in my sin, I became distressed, as the light by which I knew you was withdrawn from me.

Verses 9-10. Christ's prayer for resurrection

9. *To you, Lord, I will cry, and with my God I will plead.* I recall that time of confusion and misery, and as though set back in it I hear the voice of your First-born, my Head who is to die for me, as he prays, *To you, Lord, I will cry, and with my God I will plead.*

10. *What use is there in my blood, if I sink down into corruption?* What is the point of spilling my blood, if I sink into decay? *Will dust confess to you?* If I do not rise immediately, if my body decays, *will dust confess to you?* By *dust* I mean the great crowd of the ungodly whom I shall make righteous by my resurrection. Otherwise, *will it proclaim your truth?* If I do not rise again, will it preach your truth for the salvation of all the rest?

Verses 11-13. Sadness turned to joy

11. *The Lord heard, and took pity on me, the Lord has become my helper.* He did not allow his holy one to see corruption.[4]

12. *You have turned my lamentation into joy.* I, the Church, have followed him, the firstborn from the dead,[5] and now at the dedication of your house I say, *You have turned my lamentation into joy; you have torn up my sackcloth and girded me with happiness.* You have torn up the sacking that cloaked my sins, the sad garb of my mortal state, and have clothed me in the first robe,[6] the raiment of undying happiness.

So that my glory may sing to you, and I may be pierced no more. May it lament before you no longer, but sing to you, not my lowly condition but my glory, for you have raised me from that lowly state and I shall no longer endure compunction from any consciousness of sin, or from fear of death, or from dread of judgment. *Lord my God, I will confess to you for ever.* This is my glory, Lord my God, that for ever I may confess to you that nothing I have derives from myself, but that all good things are from you, who are God, all in all.[7]

---

4. See Ps 15(16):10.
5. See Col 1:18; Rv 1:5. The phrase, *quem primogenitum a mortuis consecuta ecclesia . . . dico* could also mean "I, the Church, have won him back as the firstborn from the dead. . . ."
6. Allusion to Lk 15:22: the "first robe" is brought out to clothe the prodigal son. Some of the Fathers used this text in association with the white garment given to the newly baptized.
7. See 1 Cor 15:28.

Exposition 2 of Psalm 29

A Sermon to the People

Verse 2. How does Christ pray?

1. *I will exalt you, Lord, because you have taken me up, and have not let my enemies gloat over me.* Now that is certainly what we have just sung, and if we know from the holy scriptures who our enemies are, we shall be well aware of the truth contained in this song. But if we are led astray by a wisdom that is no more than human, so that we do not know against whom we are struggling, we find at the very opening of this psalm a question we cannot answer. Whose voice do we think it is, praising God and giving thanks and declaring, *I will exalt you, Lord, because you have taken me up, and have not let my enemies gloat over me*? Let us take it first as the voice of the Lord himself, who was able to adopt as his own those words of prophecy, and this by virtue of having stooped to become a man. By the fact of being human, he was also weak, and in virtue of his weakness, he prayed. When the gospel was being read just now, we heard how he went so far as to withdraw into the desert away from his disciples, and that they followed him and found him. Having gone apart to that lonely place *he was praying there*, and when his disciples found him they told him, *People are looking for you.* But he responded, *Let us go to other places to preach, and into the towns, for that is what I have come for* (Mk 1:35. 37. 38). If you consider the divinity of our Lord Jesus Christ, you have to ask, Who is praying? To whom is he praying? Why is he praying? Is God praying? Is God praying to God? What reason does he have to pray, he who is always blessed, always omnipotent, always unchangeable, eternal, co-eternal with the Father? If we listen to what he himself thundered through John, as though making use of a cloud that did his bidding, we hear that *in the beginning was the Word, and the Word was with God; he was God. He was with God in the beginning. Everything was made through him; no part of created being was made without him. What was made was alive with his life, and that life was the light of humankind. The light shines in the darkness, and the darkness has never been able to master it* (Jn 1:1-5). So far we find in that no prayer, nor any reason for praying, nor any place for prayer or disposition to pray. But a little later the gospel says, *The Word was made flesh, and dwelt among us* (Jn 1:14). There you have both the majesty to which you pray, and the humanity that can pray for you. Referring even to the time after his resurrection, the apostle Paul said of Christ, *He is at God's right hand, and intercedes for us* (Rom 8:34).

Why does he intercede for us? Because he consented to be a mediator. What does it mean to be a mediator between God and humankind?[1] Notice that scripture does not say, "between the Father and humankind," but between God and human-kind. What is God? Father, and Son, and Holy Spirit. What are human beings? Sinners, godless creatures, mortals. Between that Trinity and the weakness and sinfulness of men and women came the Mediator, made human, not sinful but nonetheless weak, so that he might unite you to God by virtue of his sinlessness, and might draw near to you by being weak. In this way, then, *the Word was made flesh*, that is, the Word became a human being, so that a Mediator might arise between humanity and God. Men and women are called "flesh"; that is why the gospel says, *All flesh shall see the salvation of God* (Lk 3:6). All flesh, that means everyone. The apostle Paul uses this same idiom when he says, *It is not against flesh and blood that you have to struggle*, that is, against men and women, *but against principalities and powers and the rulers of this world of darkness* (Eph 6:12). We will talk about these later, please God.

The distinction we have just made is important for the explanation of the psalm which in the name of the Lord we have undertaken to unravel for you, holy brethren.[2] I have mentioned these examples to help you realize that "flesh" means men and women, and so understand that the statement, *the Word was made flesh*, means *"the Word became human."*

The Apollinarian heresy

2. I have good reason for emphasizing this. You all[3] know that there was a heresy about it in the past, and indeed there are still remnants of it around the people called Apollinarians.[4] Some of them held that the human nature which the Wisdom

---

1. See 1 Tm 2:5.
2. *Sanctitati vestrae*, "Your holiness."
3. "Your holiness."
4. Apollinaris, who became Bishop of Laodicea around A.D. 360, was a brilliant thinker and theologian, a friend of Saint Athanasius and a champion of the latter's anti-Arian doctrines. His central idea seems to have been that the restoration of humanity could, like its first creation, be the work of God alone. He was therefore concerned above all to assert the full divinity of Christ, and the unity of godhead and humanity in the one person of Christ. He understandably reacted against views current at Antioch which would later develop into Nestorianism: the doctrine of "the two Sons," divine and human. However, despite confusion over the meaning of such terms as "person" and "nature," it appears that Apollinaris denied the existence of a human spirit in Christ, this being rendered unnecessary by the presence of the Logos. The Christ of Apollinaris' system was therefore fully and perfectly God, but not fully man, and his system seemed to leave little room for any genuinely human experience in Christ, and therefore for the transformation of what is most human in us. The orthodox Fathers loved to repeat the axiom, "What was not assumed [by God the Son] has not been healed." Apollinaris seceded from the Church, and his doctrine was condemned at the Council of Constantinople in 381. Some of his followers probably distorted his teaching and pushed it to extremes he would not himself have countenanced; Augustine here suggests degrees of denial among them.

of God assumed when the Word became flesh had no human mind; there was nothing but a soul without human understanding.

Now it is unquestionably true that in his humanity Christ gave expression to his person, not as the rest of men and women do, but in the unique way expressed in another psalm: *God, your God, has anointed you with the oil of joy, more abundantly than your companions* (Ps 44:8(45:7)): in other words, differently from your peers. This was said to rule out any misunderstanding that Christ was anointed in the same sense as other righteous people, such as the patriarchs, the prophets, the apostles, the martyrs, and any other distinguished branch of the human race. It is certain that there was no one greater in our race than John the Baptist, nor did anyone equal him among the offspring of women.[5] If you are looking for human excellence, look to John the Baptist. Yet there was someone else, of whom John said that he was unworthy to loosen his sandal-strap.[6] What was this someone else, then, if not greater than the rest of humankind? Even in his humanity he was greater than all the rest of us. But if you think of him as God, and consider his godhead, in relation to the truth that he was the Word in the beginning, the Word who was with God, the Word who was God, then he is the Father's equal, far above every created thing.

However, we are concerned now with his human nature. Perhaps, brothers and sisters, one or other of you might think that the humanity assumed by the Wisdom of God was on the same footing as the rest of humankind. But even in the case of your own bodily frame there is a vast difference between your head and your other members. Although all the parts constitute one body, there still remains a great difference between the head and all the rest of you. In the other parts you have no sensation other than that of touch. So only through touch do you have feeling in the other parts of your body; but in your head you hear and see and smell and taste and touch. If the pre-eminence of the head over the other members is so marked, how great must be the pre-eminence of the Head of the whole Church, that is, of the one man who by God's decision was to be the Mediator between God and the human creation?

But, as I was saying, those heretics asserted that the nature which the Word took to himself when the Word became flesh did not have a human mind, but only a soul devoid of human understanding.[7] Now you can see what a human being consists of: he or she is made up of soul and body. But the human soul has a power which the souls of beasts do not have. Beasts do have souls, yes, and they are called animals for that reason; they would not be called animals[8] if they did not have souls,[9] and we

---

5. See Mt 11:11.
6. See Mk 1:7.
7. And so not spirit, but merely an animating principle of the body, almost equivalent to "life," and analogous to the animal soul, as he goes on to say.
8. *Animalia.*
9. *Nisi ab anima.*

can see that they too are living, animated creatures. But what does a human being have over and above, which makes him or her an image of God? It is this: we have understanding and wisdom, we can distinguish good from evil, and so we are made in God's image and likeness. We have, then, something which the beasts do not have. But if we despise that quality in ourselves which makes us better than the beasts,[10] we destroy or impair or in some sense degrade the image of God in ourselves. This is why scripture gives the warning, *Do not be like a horse or a mule, devoid of understanding* (Ps 31(32):9).

These heretics said that our Lord Jesus Christ did not have a human mind, that faculty the Greeks call λογικόν and we call rational, the power by which we reason, the power other animals[11] lack. But what exactly do the heretics say? That in the man Christ, the Word of God himself took the place of a human mind.[12] Well, they were banished, the Catholic faith spat them out, and they set up a heresy. Within the Catholic faith it was affirmed that the nature assumed by the Wisdom of God had nothing less than all the rest of humanity as far as the integrity of that nature was concerned, though with regard to the pre-eminence of his person, he is other than the rest of humanity. All the rest of us can be said to be partakers of the Word of God, but none of us can be called the Word of God, which is what he is called when scripture says, *The Word was made flesh.*

A variant on Apollinarianism

3. There were others too, from that same misguided stable, who not only denied that Christ, the Mediator between God and humankind, had a human mind; they held that he had no human soul either. All they would say was: "He was Word and flesh; there was no human soul in him, and no human mind either." This is what they said. What was he then? The Word plus flesh. The Catholic Church spat them out too,[13] and banished them from its sheep, from the straightforward, true faith. As I said, it was confirmed as Catholic doctrine that the man who was our mediator had all the characteristics of any other human being, apart from sin. For if Christ Jesus performed many bodily actions, from which we know that he had a body, not a fake body but a real one—well, think about it, how do we know that he had a body? Because he walked about, he sat down, he slept, he was arrested, he was scourged, he was beaten about the head, he was crucified, he died. Dispense with the body, and none of these could have happened. It is from these pieces of evidence that we recognize in the gospel that he had a real body, just as he pointed out himself after his resurrection: *Handle me and see: a ghost does not have flesh and bones, as you*

---

10. Or "despise the fact that we are better. . . ."
11. *Animalia.*
12. That is, that the Logos took the place of the *logikon* Augustine has just mentioned.
13. *Istos respuit*; a variant has *istis respondit*, "replied to them."

see I have (Lk 24:39). From these facts, these actions, we believe, and understand, and know for certain that the Lord Jesus had a body; and so too from certain other natural activities we know that he had a soul. Being hungry and thirsty have to do with the soul. Dispense with the soul,[14] and all you have is an inanimate body that could not feel these things. If the heretics assert that these activities were bogus, all that we believe about his body must be bogus too. But if the principle is that the body is real because the actions of the body are real, so too the soul is real because its actions are real.

The gloating of Christ's enemies over his passion

4. What follows from this? Just because the Lord became weak for your sake, you—yes, you there, listening to me—must not put God on the same footing as yourself. The plain fact is that you are a creature and he is your Creator. Do not think yourself equal to that man either, because your God, the Word, the Son of God, became human for your sake. Rather you must regard that man as superior to yourself, as the Mediator indeed but as God over all his creation. Accordingly you must understand that it is not inappropriate for him who became human for your sake to pray for you. And if it is not inappropriate for him to pray for you, he could quite reasonably say these words also on your behalf: *I will exalt you, Lord, because you have taken me up, and have not let my enemies gloat over me*. But those words will be untrue if we do not understand *enemies* aright, when we think about our Lord Jesus Christ. How can it be true, when Christ the Lord says, *I will exalt you, Lord, because you have taken me up, and have not let my enemies gloat over me*? In his human capacity, in the weakness of his humanity, in his flesh, how is it true? Surely everyone knows that his enemies did gloat over him when they crucified him, held him prisoner, flogged him, beat him about the head, and taunted him, *Play the prophet for us, Christ!* (Mt 26:68)? Such gratification on their part almost forces us to think that the words of the psalm have no meaning: *you did not let my enemies gloat over me*. Then when he was hanging on the cross they were walking past, or just standing there and watching, and shaking their heads, and saying, "Look at the Son of God, *he saved others, but he can't save himself. Let him come down from the cross*, then we'll believe in him" (Mt 27:42). Surely in saying these things they were gloating over him. Where does that leave the words of the psalm, *I will exalt you, Lord, because you have taken me up, and have not let my enemies gloat over me*?

---

14. *Animam.*

Their gloating over the martyrdom of Christians

5. Perhaps those are not the words of our Lord Jesus Christ, not the words, that is, of him as an individual, but the words rather of the whole Christian people, because all of us are one single person in Christ, and the unity of all Christian people forms one person. Perhaps this person is speaking then, that is, the unity of all Christian people, when it says, *I will exalt you, Lord, because you have taken me up, and have not let my enemies gloat over me.* How are the words true of them? Were the apostles not arrested, were they not butchered, were they not scourged, were they not killed, were they not crucified, were they not burned alive, did they not fight with wild beasts, those whose memorials we celebrate? And when people did these things to them, surely they gloated over them? So neither can the Christian people say, *I will exalt you, Lord, because you have taken me up, and have not let my enemies gloat over me*, or so it seems.

Human malevolence, divine dispensation

6. We shall be better able to understand this if we look first at the title of the psalm. It reads: *To the end, a psalm sung for the dedication of the house, for David himself.* In this title is all our hope, and the whole hidden mystery[15] that is the key to the problem. The house which is in the process of being built will one day be dedicated. At present the house, that is, the Church, is under construction, but it will be dedicated at a later date. At its dedication the glory of the Christian people will be clearly seen, the glory which for the present lies hidden. For the time being let the enemies of God rage, let them denigrate the Church, let them do not what they want but whatever is conceded to them from above. For not everything we may have to suffer at the hands of our enemies is to be attributed to those enemies, as though the Lord our God had no say in the matter. As the Mediator showed us in his own case, when he allows others to harm us, it is not the will to do harm that he gives them from heaven, but only the ability. Every evil person has within himself the will to do harm, but the capacity to do harm that is something not within his power. He is already guilty by simply wanting to; but the power is granted to him by the secret economy of God's providence. In one case the harm is permitted as a punishment for someone, in another as a test, in another so that the sufferer may receive a crown. For harm permitted as a punishment we could take this case of the ἀλλόφυλοι, that is, the foreigners who were allowed to seize power over the people of Israel because they had sinned against God.[16] In Job's case the devil was given free rein in order to test him; but Job was refined by it and the devil thrown into disarray. In the martyrs' case the persecutors were let loose on them so that they

---

15. *Sacramentum.*
16. See Jgs 10:7; 13:1, etc.

might win their crowns; the martyrs were killed and the persecutors thought they had come out on top. The persecutors triumphed in appearance, but not in reality, while the martyrs were crowned truly but in secret. Whenever permission is granted, then, it is by the secret economy of God's providence; but that someone should will to do harm derives from the individual himself or herself; and such persons cannot immediately kill anyone they choose.

The example of Job

7. The Lord himself, who is judge of the living and the dead, stood before a human judge, to give us a lesson in humility and endurance. He was not defeated, but was providing every soldier with a model of how to fight. A threatening judge, swollen with self-importance, demanded, *Are you unaware that I have power either to release you or to put you to death?* (Jn 19:10). But the Lord deflated him completely with a retort that punctured his puffed-up conceit: *you would have no power over me, had it not been given you from above* (Jn 19:11). Take Job, too. Remember that the devil had killed his children and taken away everything he had. What had Job to say? *The Lord gave, and the Lord has taken away. This has happened as the Lord willed: may the Lord's name be blessed* (Jb 1:21). The enemy has no grounds for feeling triumphant because it was he who did it. "I know," says Job, "who gave him permission; the will to do harm belongs to the devil, but the power to test me to my Lord." In his state of bodily affliction he had to put up with his wife's contribution too: feeling neglected, she, like Eve, made herself the devil's accomplice, instead of her husband's support. She tempted him, and among other taunts she urged him, *Curse God, and die* (Jb 2:9). But this Adam in the mire was more cautious than the original Adam in paradise; for Adam-in-paradise complied with his wife's suggestion, and in consequence was banished from paradise, but Adam-in-the-mire spurned his wife's remark, so as to be admitted to paradise. Job, the Adam-in-the-mire, had the seeds of immortality within him,[17] though outwardly he was awash with worms. What did he say to his wife? *You have spoken like the silly woman you are. If we have received good things from the Lord's hands, should we not endure the bad too?* (Jb 2:10). On another occasion Job even acknowledged that the hand of the Lord was upon him when the devil had struck him down; he did not concern himself with asking who had struck him, but only who had allowed it. Even the devil himself referred to that same power, which he was seeking for himself, as the hand of God. In laying a charge against a just person, and one to whom the Lord was giving testimony, the devil alleged, *Job hardly worships the Lord for nothing, does he? Have you not surrounded him and his household and all his property with your protection? You have blessed the work*

---

17. Literally "was giving birth to immortality within."

of his hands, and his possessions have grown and grown in the land. You have given him great rewards, and that is why he pays cult to you. *But just stretch out your hand and touch all his belongings, and see if he does not curse you to your face* (Jb 1:9-11). Why does he say, *Stretch out your hand,* when what he wanted was to come down heavily with his own? Because he had no power of himself to do so, and so he called the power he received from God, "God's hand."[18]

Holding out for God in our tribulation

8. Well, then, brothers and sisters, what are we to make of the fact that enemies have done such terrible things to Christians, and have rejoiced in it and gloated over them? When will it be clear that their rejoicing was hollow? When the wicked have been thrown into disarray, and the just exult at the coming of our Lord God; for he will come bearing in his hand the proper recompense for each: for the ungodly, damnation, and for the just, kingly rule; for the wicked, communion with the devil, and for the faithful, communion with Christ. When he reveals this, when the just stand with unshakable firmness ... I am going to quote from scripture now: remember the reading from the Book of Wisdom: *Then the just will stand with great constancy against those who have been tormenting them. But the wicked, groaning within themselves in anguish of spirit, will ask, "What good has our pride done us, and what has come to us from our vaunted wealth? All these things have passed away like a shadow."* And what will they say of the just? *Look how they are reckoned among the children of God, and their lot is among the saints!* (Wis 5:1.3.8.9.5). That will be the time for the dedication of the house which at present is being built amid tribulations. Then the people of God will have good cause to say, *I will exalt you, Lord, because you have taken me up, and have not let my enemies gloat over me.* God's people will say this in all truth, God's people that is now sorely afflicted, and suffers tribulation from being so fiercely tempted, from such great scandals, persecutions and oppression. People who are making no progress in the Church are unaware of these spiritual torments; they think there is peace. But only let them begin to advance and they will experience the oppression under which it labors, because it was when the crop had grown and begun to yield its grain that the tares also appeared.[19] Fuller knowledge means increased sorrow. Let them make some progress and they will see where the trouble lies; let the good grain come up and the needs will too. There is a true saying of the apostle Paul, one which is verified from first to last: *all who want to live devoted to God in Christ suffer persecution. People of ill-will and seducers go from bad to worse, in error them-selves and leading others into error* (2 Tm 3:12-13). Why should the psalm urge us,

---

18. Throughout this paragraph there is a sense that both Adam and Job are types of Christ.
19. See Mt 13:26.

Hold out for the Lord, bear yourself manfully; let your heart be strengthened, and hold out for the Lord (Ps 26(27):14)? It was not enough to say, *Hold out for the Lord* once only. It had to be repeated, for the psalmist might have to wait bravely for two or three or four days, and the oppression and tribulation would still be going on. So he added, *Bear yourself manfully*, and *let your heart be strengthened*. And because it will be like this from first to last, the same expression is to be found at both head and tail of that verse: *hold out for the Lord*. The things that are oppressing you pass away, and the one whom you hold out for will come; he will wipe away the sweat, and dry your tears, and you will weep no longer. But for the present we must groan amid our tribulations; as Job said, *Is not human life on earth all temptation?* (Jb 7:1).

Types of building material

9. However, brothers and sisters, while we await the day of the dedication of the house, let us not forget that our Head has been dedicated already. The dedication is achieved already as far as he is concerned, for in him its foundation has been dedicated. But since ordinarily we expect the head to be at the top, and a foundation below, perhaps we are wrong to speak of Christ as our foundation? Would it not be better to think of him as the topmost pinnacle, since he has ascended into heaven, and sits at the right hand of the Father? No, I do not think we have made a mistake, for the apostle Paul said, *No one can lay any other foundation than that which is laid, which is Christ Jesus. But one person builds in gold, silver and precious stones . . .* (1 Cor 3:11-12). Those who live upright lives, who honor and praise God, who are patient under trials, who are homesick for their fatherland, these are the people who build in gold, silver and precious stones. But there are others who are still in love with the things of this world, and are enmeshed in[20] earthly affairs, and tied up in various attachments, such as the desires of the flesh, their homes, their spouses, and their possessions. They are Christians notwithstanding, for their hearts do not desert Christ, and they put nothing before Christ, just as when we build we put nothing else in before the foundation. These people are building with wood, hay and straw. But how does Paul continue? *The work of each one will be disclosed for what it is, for it will be revealed by fire* (1 Cor 3:13), the fire of tribulation and temptation. This fire has already proved the worth of many martyrs, but it will put the whole human race to the test in the end. There have been martyrs who possessed the good things of this world. How many rich people and senators have suffered! Some of them had been building in wood, hay or straw by their self-indulgence and worldly concerns; nonetheless because they had Christ as the foundation on which they built, he set fire to the hay, and they remained firm on the foundation.

---

20. *Implicati.* Variant: *occupati*, "taken up with."

This is what the apostle says about it: *If the work anyone has put into building survives, that builder will be rewarded. If anyone's work is burnt up, he will suffer the loss; but he himself will be saved indeed, though it be through fire* (1 Cor 3:14-15). There is quite a difference between being unharmed by the fire, and being saved through it. And saved—how? On account of the foundation. So do not let the foundation be shaken loose from your heart. Do not lay your foundation on top of straw, that is, do not give straw preference over the foundation, allowing straw first place in your heart, and Christ second. Perhaps it is not possible at present to get rid of straw altogether; well then, still let Christ have first place, and straw only after him.

Weight and order

10. Christ is the foundation. As I have pointed out, our Head has been dedicated already, and the Head is the foundation. But the foundation is usually at the bottom. You must all try to understand what I am saying, holy brethren,[21] and perhaps I may be able to explain the matter, in the name of Christ. There are two kinds of weights. Weight is like a force within each thing that seems to make it strain toward its proper place.[22] This is what I mean by "weight." You are carrying a stone in your hand. You feel its weight; it presses on your hand because it is seeking its appropriate place. Do you want to see what it is looking for? Take your hand away; it plummets to the earth, it comes to rest on the ground. It has reached the goal it was tending toward, it has found the place proper to it. In that case "weight" was something like a spontaneous movement, without life, without sensation. There are other things which seek their own place by pushing upward. If you pour water onto oil, it pushes downward by its own weight, for it is seeking its proper place, seeking to be set in order. It is contrary to order for water to be on top of oil, so until the proper order is established there is uneasy movement, and then it takes up its position. But now look at it the other way round. Pour oil underneath water. Let us suppose a container of oil falls into water, into the ocean, say, or the sea, and it

---

21. *Sanctitas vestra.*
22. Depending perhaps on Plato, who had envisaged the human soul as poised between God and the material world, Augustine developed the idea of a natural "love" within all creatures; like a weight it inexorably bears them toward their proper places, which does not always mean downward, as he remarks here, since oil rises above water, and fire (significantly) leaps upward. So human beings should be borne inexorably upward by the weight of their love, but since the fall they are the battlefield of conflicting "loves." Our loves therefore need to be ordered, as he briefly suggests here. In his *Confessions* he states the same doctrine in more personal terms: "Our true place is where we find rest. We are borne toward it by love, and it is your good Spirit who lifts up our sunken nature from the gates of death. . . . [Things] are not at rest as long as they are disordered, but once brought to order they find their rest. Now, my weight is my love, and wherever I am carried, it is this weight that carries me. Your Gift sets us afire and we are borne upward; we catch his flame and up we go" (*Confessions* XIII,9,10).

breaks. The oil will not consent to remain underneath. Just as when water was poured on top of oil it sought its own place at the bottom, so now, if oil is poured out underneath water, it will seek its proper place at the top. If this is a fair statement of how things behave, brothers and sisters, where do fire and water go? Fire is borne upward in its quest for its own place; water seeks by its weight to find its place at the bottom. A stone gravitates downward, and wood likewise, and pillars and clay, all the things of which our houses are built. They come from that class of things whose weight carries them downward. Clearly, then, they need a foundation beneath them, because the component parts of a house press downward, and were there not something there to support them, the whole edifice would collapse, because it is all pressing down toward the earth. For things which strain in a downward direction the foundation is placed at the bottom. But God's Church, though established here below, strains toward heaven, and so our foundation is laid there, where our Lord Jesus Christ sits at the Father's right hand. If you have understood now, holy brethren,[23] that our foundation is already dedicated, let us listen to the psalm briefly, and then run through it.

Enemies of the Church

11. *I will exalt you, Lord, because you have taken me up, and have not let my enemies gloat over me.* Which enemies? The Jews? In the dedication of the foundation, let us understand that the dedication of the whole house, yet to come about, is implied. What is said now in the person of the foundation will then be said by the whole house. Which enemies, then? The Jews? Hardly. Rather the devil and his angels, who fled in confusion when the Lord had risen. The provost of death mourned the defeat of death. *You have not let my enemies gloat over me*, because I could not be held prisoner by death.

Verse 3. Christ prays for healing, in our name

12. *Lord my God, I cried to you, and you healed me.* The Lord prayed on the mountain before his passion,[24] and God healed him. Who was it that he healed— the Word of God, the divine Word who had never been ill? No; but he carried the death of the flesh, he carried your wound, in order to cure your wound. And his flesh was healed. When? When he rose from the dead. Listen to the apostle, and hear what true health is like: *Death is swallowed up into victory. Where, O death, is your sting? Where is your strife, O death?* (1 Cor 15:54-55). At that future date it will be our voice singing its triumph, but at present the triumph is Christ's.

---

23. *Sanctitas vestra.*
24. See Mt 26:39 and parallels.

Verse 4. Descent into the pit

13. *Lord, you have brought my soul back from the depths.* This needs no detailed explanation. *You have saved me from those who go down into the pit.* Who are those who go down into the pit? All sinners who are sinking deep, for the pit is the deep recesses of this world. And what are the deep recesses of the world? Excessive luxury and wickedness. Those who immerse themselves in sensual cravings and earthbound desires go down into the pit. Such were the people who persecuted Christ. But what does the psalmist say? *You have saved me from those who go down into the pit.*

Verse 5. Head and limbs

14. *Sing to the Lord, you who are his saints.* Because your Head is risen, you, his other members, must hope for yourselves what you believe to have been wrought in him. Hope, you members, for what you believe of your Head. There is an old proverb, and a true one: where the head is, there also are the rest of the limbs. Christ has ascended into heaven and we shall follow him there; he did not remain in the underworld, he rose, and he can never die again. When we too rise we shall no longer be subject to death. Holding these promises, then, *sing to the Lord, you who are his saints, and make the remembrance of his holiness your confession.* What is meant by *make the remembrance?* You had forgotten him, but he has not forgotten you.

Verse 6. Anger and the gift of life

15. *Because he is provoked, there is anger, but in his will there is life.* He is angry when a sinner provokes him: so he says in scripture, *If ever you eat of it, on that day you will die* (Gn 2:17). They took the forbidden fruit, and they died; they were banished from paradise because *when he was provoked there was anger,* but hope was not denied them, because *in his will there is life.* What is meant by *in his will?* Not in our strength, not in our merits. Because God willed it he has saved us, not because we were worthy of it. What does a sinner deserve other than punishment? But instead of punishing us, he gave his life. And if he gave life to the wicked, what must he be keeping in reserve for the faithful?

Evening tears, morning joy

16. *Weeping will linger in the evening.* Do not worry because just now the psalmist invited us to sing, and here we are being told there is to be lamentation. When we are happy we sing, when we lament, we pray. Lament for the things of the present, sing of what is to come in the future. Pray about what already is, sing about

what you hope for. *Weeping will linger in the evening*: what does that mean? The evening is when the sun sets. Now the sun, which means the light of righteousness and the presence of God, set on the human race; for what does Genesis tell us about the time when Adam was driven out of the garden?[25] It was when God was taking a walk in paradise, and he was walking about there toward evening. The sinner had already hidden himself among the trees; he did not want to see God's face, though that had formerly been his delight, for the sun of righteousness had set for him and he no longer found any joy in the presence of God. From that point the whole of this mortal life was launched. *Weeping will linger in the evening.* You will be in tears for a long time, humankind, for you were born from Adam. We too are from Adam, and as many as have procreated offspring, and will do so in the future, procreate children who, just like their parents, are descendants of Adam. *Weeping will linger in the evening, but toward morning there will be rejoicing*, when the sun which had set on sinners has begun to dawn on the faithful. This is why the Lord Jesus Christ rose from the tomb in the morning, to promise to the whole house what he has already dedicated in the foundation. In the case of our Lord there was evening, when he was buried, and morning when he rose, on the third day. You too were buried in the evening, in paradise, and you have risen on the third day. How is it the third day for you? Well, if you think of the history of the world, day one is the time before the law, day two is the time under the law, and day three is under grace. What your Head has shown in his three-day mystery is revealed in you by these three ages of the world. But when is this revealed? You must look forward in hope to the morning, and be joyful in it; but for the present you have to grit your teeth and lament.

Verse 7. Immovable amid plenty

17. *I said in the midst of my plenty, I shall be unmoved for ever.* What is this plenty in which someone said, *I shall be unmoved for ever*? We must understand this, brothers and sisters, as spoken from the lowly human condition. Which of us here has plenty? No one. What do human beings have plenty of? Hardship, disaster. But surely the rich have plenty? No. The more they have, the more they want. They are ravaged by desires, fragmented by cravings, tormented by their fears; they fret and are depressed. What sort of plenty is that? There was plenty when humankind was at home in paradise, when Adam lacked nothing, when Adam enjoyed God. But he said, *I shall be unmoved for ever.* How could he say, *I shall be unmoved for ever* when he bent a willing ear to the suggestion, *Taste, and you shall be like gods*; when God said to him, *If ever you eat of it, on that day you will die*; and when the

---

25. See Gn 3:8.

devil assured them, *No, you will not die* (Gn 3:5; 2:17; 3:4)? So he was beguiled by the devil's persuasion and said, *I shall be unmoved for ever.*

Verses 8-9. Strength and beauty are from God

18. But God had spoken the truth when he said that he would take away from the proud what he had given to the humble at their creation, and so the psalmist goes on to say, *Lord, in your kindly will you have added strength to my beauty.* I was neither good nor strong from within my own resources, but I was both beautiful and strong because of what you did for me, for you added strength to my beauty of your own free will, that will by which you had made me. And to show me that I was such only by your will, *you turned your face away from me, and I became distraught.* God turned his face away from the humans he banished from paradise. From their exile let them shout their entreaty: *To you, Lord, I will cry, and with my God I will plead.* You did not cry in paradise, there you only praised God; you did not groan, you enjoyed him.[26] Now that you are shut out, groan and cry. The God who abandoned humankind when it was full of pride comes close to us now in our distress. *God thwarts the proud, but gives grace to the humble* (Jas 4:6; 1 Pt 5:5). *To you, Lord, I will cry, and with my God I will plead.*

Verse 10. Confession, of sin or of praise

19. What follows next is said in the person of the Lord, our foundation: *What use is there in my blood, if I sink down into corruption?* What is he praying for? To rise again. For if I descend into corruption, he says, if my flesh is to decay in the same way as the flesh of other men and women, and to rise only at the end of time, to what purpose have I shed my blood? If I do not rise immediately, I shall not preach to anyone, I shall not win anyone over. If I am to proclaim to people your wonderful deeds, your praises, the good news of life eternal, let my flesh rise, let it not descend into corruption. Were it to go the same way as that of others, what advantage would there be in my blood-shedding? *Will dust confess to you, will it proclaim your truth?* Confession is twofold; it can be of sin or of praise. When things are going badly for us, in the midst of our tribulations let us confess our sins; when things are going well for us, in our joy at his righteousness let us confess praise to God. Only, let us never give up confession.

---

26. *Fruebaris.* Augustine famously distinguished between *uti*, "to make use of," and *frui*, "to enjoy." The latter means to cling by love to something for its own sake, not as a means to anything else.

Verse 11. The Lord takes pity

20. *The Lord heard, and took pity on me.* How? Think of the dedication of the house. He heard, and took pity. *The Lord has become my helper.*

Verse 12. The hair-shirt of mortality

21. Listen now to the resurrection: *You have turned my lamentation into joy, you have torn up my sackcloth, and girded me with happiness.* What is this sackcloth?[27] Mortality. Sackcloth is woven from the hair of she-goats and kids; but she-goats and kids are consigned to the ranks of sinners.[28] The Lord received from us only the sackcloth; he did not take on what had merited the sackcloth. What deserved sackcloth was sin, and that sackcloth is mortality. He who had nothing in him deserving of death took on mortality for your sake. Whoever sins deserves to die, but he who committed no sin did not deserve sackcloth. In another place we hear his voice declaring, *When they were troublesome to me, I clothed myself in goats' hair*[29] (Ps 34(35):13). What does that mean, *I clothed myself in goats' hair*? "I confronted my persecutors with it." To make them think he was only a human being he hid himself from the eyes of his persecutors, because they were unworthy to see the one who was disguised under that lowly garb. But now *you have torn up my sackcloth, and girded me with happiness.*

Verse 13. May my glory sing to you

22. *So that my glory may sing to you, and I may be pierced no more.* What happens to the Head happens also to the body. What is the meaning of *that I may be pierced no more*? That I may never die again. Christ Jesus was stabbed as he hung on the cross; he was pierced through with a spear. This is why our Head says, "Let me be pierced no more," meaning, "Let me never die again." But what must we pray for, if the house is to be dedicated? That our conscience may not stab us with the sting of our sins. They will all be forgiven, and then we shall be free. *So that my glory*, not my lowliness, *may sing to you.* If the lowliness is ours, it is Christ's too, for we are Christ's body. Why? Because although Christ is enthroned in heaven, he will say to some, *I was hungry, and you fed me* (Mt 25:35). So he is both there and here, there in himself, here in us. What does he say, then? *That my glory may sing to you, and I may be pierced no more.* My humble state laments to you, my glorious state will sing to you. Now we have reached the end: *Lord my God, I will confess to*

---

27. "Sack" is a very old word, probably derived by Greek and Latin from a Semitic root, and still obviously related to the Hebrew *saq.*
28. See Mt 25:32.
29. *Cilicio*, originally the hair of Cilician goats.

you for ever. What does it mean, *I will confess to you for ever?* It means, "I shall praise you for ever." I have explained that there is confession of praise too, not only of sins. Confess now what you have done to God, and in the future you will confess what God has done for you. What have you done? You have committed sins. What has God done? He forgives you your sins when you confess your unrighteousness, so that hereafter you may confess his praises for ever and be pierced no more with compunction for your sin.

Exposition 1 of Psalm 30

Verse 1

1. *To the end, a psalm for David himself, an ecstasy.* This is a psalm to the end for David, the strong-armed mediator amid persecutions. The word "ecstasy" which has been added to the title indicates some abnormal state of mind, such as may be induced by panic, or by a revelation. But in this psalm panic is characteristic principally of the distressed people of God, under persecution by all nations, and dismayed by a falling-off of faith throughout the world. The Mediator himself speaks first; then the people redeemed by his blood gives expression to its thankfulness; and finally this same people speaks for a long time in its distress, which is where the panic comes in. The voice of the prophet breaks in twice, once near the end and again in the final verse.

Verses 2-6. The Mediator speaks

2. *In you, O Lord, have I put my trust; let me not be shamed for ever.* "In you, Lord, I have hoped, so let me not be finally shamed," he prays, thinking of the time when he will be insulted as though he were only an ordinary person. *In your justice set me free and rescue me.* In your justice free me from the pit of death, and rescue me from those who belong there.

3. *Bend your ear toward me.* Hear me in my humility, for you are very close to me. *Make haste to rescue me.* Do not make me wait until the end of time to be set apart from sinners, as all who believe in me must wait. *Be to me a protecting God.* O God, be a protector to me *and a home of refuge, to save me*, like a home I can flee to and be safe.

4. *For you are my fortified place and my refuge.* You are for me both fortitude to endure my persecutors, and my place of refuge so that I can leave them behind. *For the honor of your name you will be my leader, and you will nourish me.* May I follow your will in all I do, so that through me you may become known to all nations. Little by little you will build up my body by uniting your holy ones to me, until I attain my full stature.[1]

---

1. See Eph 4:13.

5. *You will lead me out of this trap they have hidden for me.* You will lead me clear of the snares they have concealed in my path. *For you are my protector.*

6. *Into your hands I commit my spirit.* To your power I entrust my spirit, knowing that I will swiftly receive it back.

Verses 6-9. The redeemed people gives thanks

6 (contd). *You have redeemed me, Lord God of truth.* The people redeemed by its Lord's passion, and joyful in the glory that has come to its Head, must also say, *You have redeemed me, Lord God of truth.*

7. *You hate all those who pay futile regard to vain things.* You hate those who hold the world's false happiness in high esteem. *But I have put my trust in the Lord.*

8. *I will exult and be glad in your mercy,* which does not let me down. *Because you have looked kindly on my humble state,* that state in which you have subjected me to futility, but in hope,[2] *you have saved my soul from its constraints*: saved it from the constraints of fear, that it may serve you in the freedom of charity.

9. *And have not shut me up into the clutches of my enemy.* You have not imprisoned me with no possible hope for liberty; you have not handed me over to the endless power of the devil, who ensnares us with greed for this life and terrifies us with death. But *you have guided my feet into open spaces.* The charity that is in me has been released from cramping fear, and can walk unhindered for ever into the broad stretches of freedom, for I know my Lord's resurrection and the promise of my own.

Verse 10. The cries of distress begin

10. *Have mercy on me, Lord, for I am in distress.* What is this unlooked-for cruelty on the part of my persecutors, that strikes hideous terror into me? *Have mercy on me, Lord.* I am not afraid now of dying, but I am terrified of torture and agony. *Under your anger my eye is confused.* I was keeping an eye on you, to make sure you would not abandon me, but you were angry and clouded my vision. *My soul too, and my belly.* Menaced by that same anger my soul is in turmoil, and also my memory,[3] where I kept hold of what my God suffered for me and promised to me.

---

2. See Rom 8:20.

3. The memory is for Augustine like a stomach in which the contributions from the senses are stored. In his long book on *memoria* in his *Confessions* he wonders why the mind can recall past emotional states without experiencing the same emotion now: "The memory is like the mind's stomach, while joy and sorrow are like delicious or bitter food. When they are committed to memory they are transferred to the stomach, as it were, and can be kept there, but cannot be tasted" (*Confessions* X,14,21).

Verses 11-14. Death would be preferable

11. *My life was imperiled by the pain* because my soul's life consists in confessing you, but it faltered in the pain, for my enemy had decreed, "Let them be tortured until they deny him." *And my years faded amid sighs.* The long years I am spending in this world are not taken from me by death; they go on and on, and are passed amid groaning. *My vigor is undermined by want.* What I want is health for this body of mine, yet pains are provided liberally; or else what I want is the dissolution of my body in death, but death is not allotted to me. In this need my confidence is weakened, *and my bones are jarred.* The firm supports of my being are shaken.

12. *I have become an object of scorn, more so than all my enemies.* My enemies are all the unjust; yet while they suffer anguish only until they confess, and I have therefore surmounted their scorn, my confession is not followed by death, but only met with more torments. *Beyond bearing, in my neighbors' eyes.* My suffering seems excessive to those who were already drawing near, ready to recognize you and embrace the faith I hold. *And a source of fear to my acquaintances.* I have struck fear even into those who know me, by the spectacle of my horrifying distress. *Those who saw me fled outside away from me:* having no inkling of my inward, invisible hope, they fled away from me to external and visible things.

13. *I am consigned to oblivion, as though I had died out of their hearts,* for they have forgotten me; it is as though in their hearts I am dead. *I am no better than a pot thrown away.* I seemed to myself to be no use any longer for the Lord's purposes, living on in this world but winning no one over to him, since they were all afraid to be associated with me.

14. *I have heard hostile criticism from those who encircle me.* I have heard many of them censuring me; though near me in this earthly pilgrimage they pursue time's cyclic courses and refuse to travel with me straight to our homeland in eternity. *Colluding against me, they planned to let me live.* My soul could easily have escaped from them by death, so in the hope that it could be brought to compliance they hatched a plot to keep me alive.

Verses 15-16. But my fate is in your hands, Lord

15. *But I trusted in you, Lord; I said, "You are my God."* You have undergone no change, so you will not fail to save me, though you discipline me.

16. *The fate allotted to me is in your hands,*[4] *my lot is within your power, for I am conscious of no merit to explain your choice of me in particular for salvation, out of the universal godlessness of the human race. If the just and secret plan of election*

---

4. Variant: "My times are in your hands."

in your mind is concealed from me, I know this nonetheless: that through the casting of lots the Lord's tunic has fallen to me.[5] *Rescue me, then, from the hands of my enemies, and from my persecutors.*

Verses 17-19. Vindication

17. *Let your face shine over your servant.* Let them know, all those who think I do not belong to you, that your countenance is watching over me and that I am your servant. *Save me in your mercy.*

18. *Let me not be put to shame, Lord, for I have called upon you.* Lord, do not let me be shamed before those who insult me; let it not happen, because I have invoked you. *Let the godless blush with shame and be dragged down to hell:* rather let them be shamed who invoke stone idols. May they become companions of the shades.

19. *Let lying lips be struck dumb.* Make your mysterious workings[6] in me known to the peoples, and so befuddle the speech of those who fabricated lies against me, *the lips that speak wickedly against the righteous one, in their pride and scorn.* These are the people who speak wickedly against Christ, proudly strutting and scorning him as a crucified man and no more.

Verses 20-22. The prophet intervenes

20. *How great, how immense, is your sweetness, Lord!* This is the voice of the prophet, exclaiming in wonder as he discerns how abundant and how varied are the expressions of your sweetness, O Lord, *which you have hidden from those who fear you.* You dearly love even those you discipline, but to ensure that they do not relax their guard and behave carelessly you hide the sweetness of that love from those who will profit by fearing you. But *you have brought it to perfection for those who trust in you.* You have shown the perfection of your sweetness to those who trust in you, for you do not withhold it from those who persevere in hoping for it to the end. *In the sight of the children of men,* for it is not hidden from those "children" who live no longer in imitation of Adam, but after the example of the Son of Man. *You will hide them in the hidden recess of your face:* may you reserve an everlasting throne for those who set their hope in you, in a secret place where they may know

---

5. Compare Jn 19:24. Augustine's view of predestination is evident here. On the basis of many biblical texts, notably the teaching of Saint Paul, and partly under the pressure of the Pelagian controversy, Augustine developed the doctrine of God's predestination of his elect to grace and to glory, which necessarily includes the gift of final perseverance. The divine decision is infallible and completely just, though inscrutable to the human mind. It does not violate human freedom. The relationship between predestinating grace and human freedom was to be the subject of long, and at times acrimonious, controversy.

6. *Sacramenta tua.*

you *far from human disturbance*, so that they may be subject to harassment from their fellows no more.

21. *You will shield them in your tent against wrangling tongues.* Meanwhile scurrilous tongues clamor to them, "Who knows the latest? Do you know who has arrived from such-and-such a place?" But you will shield them in the tent of faith, faith in what our Lord during his time on earth did and suffered for us.

22. *Blessed be the Lord, for he has wrought wonderful mercy in the city that lies around us.* Blessed may the Lord be, because after the Church had undergone the discipline of such bitter persecutions, he made his mercy wonderful all around the world, through the widest circles of human society.

Verse 23. The Church concurs

23. *Beside myself with fear . . . :* here the people takes up the tale again, saying, "In my fear, as the pagans raged horribly against me, *I said, I have been flung far out of your sight,* for if your eyes were upon me, you would not allow me to suffer like this." *Therefore you heard the sound of my prayer, Lord, as I cried to you.* You heard it, this sound of my prayer as I lifted my voice up with great intensity in my distress, and you set a limit to my correction, proving that you were indeed taking care of me.

Verses 24- 25. The prophet again: final certainty

24. *Choose the Lord as your love, all you who are his saints.* Here we have the prophet intervening again with his exhortation as he considers these events. *Choose the Lord as your love, all you who are his saints,* he bids us, *because the Lord will search out the truth.* If the righteous will scarcely be saved, what will become of the sinner and the godless?[7] *And he will requite those who persist in their pride.* People who even though defeated will not turn to him he will punish, for their pride is beyond measure.

25. *Act manfully*[8] *and let your hearts be strengthened*, doing good without weakening, so that in due season you may reap your harvest, *all you who hope in the Lord.* You who fear him and worship him aright, hope in the Lord.

---

7. See 1 Pt 4:18.
8. See Exposition 2 of Psalm 26, 23, and note there.

Exposition 2 of Psalm 30

The First Sermon to the People[1]

Verse 1

1. Let us try to probe the secrets of this psalm we have just sung, and chisel out from it a sermon to offer to your ears and minds. The title of the psalm is *To the end, a psalm for David himself, an ecstasy.* If we have come to know Christ, we know what *to the end* means, because the apostle tells us that *Christ is the end of the law, so that everyone who believes may be justified* (Rom 10:4). He is an "end" not in the sense of finishing it off, but of bringing it to its perfection. You know how we speak of the "end" of something in two different ways: either what puts out of existence something that did exist, or what brings to full perfection something that had only begun to exist. So you can see that *to the end* means "to Christ."

What does "ecstasy" imply?

2. *A psalm for David, an ecstasy.* The word *ecstasy* is Greek. Its meaning is best conveyed for us by the phrase "standing outside," but ecstasy strictly means being out of one's mind, or "being beside oneself." Now, we can think of two possible reasons for this condition: one is fear; the other is the contemplation of heavenly things so intense that the realities of life here below seem to slip out of the mind. The saints experienced this kind of ecstasy, all those saints at least to whom were revealed the hidden mysteries of God that transcend this world. Paul spoke about being beside oneself, being in ecstasy, and hinted that he was referring to himself, when he said, *Whether we are beside ourselves, for God, or in our right mind, for you, the charity of Christ constrains us* (2 Cor 5:13-14). What he means is: "If we choose to do nothing else, and simply contemplate what we see when we are beside ourselves, we would not be available to you, but would be so rapt in heavenly things as to seem uncaring about you. And when you with your uncertain steps tried to follow us to those higher, heavenly realms, would we not still seem uncaring, but for the fact that the charity of Christ constrains us, so that we consider ourselves your servants? And so out of gratitude to him who had granted us higher graces we

---

1. Probably preached at a country church near Carthage, possibly in the summer of 411.

would not disdain lower needs for the sake of the weak, and would accommodate ourselves to people who could not join us in the vision of heavenly realities, like Christ, who *being in the form of God, deemed it no robbery to be God's equal, yet emptied himself and took on the form of a slave"* (Phil 2:6-7).[2] You notice that Paul says, *Whether we are beside ourselves, for God,* because God alone sees his own mystery and only he can reveal his secrets; we only see them in ecstasy. And the man who is speaking here is the one who testifies that he was seized and carried off to the third heaven, where he heard inexpressible words, which no human being may utter.[3] So completely was he beside himself that he could say, *Whether in the body or out of the body I do not know; God knows* (2 Cor 12:2).

If the title of our psalm refers to ecstasy like this, if it envisages this mode of being beside oneself, we must certainly expect its author to have weighty and profound things to say. The author is the prophet, but more truly the Holy Spirit who spoke through the prophet.

Could Christ be genuinely afraid?

3. But suppose "ecstasy" means fear? The text of our psalm will have plenty of relevance to this other meaning of the word, for it looks as though it is going to talk about the passion, in which fear played a part. Whose fear? Christ's certainly, since the psalm was entitled, *to the end,* and we understand "the end" to be Christ. Or our fear, perhaps? Surely we cannot attribute fear to Christ as his passion loomed, when we know that was what he had come for? When he had reached that suffering for which he had come, was he afraid of imminent death? Surely even if he had been human only, not God, he could have been more joyful at the prospect of future resurrection than fearful because he was about to die, couldn't he?

Head and body speak as one

But in fact he who deigned to assume the form of a slave, and within that form to clothe us with himself, he who did not disdain to take us up into himself, did not disdain either to transfigure us into himself, and to speak in our words, so that we in

---

2. The preceding passage could be understood in a slightly different way: " . . . when you with your uncertain steps tried to follow us to those higher, heavenly realms, would we consider ourselves your servants? Would we not deem it right, and not ungrateful to him who had granted us higher graces, to refuse to neglect lower needs and our ministry to the weak? Would we accommodate ourselves to people who could not join us in the vision of heavenly realities—would we, if the charity of Christ did not constrain us? This is the Christ who. . . .", etc.

3. See 2 Cor 12:2.4.

our turn might speak in his.[4] This is the wonderful exchange, the divine business deal, the transaction effected in this world by the heavenly dealer. He came to receive insults and give honors, he came to drain the cup of suffering and give salvation, he came to undergo death and give life. Facing death, then, because of what he had from us, he was afraid, not in himself but in us. When he said that his soul was sorrowful to the point of death,[5] we all unquestionably said it with him. Without him, we are nothing, but in him we too are Christ. Why? Because the whole Christ consists of Head and body. The Head is he who is the savior of his body,[6] he who has already ascended into heaven; but the body is the Church, toiling on earth. Were it not for the body's linkage with its Head through the bond of charity, so close a link that Head and body speak as one, he could not have rebuked a certain persecutor from heaven with the question, *Saul, Saul, why are you persecuting me?* (Acts 9:4). Already enthroned in heaven, Christ was not being touched by any human assailant, so how could Saul, by raging against the Christians on earth, inflict injury on him in any way? He does not say, "Why are you persecuting my saints?" or "my servants," but *Why are you persecuting me?* This is tantamount to asking, "Why attack my limbs?" The Head was crying out on behalf of the members, and the Head was transfiguring the members into himself. It is like the tongue speaking in the foot's name. It may happen that someone's foot is trodden on in a crowd, and it hurts: the tongue cries out, "You"re treading on me!" It does not say, "You are treading on my foot"; it says it is being trodden on. Nobody has touched it, but the crushed foot is not severed from the tongue.

This will help us to understand about the ecstasy of fear. What am I to say, brothers and sisters? If people who were destined to suffer were completely fearless, why would that prophecy have been made to Peter, the one we heard on the feast day of the apostles? The Lord foretold Peter's future passion by saying to him, *When you were younger you fastened your belt and went where you liked; but when you have grown old, someone else will fasten it for you, and take you where you do not want to go. He said this*, scripture asserts, *indicating how Peter would die* (Jn 21:18-19). If the apostle Peter was so perfect that he willingly went where he did not want to[7] (I mean he did not want to die, but he did want to win his crown), why wonder if there is some fear when the righteous suffer, even the saints? Fear springs

---

4. Here and in the following paragraphs Augustine articulates his most profound conviction on the psalms: the "I" who speaks is always Christ, either Christ in his own person, or Christ in the person of his members, or the *totus Christus*, Head and members, Bridegroom and bride. The texts he quotes (Acts 9:4; Eph 5:31-32; Is 61:10) are among his favorites for making the point, and recur frequently, as do the key phrases, *transfigurare nos in se, una quaedam persona, una vox*.

5. See Mt 26:38

6. See Eph 5:23.

7. Variants: "unwillingly went where he did not want to"; "went as though willingly where he did not want to"; "was led where he did not want to go, though also willing it."

from human weakness, hope from the divine promise. Your fear is your own, your hope is God's gift in you. In your fear you know yourself better, so that once you are set free you may glorify him who made you. Let human weakness be afraid, then, for divine mercy does not desert us in our fear.

So it is a frightened person who begins the psalm: *In you, O Lord, have I put my trust; let me not be shamed for ever.* He or she is both afraid and trustful, you see; and you see too that the fear is not devoid of hope. Even if there is some turmoil in this human heart, divine comfort has not left it alone.

4. Christ is speaking here in the prophet; no, I would dare to go further and say simply, Christ is speaking. He is going to say certain things in this psalm that we might think inappropriate to Christ, to the excellent dignity of our Head, and especially to the Word who was God with God in the beginning. Some of the things said here may not even seem suitable for him in the form of a servant, that form which he took from the Virgin; and yet it is Christ who is speaking, because in the members of Christ there is Christ. I want you to understand that Head and body together are called one Christ. To make this quite clear he says, when speaking of marriage, *They will be two in one flesh; so they are two no longer, but one flesh* (Mt 19:5-5). But perhaps it might be thought that he only means this to apply to any ordinary marriage? No, because listen to what Paul tells us: *They will be two in one flesh*, he says. *This is a great mystery, but I am referring it to Christ and the Church* (Eph 5:31-32). So out of two people one single person comes to be, the single person that is Head and body, Bridegroom and bride. The wonderful, surpassing unity of this person is celebrated also by the prophet Isaiah, for Christ speaks prophetically in him too: *The Lord has arrayed me like a bridegroom adorned with his wreath, or a bride decked with her jewels* (Is 61:10). He calls himself bridegroom and he calls himself bride: how can he say he is both bridegroom and bride, except because they will be two in one flesh? And if two in one flesh, why not two in one voice? Let Christ speak, then, because in Christ the Church speaks, and in the Church Christ speaks, and the body speaks in the Head, and the Head in the body. Listen again to the apostle as he expresses this even more plainly: *As the body is a unit and has many members, and yet all the members of the body, many though they be, are one body, so too is Christ* (1 Cor 12:12). He was speaking about Christ's members—the faithful, that is—but he did not say, "So too are Christ's members." He called the whole entity he had spoken about, "Christ." A body is one single unit, with many members, but all the members of the body, numerous as they are, constitute one body; and it is the same with Christ. Many members, one body: Christ. All of us together with our Head are Christ, and without our Head we are helpless. Why? Because united with our Head we are the vine, but if cut off from our Head (God forbid!) we are only loppings, of no use to the vine-tenders and fit only for the bonfire. This is why Christ himself says in the gospel, *I am the vine, you are the branches, and my Father is the vine-dresser*; and he warns us, *Without me you can do nothing* (Jn 15:5.1). If we can achieve nothing without you, Lord, we can do

everything in you. Yes, because whatever work he does through us seems to be our work. He can do plenty, or rather everything, without us, but we can do nothing without him.

Verse 2. Profitable shame

5. Whether the speaker's ecstasy is the product of fear or of being beside himself, let him speak on, then, because either way what is to be said befits him. Let us who are within Christ's body say—and let us all say it as one, because we are a unity—*In you, O Lord, I have put my trust; let me not be shamed for ever.* The shame I truly dread, he says, is the shame that lasts for eternity. There is a temporary shame that is profitable to us, the shame of the mind that reviews its sins, and is horrified by the review, and ashamed at the horror, and is shamed into correcting itself. This is why the apostle too asks, *What glory did you have in those doings of which you are now ashamed?* (Rom 6:21); he is saying that the believers are ashamed not of their present gifts, but of their past sins. A Christian does not fear that kind of shame; indeed, if we have not undergone it, we shall be ashamed for ever. What is eternal shame? That of which scripture says, *Their lawless actions will convict them to their faces* (Wis 4:20). The wicked flock will gather at the Lord's left hand as their iniquities convict them to their faces and the goats are separated from the sheep, and they will hear their sentence: *Depart from me, you accursed, into the eternal fire which was prepared for the devil and his angels.* And if they ask why? *I was hungry and you did not feed me* (Mt 25:41.42). They were contemptuous, then, when they refused food to Christ in his hunger, refused him a drink when he was thirsty, gave him no clothing when he was naked, did not take him in when he was a traveler, failed to visit him when he was sick; they were contemptuous then. But when this list begins to be read out to them they will be ashamed, and this shame will last for all eternity. This is the shame that the speaker in the psalm fears when he is either terrified out of his mind, or beside himself for God, and prays, *In you, O Lord, have I put my trust; let me not be shamed for ever.*

Justification is God's work

6. *In your justice set me free, and rescue me,* for if you take my "justice" into account, you cannot but damn me. *In your justice set me free.* There is a justice that belongs to God, but becomes ours as well when it is given to us. It is called God's justice to ensure that humans do not imagine that they have any justice as from themselves. Paul affirms this by saying, *When someone believes in him who justifies the impious, that faith is reckoned as justice to the believer* (Rom 4:5). What does that mean, God who "justifies the impious"? It means he changes one who was impious into a just person.

The Jews, on the contrary, assumed that they were able to achieve perfect justice by their own efforts, and in consequence they tripped over the stumbling-stone, the rock of scandal,[8] and failed to recognize the grace of Christ. All they received was a law that could show them up as guilty, not one by which they could be freed from their guilt. What does the apostle have to say about that? *I bear this witness against them: they have zeal for God, indeed, but it is not informed by knowledge* (Rom 10:2). What does he mean by saying that the Jews *have zeal for God*, but then adding that *it is not informed by knowledge*? Listen: he goes on to point out the consequence of this lack of knowledge: *They failed to recognize the righteousness that comes from God, and by seeking to set up a righteousness of their own, they did not submit to God's righteousness* (Rom 10:3). If their uninformed zeal for God consists in ignorance of God's justice and the wish to set up their own, as though they could become just by their own efforts, it follows that the reason why they did not recognize God's grace was that they did not want to be saved gratis. For who is saved gratis? Everyone in whom the Savior has found nothing to crown, but only what he must condemn, one in whom he has found nothing that deserves rewards but only what merits torments. If he is to act as the law's provisions truly demand, the sin must be condemned. If he were to act on that principle, whom could he acquit? He found all of us to be sinners; he alone, who found us sinners, himself came without sin. The apostle confirms this: *All have sinned, and are in need of the glory of God* (Rom 3:23). And what does that mean, *are in need of the glory of God*? That you need him to set you free, for you cannot do it by yourself. Because you have no power to liberate yourself you need a liberator. What have you to boast about? How can you give yourself airs about the law and righteousness? Do you not see what the law collides with inside you, what it testifies about you, and against you? Do you not hear someone fighting, confessing, and imploring help in the struggle? Do you not hear the Lord's athlete begging the superintendent of the games to help him in his contest? God does not look on as you compete, in the same way as the one who puts on the games watches you if you are fighting in the amphitheatre. This man can award you the prize if you win, but cannot help you if you are in danger. God does not look on like that. No, indeed not; notice what Paul says: *I take great delight in God's law as far as my inner self is concerned, but I am aware of a different law in my members that opposes the law of my mind, and imprisons me under the law of sin inherent in my members. Who will deliver me from this death-ridden body, wretch that I am? Only the grace of God, through Jesus Christ our Lord* (Rom 7:22-25). Why call it "grace"? Because it is given gratis. And why is it given gratis? Because there were no preceding merits on your part; God's benefits forestalled you. To him, then, be the glory, to him who sets us free, *for all have sinned, and are in need of the glory of God.*

---

8. See Rom 9:32.

With this in mind, *in you, O Lord, have I put my trust*, not in myself. *Let me not be shamed for ever*, because I trust in him who does not shame me.[9] *In your justice set me free, and rescue me*. Because you have found in me no justice of my own, set me free in yours; let me be freed by what renders me just, what makes a godless person godly, what enables a blind person to see, what raises up one who is falling, what makes a mourner rejoice. That is what sets me free; I do not liberate myself. *In your justice set me free, and rescue me*.

Verse 3. Time is very short

7. *Bend your ear toward me*. God did this when he sent Christ himself to us, for he sent one who bent his head low and wrote in the earth when an adulterous woman was presented to him as deserving of punishment.[10] Already he had bent down to the earth; for God had bent down to the humans who had been told, *Earth you are, and back to earth you shall go* (Gn 3:19). God does not bend his ear to us by some kind of shift in bodily position, nor is he confined by a determined bodily shape, as we are. We must exclude any human fantasies of this kind when thinking about God. God is Truth. Now truth is neither square, nor round, nor long. Truth is everywhere, if the eye of the heart is open to it. But God bends his ear to us when he pours down his mercy upon us. What greater mercy could there be, than that he should send his only Son, not to live with us, but to die for us? *Bend your ear toward me*.

8. *Make haste to rescue me*. His prayer, *make haste*, is heard. This verb was used to help you understand that the whole stretch of time during which the world rolls on its way, this time that seems to us so long, is really no more than a moment. Anything that has an end is not long. The time from Adam to the present day is over and done with, and certainly far more time has passed than remains ahead, yet if Adam were still alive, and were to die today, what difference would it have made to him to have been here so long, to have had such a long life? So why this prayer for haste? Because the years are flying past, and what seems to you long-drawn is very brief in God's eyes. In his ecstasy the psalmist had understood how quickly time passes.

You cannot escape from God

Make haste to rescue me. Be to me a protecting God, and a home of refuge to save me. Be a home of refuge for me, O God my protector, a home of refuge; for sometimes I am in peril, and I want to flee—but where? What place can I flee to,

---

9. Variant: "because whoever trusts in him is not shamed."
10. See Jn 8:6.

and be safe? A mountain? A cave somewhere? Some fortified building? What fortress can I hold? What defensive walls put up around me? Wherever I go, there is someone following me: myself. You can flee from anything and everything, poor mortal, except your conscience. Go into your house, lie down on your bed, seek the ultimate privacy: you will find no secret place to run to from your conscience, if your sins are gnawing you. But in saying, "Make haste to rescue me, and set me free by your justice, forgive my sins and build up your own justice in me," he is saying, "You will be the home where I can take refuge, and to you I flee for safety; for where else can I run to, away from you?" If God is angry with you, where will you run? Listen to what is said in another psalm by someone who fears God: *Whither shall I go from your spirit, and whither flee from your face? If I mount to heaven, you are there; if I sink down to hell, even there you are present* (Ps 138(139):7-8). Wherever I go, I find you there. If you are angry, I find you as an avenger, if you are appeased, as a helper. Nothing is left to me but to flee, not from you but to you. My brothers and sisters, if any one of you is a servant, and you want to evade your master, you run to some place where your master is absent; but if you want to evade God, it is to the Lord that you must run, for there is no place where you can go to escape God. All things are immediately present and naked to the eyes of the Almighty.[11]

The Lord is the good Samaritan

"Do you yourself be my home, then," prays the psalm, "a home where I can take refuge. If I have not been saved, how can I escape? Heal me, and I will take refuge in you. I cannot walk unless you heal me, so how will I be able to run?" Where could a person go, or run to, if he was unable to walk and lying half-dead in the road, after being wounded by robbers? A priest passed him by, a Levite passed him by, but a Samaritan who chanced that way took pity on him (see Lk 10:30-35); and this is our Lord, who took pity on the human race. The word "Samaritan" means "guardian." And who will guard us, if he abandons us? The Jews said to him, *Are we not right to say that you are a Samaritan, and that you have a demon?* and they spoke truly, even though they meant it as vilification. The Lord rejected one charge but embraced the other: *I have no demon*, he said (Jn 8:48-49); but he did not say, "I am no Samaritan," because he wanted it to be understood that he is our guardian. In his loving pity he drew near to the wounded traveler, healed him, took him to the tavern, and lavished his mercy on him in every way. The patient can now walk, and therefore can also run, and where should he run to, if not to God, where there is a home of refuge waiting for him?

---

11. See Heb 4:13.

Verse 4. God our mother

9. *You are my fortified place and my refuge. For the honor of your name you will be my leader, and you will nourish me.* Not for my deserts, but *for the honor of your name*, so that you may be glorified; and not because I am worthy of it, *you will be my leader*, so that I do not stray away from you; and *you will nourish me*, so that I may be strong enough to eat the food you give the angels. He who has promised us the food of heaven has nourished us here below with milk, in his motherly mercy. A nursing mother causes the food which her child is not yet capable of eating to pass through her own flesh, and pours it out again as milk; the baby gets the same food he would have received at table, but because it has passed through her flesh it is suitable for a young child. So too the Lord put on flesh and came to us, to make his wisdom palatable for us as milk. The body of Christ speaks here: *You will nourish me.*

Verse 5. Temptation

10. *You will lead me out of this trap*[12] *they have hidden for me.* Already there is a hint of the passion here: *you will lead me out of this trap they have hidden for me.* But it does not refer only to the passion of our Lord Jesus Christ, for the devil has set his trap for all time. Woe betide anyone who falls into that trap; and fall into it anyone will, who does not trust in the Lord, and does not say, *In you, O Lord, have I put my trust; let me not be shamed for ever. In your justice set me free, and rescue me.* The enemy's trap is stretched out ready; there are twin loops in it, error and terror: error to entice, terror to break and grip us. You must shut the door of greed against error, and the door of fear against terror; and then you will be led clear of the trap.

Your Commander gave you an example of how to fight in this way. He deigned even to be tempted for your sake, and displayed the example in himself. At first he was tempted by alluring possibilities, as the devil tried the door of greed in him, suggesting, *Say to these stones, "Become loaves of bread." Worship me, and I will confer these kingdoms on you. "Throw yourself down, for scripture says, 'He has charged his angels to take care of you, and they will carry you in their hands, so that you will not even stub your foot on a stone'"* (Mt 4:3.9.6). All this was enticement, meant to tempt him to greed. But when the devil discovered that in Christ, who was being tempted for us, the door of greed was closed, he changed his tactics and tried the door of fear instead, preparing the passion for him. That is why the evangelist ends the story with the words, *when all the temptation was finished, the*

---

12. *Muscipula*, literally a mousetrap.

devil left him, biding his time (Lk 4:13). What does that suggest, *biding his time*? That he meant to return and try the door of fear, having found the door of greed shut.

Now the whole body of Christ undergoes temptation to the very end. Think, my brothers and sisters, how it was when some harmful measure was enacted against Christians. The whole body was hit at once, the whole body took the thrust; that is why a psalm contained the words, *I was pushed at like a heap of sand to make me topple, but the Lord held me up* (Ps 117(118):13). Then when all those attempts to strike down the whole body were over, temptation began to assail separate parts. The body of Christ is still tempted: although one church may not be suffering persecution, another will be feeling the blows. It no longer has to suffer the fury of an emperor, but it endures the rage of a wicked populace. How much devastation has been caused by mobs?[13] How much harm has been done to the Church by bad Christians? They are like the fish that were caught in the net and became so numerous that they weighed down the fishermen's boats, on that occasion when the Lord aided their catch before his passion.[14] A similar load of temptation is never lacking. Let none of us tell ourselves, "This is not a time of temptation." Any who think so are promising themselves peace, but those who promise themselves peace are invaded unawares. Let the whole body of Christ pray, *You will lead me out of this trap they have hidden for me*, for our Head has been led out of the trap they concealed for him, those people we heard about just now in the gospel. They were all ready to say, *This is the heir. Come on, let's kill him and the inheritance will be for us.* But when the Lord questioned them they pronounced sentence against themselves. *"What will the landlord do to those rascally tenants?" "He will bring those wretches to a wretched end, and let the vineyard to other gardeners." "What? Have you never read the text, The stone rejected by the builders has become the headstone of the corner?"* The phrase, *rejected by the builders,* has the same implication as *they threw him out of the vineyard and killed him* (Mt 21:38.40-42.39). Christ was delivered; our Head is there on high, and free. Let us cling to him now by love, so that later on we may be even more strongly cemented to him by immortality; and let us all say, *You will lead me out of this trap they have hidden for me, for you are my protector.*

Verse 6. Christ is speaking in the psalms

11. Let us listen now to something our Lord said on the cross: *Into your hands I commit my spirit* (Lk 23:46). When we hear those words of his in the gospel, and recognize them as part of this psalm, we should not doubt that here in this psalm it is Christ himself who is speaking. The gospel makes it clear. He said, *Into your hands*

---

13. Perhaps an allusion to the Circumcellions; see note at Exposition of Psalm 10, 5.
14. See Lk 5:7.

I commit my spirit; and bowing his head he breathed forth his spirit (Lk 23:46; Jn 19:30). He had good reason for making the words of the psalm his own, for he wanted to teach you that in the psalm he is speaking. Look for him in it. Bear in mind how he wanted you to look for him in another psalm, the one "for his taking up in the morning,"[15] where he said, *They dug holes in my hands and my feet, they numbered all my bones. These same people looked on and watched me. They shared out my garments among them, and cast lots for my tunic* (Ps 21:17-19(22:16-18)). He wanted to make sure you would understand that this whole prophecy was fulfilled in himself, so he made the opening verse of that same psalm his own cry: *O God, my God, why have you forsaken me?* Yet all the same he transfigured the body's cry as he made it his own, for the Father never did forsake his only Son. *You have redeemed me, Lord God of truth*, carrying through what you promised, unfailing in your pledge, O God of truth.

Verse 7. Futile preoccupations

12. *You hate all those who pay futile regard to vain things.* Who does so? Anyone who dies by fearing death. Such a person tells lies out of fear of dying, and so dies before the time comes for death, even though the object of the lies was to carry on living. You are afraid to die, and so you want to tell lies, so you tell lies and you die! While attempting to evade one death, which you may postpone but cannot banish altogether, you fall into two deaths, dying first in your soul and later in your body. How does this come about, if not through paying futile regard to vain things? And all because this passing day is pleasant to you, and those years that fly by are pleasant; yet you can catch hold of no part of them and, what is more, you are caught yourself. *You hate all those who pay futile regard to vain things. But I*, who do not, *have put my trust in the Lord.* If you put your trust in money, you are paying futile regard to vain things; if you put your trust in high office or some exalted rank in human government, you are paying futile regard to vain things; if you put your trust in some powerful friend, you are paying futile regard to vain things. When you put your trust in all these, either you expire, and leave them all behind, or they will crumble while you are still alive, and what you trusted will have let you down. Isaiah points to futility like this: *All flesh is but grass, and all its splendor like the flower of the field; the grass is dried up and its flower wilted, but the word of the Lord abides for ever* (Is 40:6-8). For my part, I do not put my trust in empty things as they do, nor pay futile regard to them; I have put my trust in the Lord, who is not empty.

---

15. See the title of Psalm 21(22).

Verse 8. The soul's constraints

13. *I will exult and be glad in your mercy*, not in any righteousness of my own. *Because you have looked kindly on my humble state, you have saved my soul from its constraints, and have not shut me up into the power of the enemy.* What are these constraints, from which we want our souls plucked free? Could anyone list them? Or heap them up, so that we can size them aright? Or suggest suitable means to avoid or escape them? The first constraint that hems in the human race, and a harsh one it is, is our ignorance of anyone else's heart, our tendency often to think badly of a faithful friend and to value an unfaithful one. This is a hard constraint indeed! What are you going to do about it, to gain insight into the hearts of others? What kind of eye can you bring to the job, you weak, pathetic mortals? What do you propose to do today, to read the heart of your brother or sister? You have not the wherewithal.

Another major constraint is that you do not even see what your own heart will be like tomorrow. And what am I to say about the constraints of mortality itself? We are constrained to die, and no one wants to. Nobody wants something that constrains us all. No one wants something that will happen whether we like it or not. That is a mighty constraint, to dislike something unavoidable. If it were possible, we would certainly choose not to die; we would wish to become like the angels, but by some transformation that did not involve dying, as the apostle suggests: *We have a building from God, a home not made by hands, an everlasting home in heaven. We groan over our present condition, longing to have our heavenly dwelling put on over this one, so that being clothed in it we may not be found naked. Yes, we who are still in this earthly dwelling groan under our burden; not that we want to be stripped of it, but wishing to be invested with the other one on top, so that what is mortal may be swallowed up by life* (2 Cor 5:1-4). We want to reach God's kingdom, but not to travel there through death; yet constraint stands there saying, "This way." Do you hesitate to go that way, poor mortal, when by that same route God has come to you?

Then what about the constraints of overcoming bad habits? Conquering a habit entails a hard fight, as you well know. You see that your behavior is wrong, that it is detestable and makes you unhappy, yet you go on behaving in the same way. You did so yesterday, and you will today. If you are so uncomfortable when I put it to you like this, how much more uncomfortable does it make you to think about it yourself? Yet you will go on doing it. What is dragging you along? Who is leading you off captive? Could it be the law in your members that is in conflict with the law in your mind? If so, cry out, *Who will deliver me from this death-ridden body, wretch that I am? Only the grace of God, through Jesus Christ our Lord* (Rom 7:24-25). Then the psalm-verse we have just read will be true for you: *I have put my trust in the Lord. I will exult and be glad in your mercy. Because you have looked kindly on my humble state, you have saved my soul from its constraints.* How was it saved from its constraints? Only because he looked kindly on your humble state. He who had the power to free you from constraints would not have heard your plea unless you had first humbled yourself, as that man humbled himself who cried, *Who will deliver me from this death-ridden body, wretch that I am?* But the Jews were not humbled, the Jews who *failed to recognize the righteousness that comes from God, and by seeking to set up a righteousness of their own, did not submit to God's righteousness* (Rom 10:3).

Verse 9. Freedom from the real enemy

14. You have not shut me up into the clutches of the enemy. This does not mean the clutches of your neighbor, or your business-partner, or someone you fought with and wounded, or someone you may have chanced to injure in your town. For people like that we are bound to pray.[16] We have a different enemy, the devil, the ancient serpent. All of us are set free from his clutches when we die, provided we meet death well; but any who die a bad death, who die in their iniquities, are shut up into his power, to be damned with him at the end. The Lord our God delivers us from the clutches of our enemy, but the enemy tries to entrap us through our lusts. When these lusts are powerful, and we submit to them, they are justly called constraints. So if God sets us free from our constraints, what will there be in us for the enemy to grab? How can we then be imprisoned in his clutches?

15. *You have guided my feet into open spaces.* Well, yes, the path is narrow.[17] To the laborious plodder it is narrow, but to the lover it is wide. The same path which seemed narrow now seems to have widened. *You have guided my feet into open spaces,* says the psalm, for if my feet were squeezed too close together they might tread on each other and trip me up. So what does he mean by saying, *You have guided my feet into open spaces?* It must mean, "You have made right living easy for me, though it was once so difficult." That is what the line means: *you have guided my feet into open spaces.*

Verses 10-11. A hurried conclusion

16. *Have mercy on me, Lord, for I am in distress. Under your anger my eye is confused, my soul too and my belly. For my soul faltered in the pain, and my years faded amid sighs.* This will have to do for now, dearest friends.[18] With the Lord's help I may be able to make up what is still due, and go home with the psalm finished.[19]

---

16. See Mt 5:44.
17. See Mt 7:14.
18. *Caritati vestrae.*
19. Apparently the foregoing sermon, and the two following sermons on the same psalm, were preached at some country church away from Hippo.

Exposition 3 of Psalm 30

The Second Sermon to the People

Verse 10. Varied experiences, common sympathy

1. We must turn our minds to the rest of the psalm now, and see if we can recognize ourselves in the words of the prophet. If we have examined ourselves when we are in trouble, we shall rejoice when the time comes for apportioning rewards. While explaining the earlier verses of the psalm I reminded you, beloved,[1] that it is Christ who is speaking; and I stressed that we must understand this as the whole Christ, Head and body. I established this solidly, I think, with appropriate and crystal-clear texts from the scriptures, so that there could be absolutely no doubt that Christ consists of Head and body, Bridegroom and bride, the Son of God and the Church, the Son of God who became Son of Man for our sake, to make us who are children of men children of God. So by a great sacrament[2] these two were to be united in one flesh, the two who are hailed by the prophets as two in one voice. This voice exclaimed in grateful joy earlier, *Because you have looked kindly on my humble state you have saved my soul from its constraints, and have not shut me up in the clutches of my enemy, but have guided my feet into open spaces.* This is the grateful relief of someone freed from distress, the cry of Christ's members liberated from affliction and subtle attacks. Yet here is the speaker again, and now he is praying, *Have mercy on me, Lord, for I am in distress.* But being distressed is like being cramped in a narrow place, so how could he have said, *You have guided my feet into open spaces?* If he is still distressed, how can his feet be in open spaces?

The answer may be that there is, certainly, one single voice, because there is one body; but in some members there is a sense of spacious freedom, while others are squeezed and confined. Some live righteous lives and experience it as easy, but others toil away amid troubles. It must be like this, that different members suffer differently, because otherwise the apostle would hardly have told us, *If one member suffers, all the members suffer with it, and if one member is honored, all the rest rejoice too* (1 Cor 12:26). Some churches, for instance, enjoy peace; others are harassed. Those that are at peace have their feet in open spaces, while the harassed

---

1. *Caritati vestrae.*
2. *In sacramento magno*: probably the mystery of the incarnation, the "great sacrament" from which all sacraments derive, particularly as evoked by Eph 5:32, which he has already mentioned; but possibly an allusion also to the eucharist.

ones are confined and squeezed. But the distress of one group saddens the other, while the peace of some brings the distressed ones comfort. The body is one, so much so that it is not torn apart by this difference; the only thing that tears it apart is discord. Charity ensures the close connection of the parts; these organic links hold them together in unity; unity fosters charity; and charity brings us all to glory. From some members, then, it is right that the cry should go up: *Have mercy on me, Lord, for I am in distress; my eye is confused by anger, my soul too, and my belly.*

Why the distress or anger?

2. We may wonder all the same what this distress is, since not long ago the speaker seemed to be happy about the righteousness freely bestowed by God's gift, and the ample room it gave to his feet in the wide spaces of charity. What can be the source of his distress now? Perhaps that state of affairs which the Lord mentioned: *With iniquity increasing mightily, the love of many will grow cold* (Mt 24:12). It is hinted first of all that the saints are few, but since the nets have been cast widely and the Church has grown, countless numbers have been caught, as another psalm foretold: *I announced the news and spoke the message, and they were multiplied, in numbers beyond reckoning* (Ps 39:6(40:5)). They have overloaded the boats and burst the nets, as that passage in the gospel tells us, when the Lord helped the fishermen's catch, before his passion.[3] These crowds have accumulated, and now they cram the churches full at Easter, until the walls can scarcely contain them. But the psalmist grieved over these crowds, and how could he not, when he also saw them filling up the playhouses and amphitheaters, the same people who so recently filled the churches? Or when he saw them committing sins, so soon after sharing in the praises of God? Or when he heard them blaspheming, after responding to God with their "Amen"?

But he must hold firm, stick it out and not weaken, even at the sight of this vast multitude of unworthy people; for the wheat does not give up hope when it views the quantity of straw, but waits for the day when after the harvest it will be stored in the barn, where it will have the company of the saints to enjoy, and no more harm to fear from whirling dust. The psalmist must stand fast, then, for the Lord has more to say. After his warning that *with iniquity increasing mightily, the love of many will grow cold*, the Lord immediately added something else, lest our feet should slip or waver at the increase of iniquity he had mentioned. He added something designed to uplift believers, to comfort and steady them. He said, *Whoever perseveres to the end will be saved* (Mt 24:13).

---

3. See Lk 5:6. Augustine thought of this episode, before the Lord's passion, as symbolizing the inclusion of both good and bad within the Church, to the danger of the nets. He contrasts it with the other fishing episode, after the resurrection (Jn 21:1-8), where the nets did not break; the catch there symbolizes the elect. See his Exposition of Psalm 49, 9.

3. Let us turn our attention now to the speaker who, as I think, has found himself in such straits. If he was indeed in distress, surely he ought to have been sorrowful? Sorrow is the emotion appropriate to distress. But no, he is not sorrowful; he says he is angry: *Have mercy on me, Lord, for I am in distress; my eye is confused by anger.* If you are distressed, why are you angry?[4] He is angered by the sins of others. And who would not be angered by seeing people who confess God with their lips denying him by their conduct? Who could fail to be angry on seeing people renounce the world by their words, but not by their deeds? Who would not be angered by seeing brothers and sisters plotting against each other, betraying the trust they express by exchanging the kiss during God's holy mysteries? And who could possibly count all the things that anger Christ's body, the body that inwardly lives by Christ's Spirit, but groans like wheat nearly choked by chaff? The people who are groaning are scarcely visible, just as the wheat is scarcely visible on the floor at threshing-time. Anyone who did not know how many ears had been thrown in would think there was nothing there but straw, yet from this massive bulk that looks like all straw, a great heap will be sifted out. These half-hidden groaners feel angry. In another passage they declare, *Zeal for your house has devoured me* (Ps 68:10(69:9)); and in similar vein they say elsewhere, *Disgust possessed me at the sinners who abandon your law*, and again, *With chagrin I watched the fools* (Ps 118(119):53.158).

Anger is not hatred

4. Now, about this anger: we must take care that our anger is not so vehement as to turn into hatred. Anger is not yet hatred. You may be angry with your son, but you do not hate your son. He is aware that you are angry with him, but all the while you are safeguarding an inheritance for him; indeed the reason why you are angry with him may be that you fear he may lose by his bad behavior what you are saving up for him. So anger is not yet hatred; we do not yet hate those with whom we are angry; but if the anger remains and is not quickly uprooted, it grows into hatred. This is why scripture bids us, *Do not let the sun set on your wrath* (Eph 4:26); it is urging us to pluck out newly-aroused anger before it turns into hatred. Sometimes you come across one of the faithful who really does hate, and yet rebukes a brother or sister for being angry. The one is nurturing hatred, yet condemns anger in another; the one has a beam in his eye, but finds fault with the splinter in the eye of a brother or sister.[5] All the same, that splinter is a little shoot that may grow into a beam if it is not plucked out at once. This is why the psalmist does not say, "My eye has been blinded by anger"; he says it is *confused*. If it were being blinded, that

---

4. Throughout this sermon Augustine understands it to be the speaker who is angry; in his first Exposition of the psalm he took it to be God's anger that caused the speaker's distress.
5. See Mt 7:3-5.

would mean there was hatred there already, not anger. I can prove to you that hatred really does blind our eyes, for John says, *Whoever hates his brother is still in darkness* (1 Jn 2:11). Before we go off into darkness our eye is confused by anger, and we must be careful that anger does not develop into hatred, and blind us.[6] The psalmist therefore says, *My eye is confused by anger, my soul too, and my belly*, which means, "Everything inside me is in turmoil." By his belly he means his inner life. It is sometimes legitimate to be angry with wicked and perverse people, and with those who transgress the law and lead bad lives, but we may not lose our temper with them. When we feel anger but are not allowed to lose our temper, all our inner being is confused. Sometimes perversity has gone so far that it is past correction.

Verse 11. The Church's hunger

5. *My life was imperiled by sorrow, and my years faded amid sighs.* He complains, *My life was imperiled by sorrow.* Remember how the apostle declared, *We are alive now, if you are standing firm in the Lord* (1 Thes 3:8). All those who have been made perfect through the gospel and the grace of God live on in this world only for the sake of others, for their life here is no longer necessary to themselves. Because what they have to give is necessary for others, that cry of the apostle comes true in them as well: *I long to die and to be with Christ, for that is much the best; but it is necessary for you that I remain in the flesh* (Phil 1:23-24). But when, on the contrary, someone sees that what he tries to give, through hard work and preaching, is of no profit to other people, his life is weakened and in want. And a miserable sort of want and hunger that is. When we win people over to the Lord, it is as though the Church eats them. How is that? Well, the Church draws them into its own body. Whatever we eat, we assimilate into our bodies. This is what the Church does, through the saints: it is hungry for those it longs to win over, and in a sense it eats those it has somehow won. Peter represented the Church when a dish was lowered to him from heaven full of all kinds of living creatures, all four-footed things, and crawlers, and flying creatures that by their diversity signified all the Gentiles. The Lord was foreshadowing the Church, which was destined to swallow down all nations and convert them into its own body. So he said to Peter, *Slaughter and eat* (Acts 10:13). "Go on, Church," he said (he could call Peter, "Church," because he had said to him, "On you, the rock, I will build my Church"),

---

6. At this point a Louvain manuscript inserts the following: "Let everyone be careful about this, everyone who has been called in peace, that is, in Christ who bequeathed to us the peace of God, in Christ at whose birth supreme peace was proclaimed to the human race by angels. If such a person breaks out into hatred for any reason, light or grave, he or she will be unable to have any fellowship with peace, which means with Christ, except through penance and worthy amendment."

"go on, Church, slaughter and eat. Slaughter them first, then eat them; kill what they are of themselves, then make them what you are."

When the gospel is preached, then, and the preacher sees that it is doing no good to people, he has reason to cry out, *My life is imperiled by sorrow, and my years have faded amid sighs. My vigor is undermined by want and my bones are jarred.* These years of ours that we spend here are passed amid groaning. Why? Because with the mighty increase of iniquity, the love of many grows cold. But it is groaning, rather than articulate complaints. When the Church watches many people going wrong, it swallows down its groans so silently that it can say to God, *My groaning is not hidden from you* (Ps 37:10(38:9)). That is said in another psalm, but it fits well here, and the meaning is: "My groaning is hidden from human beings, but never from you." *My vigor is undermined by want, and my bones are jarred.* We have spoken already about this want. The bones are the strong churches which, although undisturbed by any persecutions from outside, are shaken by the iniquities of their own members.

Verse 12. The deterrent effect of bad example

6. *I have become an object of scorn, more so than all my enemies, beyond bearing in my neighbors' eyes, and a source of fear to my acquaintances.* When he says, *I have become an object of scorn, more so than all my enemies,* whom does he mean? Who are the Church's enemies? Pagans? Jews? Bad Christians live worse than all those. Shall I show you how much worse bad Christians are than all the rest? The prophet Ezekiel compares them to useless branches.[7] Imagine that the pagans are woodland trees, outside the Church's garden. Something may still be made of them. From trees suitable for timber comes wood apt for the joiner's craft; it may still be knotty, or warped, or covered with bark, but he can work on these unsatisfactory features, and plane it, and in the end turn it into some object for human use. But a joiner can do nothing with the branches cut off from a tree; they are fit only for the fire. Think about it, brothers and sisters. As long as the branch remains attached to the vine, it is vastly superior to the forest tree, because the branch can bear fruit, and that tree bears none; but if the branch is lopped off the vine, and then compared with the forest tree, it is clear that the tree is better, because the joiner can make something out of it, whereas no one wants the branch, except someone who has to supply his hearth.

In the light of this the psalmist considers the hordes of people who lead bad lives in the Church, and exclaims, *I have become an object of scorn, more so than all my enemies.* "These people who frequent my sacraments live more disgracefully than others who have never approached them," he laments. Why should we not admit

---

7. See Ezk 15:2-5.

this openly, in plain English,[8] at least now, while we are expounding this psalm? We might shrink from saying it at other times, but the present need to comment gives us the freedom to correct. *I have become an object of scorn, more so than all my enemies.* The apostle Peter says of such people, *Their later doings are even worse than what they did earlier; for it would have been better for them not to have known the way of righteousness than having known it to be turned away from the holy commandment delivered to them* (2 Pt 2:20-21). In saying, *It would have been better for them not to have known the way of righteousness,* he has judged the enemies outside to be better than those inside who lead sinful lives, and weigh down the Church so heavily. *It would have been better for them not to have known the way of righteousness,* he says, *than having known it to be turned away from the holy commandment delivered to them.* And as if this were not plain enough, look at the horrible comparison he offers: *the proverb is proved true by what happens to them: the dog has returned to its vomit* (2 Pt 2:22). Since the churches are full of such people, is it not a true lament that the few utter, or, rather, that the Church utters through those few, *I have become an object of scorn, more so than all my enemies, beyond bearing in my neighbors' eyes, and a source of fear to my acquaintances?* I have become the object of intense scorn to my neighbors, to those, that is, who had begun to approach me to find faith. These neighbors of mine have been thoroughly put off by the evil lives of bad and spurious Christians. How many people do you think would like to become Christians, my brothers and sisters, but are scandalized by the disgraceful way they see Christians behaving? These are the "neighbors" who had begun to approach the Church; but we have become an object of intense scorn in their eyes.

Scandals, and how not to react to them

7. *I have become a source of fear to my acquaintances.* What can be more frightening to one who sees others leading bad lives, than to find that even those for whom he had high hopes are also guilty of many bad deeds? Such a person is afraid that everyone who was considered good may after all be no better than the rest, and the result is that nearly all good people fall under suspicion. "What a fine fellow that man was! Then how comes it that he has fallen? How did it happen that he could be found out in that base dealing, that crime, that disgraceful business? Perhaps everyone is like that?" This is what *a source of fear to my acquaintances* implies, this is how we often come to be doubted even by those who know us well.

But it is only if you feel smug about your own virtue (supposing you have any) that you can suspect someone else of being bad like all the rest. Complacency of conscience, whatever form it takes, is so flattering to a good-living person that he

---

8. He says, of course, "In plain Latin."

may say to himself, "You were anxious just now lest everyone may be bad like that. So what about yourself? Are you like that?" Conscience replies, "Oh no, not me." "So if you aren't, you must be the only one who isn't?" When that happens you need to be on your guard lest pride of this kind be worse than the original wrong-doing. Beware of considering yourself the only one. Even Elijah, in his disgust at the vast number of the godless, once complained to God, *They have slain your prophets and undermined your altars. I am abandoned and alone, and they are seeking my life.* And what is God's reply to him? *I have seven thousand men left to me who have not bent their knees to Baal* (Rom 11:3-4).[9] So among all these scandals we have only one remedy, brothers and sisters: to believe no evil of our neighbor. Humbly try to be yourself what you want him or her to be, and then you will not think him or her to be what you are not. All the same, we must admit that such a person does necessarily arouse fear in his acquaintances, even those most familiar with him.

Scripture is clear on the Church

8. *Those who saw me fled outside away from me.* If those who had never truly seen me had fled outside away from me, that would have been excusable; but it is even those who did see me who fled outside. The flight of those who had not truly seen me would have been bad enough (though strictly speaking we should not say that they fled out of doors, because they had never truly been indoors. If they had been inside they would have known the body of Christ, the members of Christ, and our unity in Christ). But far more lamentable, indeed altogether beyond bearing, is that many who did see me fled away outside. Many who well knew what the Church was went outside and left it, and set up heresies and schisms in opposition to the Church. You may find someone today, for example, who was born within the Donatist party and does not know what the Church is. People like that hold fast to the sect in which they were born, and you will have a hard job to uproot from their minds a habit of thought which they imbibed with their mothers' milk.[10] But what about the person who is thoroughly versed in the scriptures, who reads them constantly and preaches on them? Has he never come upon the text, *Ask of me, and I will give you the nations as your heritage, and the ends of the earth for your posses-sion?* Will he not also light on the promise, *All the ends of the earth will be reminded and will turn to the Lord, and all the families of the nations will worship in his presence* (Pss 2:8; 21:28(22:27))? If you see the unity of the entire world fore-

---

9. See 1 Kgs 19:10,18.
10. Their nurses' milk, literally. In this paragraph he is contrasting the invincible ignorance of some with the more culpable blindness of others who should be capable of finding the true Church prophesied in scripture.

told in scripture, what right have you to run out of doors away from it, so that you not only incur blindness yourself, but also inflict it on others?

Those who saw me—that is, those who knew what the Church is, and contemplated it in the scriptures—*fled outside, away from me*. Do you really think, my brothers and sisters, that all those people who set up their little local heresies and sects were unaware that when the Church was prophesied in God's scriptures, it was always as a Church spread throughout the world?[11] By no means! I tell you, beloved,[12] we are all Christians, we and they, or at any rate we are all called Christians, and all of us are signed with Christ's sign. Yet the prophets spoke more clearly about the Church than about Christ, because, I think, they saw in spirit that it was in opposition to the Church that people would found their conventicles. They would not engage in such intense argument about Christ himself; it would be about the Church that they would raise the fiercest quarrels. Accordingly the clearest predictions were made and the most open prophecies pronounced about this matter on which the most serious controversies would focus, so that the prophecies could convict those who had indeed seen, yet fled outside.

In Abraham's sacrifice Christ was prophesied obscurely, the Church plainly

9. I will mention one instance of this. Abraham is our father, not because we are descended from him in the flesh, but because we imitate his faith (see Rom 4). He was a just man, and pleasing to God. Through his faith he received Isaac, the son who had been promised to him and to his sterile wife, Sarah, in their old age.[13] Then he was ordered to immolate this very son to God. He did not hesitate, or argue, or question God's command, or think ill of what had been enjoined by one who had the best possible right to give the order. He led his son to the sacrifice; he laid the wood for the fire on the boy; he arrived at the place and raised his right hand to strike. At God's bidding he dropped it, as at God's bidding he had lifted it. As he had obeyed in preparing to slay the boy, so he now obeyed in sparing him. At every point he was obedient, at no point afraid. Yet in order that the sacrifice might be duly offered, and that he might not depart without some blood-shedding, a ram was found stuck by its horns in a thornbush. It was immolated, and so the sacrifice was carried through. Now what is this ram? It is a symbol of Christ, but one wrapped in mysteries. It is a symbol that needs discussion in order that the meaning may come clear; it has to be studied carefully so that it may be made plain to us, and what was wrapped in obscurity be unwrapped. Isaac as the only son, the dearly-loved son, prefigured the Son of God, and carried the wood for his sacrifice as Christ carried

---

11. A favorite point in Augustine's polemic against the Donatists who, though powerful, were essentially an African phenomenon, in contrast to the catholicity of the Church.
12. *Caritati vestrae.*
13. See Gn 21.

his cross. We can even say that the ram was a symbol of Christ, for to be held fast by the horns is like a crucifixion. So all this obscurely prefigures Christ. But it was necessary that the Church too be proclaimed, and proclaimed immediately; no sooner had the Head been foretold than the body must be too. The Spirit of God began—God himself began—to want to preach to Abraham about the Church, and to do so he discarded figurative language. He proclaimed Christ in a figurative way but foretold the Church quite openly, saying to Abraham, *Because you have hearkened to my voice, and for my sake have not withheld your beloved son, I will bless you exceedingly, and multiply your seed more and more, like the stars in the sky and the sand on the seashore; and in your seed shall all the nations of the earth be blessed* (Gn 22:16-18). The same is true nearly everywhere else: Christ was proclaimed by the prophets under a veil of mystery, but the Church clearly, so that even those who later would oppose the Church would see it, and in them would be realized that prophecy of wickedness in the psalm: *those who saw me fled outside, away from me.* As the apostle John said of them, they went out from our midst, but they never truly belonged to us.[14]

Verse 13. Forgotten and useless

10. *I am consigned to oblivion, as though I had died out of their hearts.* I am forgotten, I have fallen into oblivion, those who once saw me have forgotten me. They have forgotten me so completely that it is as though in their hearts I have died. *I am consigned to oblivion, as though I had died out of their hearts; I am no better than a pot thrown away.* Why does he think he has become *no better than a pot thrown away*? He had been working hard, but doing no good to anyone; he saw himself as a tool or vessel fit to serve no one's purpose, so he calls himself a discarded pot.

Verse 14. Indiscriminate blame

11. *I have heard hostile criticism from those who encircle me.* Plenty of people live close around me, and every day they find fault with me. How many accusations are leveled against bad Christians, only to fall as curses upon all Christians! Do you find anyone who speaks ill of Christians, or rebukes them, saying, "Look what they are doing, those among the Christians who are unworthy"? No, not at all; they just say, "Look what the Christians are doing." They make no distinction, they tar us all with the same brush. The critics who talk like this live close by us, all around; that is, they walk round and round the church, but do not enter it. Why is that? Why do they walk round the church without entering? Because they are enamored of cyclic

---

14. See 1 Jn 2:19.

time; they are unwilling to enter and find the truth because they do not love eternity. They are given over to temporal concerns as though bound onto a wheel, and consequently another text says of them, *Whirl them round like dust*, and another again, *the wicked walk round in a circle* (Pss 82:14(83:13); 11:9(12:8)).

Colluding against me, they planned to seize my soul. What does that suggest, *they planned to seize my soul*?[15] It means that they planned to make me consent to their depraved acts. For those who curse the Church and do not enter it, merely refusing to enter is insufficient; they also want to drive others out of the Church by disparaging it. If they succeed in driving you out of the Church they have seized your soul; that is, they have secured your acquiescence. And then you will be wandering around the Church, not at home in it.

Verse 15. Put your trust in the Lord alone

12. What about me? Amid all these reproaches, all the scandals, all the calamities, amid all that would lead me astray, whether unjust treatment from without or crooked dealings within, amid all this I thought to find righteous people whom I might imitate. I looked for them, and there were none; so what did I do? *I trusted in you, Lord*. Nothing is more conducive to salvation, nothing safer. You wanted to imitate someone, and you found that person no good. Have done with imitation, then. You went on to look for someone else, but found in him or her something that displeased you. You sought out a third, and that one did not satisfy you either. Does that mean that you are destined to be lost, because this, that, or the other person has let you down? By no means. Switch your hope away from human beings, because all who fix their hopes on mortals are under a curse.[16] If you are still looking to some mortal, seeking to imitate him and to hang on his words, you are still thirsting for milk as your nourishment, and in danger of becoming a milksop,[17] as children are called who go on sucking too long, which is bad for them. What else is a persistent use of milk but a desire to get your food through the flesh of someone else? And that is to live off another human being. Grow up and eat at table; take your food from the same source where your hero took his (or perhaps failed to take it). It may have been lucky for you that you fell in with a bad fellow whom you believed to be good, so that you found only bitterness in what passed for a mother's breast, and were put off and disgusted by it, because then you were enticed to more sustaining fare. Nurses use this trick with milksops. They put something with a bitter taste on their

---

15. *Ut acciperent animam meam consiliati sunt*. In his first Exposition Augustine understands *animam* to mean "life" and *acciperent* to mean "spare," so extracting the idea that the persecutors cruelly prolonged the life of the just sufferer who longed for death. He takes the words differently here.
16. See Jer 17:5.
17. *Mammothreptus*.

nipples, so that the babies recoil from the breast in disgust, and struggle open-mouthed toward the table.

Let the psalm declare, then, *I trusted in you, Lord; I said, "You are my God."* You are my God. Begone, Donatus! Begone, Caecilian![18] Neither of them, nor my latest paragon, is my God. I am not walking under the banner of any ordinary name; I hold to the name of Christ. Listen to Paul's question: *was Paul crucified for you, or were you baptized in Paul's name?* (1 Cor 1:13). I would have been lost if I had thrown in my lot with Paul; shall I not be lost if I align myself with Donatus? Let human names, human claims and human devices fade away. *I trusted in you, Lord; I said, "You are my God."* Not any mere human, but you alone are my God. One human model fails, one perhaps makes some progress; but my God neither fails nor makes progress. He who is perfect has no scope for improvement, and the eternal cannot possibly fail. *I said to the Lord, "You are my God."*

Verse 16. God's will in the casting of lots

13. *The fate allotted to me is in your hands.* Not in other people's hands, but in yours. Now what is this talk about being allotted? Why lots? When lots are mentioned we must not think of soothsayers. The casting of lots is not a bad thing in itself; it is the means by which God's will is indicated when human beings are in doubt. Even the apostles drew lots after the death of Judas, who had betrayed the Lord and, as was written of him, had *gone to his own place* (Acts 1:25). The question arose as to who should be appointed in his stead. Two were chosen by human judgment, and from these two one was chosen by divine judgment. God was consulted as to which of them he wanted, *and the lot fell to Matthias* (Acts 1:26). So then, what does the psalm mean by *the fate allotted to me is in your hands*? He has called the grace by which we have been saved his "lot," or so I think. Why would he call God's grace a lottery? Because where lots are concerned, it is not our choice that operates, but God's will. Where it is a case of saying, "This person has this recommendation, but that one does not," we are weighing their merits, and where merits are taken into consideration there is choice, not lot. When God, though, found no merits on our part, he saved us by the "lot" of his will, saved us because he willed it, not because we were worthy. That is our lot. It was no accident that the Lord's tunic, woven throughout from the top to signify the heavenly charity that will last for ever, could not be divided by his persecutors.[19] So they drew lots for it. Those on whom the lot has fallen appear to be destined to share the lot of the saints.[20] *By grace you have been saved, through faith*, says Paul, the apostle. *By grace you have been saved, through faith, and this is not your own doing* (it is by

---

18. See note at Exposition of Psalm 10, 1.
19. See Jn 19:23-24.
20. See Col 1:12.

lot, then), *and this is not your own doing, but the grace of God. It does not come from works* (as though you had behaved so well that you were worthy to attain it). *It does not come from works, lest anyone boast. We are his own handiwork, created in Christ Jesus for good works* (Eph 2:8-10). In a sense God's will is like a secret lottery held in the human race, a lottery decided by the hidden will of God, in whom there is no unfairness,[21] for he takes no account of human pretensions. Your lot comes from his hidden justice.

Grace is not for sale

14. Let me have your attention now, dearly beloved.[22] Notice how what we have been saying is confirmed by the apostle Peter. Simon the magician had been baptized by Philip, and he attached himself to Philip, believing in the divine miracles he had himself witnessed.[23] The apostles came to Samaria, where the magician was and where he had been baptized. They laid their hands on the newly-baptized, who received the Holy Spirit and began to speak in tongues. Simon was amazed and dumbfounded at this divine miracle, that at the imposition of human hands the Holy Spirit should come and fill people; and he lusted after the power, not the grace. What he wanted was not something to set him free, but a gift to enhance his own reputation. But as he craved it his heart filled up with pride and devilish impiety and a haughtiness that needed to be taken down a peg. He asked the apostles, "How much money do you want from me for the power to lay my hands on people and cause them to receive the Holy Spirit?" This man lived close by, near the Church; he was after secular honors, and thought he could buy God's gift with money. And in thinking he could get the Holy Spirit with money he also judged the apostles to be avaricious, just as he was himself impious and proud. Peter immediately addressed him: *Take your money with you to perdition for thinking you could buy God's gift with it. You have no share or lot in this faith* (Acts 8:20-21). You, he implies, have no share in this grace which we have all received freely, because you think to purchase what is given gratis. Now grace is called a "lot" precisely because it is given gratis. *You have no share or lot in this faith.*

I have explained this to show that we have no need to be afraid when the psalm says, *The fate allotted to me is in your hands.* What is our allotted fate? The Church's inheritance. But how far does that stretch? Even to the furthermost coasts: *I will give you the nations as your heritage, and the ends of the earth for your possession* (Ps 2:8). I don't want some fellow promising me a little parcel of land: O my God, *the fate allotted to me is in your hands.*

---

21. See Rom 9:14.
22. *Caritas vestra.*
23. See Acts 8:13-24.

Let that be enough for now, beloved ones.[24] We will finish it tomorrow, in the Lord's name and with his help.

---

24. *Caritati vestrae.*

Exposition 4 of Psalm 30

The Third Sermon to the People

Let us not delay long over the easy verses

1. I have preached two sermons already on this psalm, yet there is still more than a third of it left. And I must complete today what is still owed to you. So I must ask you not to mind, beloved friends,[1] if I do not linger over the easily accessible verses, so that we can spend more time on those which need explanation. Many of the verses in this psalm will make their point without more ado in the minds of believers, and many require no more than a brief comment; but there are some, though far fewer, on which we must work hard if they are to be intelligible. So to ensure that we have enough time, and that both I and you have enough stamina, try to see how plain and obvious most of the verses are, and that it is more a matter of your grasping them together with me, and praising God for them along with me. If the psalm is praying, pray yourselves; if it is groaning, you groan too; if it is happy, rejoice; if it is crying out in hope, you hope as well; if it expresses fear, be afraid. Everything written here is like a mirror held up to us.

Verse 16. Two kinds of enemies

2. *Rescue me from the hands of my enemies, and from my persecutors.* Let's all make this prayer, each one of us with regard to our own enemies. It is a worthy petition, for we are bound to pray that God will rescue us from our enemies' clutches. But we have to distinguish between enemies for whom we must pray and enemies against whom we must pray. Human enemies, of whatever kind, are not to be hated, lest when a good person hates a bad person who is causing trouble, the result is two bad people. A good person must love even the bad person he or she has to put up with, so that at any rate there is only one who is bad.

The enemies against whom we need to pray are the devil and his angels. They envy us the kingdom of heaven and are unwilling that we should ascend to the place from which they were thrown out; so let us pray indeed that our souls may be rescued from them. Even when human enemies assail us, it is only as the instruments of these evil spirits. When the apostle Paul warns us how careful we must be to guard against those enemies, he is speaking to God's servants who are being

---

1. *Caritatem vestram.*

harassed, and probably by the factions and dishonesty and hostility of human beings; yet he says to them, *It is not against flesh and blood that you have to struggle*—not against human enemies, then—*but against principalities and powers and the rulers of this world* (Eph 6:12). This world? What world? Not heaven and earth—God forbid! This world has no ruler other than its Creator. What "world" did he mean, then? The lovers of the world, worldlings. He went on to explain this by adding, "When I say world, I mean *this world of darkness*." And what darkness is that? The darkness of unbelievers and godless persons. This is obvious, because when the apostle talks to those who were once godless unbelievers, but are now faithful and devout servants of God, he reminds them, *You were darkness once, but now you are light in the Lord* (Eph 5:8). Your warfare, he tells them, is against wicked spirits in the heavens, against the devil and his angels. You do not see your enemies, yet you can defeat them. *Rescue me from the hands of my enemies, and from my persecutors.*

Verse 17. Light for discernment

3. *Let your face shine on your servant; save me in your mercy.* Those of you, my beloved friends,[2] who were here yesterday remember how in the instruction I gave you then I repeatedly said that the Church's worst persecutors are Christians who refuse to live good lives.[3] They bring the Church into disrepute, and it has to endure their animosity. When they are rebuked, when they are not permitted to continue in their disgraceful way of life, when even a mere verbal remonstrance is given them, they turn over wicked plans in their hearts and look for an occasion to spew out their venom. The man who is groaning in our psalm finds himself beset by such people, and we can groan with him if we like. There are very many of them, so many that good people can scarcely be seen among them, just as the grains are scarcely visible on the threshing-floor, even though it is with these sifted grains that the Lord's barns are to be filled. Surrounded by such people, and groaning about it, the psalmist says, *Let your face shine over your servant*; for he thinks it is all such a mix-up, with all of these being called Christians, both those who lead good lives and those who do not. All are imprinted with the one sign, all approach one altar, all are washed in the same baptism, all repeat the same Lord's Prayer, and all are present at the celebration of the same mysteries. When are the ones who groan to be distinguished from the ones groaned over, unless God causes his face to shine over his servant? Well then, what exactly does it mean, *let your face shine over your servant*? Perhaps this: "Let it be evident that I belong to you. Let it be impossible for a wicked Christian to make the same claim to belong to you, lest the prayer I made

---

2. *Caritas vestra.*
3. Compare his Second Sermon to the People on this psalm, 2-8.

to you in another psalm go unanswered: *Judge me, O God, and distinguish my cause from that of an unholy people*" (Ps 42(43):1). There he prayed, *Distinguish my cause*; here he begs, *Let your face shine over your servant*. But he steers clear of pride and any trace of self-justification by adding, *Save me in your mercy*: save me, not because I deserve it but because you are merciful. Give me a hearing, not with the severity of a law court but in keeping with your most merciful goodness.

Verse 18. What does it mean to "invoke God"?

4. *Let me not be put to shame, Lord, for I have called upon you.* He has produced a weighty reason for his request: *let me not be put to shame, for I have called upon you.* Do you want someone who has invoked you to be shamed? Do you want others to say, "Where is the God he relied on?"

But is there anyone, even among the impious, who does not invoke God? Surely not. It seems, then, that the psalmist must have been able to say, *I have called upon you*, in some special sense, some sense that has nothing to match it in the invocations offered by most people, because otherwise he could not possibly have dared to demand so great a reward just for making his invocation. God might have answered him in his mind, "What do you think you are asking of me, when you beg not to be put to shame? Why should you not be? Just because you have invoked me? Don't people invoke me every day, begging my help in achieving the adulteries they lust after? Don't people call upon me every day, asking for the death of those from whom they hope for legacies? Don't people who are planning frauds invoke me every day, asking that they may bring their schemes to a successful conclusion? So how can you request so great a reward just for invoking me; how can you ask, *Let me not be put to shame, for I have called upon you?*"

Yes, they invoke, but they do not invoke you, Lord. To invoke God is to call God into yourself,[4] for this is what "invocation" means, to "call him into." But you would not presume to invite a person of such authority[5] into your home, unless you knew how to prepare a fit place in which to entertain him. So what if God were to say to you, "Well now, you called me in, and here I am. What kind of place am I to enter? Am I expected to put up with such disgusting filth in your conscience? If you were inviting a servant of mine[6] into your home, would you not take care to clean it up first? Yet you invite me into your heart, and it is like a robbers' den. The place where God is invoked is full of blasphemy, full of adulteries, cluttered with dishonest dealings, littered with wicked lusts, and you call me in there!"

It was obviously of people like this that another psalm was speaking when it declared, *They have not invoked the Lord* (Ps 13:5(14:4); 52:6(53:4)). They did

---

4. The point is clearer in Latin: *in-vocare*, to "call into."
5. *Patrem familias*: a householder or a father of a family or an owner of an estate.
6. Possibly he means a bishop or someone else of good standing in the Church.

invoke him in a sense, but they did not truly invoke him. I want to explain this point briefly, because the question is raised by this man's claiming such a great reward for the sole merit he can allege: *because I have called upon you.* This evidently does give rise to questions, when we see that God is invoked by so many bad people; so we cannot dismiss the problem. I would put this simple question to an avaricious person: "Do you invoke God, and if so, why?" "So that he will help me to make money." "Then what you are invoking is money, not God. You cannot get the money you covet through the agency of your servant, or the tenant of your farm, or any of your hangers-on, or your friend, or some partisan who supports you; so you call God in to help. By making God the agent of your enrichment, you have cheapened God for yourself. Do you really want to invoke God? Then invoke him disinterestedly. Is it too little for you, you miser, that God himself should fill you? Is God unacceptable to you, if he comes without gold and silver? How can you find satisfaction in the things God has made, if God himself does not satisfy you?"

The psalmist is justified, then, in making his prayer, *let me not be put to shame, for I have called upon you.* Call upon the Lord, brothers and sisters, if you do not want to be put to shame, for the shame the psalmist fears is that shame mentioned earlier in the psalm: *In you, O Lord, have I put my trust; let me not be shamed for ever.* To show that it is still this kind of shame he has in mind, he adds something further after praying, *Let me not be put to shame* for ever, *for I have called upon you.* What does he add? *Let the godless blush with shame and be dragged down to hell.* Clearly he is referring here to the shame that lasts for eternity.

Verse 19. Christ is scorned, Head and members

5. *Let lying lips be struck dumb, lips that speak wickedly against the righteous one, in their pride and scorn.* The righteous one is Christ, and plenty of lips there are that speak wickedly against him in their pride and scorn. But why in pride and scorn, especially? Because he who came so humbly appeared contemptible to the proud. Are you unwilling to see him scorned by the lovers of prestige, him who was so abused? Do you shrink from seeing him who died scorned by those who think this life is everything? Are you reluctant to see him who was crucified scorned by those who think it a disgraceful thing to die like a criminal on a cross? Does it offend you to see him, who led a poor life in this world although he was the world's Creator, scorned by the rich? Christ renounced all that human beings hold dear, not because he lacked the power to possess them, but because he chose not to have those things in order to show us that they are to be treated as unimportant; and therefore all who set store by such things despise him. Anyone among his servants who has chosen to follow in his footsteps and walk in the same humility that, as we are taught, was our Lord's own way is scorned in Christ and as a member of Christ. And when both Head and members are scorned, it is the whole Christ who is scorned, because the righteous one consists of Head and body all together. Inevi-

tably the whole Christ is scorned by the proud and godless, so that they may incur the punishment foretold in the psalm: *let lying lips be struck dumb, the lips that speak wickedly against the righteous one, in their pride and scorn.* When will such lips be struck dumb? In this age? Never. Daily they rant against Christians, especially the lowly ones; they blaspheme daily; every day they bark their insults; and they are storing up torments for those very tongues of theirs which will thirst in hell, pining for a drop of water, but in vain.[7] Not in this present age are their lips struck dumb. When will it happen? When their iniquities confront them to their faces, as the Book of Wisdom describes: *Then the just will stand with great constancy against those who have been tormenting them. Then the persecutors will say, "And these are the people we once held in derision, as a byword and a butt for our mockery! How have they come to be reckoned among the children of God, with their lot among the saints? Fools that we were, we thought their life madness"* (Wis 5:1,3,5,4). Only then will their lips be struck dumb, the lips that speak wickedly against the righteous one, in their pride and scorn. But for the present they go on saying to us, "Where is your God? What do you worship? What do you see? You believe, yet you have a hard life; your hard life is certain, but what you hope for is far from certain." But when that certainty for which we hope has become real, those lying lips will be struck dumb.

Verse 20. Tasting the sweetness of the Lord

6. Let us see what the consequence is, now that we know the lying lips will fall silent, those lips that speak wickedly against the righteous one. The psalmist who groans this prayer is waiting; he has seen the good things of God inwardly, in spirit, he has seen those good things which are only seen in this secret way and are not seen by the godless. This is precisely why he hears the godless maligning the righteous one in their pride and scorn: they know well enough how to see the good things of this world, but do not know even how to think of the goods that belong to the world to come. But the psalmist wanted to whet an appetite for those good things of eternity in people whom he encouraged to endure what the present offers, but not to love it, so he exclaimed, *How great, how immense, is your sweetness, Lord!* And if some godless fellow retorts, "Where is this immense sweetness, then?" I will answer, "How can I demonstrate this immense sweetness to you, who have lost your faculty of taste in the fever of sin? If you had never come across honey before, you would not exclaim how delicious it is unless you had first tasted it. You have no palate in your heart capable of tasting the good things I am telling you about, so what can I do for you? It is useless for me to say, *Taste and see that the Lord is very sweet* (Ps 33:9(34:8)) to one who is not capable of doing so."

---

7. See Lk 16:24.

But still, *how great, how immense, is your sweetness, Lord, which you have hidden from those who fear you!* What does that mean—you have hidden it from them?[8] You have not refused it, but stored it up for them, this good which cannot be shared by the just and the godless alike; and you have so stored it that only those who travel toward it by way of fear may reach it. As long as they are still afraid, not even they have arrived; but they believe that they will arrive, and they set out from fear. Nothing is more delicious than immortal wisdom, but the first stage of wisdom is fear of the Lord.[9] That sweetness *you have hidden from those who fear you.*

7. *But you have brought it to perfection for those who trust in you in the sight of the children of men.* Notice that it does not say, "You have brought it to perfection in the sight of the children of men," but *for those who trust you in the sight of the children of men*; that is to say, you have brought your sweetness to perfect fullness for those who trust you in a way the children of men can see. It is the same point that the Lord is making when he says, *Anyone who disowns me in front of other people, I also will disown before my Father* (Mt 10:33). So if you hope in the Lord, make sure you hope so that others can see you; do not hide that hope of yours away in your heart, do not fear to confess it when you are accused of being a Christian. But is anyone accused of being a Christian nowadays? So few people remain who have not become Christians that it is more a case of those few being charged with not being Christians than of their daring to accuse others who are. All the same, my brothers and sisters, I must warn you of this: whoever you may be who are listening to me, just begin to live as a Christian should, and see if it is not cast up against you, even by those who are Christians, but in name only, not in their manner of life or their morals. No one will credit this, except from experience.

Think about it now, and see how true it is. Do you want to live like a Christian? Do you want to follow in your Lord's footsteps? No doubt you do; but suppose someone taunts you about it, and you blush for shame, and rebut the charge out of embarrassment? You have lost your way.[10] You thought you had in your heart the faith that leads to justification, but it is with the lips that confession is made that leads to salvation.[11] If, then, you want to walk in the way of the Lord, hope in God even in the sight of the children of men; that is, do not blush with shame over your hope. As it is alive in your heart, let it find a home in your mouth. Not for nothing has Christ willed to place his sign on our foreheads, where embarrassment shows itself, for he does not want a Christian to blush when Christ is taunted. If you have

---

8. *Abscondisti timentibus te* could equally well, and perhaps more naturally, mean "you have hidden it *for* those who fear you"; but in his first Exposition of this psalm Augustine seems to favor the meaning "from."

9. See Prv 1:7; Ps 110(111): 10.

10. Or "the Way."

11. See Rom 10:10.

conducted yourself boldly like this in the sight of other people, if you have not been ashamed of Christ in their presence, if you have not denied him by either word or deed in front of the children of men, then hope that for you the sweetness of God may reach its full perfection.

Verse 21. Tent and home

8. What comes next? *You will hide them in the hidden recess of your face.* What kind of place is that? He does not say, "You will hide them in your heaven," or "you will hide them in your paradise," or "you will hide them in Abraham's bosom." The future abode of holy people is called by a variety of names[12] in holy scripture, but let us hold cheap whatever is not God. May he who keeps guard over us in our place in this life be himself our place after this life; indeed, this same psalm prayed to him in an earlier verse, *Be to me a protecting God, and a home of refuge.* We shall be hidden, then, in the face of God. Do you expect to hear from me what shelter there is in God's face? Purify your heart so that he may himself enlighten you, and he whom you invoke may enter it. Be a home for him, and he will be a home for you; let him dwell in you, and you will dwell in him. If you have welcomed him with your heart in this age, he will welcome you with his face when this age is past.

You will hide them, says the psalm. Hide them where? *In the hidden recess of your face, far from human disturbance.* Once hidden there, they will fear no disturbance; in the hidden place of your countenance it will not come near them. Do you not think, brothers and sisters, that there may be some who even in this world are so blessed that when they begin to hear themselves reviled by other people, simply because they are servants of Christ, they can flee to God in their hearts and have some initial hope of his sweetness? Do you not think they can flee from human disturbance and the insults they hear with it, and enter with their consciences into the face of God? Enter they do, certainly, provided they have the kind of consciences that permit entry; that is, if their consciences are not overloading them, and laying on them a burden too wide to pass through a narrow gate. *You will hide them in the hidden recess of your face, far from human disturbance. You will shield them in your tent against wrangling tongues.* One day in the future you will surely hide them in the hidden recess of your face, far from human disturbance, so that no harassment from human beings will ever have power to trouble them again; but what of this time in between, while they are still on pilgrimage in this world? Those who serve you have to endure many wrangling tongues; what do you do for them now? *You will shield them in your tent.* What tent is that? The Church in this present age. It is called a tent because the Church is still traveling on earth; for a tent is

---

12. Following a variant in one manuscript. Instead of *nominibus* other codices have *fidelibus* which could yield the meaning, "the future abode of holy people is promised to many of the faithful."

where soldiers live while they are on active service. Their lodgings are called tents. A tent is not one's home. So then, traveler, fight while you are on active service, so that after being saved in your tent you may be welcomed gloriously into your home. There will be an eternal home for you in heaven, if you have lived a good life here in this tent.

In this tent you, Lord, will protect them from wrangling tongues. Wrangling tongues there are aplenty. Various heresies and schisms set up their din; many tongues contradict true teaching. As for you, you must run to God's tent. Hold fast to the Catholic Church and do not depart from the rule of truth. Then you will be shielded in the tent from wrangling tongues.

Verse 22. The spread of the fire

9. *Blessed be the Lord, for he has wrought wonderful mercy in the city that lies around us.* What city is this, that lies all around? God's people was established in the one country, Judea, as though in the center of the world. There the praises of God were sung, and sacrifices were offered to him, and there prophecy was never lacking; it sang of the future, and we now see those predictions fulfilled. This people was established in the middle of the Gentiles. Now our prophet considered its position, and saw that in the future the Church of God would be found among all nations. But he saw too that in his own day the Gentiles surrounded him on every side, so making the Jewish race the center point, and so he called the encircling nations "a city that lies around us." Indeed, Lord, you wrought wonderful mercy in the city of Jerusalem, for there Christ suffered, there he rose from the dead, there ascended into heaven and there performed many miracles; but we have far more reason to praise you for the wonderful mercy you have wrought in the city that lies all round it, for you have poured out your mercy over all the Gentiles. You did not confine it to Jerusalem, as though holding your ointment sealed in a vessel; you broke the jar and the ointment gushed out all over the world, so that the prophecy of holy scripture might be fulfilled: *Your name is like ointment poured out* (Sg 1:2). That was how you wrought your wonderful mercy in the city that lay round about. Christ ascended into heaven to take his place at the Father's right hand, and after ten days he sent the Holy Spirit. The disciples were filled with the Holy Spirit and began to proclaim the mighty deeds of Christ. Some were stoned, some killed, some dispersed.[13] But they were like torches burning with divine fire, and when driven out from that one place, they filled the entire forest of the world, setting it alight with the radiant heat of the Spirit and the light of truth. And so the Lord wrought wonderful mercy throughout the city that lay all around.

---

13. See Acts 8:1.

Verse 23. Fear and mercy

10. *Beside myself with fear, I said. . . .* Remember how "ecstasy" was mentioned in the title of the psalm: well, here it is. Listen to what the psalm says now: *Beside myself with fear, I said, "I have been flung far out of your sight."* It was in dread that I spoke, *beside myself with fear.* The psalmist experienced inner dread on account of some calamity (and such are never lacking); he regarded his frightened and worried heart, and said, *I have been flung far out of your sight.* If I were hidden in your face, I would not be so afraid; if you were looking at me, I would not be full of dread. But in another psalm he declared, *Whenever I said, "My foot has slipped," your mercy, Lord, always supported me* (Ps 93(94):18), and here too he immediately adds, *Therefore you heard the sound of my prayer.* Because I made confession, because I said, *I have been flung far out of your sight*, because I did not stiffen in pride, but acknowledged my heart's weakness, and cried out to you even as I staggered in my trouble, you heard my prayer. That declaration I made in the other psalm held good here too. My words here, *beside myself with fear, I said, "I have been flung far out of your sight,"* come to the same as what I said there: *whenever I said, "My foot has slipped."* And just as I proclaimed there, *Your mercy, Lord, always supported me*, so too now I can say, *Therefore you heard the sound of my prayer, Lord.*

Think what a good illustration of this we have in Peter.[14] He sees the Lord walking on the waters, and thinks it is a ghost. The Lord calls out, "It is I, don't be frightened." Peter takes heart, and replies, "If it is you, command me to come to you over the water. I will be sure that it is you, if at your word I am able to do what you can do." Jesus says, "Come." And the word of him who commanded empowered him who heard. "Come," he said. Peter climbed out of the boat and began to walk. He went bravely, trusting in the Lord; but when he felt the force of the wind, he was frightened. *Beside myself with fear, I said, "I have been flung far out of your sight."* Beginning to go under, he cried, "I'm sinking, Lord!" And Jesus stretched out a hand to him and pulled him up, saying, "Why did you hesitate? Is that all the faith you have?" So I too said in my alarm, *I have been flung far out of your sight*, and you, Lord, *heard the sound of my prayer*, as you listened to those who were all but wrecked at sea. But you heard it *as I cried to you.* Crying to God is done not with the voice but with the heart. Many people whose lips were silent have cried to him in their hearts, while many who produced plenty of noise from their throats have been able to get nothing because their hearts were turned away from him. If you cry to him, then, cry inside yourself, where God hears. *When I cried to you*, says the psalmist, *you heard the sound of my prayer.*

---

14. See Mt 14:26-32.

Verse 24. Choosing your love

11. The man talking to us is experienced, clearly, so what advice does he give us? *Choose the Lord for your love, all you who are his saints.*[15] It is as though he is telling us, "Believe me, I know what I am talking about. I was in trouble, I called upon the Lord, and he never let me down. I hoped in God, and was not put to shame; he enlightened my mind and steadied my nerves." *Choose the Lord as your love, all you who are his saints.* Yes, you choose to love the Lord, you who do not choose the world, for that is what it means by *all you who are his saints.* To whom could I say, "Choose the Lord for your love," if they are still choosing to love the amphi-theater? Whom could I invite to choose the Lord for their love, if they are still choosing to set their love on farce,[16] or on the pantomime,[17] or on excessive drinking, or if they still choose worldly ostentation as their love, or the whole gamut of empty show and deceptive trumperies? I could say it only to someone to whom I could also say, "Unlearn your love of those things, that you may truly learn love; turn away from them, that you may turn to the Lord; pour out the rubbish, that you may be filled." *Choose the Lord for your love, all you who are his saints.*

Apparent and real humiliation

12. *Because the Lord will search out the truth.* You are aware of the number of wizards and magicians that make their appearance, and you know what a high reputation they gain by their empty shows; but the Lord will search out the truth, *and he will requite those who persist in their pride.* Bear with them until you can bury them, have patience till you can have done with them; it must happen that the Lord who searches out the truth will requite those who persist in their pride. But you will be asking me, "When will he requite them?" When he wishes. Be quite certain that he will requite them; you must have no doubt about the retribution, but neither must you presume to give God advice about the timing of it. Of course he will search out the truth, and punish those who persist in pride. In some cases he will punish them even here. We have seen this happening, or at least heard about it.

Now what about those cases where people who fear God are humiliated, people who perhaps were formerly illustrious in some high office in this world? Brought low they may be, but they have not fallen, because they have not shut God out of their hearts, and God is their high dignity. Job seemed to be humiliated when he had lost all his wealth, and lost his children; he had lost both what he was saving up and

---

15. Throughout this paragraph Augustine uses the verb *diligo* for "love," a verb connoting more of choice, esteem and value than the more common *amo*. The translation attempts to reflect this nuance.

16. *Mimum.*

17. *Pantomimum*, a show in which a chorus and instrumental music accompanied a dancer who mimed a part.

those for whom he was saving it. He was left without an inheritance and, sadder still, without an heir. He was left in the company of his wife alone, and she acted not as his comforter but rather as the devil's accomplice. He appeared, but only appeared, to be brought low; but judge for yourselves whether he was made unhappy, whether he was not in the hidden recess of God's face. *Naked I came from my mother's womb*, he said, *and naked I will return to the earth. The Lord gave, and the Lord has taken away. This has happened as the Lord willed: may the Lord's name be blessed* (Jb 1:21). These are pearls of praise for God; where did they come from? Look at him outwardly—a poor man, but a rich one within. Could those pearls of praise for God have come from his lips, if he had no treasure house in his heart?

If any of you hope to be rich, aspire to riches like that, riches that you cannot lose in a shipwreck. So when people of this calibre are brought down, do not think them unhappy. You are mistaken, for you do not know what resources they have within themselves. You who choose the world for your love are judging by your own standards, because when you lose worldly goods you are indeed unhappy and remain so. But you are quite wrong about people like Job, for they have the source of their joy within them. They have an inner ruler, a shepherd and comforter who is in their hearts.

The people who fall badly are those who pin their hopes on this world. Showy external glitter is stripped away, and nothing is left inside them except the reek of a bad conscience. They have nothing to comfort them, nowhere to go if they venture out, nowhere to go if they return within. Despoiled of worldly trappings and devoid of spiritual grace, they truly are humiliated. God deals like this with many people in this present time, but not with all. If he punished no one in this way, we might think divine providence had gone to sleep; if he punished all of them now, what would have become of divine patience?

All the same, you as a Christian have learned to bear wrongs, and not seek revenge. Do you thirst to be avenged, Christian? But Christ has not yet been avenged. Have you suffered reproach, and he not? Did he not first suffer it for you, he who had no reason to suffer? Unlike you: for in you tribulation is the goldsmith's furnace which (as long as you are gold, and not straw) ensures that you are refined from your impurities. It is not meant to burn you to ashes.

Verse 25. Encouraging conclusion

13. *Choose the Lord as your love, all you who are his saints, because the Lord will search out the truth, and he will requite those who persist in their pride.* But when will he requite them? If only it could be now! I would simply love to see them humiliated and flattened immediately! But listen to what comes next: *act manfully.* Do not let your hands fall limp when troubles come, do not let your knees sag. *Act manfully, and let your hearts be strengthened.* To bear up and endure all the woes

of this world, your hearts need to be strengthened. But to whom does the prophet address his encouragement, *act manfully, and let your hearts be strengthened*? To those who choose the world as their love? No. The next line tells you whom he is addressing; listen to it: *all you who hope in the Lord.*

Exposition 1 of Psalm 31

Verses 1-2. Forgiveness

1. *For David himself, for understanding.* The psalm is so called because it enables us to understand that we are set free not because we earned it, but by God's grace, as we confess our sins.

2. *Blessed are those whose iniquities are forgiven, and whose sins are covered,* those people, that is, whose sins have been consigned to oblivion. *Blessed is the one to whom the Lord has imputed[1] no sin, and in whose mouth is no guile.* Such a person does not indulge in a loud-mouthed parade of righteousness, since he or she has a conscience full of sins.

Verses 3-4. Consciousness of guilt

3. *My bones grew old because I kept silence.* Because I uttered no saving confession with my mouth[2] all the strength that was in me declined into the weakness of old age, *in consequence of my shouting all day long,* when I was ungodly, and blasphemed God by raising my shouts against him, wishing to defend and excuse my sins.

4. *For day and night your hand lay heavy upon me.* Under the relentless scourging to which you subjected me *I was reduced to bitterness, when the thorn stuck fast in me.* I was made more wretched by the recognition of my wretched state, as my bad conscience stabbed me.

Pause

Verse 5. Confession

5. *I perceived my sin, and did not cloak my unrighteousness;* that is, I did not hide it. *I said, I will declare my unrighteousness against myself to the Lord.* Yes, this is what I said: I will make my declaration, not against God, as I did when by keeping silence I raised my impious hubbub; rather I will declare my unrigh-

---

1. Variant: "will impute."
2. See Rom 10:10.

teousness against myself and to the Lord. *And you have forgiven the impiety of my heart*, because you hear the heart's confession before ever it is spoken aloud.

Verses 6-7. Redemption

6. *Every holy person will pray*[3] *to you about this matter when the time is right.* Everyone who is holy will pray to you about this impiety in the heart, for the saints are not holy by their own merits, but only when the time is right, which means at the coming of him who redeemed us from our sins. *Yet they will not draw near to him amid the flood of many waters.* All the same, no one must assume that when the end comes suddenly, as it did in Noah's day, an opportunity will remain for the confession by which we may draw near to God.

7. *You are for me a refuge from the distress that besets me.* You are my refuge from the oppressive sins that beset my heart. *You who make me dance with happiness, save me from those that hem me in.* In you there is joy for me, so redeem me from the sadness my sins cause me.

Pause

Verses 8-9. God's reply

8. Now comes God's answer. *I will give you understanding, and set you on this road you must enter.* You have made your confession, so now I will give you understanding, so that you may not leave the road where you are beginning to walk, in an attempt to regain disposal of yourself. *I will keep a firm eye on you*, and so confirm my loving choice of you.

9. *Do not be like a horse or a mule, devoid of understanding*, and therefore wanting to be its own master. Here the voice of the prophet breaks in, praying, *Rein in their jaws with bit and bridle*: deal with them, O God, as horses and mules are dealt with, compelling them by punishment to submit to your control, those *who will not approach you.*

Verses 10-11. Contrasting fortunes

10. *There is many a scourge for the sinner.* Those who refuse to confess their sins to God, and want to be their own rulers, find plenty to scourge them. *But everyone who hopes in the Lord is encompassed with mercy.* Those who trust in the Lord and submit themselves to his rule find his mercy all around them.

---

3. One manuscript has "has prayed."

11. *Rejoice in the Lord and dance for joy, you just.* Rejoice and dance for joy, you just, not in yourselves but in the Lord. *And make him your boast, all you who are right of heart.* Boast in him, all you who have understood that it is right to submit to him, that you may assert your dignity over everything else.

Exposition 2 of Psalm 31

A Sermon to the People, preached on a Thursday in the Restored Basilica[1]

Treading a fine line between different kinds of presumption

1. This is a psalm about God's grace, and about our being justified by no merits whatever on our own part, but only by the mercy of the Lord our God, which forestalls anything we may do. It is a psalm to which the apostle's teaching has called our attention in a special way, as the reading that preceded the psalm has made clear to us all.[2] And this is the psalm which I, insignificant though I am, have undertaken to expound to you, dearest friends.[3] So I must begin by commending my weakness to your prayers. As the apostle says, *May the right word be given me when I open my mouth* (Eph 6:19), so that I can speak in a way that will not be perilous for me, and will be salutary for you. The human mind dithers between opposite dangers, wavering between confession of its weakness and rash presumption, and for the most part it is tossed between these two and battered on either side, and whichever way it is driven there is a ruinous fall awaiting it. If it veers entirely to the side of its own weakness, it begins to think that God in his mercy forgives all sinners, provided only they believe that God sets them free, so that at the end his mercy is ready to ensure that no one among sinful believers shall perish. In other words, no one will be lost of those who promise themselves, "I can do anything, I can defile myself with any crimes or shameful deeds, I can sin as much as I like. God frees me in his mercy because I have believed in him." Now if a person takes the view that no one in these circumstances will perish, he will be inclined by this evil notion to think he can sin with impunity. And then our just God, whose mercy and judgment are sung about in another psalm[4]—and it is not mercy alone, mind you, but mercy and

---

1. *Basilica Restituta*, the most famous of the Carthaginian basilicas, also called *Basilica Maior*. In it were held the African Councils of 390 and 401. This sermon has been tentatively assigned to the winter of 412-413.
2. An indication that the reading had been from Romans 4, by Augustine's choice, as appears from 2 below.
3. *Cum vestra Caritate.*
4. See Ps 100(101):1.

judgment—finds this person self-deceived by presumption and abusing the divine mercy to his own destruction, and then God must necessarily condemn.

An attitude like this brings a person crashing down. But then, suppose someone is terrified of that, and exalts himself in rash self-assurance, trusting in his own strength of character, and mentally resolving to fulfill all the righteous requirements of the law and to carry out all it enjoins without offending in any point whatever. If such persons think they can keep their lives under their own control and slip up nowhere, fall short nowhere, with never a wobble, never a blurring of vision, and if they claim the credit for themselves and their own strength of will, then even if they have carried out the whole program of righteous conduct as far as human eyes can discern, so that nothing in their lives can be faulted by other people, God nonetheless condemns their presumption and boastful pride.

What happens, then, if someone has thought to justify himself, and takes his stand on his own virtue? He falls. But if anyone considers himself and thinks about his weakness, and presumes on God's mercy, neglecting to purify his life from sin and sinking into a whirlpool of iniquity, he too falls. Presuming on one's righteousness is the danger on the right hand; thinking that one's sins will go unpunished is the danger on the left. We need to listen to God's voice warning us, *Turn not aside, to right hand or to left* (Prv 4:27). Do not presume on your virtue to get you into the kingdom; but do not presume on God's mercy and go on sinning. The divine command calls you back from both: from trying to climb the steep bank on the one hand, and from sliding down on the other. If you scramble up to the first you will fall headlong; if you slip down the second you will drown. *Turn not aside, to the right hand or to the left*, scripture warns us. I will say it again so that you can all fix it in your minds in a brief formula: don't presume on your virtue to win the kingdom, don't presume on God's mercy and think you can get away with sinning.

This psalm indicates the fine line

You will ask me, "What am I to do, then?" This psalm teaches us. Once we have read it through and discussed it, I think that with the help of the Lord's mercy we shall see the road clearly, the road on which we may be walking already, or which we must take. Each of us must listen according to our own capacity and, as our conscience dictates, either bemoan our need for correction or rejoice that we have something that deserves approval. Any who find that they have gone astray must return to the road and walk on it; and any who find that they are on the road must go on walking until they arrive. Do not be stubborn if you are off the road, or dilatory if you are on it.

Abraham and faith: Paul's teaching

2. The apostle Paul bore witness to the fact that this psalm deals with the grace that makes us Christians; that is why we arranged for this particular passage to be read to you. When the apostle was explaining about the righteousness that depends on faith, in opposition to those who boasted about a righteousness derived from works, he asked, *What are we to say that Abraham obtained, he who was our father according to the flesh? If Abraham was justified by works, he has ground for pride, but not before God* (Rom 4:1-2). May God keep that kind of pride far from us! Let us listen to a different injunction: *Let anyone who boasts, boast of the Lord* (1 Cor 1:31). Many people do boast about their works, and you will find plenty of pagans who are unwilling to become Christians because they think their upright lives are enough. "The important thing is to live a good life," such a pagan will tell you. "What further command would Christ lay upon me? That I should live a good life? But I am doing that already, so why do I need Christ? I commit no homicide, no theft, no robbery; I do not covet anyone else's property, or defile myself by adultery. Let anything that deserves rebuke be found in my way of life, and the one who rebukes me for it shall make me a Christian." A person like this has ground for pride, but not before God.

Not so our father Abraham. This passage of scripture is meant to draw our attention to the difference. We confess that the holy patriarch was pleasing to God; this is what our faith affirms about him. So true is it that we can declare and be certain that he did have grounds for pride before God, and this is what the apostle tells us. It is quite certain, he says, and we know it for sure, that Abraham has grounds for pride before God. But if he had been justified by works, he would have had grounds for pride, but not before God. However, since we know he does have grounds for pride before God, it follows that he was not justified on the basis of works. So if Abraham was not justified by works, how was he justified?" The apostle goes on to tell us how: *What does scripture say?* (that is, about how Abraham was justified). *Abraham believed God, and it was reckoned to him as righteousness* (Rom 4:3; Gn 15:6). Abraham, then, was justified by faith.

Paul and James do not contradict each other: good works follow justification

3. Now when you hear this statement, that justification comes not from works, but by faith, remember the abyss of which I spoke earlier. You see that Abraham was justified not by what he did, but by his faith: all right then, so I can do whatever I like, because even though I have no good works to show, but simply believe in God, that is reckoned to me as righteousness? Anyone who has said this and has decided on it as a policy has already fallen in and sunk; anyone who is still considering it and hesitating is in mortal danger. But God's scripture,

truly understood, not only safeguards an endangered person, but even hauls up a drowned one from the deep.

My advice is, on the face of it, a contradiction of what the apostle says; what I have to say about Abraham is what we find in the letter of another apostle, who set out to correct people who had misunderstood Paul. James in his letter opposed those who would not act rightly but relied on faith alone; and so he reminded them of the good works of this same Abraham whose faith was commended by Paul. The two apostles are not contradicting each other. James dwells on an action performed by Abraham that we all know about: he offered his son to God as a sacrifice. That is a great work, but it proceeded from faith. I have nothing but praise for the superstructure of action, but I see the foundation of faith; I admire the good work as a fruit, but I recognize that it springs from the root of faith. If Abraham had done it without right faith it would have profited him nothing, however noble the work was. On the other hand, if Abraham had been so complacent in his faith that, on hearing God's command to offer his son as a sacrificial victim, he had said to himself, "No, I won't. But I believe that God will set me free, even if I ignore his orders," his faith would have been a dead faith because it did not issue in right action, and it would have remained a barren, dried-up root that never produced fruit.

Apparent good works before faith are wide of the mark

4. What are we to make of this? That no good actions take precedence of faith, in the sense that no one can be said to have performed good works before believing? Yes, that's right, because although people may claim to perform good works before faith, works that seem praiseworthy to onlookers, such works are vacuous. They look to me like someone running with great power and at high speed, but off course. This is why no one should reckon actions performed before belief as good; where there was no faith, there was no good action either. It is the intention that makes an action good, and the intention is directed by faith. You should not pay too much attention to what a person does, but consider where he is aiming as he does it, and whether he is directing his efforts toward the right harbor, like a skilled pilot. Imagine a very expert steersman who has lost his bearings. What is the use of keeping a firm hold on the jib, making fair speed, putting the vessel's prow to the waves, and taking good care that she is not caught sideways onto their force? Such a pilot may be so competent that he can turn the ship whatever way he will, and turn her away from anything he wants to avoid; but if you ask him, "Where are you making for?" he replies, " I don't know." Or rather, he does not say, "I don't know," but "I am making for such-and-such a port," when in fact he is speeding not into port but onto the rocks. The more handy and efficient he thinks he is in steering his ship, the more dangerous is his mastery of her, surely, since it just brings her more swiftly to

shipwreck. A swift athlete who is off course is just like him. Would it not be better and safer if the pilot were somewhat less skilled, so that he steered the vessel laboriously and with difficulty, and yet held her to a straight and proper course, and if the athlete were running more lazily and feebly, but keeping to the track, rather than running so impressively off it? The best thing of all is to keep to the right road and maintain a good pace on it; but we may have good hopes for someone who straggles along in the rear, limping a little perhaps, but not so badly as to lose the way altogether or just sit down. Such walkers do make progress, even though slowly, and we may be confident that they will reach the goal sooner or later.

But faith cannot be sterile: it works through love

5. Well now, brothers and sisters, Abraham was justified by faith, but if no good works preceded his justification, they certainly followed it. Is your faith sterile? No, of course not. You are not sterile yourself, and neither is your faith. If you believe something bad, you scorch the root of your faith in the fire of that bad belief. So make sure to hold fast to your faith with a mind to work. You may object, "But that is not what the apostle Paul tells us." Oh, but it is. Paul speaks of *faith that works by choosing to love*[5] (Gal 5:6). In another place he says, *The fullness of the law is charity* (Rom 13:10); and elsewhere, *The whole law is summed up in one word, when scripture says, "You shall lovingly cherish*[6] *your neighbor as yourself"* (Gal 5:14). Can you really contend that Paul does not want good works from you, when he says, *You shall not commit adultery. You shall not murder. You shall not covet. And if there is any further commandment, it is covered by this one word, "You shall lovingly cherish your neighbor as yourself." Love of one's neighbor prompts no evil. The fullness of the law is charity* (Rom 13:9-10)? Does charity allow you to do anything harmful to a person whom you lovingly cherish? Perhaps, though, you refrain from doing harm, but do no good to your neighbor either. Does charity allow you to withhold from someone you lovingly cherish anything that it is in your power to give? Is it not charity that impels us to pray even for our enemies? Can charity leave a friend in the lurch, when it wishes well to an enemy?

If faith is devoid of the will to love,[7] it will equally be devoid of good actions. But don't spend too much time thinking about the works that proceed from faith:

---

5. Augustine uses three different words for love in this section: *dilectio*, the love that is directed by choice, a cherishing love; *caritas*, charity; and *amor*, a general word for love which may have connotations of sensuality or lust, in some contexts.
6. *Diliges.*
7. *Dilectione.*

add hope and the will to love[8] to your faith, and you will have no need to ask yourself what kind of works you should perform. This deliberate love[9] cannot remain idle. After all, what is it in any one of us that prompts action, if not some kind of love?[10] Show me even the basest love[11] that does not prove itself in action. Shameful deeds, adulteries, villainies, murders, all kinds of lust—aren't they all the work of some sort of love?[12] Purify this love, then, divert onto your garden the water that is going down the drain, let the current that drove you into the arms of the world be redirected to the world's Maker. Do you want people to ask you, "Don't you love anything, then?" Of course not. If you loved nothing you would be sluggish, dead, loathsome and unhappy. Love[13] as much as you like, but take care what you love. Love of God and love of your neighbor are called charity; but love of the world, this passing world, is called greed or lust. Lust must be reined in, charity spurred on.

A good conscience and hope

Now when people perform good actions their charity endows them with the hope that proceeds from a good conscience; for it is a good conscience that gives rise to hope. As a bad conscience plunges a person into complete despair, so a good conscience fills us entirely with hope. Then there will be the three realities of which the apostle speaks: *faith, hope and charity* (1 Cor 13:13). In another place he mentions this triad again, but this time he substitutes a good conscience for hope. He refers to *the finishing of the commandment* (1 Tm 1:5). What does he mean by its being finished? He is thinking of the commandments being perfectly fulfilled, not done away with. We have two different ways of speaking about a thing being finished: we say, "The food is finished," and in a different sense, "This tunic which I was weaving is finished." Food is finished up and so exists no longer, but the tunic is finished by being brought to completion. Yet we use the word, "finished," in both cases. So when Paul spoke about the commandment being finished he did not mean that the commandments were being abolished, but that they were being brought to perfection, accomplished, not abrogated.[14] The commandment is "finished," then, because of these three realities: *the finishing of the commandment is single-hearted charity, and a good conscience, and unfeigned faith* (1 Tm 1:5). The apostle substituted "a good

---

8. *Dilectionem.*
9. *Dilectio.*
10. *Amor.*
11. *Amorem.*
12. *Amor.*
13. *Amate.*
14. *Consummentur, non consumantur.*

conscience" for hope, because anyone whose conscience is clear does have hope. Those who suffer from a bad conscience, on the contrary, have estranged themselves from hope, and can look for nothing but damnation. If we are to hope for the kingdom we must have good consciences, and in order to have good consciences we must both believe and do good. Believing is the province of faith, good work that of charity. So in one text the apostle began from faith, saying, *Faith, hope, and charity*; but in the other text he made charity itself his starting-point: *single-hearted charity, and a good conscience, and unfeigned faith*. But we began just now with the middle term, conscience and hope. Yes, and rightly, because anyone who wants to have good hope needs to have a good conscience, and to have a good conscience we must both believe and work. So from this middle term, hope, we can work backward to the beginning, that is, to faith; and forward to the end, which is charity.

Paul himself gives the complementary teaching on "works"

6. How can the apostle assert that a person is justified by faith, independently of works, when in another place he speaks of *faith that works by choosing to love* (Gal 5:6)? It is not just a case of pitting the apostle James against Paul; we can pit Paul against himself, and challenge him like this: "On the one hand you seem to give us permission to sin with impunity by saying, *Our argument is that a person is justified by faith, apart from any works* (Rom 3:28); and on the other hand you speak of *faith that works by choosing to love*. How can I be free from anxiety on the basis of the first, having done no good works, while according to the second I do not seem to have either sound hope or even sound faith itself, if I have performed no good works in love? I am listening to you, apostle. You obviously want to urge upon me faith without works, but faith's work is willed love,[15] and this willed love cannot remain idle; it must refrain from doing evil and do all the good it can. What does love do? *Turn away from evil, and do good* (Ps 36(37):27). You extol faith apart from works, yet in another place you declare, *If I have such perfect faith that I can move mountains, but have no love, it profits me nothing* (1 Cor 13:2). So if faith profits us nothing without charity, and charity must always be at work wherever it is found, then faith itself works by choosing to love. How then is it possible for anyone to be justified by faith apart from works?"

The apostle has an answer for us. "I told you this, stupid, to save you from the mistake of relying on your achievements and thinking that you earned the grace of faith by your works. Put no reliance on works accomplished before faith. You

---

15. *Dilectio.*

know well that when faith came to you it found you a sinner, and although it is true that once faith was given it made you righteous, it was an ungodly person that faith found to transform into a righteous one." *When someone believes in him who justifies the impious, that faith is reckoned as justice to the believer*—so says Paul (Rom 4:5). If the impious is justified, then the impious person is changed from being impious into being righteous, but in that case what good works can he or she have performed while still impious? An impious, ungodly person may boast about his good deeds, claiming, "I give alms to the poor, I rob no one, I do not covet anyone else's wife, I kill nobody, I commit no fraud, I return promptly anything entrusted to me even though there were no witnesses." All right, let the unbeliever say all this, but still I ask, is the speaker a godly person, or impious? "How can I be impious," he or she will reply, "if I conduct myself like that?" In just the same way, I reply, as those of whom scripture says, *They served creatures rather than the Creator, who is blessed for ever* (Rom 3:25). In what sense are you impious? It may be that on the basis of all these good works of yours you either hope for what is worth hoping for, but not from God, from whom you should hope for it; or else you hope for something unworthy, even though you hope for it from God, from whom you should be hoping for eternal life. On the strength of your good actions you have hoped for worldly advantage, and so you are impious. The reward of faith is not like that. Faith is a precious thing, but you have cheapened it. You are impious, therefore, and those works of yours are null and void. Though you employ all your muscle in good works, and appear to pilot your ship with expertise, you are rushing toward the rocks.

But suppose what you hope for is the true object of hope, life eternal, but you do not hope for it from the Lord God through Jesus Christ, through whom alone eternal life is given, but think to arrive at eternal life through the host of heaven, through the sun and the moon, through the powers of air and sea and earth and stars? What then? You are still impious. Believe in him who justifies the impious, so that those good works of yours may be good too. I should not even have called them "good," as long as they do not spring from the root of faith. Think about it. Either you are hoping for temporal life from the eternal God, or you are hoping for eternal life from demons. Either way you are impious. Correct your faith, direct your faith, and set your course. If you have good strong feet, walk without fear, run, and stay on the road. The more strongly you run, the more easily you will arrive. Or perhaps you are slightly lame? At least do not leave the road; you may take longer, but you will get there. Only do not stand still, do not turn back, do not get sidetracked.

The grace of faith presupposes God's forgiveness

7. In the light of this, who are to be judged blessed? Certainly not people in whom God has found no sin, because he has found it in all of us. *All have sinned,*

and are in need of the glory of God (Rom 3:23). Now, if sins are found in everyone, it follows that only those can be blessed whose sins have been forgiven. This is the point the apostle made by saying, *Abraham believed God, and it was reckoned to him as righteousness. But to anyone who does some work* (that is, anyone who takes his stand on works, pretending that the grace of faith was given to him on the strength of them) *wages are given not as a free grace, but as something owed* (Rom 4:3-4). And what does that mean, if not that the only recompense we have is called grace? And if it is grace, it is given gratis. Given gratis? How is that? It consists of a free gift. You have done nothing good, but forgiveness of your sins is granted to you. If your actions are scrutinized, they are all found to be bad. If God awarded you just retribution for those actions, he would certainly condemn you, for the wage due to sin is death.[16] What is owing to evil deeds, except damnation? And what to good deeds? The kingdom of heaven. You were found in your evil deeds, so if you are awarded what is due to you, you are to be punished. But what happens? God does not mete out to you the punishment you deserve; he bestows on you the grace you do not deserve. He owed you retribution, he awards you forgiveness. So it is through being forgiven that you begin to live in faith; that faith gathers to itself hope and the decision to love[17] and begins to express itself in good actions; but not even after that may you boast and preen yourself. Remember who planted you on the right road; remember how even with your strong, swift feet you were wandering off it; remember how even when you were sick and lying half-dead by the wayside you were lifted onto a mount and taken to the inn.[18] *To anyone who does some work*, Paul tells us, *wages are given not as a free grace, but as something owed* (Rom 4:4). If you want to be excluded from the domain of grace, vaunt your own merits. But God sees what is in you, and knows what he owes to each.

But what about the person who *does no work* (Rom 4:5)? Think here of some godless sinner, who has no good works to show. What of him or her? What if such a person comes to believe in God who justifies the impious? People like that are impious because they accomplish nothing good; they may seem to do good things, but their actions cannot truly be called good, because performed without faith. But *when someone believes in him who justifies the impious, that faith is reckoned as justice to the believer, as David too declares that person blessed whom God has accepted and endowed with righteousness, independently of any righteous actions* (Rom 4:5-6). What righteousness is this? The righteousness of faith, preceded by no good works, but with good works as its consequence.

---

16. See Rom 6:23.
17. *Dilectione.*
18. See Lk 10:30-37.

Good will is needed for right understanding

8. You must pay careful attention to what I am saying, my friends, because otherwise you will hurl yourselves into that abyss I mentioned, assuming that you can sin with impunity. It won't be my fault if you do, any more than it was the apostle's fault when many people misunderstood him. They misunderstood on purpose, so that they would not need to produce any good work after justification. Do not be like those folk, my brothers and sisters. One of the psalms speaks about them (about all such people, that is, but expressing it in the singular): *He refused to understand that he should act well* (Ps 35:4(36:3)). Notice that it does not say, "He was unable to understand." As for you, you must want to understand that you should act well. What you need to understand is perfectly clear, and well within your grasp. And what is this clear truth? That no one must boast of any good actions before faith, and no one must be lazy about performing good actions once faith has been given. So then, God grants forgiveness to all the ungodly, justifying them on the basis of faith.

Verses 1-2. Forgiveness and truth: the example of Nathanael

9. *Blessed are those whose iniquities are forgiven, and whose sins are covered. Blessed is the one to whom the Lord will impute no sin, and in whose mouth is no guile.* Now we get to the beginning of the psalm, and so to the beginning of understanding. This comprehension, this understanding, teaches you that you must neither vaunt your merits nor presume that you can get away with sinning. The title of the psalm is, *For David himself, for understanding*, so this is a psalm that promotes understanding. The first stage of understanding is to recognize that you are a sinner. The second stage of understanding is that when, having received the gift of faith, you begin to do good by choosing to love,[19] you attribute this not to your own powers but to the grace of God. Then there will be no guile in your heart, which means in your inward mouth, for you will not have one thing on your lips and something different in your thoughts. You will not be one of the Pharisees to whom the Lord said, *You are like whitewashed tombs; outwardly you appear righteous to other people, but inwardly you are full of guile and sin* (Mt 23:27). When people who are wicked pass themselves off as righteous, are they not full of guile? Nathanael was not like that; of him the Lord said, *Look, there is a true Israelite, in whom there is no guile* (Jn 1:47). But why was there no guile in Nathanael? *When you were under the fig tree, I saw you*, the Lord told him (Jn 1:48). He was under a fig tree, which symbolized being subject

---

19. *Cum ex fide per dilectionem bene coeperis operari.*

to the condition of our flesh. If he was subject to the fleshly condition, being held prisoner by the impiety we all inherit by human descent, then he was under that fig tree another psalm groans about: *Lo, I was conceived in iniquity* (Ps 50:7(51:5)). But he who saw Nathanael there was he who had come to bring grace. What does "saw him" mean? He had mercy on him. So when he commends a man free from guile, what he is commending is his own grace in that man. *When you were under the fig tree, I saw you.* What is special about saying, *I saw you*? Nothing, unless you understand it in a particular sense here, because otherwise what is remarkable about seeing anyone under a fig tree? If Christ had not espied the human race under that fig tree,[20] we should either have withered away completely, or else only leaves would have been found on us, but no fruit, as with the Pharisees in whom there was plenty of guile, for they justified themselves by their words, but were wicked in their deeds. It was just such a tree that Christ saw, and cursed; and it withered. "All I can see is leaves," he said; that is, words only, and no fruit. "Let it wither," he said, "so that it may not even produce leaves."[21] Why did he strip them even of words? It is a withered tree that cannot bring forth even leaves. The Jews were like that; the Pharisees were that tree; they produced a luxuriance of words but no deeds, so they deserved to be condemned by the Lord to wither.[22]

May Christ see us too under a fig tree; may he see us in our fleshly condition producing not leaves only but the fruit of good deeds, lest we wither away under his curse. But because all fruit grows from his grace, not from any merits of ours, the psalm declares, *Blessed are those whose iniquities are forgiven, and whose sins are covered*: not those in whom no sins have been found, but those whose sins are covered. Their sins are covered over, they are out of sight, they are done away with. If God has covered our sins, he does not want to see them or be aware of them; if he does not want to be aware of them, he does not want to punish them; if he does not want to punish them, he does not want to convict us, he wants not commination but commiseration.[23] *Blessed are those whose iniquities are forgiven, and whose sins are covered.* You must not interpret this statement that our sins are covered over to mean that they are still there, still alive. Why, then, did the psalmist say that sins are covered? Because they are thrust out of sight. What would it mean for God to look

---

20. Perhaps we should translate here "under the guise of that fig tree"; see the next note.
21. See Mt 21:19.
22. When Augustine describes the climax of his struggle for conversion in *The Confessions* VIII,28, he says he flung himself down under a fig tree. At least in retrospect he must have been aware of its ambivalent symbolism, alluded to here. Adam and Eve after their fall made themselves loincloths of fig leaves, a sign of their sinful condition (see Gn 3:7); the Lord curses a barren fig tree that represents unfaithful Israel (see Mt 21:19 = Mk 11:13-14); but Nathanael's call from beneath a fig tree suggests his vocation, like Augustine's own, to grace.
23. *Noluit agnoscere, maluit ignoscere.*

at our sins? To punish our sins. I can prove to you that for God to look at our sins is the same thing as to punish them: another psalm prays to him, *Turn your face away from my sins* (Ps 50:11(51:9)). May God not look at your sins, so that he can see you. See you how? In the same way as he saw Nathanael: *When you were under the fig tree, I saw you.* The fig tree's shade was not so dense that the eyes of God's mercy could not see through it.

Forgiveness and truth: the example of the Pharisee and the tax collector

10. *In whose mouth there is no guile.* Very different is the case of those who refuse to confess their sins, and struggle vainly to excuse them. The more they exert themselves to defend their sins and brag about their merits, turning toward their sins a blind eye, the more do their strength and vigor wane. The only truly strong person is one who is strong not in himself but in God. So Paul admits that in his trouble *three times I begged the Lord to take it away from me, but he said to me, "My grace is sufficient for you."* Notice that God says, *My grace*, not "your own power." *My grace is sufficient for you, for my power finds complete scope in weakness* (2 Cor 12:8-9). Accordingly a little further on Paul himself confesses, *When I am weak, then I am strong* (2 Cor 12:10). Any who aspire to be strong, relying on themselves and displaying their own merits, whatever these may be, will be kin to that Pharisee[24] who managed to boast even about what he admitted was the gift of God, saying, *O God, I thank you.* Take note, my brothers and sisters, of the sort of pride God is warning us about here, the kind that can creep into a righteous person and sneak up even on someone of good promise. *O God, I thank you*, he kept saying. By repeating, *I thank you*, he was avowing that he had received what he had from God, for *what have you that you did not receive?* (1 Cor 4:7) Acknowledging that much, he said, *I thank you*, yes, *I thank you that I am not like other people: robbers, cheats, adulterers, or like that tax collector there.* Why was this a proud attitude? Not because he thanked God for the gifts he had, but because he was exalting himself above his neighbor on the strength of those gifts.

11. Close attention is required here, my brothers and sisters, because the evangelist tells us something at the outset to indicate what provoked our Lord's parable. Christ had asked, *When the Son of Man comes, do you think he will find faith on earth?* (Lk 18:8). But that might have given an opening to some heretics who would seize on it and think that it meant the whole world had fallen away (for all heretics are very elitist and out of touch) and might take occasion to brag that in themselves alone remained the faith that had vanished from the rest of the

---

24. See Lk 18:10-14.

world. To guard against this the evangelist added to the Lord's question, *When the Son of Man comes, do you think he will find faith on earth?* the further statement, *He spoke to certain people who considered themselves righteous and despised others the following parable. A Pharisee and a tax collector went up to the temple to pray* (Lk 18:9-10), and so on; you know the story.

So the Pharisee kept saying, *I thank you.* Was that pride? Yes. Why? Because he was despising others. How do I prove that? From his very words. The gospel tells us that the Pharisee despised another man who stood a long way off, but God came close to that man as he made his confession. *The tax collector stood a long way off,* we are told, but God was not standing a long way off from him. And why not? Because, as another verse of scripture tells us, *The Lord is close to those who have bruised their hearts* (Ps 33:19(34:18)). Ask yourselves whether this tax collector had bruised his heart, and there you will see how close the Lord is to the brokenhearted. *The tax collector stood a long way off and would not even raise his eyes to heaven, but beat his breast*—beat his breast, you see, as a token of his bruised heart—*and said, O God, be merciful to me, a sinner.* And what was the Lord's verdict? *Truly I tell you, that tax collector went down to his house at rights with God, more than did the Pharisee* (Lk 18:13-14). Why? This is God's judgment. The one boasts, *I am not like other people: robbers, cheats, adulterers, or like that tax collector there; I fast twice a week, and give tithes from everything I own.* The other does not dare to lift his eyes to heaven; he examines his conscience and stands a long way off, and he is justified rather than the Pharisee. How can this be? I beg you, Lord, to explain to us this just sentence of yours; explain to us the equity of your law. And the Lord does explain. Would you like to hear him give his judgment? *Anyone who exalts himself will be humbled, but the one who humbles himself will be exalted.*

12. Now listen, beloved.[25] We have said that the tax collector did not dare to lift his eyes to heaven. Why was he not directing his gaze heavenward? Because he was directing it toward himself. He was scrutinizing himself so that he might initially find himself displeasing, and so become pleasing to God. But you, Pharisee, you bear yourself arrogantly, standing with head held high. And the Lord says to any such proud person, "So you are not willing to take a hard look at yourself? I am looking at you. Do you want me to stop looking at you? Then look hard at yourself." The tax collector did not dare to raise his eyes heavenward because he was looking into himself, and dealing severely with his own conscience. He took the role of judge over himself so that the Lord might be the intercessor; he was punishing himself so that another might set him free; he was accusing himself so that the other might defend him. The Lord did not merely plead the

---

25. *Caritas vestra.*

case in his defense; he went further and decided it in his favor: *the tax collector went down to his house at rights with God, more than did the Pharisee; because anyone who exalts himself will be humbled, but the one who humbles himself will be exalted.* "This man looked so hard at himself," says the Lord, "that I did not want to scrutinize him. I heard him entreating me, *Turn your face away from my sins.*" Who said that? The same who also said, *I know my iniquity* (Ps 50:11,5(51:9,3)).

Obviously, my brothers and sisters, the Pharisee was a sinner too. Not because he was able to say, *I am not like other people: robbers, cheats, adulterers*, nor because he fasted twice a week, nor because he gave tithes. None of these things made him a sinner. But even if he had been free of all other sins, pride such as this would have been gravely sinful in itself, and yet he did reel off this list. But in any case, who is free from sin? Who can boast of having a pure heart, or of being clean from sin in all respects?[26] The Pharisee was indeed guilty of sin; but he was looking the wrong way, and failed to realize where he was standing. He was like someone in need of healing who had come to a doctor's surgery, but presented only his sound limbs and covered up his wounds. Let God cover your wounds; don't cover them yourself. If you cover them up out of embarrassment, the doctor will not heal them. Allow the physician to cover and cure them, because he covers them with a dressing. Under the physician's dressing the wound heals; under the patient's covering it is merely hidden. Anyway, from whom are you trying to hide it? From him who knows everything?

Verse 3. Growing old in the wrong silence

13. Take heed now, brothers and sisters, to what this psalm says about the matter. *My bones grew old because of my silence, in consequence of my shouting all day long.* What does that mean? It sounds like a contradiction: *because of my silence, my bones grew old in consequence of my shouting.* If it was due to his shouting, how can he say he kept silence? The answer is that he kept silence about one thing but not about another. He refrained from saying something that would have helped him, but did not keep quiet about something that harmed him. He kept silence from confession, but shouted his presumption. When he says, *my silence*, he means, "I did not confess." That was how he ought to have spoken. He should have kept quiet about his merits and shouted his sins; but he got it all wrong: he was silent about his sins and shouted his merits. So what happened to him? His bones grew old. If he had shouted his sins aloud, and kept quiet about his merits, you see, his bones would have been rejuvenated—his virtues, that is.

---

26. See Prv 20:9.

He would have been invigorated in the Lord, because he knew he was weak in himself. But as things were he wanted to be strong and steady in himself, and so he became weak, and his bones grew old. He was stuck in decrepitude because he refused to embrace newness by confessing. You know who are renewed, brothers and sisters: *blessed are those whose iniquities are forgiven, and whose sins are covered.* This man did not want his sins forgiven, so he piled up more sins, and defended them, by boasting about how good he was. And so, because he kept silence from confession, his bones grew old. *In consequence of my shouting all day long.* What can that mean, *shouting all day long?* Obstinately defending his sins.

Yet, after all, he does come to recognize himself. In a minute he will gain understanding, for he will turn his gaze on nothing else but himself; and in knowing himself he will find himself unlovely. You are going to hear about this, for your own healing.

Verse 4. The weight of God's hand

14. *Blessed is the one to whom the Lord will impute no sin, and in whose mouth is no guile. My bones grew old because of my silence, in consequence of my shouting all the day long. For day and night your hand lay heavy upon me.* What are we to understand by *your hand lay heavy upon me?* This is something momentous and real, my friends. Keep your eyes on that clear distinction drawn between the two of them, the Pharisee and the tax collector. What were we told about the Pharisee? That he is humiliated. And what of the tax collector? That he is exalted. Why is the former humiliated? Because he exalted himself. And why is the other exalted? Because he humbled himself. In order to humble a person who exalts himself, God puts a heavy hand on him. That person disdained to be humbled by confessing his iniquity, so he is brought low by the weight of God's hand. How could he ever endure the heavy hand that squashed him down? But how light the hand that lifts up! A mighty hand it was in both instances: powerfully pressing down the one, powerfully lifting up the other.

Verses 4-5. God forgives even before the confession is out

15. Accordingly, *day and night your hand lay heavy upon me. I was reduced to bitterness, when the thorn stuck fast in me.*[27] This heavy weight of your hand upon me, this very humiliation, has reduced me to bitterness;[28] I became

---

27. Variant: "in my bitter hardship I was converted, when the thorn. . . ."
28. Variant: "caused me to writhe in my bitterness."

wretched, the thorn stuck fast in me, and my conscience was stabbed. What happened when the thorn stuck into him? It hurt badly, and he realized his weakness. So what did he do, now that the thorn was lodged in him, this person who had kept silent from confession of sin, but shouted in defense of it, so that his strength waned and his bones wore out with age? *I perceived my sin.* Ah, so he does perceive it now. If he looks at it, God will overlook it.[29] Listen to how it goes on, and see if this is not his own admission. *I perceived my sin, and did not cloak my unrighteousness*: I explained this point just now. Do not cover it yourself, and God will cover it for you. *Blessed are those whose iniquities are forgiven, and whose sins are covered.* Those who draw a veil over their sins are stripped naked, but the speaker here stripped the cover off his so that he might be clothed. *I did not cloak my unrighteousness.* What does he mean by saying, *I did not cloak* it? Until very recently I kept my mouth shut, but now *I said....* Some reversal of his silence is taking place. *I said ....* What did you say? *I will declare against myself my unrighteousness to the Lord; and you have forgiven the impiety of my heart.* He tells us, *I said ....* Said what? He is not declaring anything yet, only promising that he will make a declaration; yet already God forgives.

Pay close attention, brothers and sisters, because this is very important. The psalmist says, *I will declare.* He does not say, "I declared"; yet you, Lord, have already forgiven him. This is what he says: *I will declare, and you have forgiven.* By the expression, *I will declare,* he made it obvious that he had not yet declared anything with his tongue, but he had made the declaration in his heart. The very resolve that *I will declare* is itself a declaration, and for that reason *you have forgiven the impiety of my heart.* My confession had not yet reached my lips; I had only got as far as saying, *I will declare against myself,* yet God heard the voice of my heart. My words were not yet in my mouth, but already God's ear was in my heart. *You have forgiven the impiety of my heart* because I said, *I will declare.*

Free will, not fate

16. It would not have been enough, though, for him to say, *I will declare my unrighteousness to the Lord.* He had good reason to say, *I will declare it against myself.* There is a difference. Plenty of people declare their unrighteous conduct, but against the Lord God himself. When they are found out in their sins they say, "God willed it so." People who say, "I didn't do it," or, "This action that you are finding fault with is no sin," are not making any declaration, either against themselves or against God. But if someone says, "Yes, I did it, to be sure, and it is a

---

29. *Si ille cognoscit, ille ignoscit.*

sin. But God willed it, so what fault is it of mine?" that is to make a declaration against God. You may object, "But no one would say that. How could anyone maintain that God willed it?" On the contrary, many people do say just that. And others there are who do not express it so bluntly, but what else does it amount to when they protest, "It was my fate. My stars were responsible"? They are simply getting at God by a roundabout route. They want to accuse God in this devious way, instead of taking a short cut to making their peace with him, so they say, "Fate did this to me." And what is fate? "Well, my stars did it." And what are the stars? "Those things we see in the sky, of course." And who made them? "God." Who set them in their courses? "God." Look what you are trying to say, then: "God made me sin." That means he is in the wrong and you are in the right, because if he had not made them, you would not have sinned! Have done with these excuses for your sins; remember the prayer in a psalm: *turn not my heart aside into dishonest words, to seek excuses in its sins with people who commit iniquity* (Ps 140(141):4).

Yet these people who defend their sins are persons of high repute, persons of good standing who count the planets, and calculate astral conjunctions and significant times; they predict who will sin, and when, and who will live honorably; when Mars will drive someone to murder or Venus someone to adultery. They are people of substance, learned men, who seem to be the privileged ones of this world. But what has the psalm to say? *Turn not my heart aside with people who commit iniquity; I will have no part with their privileged ones.* Let others call them wise, those privileged, learned ones who count the planets; let others call them wise, those pedants who fiddle human fate on their fingers[30] and map out human conduct from the stars. God created me with free will; if I have sinned, it is I myself who have sinned, so my business is not simply to declare my unrighteousness to the Lord, but to declare it against myself, not against him. *I myself said, Lord, have mercy on me*: this is a sick person crying out to the physician: *I myself said.* Why this emphasis, *I myself*? It would have been enough to write, *I said.*[31] But the emphasis is deliberate: I said it *myself*. I, I myself, not fate, not my horoscope, not the devil either, because he did not compel me, but I consented to his persuasion. *I myself said, Lord, have mercy on me; heal my soul, for I have sinned against you* (Ps 40:5(41:4)). Our psalmist made the same decision here too. He made up his mind: *I said, I will declare against myself my unrighteousness to the Lord, and you have forgiven the impiety of my heart.*

---

30. A pun: *qui digerunt in digitis.*
31. *Quare: Ego dixi? Sufficeret: dixi.*

Verse 6. The time of grace

17. *Every holy person will pray to you about this matter, when the time is right.* What time would that be? The right time for *this matter.* What matter? Impiety. And what would one pray for about that? For sins to be forgiven, obviously. *Every holy person will pray to you about this matter, when the time is right*; and the only reason why all holy persons will pray to you is that you have forgiven their sins, for if you did not forgive sins there would not be a single holy person to pray to you. But *every holy person will pray to you about this matter, when the time is right,* when the New Covenant shall be revealed and the grace of Christ be made manifest. That will be the right time. *When the fullness of time had come, God sent his Son, made from a woman* (that means one of the female sex; the ancients applied the term to married women and virgins indiscriminately),[32] *made subject to the law, that he might redeem those who were subject to the law* (Gal 4:4-5). From what did he redeem them? From the devil, from perdition, from their sins, from him to whom they had sold themselves. *To redeem those who were subject to the law.* They were indeed subjects under the law, for it weighed heavily upon them. Its terms oppressed them by showing up their guilt without saving them. It certainly forbade wrongful deeds, but since they had in themselves no power of self-justification, they were forced to cry out to God in the same way as Paul did when he knew himself to be a prisoner under the law of sin: *Who will deliver me from this death-ridden body, wretch that I am?* (Rom 7:24). All men and women were under the law, not within it, as long as it oppressed them and declared them guilty. The law brought sin into the open; it drove the thorn home, evoked compunction of heart, and warned all that they must acknowledge their guilt and cry to God for pardon. *Every holy person will pray to you about this matter, when the time is right.* That is why, says the psalmist, I pointed to a right time: *when the fullness of time had come, God sent his Son.* The apostle says elsewhere, *At the acceptable and favorable time I have heard you, and on the day of salvation I have helped you.* And since the prophet envisaged all Christians[33] when he foretold this, the apostle added, *See, now is the acceptable time, lo, this is the day of salvation* (2 Cor 6:2).[34] *Every holy person will pray to you about this matter, when the time is right.*

---

32. Augustine is alluding to the virginal conception of Christ, not excluded by the general word, *mulier.*
33. Variant: "Christian times."
34. Compare Is 49:8.

The floods that keep us from God

18. *Yet they will not draw near to him amid the flood of many waters.* What is meant by *to him*? To God. This shift from second to third person is quite usual. We have another example of it in the verse, *salvation is from the Lord, and may your blessing be upon your people* (Ps 3:9(8)). It did not say there, "Salvation is from the Lord, and may his blessing be upon his people," did it? Nor did it say, "Salvation is from you, Lord, and may your blessing be upon your people"; but having begun in the third person, *salvation is from the Lord*, speaking about him, not to him, the psalmist then turned to him and continued, *and may your blessing be upon your people.* So too in the present psalm. When you hear it beginning, *to you*, and then shifting to *to him*, you must not think it is referring to someone different. *Every holy person will pray to you about this matter, when the time is right. Yet they will not draw near to him amid the flood of many waters.* What is meant by *the flood of many waters*? It means that people who swim in the flood of many waters do not draw near to God. Well, then, what are these many flood-waters? They stand for the multiplicity of variegated teachings. Try to concentrate, my brothers and sisters. The many waters are the variety of doctrines. God's doctrine is one. There are not many waters, but one single water, whether we think of the water of baptism or the water of salutary doctrine. Of this doctrine, with which we are irrigated by the Holy Spirit, scripture says, *Drink water from your own cisterns and your own wellsprings* (Prv 5:15). The ungodly have no access to these springs, but those who believe in him who justifies the ungodly approach once they are justified. The many other waters are the many teachings that pollute human souls. I was speaking of some of them not long ago. One alien doctrine is: "Fate did this to me." Another is: "Chance made this happen to me," or "My horoscope was responsible." If human beings are ruled by chance, nothing is effected by Providence; and this too is a doctrine. Another teacher said, "There is a hostile race of darkness which has rebelled against God, and it causes people to sin." Swimmers in this flood of many waters do not draw near to God.

What is the real water, the water that wells up from the most secret inner spring, from the pure channel of truth? Yes, what is that water, my brothers and sisters? It is the water that teaches us to confess to the Lord. What other water admonishes us that *it is good to confess to the Lord* (Ps 91:2(92:1))? What water are we talking about, but the water that inspires the cry, *I said, I will declare against myself my unrighteousness to the Lord*, and *I myself said, Lord, have mercy on me; heal my soul, for I have sinned against you*? This is the water that urges us to confess our sins, the water that humbles our hearts, the water of a way of life that leads to salvation, of those who abase themselves, do not presume on themselves at all and refuse any proud attribution of their achievements to their own strength. You will not find this water in any of the books of the pagans, whether Epicurean, Stoic, Manichean or Platonist. You will find throughout those books excellent precepts of morality and self-improvement, but nowhere humility like this. The way of humility comes from no other source; it comes only from Christ. It is the way originated by him who, though most high, came in humility. What else did he teach us by humbling himself and becoming obedient even to death, even to the death of the cross?[35] What else did he teach us by paying a debt he did not owe, to release us from debt? What else did he teach us, he who was baptized though sinless, and crucified though innocent? What else did he teach us, but this same humility? He had every right to say, *I am the way, and the truth, and the life* (Jn 14:6). By this humility, then, we draw near to God, because the Lord is close to those who have bruised their hearts;[36] but amid the flood of many waters, amid the torrent of those who exalt themselves in opposition to God and peddle proud blasphemies, no one will draw near to him.

Verse 7. Joy amid groaning

19. But what about you, who are already justified: are you immersed in these flood-waters? They are all around us, my brothers and sisters; even when we confess our sins those torrential waters raise their din on every side. We are not in the flood, but it swirls all round us. Its waters splash us, yet do not swamp us; they drive against us but do not drown us. How are you going to manage, then, in the middle of the flood as you are, wading through this world? Is the psalmist deaf to those teachers, those proud professors? Does he not endure daily persecution in his heart from their pronouncements? What has this psalmist to say, already justified as he is and relying wholly on God? What is he to say, surrounded by the flood? *You are for me a refuge from the distress that besets me.* Let those others take refuge with their gods, or with their demons, or in their own strength, or in defending their sins. As for me, I have no refuge in this flood except yourself, my refuge from the distress that besets me.

20. *You who make me dance with happiness, save me.* If you are already dancing with happiness, why ask to be saved? *You who make me dance with happiness, save me.* I can hear the voice of joy when he says, *You make me dance with happiness*; and I hear groaning when he prays, *Save me.* You are joyful, yet you groan. "Quite so," he replies, "I both groan and rejoice. I rejoice in hope, but still groan over present reality. *You who make me dance with happiness, save me.*" The apostle entreats us, *Rejoice in hope*, and so the psalmist is right to pray, *You who make me dance with happiness, save me.* Paul continues, *Be patient in*

---

35. See Phil 2:8.
36. See Ps 33:19(34:18).

anguish (Rom 12:12), and the psalmist is in accord: *You who make me dance with happiness, save me.* The apostle too was already justified, and what had he to say? *Not creation only, but we ourselves, though we have the firstfruits of the Spirit, groan inwardly.* So why the psalmist's prayer, *save me?* Because we ourselves *groan inwardly as we await our adoption as God's children, the redemption of our bodies.* That is why the psalm begs, *Save me*: we are still groaning inwardly as we await the redemption of our bodies. But why then does he also say to God, *You make me dance with happiness?* The apostle's next words make it clear why: *in hope we have been saved. But if hope is seen, it is hope no longer, for when someone sees what he hopes for, why should he hope for it? But if we hope for what we do not see, we wait for it in patience* (Rom 8:23-25). If you hope, you rejoice; if you are waiting with patience, you still groan; for there is no need for patience when you have no evil to put up with. What we call endurance, what we call patience, what we call bearing up, what we call steadfastness, has no place except amid misfortunes. Where you are hard pressed, there you feel the pinch. If we are still waiting in patience, we still have reason to say, *Save me from those that hem me in*; but because we are saved in hope, we can say both these things simultaneously: *you make me dance with happiness*, and *save me.*

Verse 8. Keep your eyes on the Lord

21. Now comes God's answer: *I will give you understanding.* Remember, this is a psalm about understanding. *I will give you understanding, and set you on this road you must enter.*[37] What is meant by that: *I will set you on this road you must enter?* He does not mean to set you there so that you stay put, but so that you do not stray off it. I will give you understanding so that you may always truly know yourself, and always rejoice in hope toward God, until you arrive in your heavenly homeland, where there will be no place for hope, but only the reality.[38] *I will keep a firm eye on you.* I will not take my eyes off you, because you will not take yours off me either. Now that you are justified, now that your sins are forgiven, lift your eyes to God. Your heart went moldy when it wallowed in the mud. There is good reason for the exhortation you know well: "Lift up your hearts,"[39] because they may go bad if you don't. You, for your part, must now lift your eyes to God all the time, so that he can keep a firm eye on you. Need you be afraid that when you keep your eyes on God you may trip over something, and fail to see

---

37. Variant, in this and the following sentence: "on this road where you must walk."
38. *Ubi iam non spes, sed res erit.*
39. Familiar from the liturgy; see note on Exposition of Psalm 10, 3.

what is before your feet, and even fall into a trap? No, you need not worry, for his eyes are alert, those eyes of God that he keeps fixed on you. *Do not be anxious* (Mt 6:31), says the Lord; and the apostle Peter tells us, *Cast all your anxiety on him, for he takes care of you* (1 Pt 5:7). In this same sense God promises here, *I will keep a firm eye on you.* Raise your eyes to him, and, as I said, you will have no cause to fear that you may stumble into a snare. Listen to what another psalm recommended: *My eyes are on the Lord continually;* and then, as though someone had objected, "But how can you take care of your feet, if you are not looking where you are going?" the psalmist continued, *He will pluck my feet from the snare* (Ps 24(25):15). *I will keep a firm eye on you.*

Verse 9. Mulish obstinacy

22. God has promised to this one who prays both understanding and protection; but now he turns to the proud folk who defend their sins, and gives us an idea of what kind of understanding is in view. *Do not be like a horse or a mule, devoid of understanding.* The horse and the mule toss their heads. Neither horse nor mule is like the ox that recognizes its owner, or the ass that knows its master's manger.[40] *Do not be like a horse or a mule, devoid of understanding,* for what kind of treatment are those creatures subjected to? *Rein in their jaws with bit and bridle, those who will not approach you.* Do you aspire to be a horse or a mule; Do you want to throw your rider? Your mouth and your jaws will be reined in with bit and bridle; yes, that mouth of yours with which you vaunt your merits but keep quiet about your sins will be reined in. *Rein in their jaws with bit and bridle, those who will not approach you* by humbling themselves.

Verse 10. Breaking in the horse

23. *There is many a scourge for the sinner.* We need not wonder if after the bit has been inserted the whip is also used. The sinner wanted to be like an unbroken animal, and so must be subdued with bit and whip; and let us hope that he or she can be broken in. The fear is that such persons may resist so obstinately that they deserve to be left in their unbroken state and allowed to go their own sweet way, until of them it can be said, *Their iniquity will leak out as though from folds of fat* (Ps 72(73):7), as it is of those whose sins go unpunished for the present. May such people, when the whip catches them, be corrected and subdued, as the psalmist tells us he too was tamed. He admits that he was a horse or a mule, because he was obstinately silent; and how was he subdued? By the whip. *I was*

---

40. See Is 1:3.

reduced to bitterness, he says, *when the thorn stuck fast in me*. Whether we think of this as a whip or a spur, God tames the beast he rides, because it is to the beast's own advantage to be ridden. It is not because God is weary of walking on his own feet that he mounts. Isn't it a very mysterious episode, when a donkey is led to the Lord?[41] This donkey stands for the humble and docile people that provides a good mount for the Lord, and it is making for Jerusalem. *He will guide the meek in judgment*, as another psalm predicts; *he will teach his ways to the gentle* (Ps 24(25):9). Who are these gentle ones? Those who do not toss their heads in defiance of their trainer, who patiently accept the whip and the rein, so that later, when they have been broken in, they may walk without the whip, and hold to their course without the need for bit and bridle. If you refuse your rider, it is you who will fall, not he. *There is many a scourge for the sinner; but everyone who hopes in the Lord is encompassed with mercy*. How does the Lord prove himself a refuge from the distress that surrounds us? The person who was at first encompassed with distress is later encompassed with mercy, for he who gave the law will grant mercy too:[42] the law when he applied the whip, and mercy when he handles us gently. *Everyone who hopes in the Lord is encompassed with mercy*.

Verse 11. The true rejoicing

24. Now for the last verse. *Rejoice in the Lord and dance for joy, you just.* Woe betide you who rejoice in yourselves! You are impious and proud if you rejoice in yourselves; but once you come to believe in him who justifies the impious, your faith will be reckoned as righteousness. *Rejoice in the Lord and dance for joy, you just.* We must understand, "dance for joy in the Lord," of course. Why is that? Because they are now just. And how did that happen to them? Not by their own merits, but by his grace. In what sense are they just? Just because justified.

25. *And make him your boast, all you who are right of heart.* What is it to be *right of heart*? The right of heart are those who do not resist God. Let me have your attention, beloved ones,[43] and try to understand this rectitude of heart. I will explain it briefly, though it is a point of major importance; and I thank God that it comes at the end, so that it will stick in your minds.

This is the difference between a right heart and a crooked one. When a person has to suffer many things willy-nilly, such as sickness, grief, toil and humiliations, and attributes them solely to the just will of God, not concluding that God is unwise or that he does not know what he is doing when he chastises this one

---

41. See Mk 11:7.
42. See Ps 83:8(84:7).
43. *Caritas vestra.*

and spares others, that man or woman is right of heart. People with perverse hearts, hearts crooked and misshapen, complain that all the woes they suffer are undeserved, and so they charge God, by whose will they undergo these things, with acting unjustly. Or perhaps they do not dare to accuse him directly of injustice, so they assume that he cannot be in control. "This must be the way of it," they say, "because he cannot do anything unjust, and yet it is unjust that I should suffer while someone else is exempt. I admit that I am a sinner, but there are others who are greater sinners still, and they make merry while I am in trouble. It is unfair that those who are even worse than I should be happy, and I, who am a righteous person, or at any rate less sinful than they are, should have to put up with all this. By my reckoning this is certainly unjust, and by my reckoning it is equally certain that God cannot act unjustly. So I conclude that God is not in control of human affairs, and does not care about us."

So the people with crooked, twisted hearts propose three opinions. Either God does not exist; so the fool says in his heart, "There is no God."[44] And as I have already said in connection with the flood,[45] there has been no lack of such teaching among the philosophers, no lack of teachers who denied the existence of a God who governs all things and created all things, but postulated a plethora of gods who were engrossed in their own affairs, distanced from the world and unconcerned with it. So then, either "There is no God," which is the opinion of the impious person who is angry about anything unpleasant that happens to him or her, but does not happen to someone else deemed to be less deserving; or, secondly, "God is unjust, since he enjoys this sort of thing, and acts like this"; or, thirdly, "God is not in control of human affairs, and does not concern himself with any of them." All three of these opinions entail grave impiety, whether it is denial of God's existence, or charging him with injustice, or doubting his governance of the world. Why does anyone hold such views? Because they are crooked of heart. God is straight and true, and therefore a crooked heart is not at peace with him. Another psalm exclaims, *How good is Israel's God to those who are right of heart!* But the psalmist had once held a perverse opinion himself: *How does God know? Can any knowledge be attributed to the Most High?* and remembering that, he added, *Even I almost lost my footing* (Ps 72(73):1,11,2). If you lay a warped beam on a hard, level surface, it does not fit or square up properly or lie flat; it will always shake and wobble, not because the surface where it was placed is uneven, but because the beam itself is lopsided. So too as long as a heart remains crooked and twisted, it cannot be aligned with the rectitude of

---

44. See Ps 13(14):1.
45. See 18 above.

God; it cannot be bedded close to him and cling to him.[46] In such a heart the saying cannot come true that *anyone who clings to the Lord is one spirit with him* (1 Cor 6:17).

Make the Lord your boast, then, *all you who are right of heart.* How do right-hearted people boast? Listen to their boasting: *What is more, we even glory in our sufferings.* It is no great thing to glory amid joy or boast when we are happy; right-hearted persons glory even in tribulations. And listen to how they do it, how no one who glories amid afflictions is doomed to disappointment or boasts in vain. Look at this rightness of heart, as evinced by Paul: *we even glory in our sufferings, knowing that suffering fosters endurance, and endurance constancy, and constancy hope; but hope does not disappoint us, because the love of God has been poured out into our hearts through the Holy Spirit who has been given to us* (Rom 5:3-5).

26. This is what a right heart is like, my brothers and sisters. If any misfortune befalls right-hearted people, let them say, "The Lord gave, and the Lord has taken away." This is rightness of heart: "as it has pleased the Lord, so it has turned out. May the name of the Lord be blessed."[47] They do not say, "The Lord gave, and the devil has taken away." Pay careful attention to this, my dearest ones,[48] so that you may never say, "The devil has done this to me." No, by no means; refer the scourge that falls on you to God, because the devil does nothing to you unless by permission from our powerful God, who may allow it either as punishment or as discipline: punishment for the ungodly or discipline for God's children. God scourges every son whom he acknowledges.[49] Do not hope that you will be spared the lash, unless you also plan to be disinherited. He scourges every son he acknowledges. Every single one? Yes. Where did you think to hide? Every one without exception, every single one, will be liable to scourging. What, is no one spared? No. Do you need to be convinced that this rule admits of no exceptions? Even the only-begotten Son, he who was sinless, even he was not exempt. The only-begotten Son himself, bearing your weakness and representing you in his own person, as the Head which included the body in itself, even he was deeply saddened in his human nature as he approached his passion, in order to give you joy. He was saddened that he might comfort you. Undoubtedly the Lord could have faced his passion free from sadness. If a soldier had the power to do so, surely the commander-in-chief had? But did a soldier have that power? Yes: listen to Paul shouting with joy as he approached his suffering:

---

46. Or, with the addition of one word by the editors of the Latin text, " . . . cling to him and be straightened."
47. See Jb 1:21.
48. *Caritas vestra.*
49. See Heb 12:6.

Already I am being poured out like a sacrificial libation, he says, *and the time for my dissolution is upon me. I have fought the good fight, I have run the whole course, I have kept the faith; all that remains for me now is the crown of righteousness which the just judge will award me on that day, and not to me alone but to all those who love his coming* (2 Tm 4:6-8). Look at that for triumphant cheerfulness in the face of suffering! So the man who is due to be crowned rejoices, while the One who is to crown him is deeply saddened. What does this suggest that he was carrying? The weakness of others, who are grieved when trouble or death looms.

But observe how he leads them toward rightness of heart. Think about it: you were wanting to live, and not wanting any calamity to fall upon you; but God willed otherwise. There are two wills, then; but your will must be straightened to fit the will of God, not God's will twisted out of shape to fit yours. Yours is crooked, his is the ruler. The ruler must stand steady so that the crooked thing may be conformed to it. Our Lord Jesus Christ teaches us this. Listen to him: *my soul is sorrowful to the point of death*; and *Father, if it is possible, let this cup pass from me*. His human will shows through here. But look at his rightness of heart: *not what I will, but what you will be done, Father* (Mt 26:38,39). Do likewise yourself, and rejoice in the troubles that befall you; and if your last day is upon you, rejoice. If any of the frailty of your human will tries to take over, surrender it swiftly to God, that you may be among those to whom the psalmist says, *Make him your boast, all you who are right of heart.*

Exposition 1 of Psalm 32

Verses 1-3. Exhortation to praise

1. *Dance for joy in the Lord, you just.* You righteous folk, dance for joy, not in yourselves, which is unsafe, but in the Lord. *Praise befits the upright.* These upright ones who praise the Lord are they who submit to him; were this not so, they would not be upright, but crooked and misshapen.

2. *Confess to the Lord on the lyre*, confess to him by presenting your bodies to him as a living sacrifice.[1] *Sing psalms to him with the ten-stringed psaltery*; put your members at the service of willing love for God and your neighbor, thereby observing both the three and the seven commandments.[2]

3. *Sing him a new song,* sing him a song about the grace of faith. *Sing skillfully to him in jubilation.* In your joy, sing tunefully to him.

Verses 4-5. God's fidelity and mercy

4. *Because the Lord's word is straight.* The straight word of the Lord is able to make you what you have no power to make yourselves. *And all his works are done in faith.* This is said to correct any who think they have attained to faith on the merit of their own works; in fact all the works that have any value in God's estimation are performed within faith itself.

5. *He loves judgment and mercy*, for he delights to make an advance payment of mercy to us; but he also values judgment, by which he demands from us a return on what he advanced. *The earth is full of the mercy of the Lord*: throughout the world humankind's sins are forgiven by the Lord's mercy.

---

1. See Rom 12:1.
2. That is, the first three of the Decalogue that relate to God, and the remaining seven on relations with our neighbors. See section 6 in the sermon that follows. The division of the commandments proposed by Augustine (see *Faith and Works*, 17) became traditional in the West and is used by Catholic and Lutheran traditions. This yields the 3 + 7 alluded to here. An alternative system adopted by the Greek Fathers and used by the Orthodox and Reformed churches divides the opening precept into two (no false gods, no graven images) and joins Augustine's last two (coveting the neighbor's wife, coveting his goods) into one.

Verses 6-9. Creator of the material and spiritual universes

6. *By the word of the Lord the heavens were established,* for the righteous, represented by *the heavens,* are firmly established not by themselves but by the word of the Lord; *and all their strength by the breath of his mouth.* Their entire faith is stabilized by his Spirit.

7. *He gathers the waters of the sea together as though into a bottle.* He gathers the nations of the world together in the confession that sin has been put to death, to ensure that pride does not lead them to flow about unchecked. *Storing up the depths in his treasure-houses.* He keeps his mysteries there, like hoarded riches.

8. *Let every region of the earth fear the Lord;* let every sinner stand in awe of him, and so give up sinning. *But let it be by him that they are thrown into turmoil.* Not by threats from human beings or any created thing, but by the Lord himself, *let them be thrown into turmoil, all the world's inhabitants.*

9. *For he himself spoke, and they were made.* Those things which they might have feared were not, after all, made by anyone else save the Lord; he himself spoke, and they came to be. *He gave the order, and they were created.* In speaking his word he himself gave the order, and they were created.

Verses 10-15. The Lord's saving design

10. *The Lord frustrates the plans of the nations* who seek not his kingly rule, but kingdoms of their own. *He rebukes the thoughts of the peoples* who long for earthly happiness, *and rejects the designs of rulers* who seek to dominate such peoples.

11. *But the Lord's plan abides for ever.* The Lord's plan, according to which he grants happiness only to those who submit to him, abides for ever. *The thoughts of his heart endure from age to age.* The thoughts of his wisdom are not subject to change, but abide for ever and ever.

12. *Happy the nation whose God is the Lord.* One nation alone is truly happy, the one whose home is that heavenly city which has chosen as Lord none other than its God. *The people whom the Lord has chosen as his inheritance.* This inheritance is his elect, not for any pretensions of its own but by God's gift, so that by making it his own he may not allow it to lie fallow or become derelict.

13. *The Lord looked down from heaven and saw all the children of men.* From the vantage-point of a just soul the Lord mercifully regarded all who want to be reborn into the new life.

14. *From his own prepared dwelling,* from that abode where he took on human nature, the dwelling he made ready for himself, *he looked on all the inhabitants of the earth.* He has looked in mercy on all who dwell in the flesh, willing to be their leader and rule them.

15. *He fashioned all their hearts individually*, endowing each heart with appropriate spiritual gifts, so that the body should be a whole, not consisting of an eye only, or hearing only,[3] but that each should be incorporated into Christ in its own special way. *He has understood all their actions*, for all they do is present to his intelligence.

Verses 16-17. Human resources cannot save us

16. *A king will not be saved by his extensive power.* Those who exercise royal dominion over their flesh will not be saved if they rely heavily on their own power; *nor will even a giant be saved by his immense prowess*, for those who do battle against their entrenched concupiscence, or against the devil and his angels, will not be victorious if they have trusted too much in their own valor.

17. *A horse cannot be relied on for salvation.* They are deluded who suppose that they can acquire through other human beings the salvation which is received, indeed, among humans. Equally deceived are they who think they can be preserved from ruin by their own impetuous courage. *Nor will anyone be saved by his own strength, however great.*

Verses 18-22. The Lord mercifully supports his own

18. *Lo, the Lord's eyes are upon those who revere him*, for if it is salvation that you seek, be aware that the elective love of the Lord rests on those who fear him *and trust in his mercy*, rather than putting their hope in their own strength.

19. *To deliver their souls from death, and sustain them amid famine*; for he wills to nourish them with the word and everlasting truth, which they had forfeited by presuming on their own resources, with the result that they lost even those resources in the dearth of righteousness.

20. *Our soul will wait patiently for the Lord.* In order that it may be feast hereafter on incorruptible food, our soul will wait on the Lord with patience as long as it sojourns here. *Because he is our helper and protector*: our helper as we make the effort to reach him, and our protector as we fight our adversary.

21. *For in him our heart will rejoice.* Not in ourselves, where there is nothing but vast penury without him, but in him will our heart rejoice. *We have hoped[4] in his holy name.* This is why we have hoped that we shall reach the Lord: while we are still at a distance he has put his own name upon us through our faith.

---

3. See 1 Cor 12:17.
4. Variant: "will hope."

22. *May your mercy, Lord, be upon us, as we have hoped[5] in you.* Lord, may your mercy rest on us, for hope does not disappoint us,[6] and in you we have placed our hope.

---

5. Variant: "will hope."
6. See Rom 5:5.

Exposition 2 of Psalm 32

First Sermon to the People, preached at Mappalia during the Vigil of the Feast of Saint Cyprian the Martyr[1]

Verse 1. Praising God means uniting our will to his

1. This psalm urges us to dance for joy in the Lord. But it is entitled, *For David himself.* All of us, then, who are numbered among the sacred progeny of David must listen to his words, and make those words our own, and dance for joy in the Lord. The psalm begins with the admonition, *Dance for joy in the Lord, you just.* Let the unjust dance for joy in this world, by all means; but when this world comes to an end, there will be an end to their dancing. Let the just dance for joy in the Lord, for the Lord abides for ever, and so will the exultation of the just. The most fitting way for us to dance for joy in the Lord is for us to praise him, in whom alone there is nothing whatever that can be displeasing to us, though in the eyes of unbelievers no one has so many aspects that are displeasing. There is a pithy saying: one is pleasing to God if one finds God pleasing to oneself. Do not dismiss this as frivolous, my friends. You can see for yourselves how many people argue in opposition to God, and how many are offended by what he does. When he has decided to act in a way human beings do not like, because he is the Lord and he knows what he is about, and is less concerned with our likes and dislikes than with what will be to our profit, people who want their own will carried out rather than God's seek to bend God to their will, instead of correcting theirs by aligning it with his. Such people are unbelievers, impious and wicked. I am ashamed to say this, but I will say it, for you know how true it is: an actor on stage[2] gives them more pleasure than God does.

2. With this in mind the psalmist first invites us, *Dance for joy in the Lord, you just,* because we could scarcely dance for joy in him without praising him, and we praise him by becoming more and more pleasing to him as we find him pleasing to us. Accordingly the psalmist then adds, *Praise befits the upright.* Who are the

---

1. According to the *Acta proconsularia sancti Cypriani,* after Cyprian's martyrdom his body was carried in triumph by the Christians to the *area Macrobii,* a graveyard "which is on the Mappalian Way, near the reservoirs," outside the walls of the city of Carthage. A basilica was later built there at the place of his burial, and in it the present sermon was preached, possibly on 13 September 403, though the date is disputed.
2. Literally a "pantomime performer"; see note on Exposition 4 of Psalm 30, 11.

upright? Those who direct their hearts in accordance with the will of God. If human frailty unsettles them, divine tranquility consoles them; for although they may privately in their mortal hearts want something that serves their present purpose, or promotes their business, or meets their immediate need, once they have understood and recognized that God wants something different, they prefer the will of One better than themselves to their own, the will of the Almighty to that of a weakling, the will of God to that of a human being. As God is infinitely above his human creatures, so is God's will far above the will of men and women.

This is why Christ took the mantle of humanity, set us an example, taught us how to live and gave us the grace to live as he taught. To this end he let his human will be seen. In his human will he embodied ours in advance, since he is our Head and we all belong to him as his members, as you know well. *Father*, he said, *if it is possible, let this cup pass from me*. It was his human will speaking here, wanting something individual and private, as it were. But he wanted the rest of us to be right of heart, and whatever might be even slightly warped in us to be aligned with him who is always straight, and therefore he added, *Yet not what I will, but what you will be done, Father* (Mt 26:39). But was Christ capable of wanting anything bad? Could he, in the end, will anything other than what the Father willed?

They are one in godhead, so there can be no disparity of will. But in his manhood, he identified his members with himself,[3] just as he did when he said, *I was hungry, and you fed me* (Mt 25:35), and as he identified us with himself when he called from heaven to the rampaging Saul who was persecuting God's holy people, *Saul, Saul, why are you persecuting me?* (Acts 9:4), though no one was laying a finger on Christ himself. So too in displaying the will proper to a human being he displayed your nature, and straightened you out. "See yourself reflected in me," Christ says, "because you have the capacity to want something on your own account that is at variance with God's will. This is natural to human frailty, characteristic of human weakness, and difficult for you to avoid. But when it happens, think immediately about who is above you. Think of God above you, and yourself below him, of him as your Creator and yourself as his creature, of him as Lord and yourself as servant, of him as almighty and yourself as weak. Correct yourself, subject yourself to his will, and say, *Not what I will, but what you will be done, Father*. How can you then be separated from God, when you now will what God wills? You will be straight and upright, and praise will be your fitting occupation, for *praise befits the upright*."

---

3. *Transfiguravit in se suos*, difficult to render in English, but a key phrase in Augustine's theology of Christ and the Church. Perhaps "he took us over into himself," or "he incorporated us into his own personality and will," may convey something of its richness.

Praise and thank God in adversity

3. On the other hand, if you are a bent person, you will praise God when good things come your way, and curse him when something bad happens to you; though in fact your lot cannot be bad if it is just, and it is just, because it is arranged for you by One who can do nothing unjust. But you will be like a spoiled child in its father's house, loving your father if he caresses you and hating him when he beats you, never thinking that he is all the while preparing an inheritance for you, whether caressing or beating.

Another psalm gives an example of how praise befits the upright. Listen to the voice of someone who knows how to praise in the right way: *I will bless the Lord at all times; his praise shall be in my mouth always.* In this saying *at all times* means the same as *always*, and *I will bless the Lord* is the same as saying, *His praise shall be in my mouth.* Praise him at all times and always, in good times and bad. If you praise God only in good fortune and not in adversity, how is that praising him always? We hear plenty of people making protestations like that when some happiness has come to them; they dance for joy, they are full of gladness; they sing to God and praise him. We should not disapprove of them; on the contrary, their behavior should delight us, for many people would not behave so even in the same good fortune. But people who have already begun to praise God in circumstances of prosperity must be taught to recognize their Father when he beats them too, and not to grumble under his correcting hand. Otherwise they may remain permanently warped, and deserve to be disinherited. Once straightened, however (and what does being straight mean? That nothing God does displeases them), they are enabled to praise God even when things go wrong, and to say, *The Lord gave, and the Lord has taken away. This has happened as the Lord willed: may the Lord's name be blessed* (Jb 1:21). Praise befits people of this stamp, not the kind who at first are ready to praise God, but later revile him.

4. Come on then, you just, you upright folk, dance for joy in the Lord, because praise befits you. No one should say, "Who is that? Am I just? When am I just?"[4] Do not rubbish yourselves or despair of yourselves. You are human beings made in the image of God, and he who made you human became human himself for your sake. The blood of God's only Son was poured out for you so that you, all of you, might be adopted as a great family of God's children with rights of inheritance. If you hold yourselves cheap in your earthly frailty, esteem yourselves precious by reason of the ransom paid for you. Give serious thought to what you

---

4. *Quis ego iustus? Aut quando ego iustus?* The editors of the Latin text amend this to *Quis ergo iustus, aut quando ero iustus?* which yields the clearer sense, "Who is just, though, and when shall I be just?"

eat, what you drink,[5] what you endorse with your "Amen."[6] Are we giving you this advice to prompt you to pride, or suggesting to you the audacity of attributing some perfection to yourselves? By no means; but neither must you think yourselves far removed from all righteousness. I do not mean to question you about your personal righteousness or justice; if I did, perhaps no one among you would dare to reply, "I am just." No, but I do question you about your faith. As no one among you dares to claim, "I am just," so equally no one will dare to say, "I am not a believer." I am not yet inquiring what your life is like; I am inquiring what your faith is. You will respond that you believe in Christ. Very well, then, have you not heard the apostle telling us that *the one who lives by faith is just* (Rom 1:17)? Your justice is your faith, because if you believe, you will undoubtedly be careful, and if you are careful you make efforts; and God knows your efforts, and sees deep into your will, and takes note of your struggle with the flesh, and encourages you to keep up the fight, and helps you to win, and has his heart in his mouth waiting for you[7] when you are locked in conflict, and lifts you up when you are flagging, and crowns you when you are victorious. *Dance for joy in the Lord*, then, *you just*; I should have said, "Dance for joy in the Lord, you believers," for anyone who lives by faith is just. *Praise befits the upright.* Learn to give thanks to God both in prosperity and in trouble. Learn to have in your hearts what many people have on their tongues, "As God wills."[8] That is a popular pious cliché, but even more it is the doctrine of salvation. Who is not ready to say every day, "As God wills, so may he act"? The one who says so will be upright,[9] and find a place among those who dance for joy in the Lord, those for whom praise is the fitting occupation. To such as these the psalm speaks in the following verses, inviting them to *confess to the Lord on the lyre, and sing psalms to him with the ten-stringed psaltery.* This is what we were singing just now, and as we gave expression to it with voices in unison, we were instructing your hearts.[10]

---

5. A eucharistic allusion.

6. Variant: " . . . drink, where your names are enrolled."

7. Variant: "watches you."

8. *Quod vult Deus.* So much was it a popular saying that it was sometimes given as a name; Augustine wrote at least two letters to a deacon called Quod-vult-Deus, who had asked him to compile a catalogue of heresies (Letters 222, 224).

9. Punctuating a little differently, some codices have " . . . to say every day, 'As God wills'? Let everyone do so, and he or she will be upright. . . ."

10. A variant in some codices makes better sense: " . . . just now, giving expression with voices in unison to what was in our hearts, and as we did so this is what we were teaching."

Verse 2. Praise God with both lyre and psaltery

5. Was not the purpose of the institution of these vigils in Christ's name,[11] to banish lyres from this place? Yet here we have even lyres being commanded to sound their melody: *Confess to the Lord on the lyre*, says our psalm, *and sing psalms to him with the ten-stringed psaltery.* But none of you must think that we are meant to turn to the musical instruments of the theatre. All of us have within ourselves the means of doing what we are bidden; in another place scripture says, *The vows I must perform for you, and the praises I will render you, O God, are within me* (Ps 55(56):12). Those of you who were present on a previous occasion will remember how we discussed in òur sermon, as best we could, the difference between a psaltery and a lyre, attempting throughout to make the distinction clear to everyone.[12] How far we succeeded is for those to judge who were listening then. But it is timely to repeat it now, so that we may find in the difference between these two musical instruments the difference between human activities. It is signified by the instruments but must be made real in our lives. The lyre[13] has a hollow, drum-like sounding-board with a vaulted back like a tortoise-shell. The strings are attached to the wood so that when they are plucked they yield resonant notes. I am not talking about the plectrum which is used, but about the concave sounding-chamber across which the strings are stretched, on which they lie, as it were, so that when they are set quivering they derive their resonance from the hollow cavity and yield a richer tone. Now the lyre has this wooden sounding-board below, while the psaltery has it at the top. That is the difference.

In the present passage we are commanded to confess on the lyre, and to sing psalms on the ten-stringed psaltery.[14] No mention is made of a ten-stringed lyre, either in this psalm or anywhere else, as far as I remember. The readers among my flock should look up that point, and consider it more carefully at leisure; but for my part I seem to recall that while we often find references to the psaltery with ten strings, there is nowhere any mention of a lyre with ten strings. Now, remember that the lyre has its sounding-board below, while the psaltery has it above. In our life below, our earthly life, we experience prosperity and adversity, and we have an opportunity to praise God in both, so that his praise may be in our

---

11. See the title of this sermon, and Augustine's *Sermon 311*, 5, where he reminds his hearers that the holy place where Cyprian's body rested had been invaded some years previously by dancers and singers who kept up wanton performances all night. The Bishop of Carthage had made a clean sweep, and in their place the celebration of this vigil was instituted.
12. See his Exposition of Psalm 42, 5; Exposition 2 of Psalm 70, 11; Exposition of Psalm 80, 5.
13. *Cithara*, often translated "harp," but unlike the modern instrument of that name. The *cithara* was more like a zither or lyre. Its invention was attributed to Hermes, who stretched strings of sheep-gut across a tortoise-shell.
14. *Psalterium.*

mouths always, and we may bless the Lord at all times. There is earthly good fortune and earthly misfortune, and God is to be praised whichever we find ourselves in, so that we may play the lyre for him. What is earthly prosperity? It is enjoying bodily health and an abundance of all the things we need, being kept safe and having a profusion of crops; it is when God causes his sun to rise over good and bad alike, and sends his rain on both just and unjust.[15] All these things contribute to our earthly life, and anyone who does not praise God for them is ungrateful. Just because they are earthly, are they any the less God's gifts? Or are they to be deemed the gifts of someone else, because they are bestowed on wrongdoers too? No; God's mercy is manifold. He is patient and long-suffering. By letting us see how richly he endows even the wicked, he signifies more clearly what he is reserving for the righteous.

But adversities too are certainly our lot in this lower region. They come from the frailty of the human race, from pain and sickness, from harassment and disasters and temptations. The person who plays the lyre will praise God throughout all of it. We should not simply despise these things as lower realities, but remember that they can be controlled and governed only by that wisdom which reaches powerfully from end to end, disposing all things sweetly.[16] It is not the case that he rules the affairs of heaven and disregards those of earth; does not a psalmist ask him, *Whither shall I go from your spirit, and whither flee from your face? If I mount to heaven, you are there; if I sink down to hell, even there you are present* (Ps 138(139):7-8)? If there is no place from which he is absent, can he fail us anywhere? Confess to the Lord on the lyre, then. If you have plenty of some earthly commodity, give thanks to him who has given it to you; if you lack it, or if you have lost it through some mishap, still go on playing your lyre serenely. He who gave it to you has not been taken from you, even if what he gave has been withdrawn. Yes, even in these circumstances, I tell you, go on calmly playing your lyre. You are certain of your God, so pluck the strings in your heart, and say, like a lyre that gives its sweet sounds from below, *The Lord gave, and the Lord has taken away. This has happened as the Lord willed: may the Lord's name be blessed* (Jb 1:21).

Ten commandments and ten strings

6. But when you turn your thoughts to the higher gifts of God—to the commandments he has entrusted to you, the heavenly doctrine with which he has imbued you, the admonitions he has given you[17] from the fount of his truth in

---

15. See Mt 5:45.
16. See Wis 8:1.
17. Variant: "the gifts he has given to you more than to others."

heaven—then take up the psaltery and sing psalms to God on this psaltery with its ten strings. There are ten commandments in the law, and in these ten commandments you find the psaltery. It corresponds perfectly. In the first three you have love for God, and in the other seven love of your neighbor;[18] and you certainly know, since the Lord has told us, that *on these two commandments depend all the law and the prophets* (Mt 22:40). From on high God instructs you that *the Lord your God is one God,*[19] and there you have one string. *You shall not misuse the name of the Lord your God:* there is string number two. *Observe the sabbath,* but not in carnal fashion, with the amusements the Jews indulge in, abusing their leisure to do mischief. They would be better off digging all day long than spending the day dancing. For your part you must ponder on the rest you are called to enjoy in the Lord your God, and do all you have to do with that rest in view. You must abstain from working like slaves. Anyone who commits sin is a slave of sin,[20] and it is better to be enslaved to another human being than to sin. These first three commandments are concerned with loving God. Think about his unity, his truth, and the enjoyment to be found in him;[21] for there is indeed pleasure for us in God, in whom we enjoy the true sabbath and true rest. This is why another psalm bids us, *Delight in the Lord, and he will grant you your heart's desire* (Ps 36(37):4). Can anyone else provide us with such delight as he can, who made everything that delights us?

In these first three commandments charity toward God is enjoined, and in the remaining seven charity to your neighbor, as you are taught to do nothing to another that you would not wish to suffer yourself. *You shall honor your father and mother,* because you hope to be honored by your own children. *Do not commit adultery,* because you would not want your wife committing adultery behind your back. *Do not kill,* because you do not want to be killed yourself. *Do not steal,* because you do not want your things stolen. *Do not bear false witness,* because you hate anyone who gives false evidence to damage you. *Do not lust after your neighbor's wife,* because you do not want anyone lusting after yours either.[22] *Do not covet anything that belongs to your neighbor,* because if anyone covets your property, you are annoyed. Turn against yourself the denunciation you hurl against anyone who hurts or offends you.

---

18. See Ex 20:2-17; Dt 5:6-21; and note at the first Exposition of this psalm, verse 2.
19. Compare Dt 6:4.
20. See Jn 8:34.
21. Perhaps a trinitarian allusion, but also a reflection on the first three commandments.
22. In the Deuteronomic text of the commandments (Dt 5:6-21), which Augustine is following in preference to the text in Exodus, a wife is mentioned first, and a man's other possessions after her; this makes possible the division of the commandment against covetousness into two, as noted earlier. Ex 20:17 regards a wife as one of the chattels.

Fear and love as motives for obedience

All these commandments are from God. They were granted to us as the gift of divine wisdom, and are trumpeted from heaven. Pluck your psaltery, then, and fulfill the law, for the Lord your God came not to supersede it but to bring it to perfect fulfillment.[23] You will fulfill through love what was beyond your powers through fear. A person who refrains from a bad action out of fear would really like to do it, if it were allowed; so even if the possibility of carrying it out is absent, the person's will is attached to the bad deed. "I'm not doing it," he or she will say. Why not? "Because I'm afraid to." Then you do not yet love righteousness, you are still a slave. Become a son or a daughter. Nonetheless a good slave may become a good son or daughter, so go on refraining from sin out of fear, and you will gradually learn to refrain also out of love, for there is beauty in righteousness. Let the fear of punishment deter you; but righteousness has its own fair character; it catches the eye and sets its lovers on fire. For love of it the martyrs trod this world underfoot and shed their blood. What were they in love with, when they renounced everything? They were truly lovers, I tell you. Am I trying to discourage you from loving? No, of course not. Anyone who does not love is a cold character, frozen stiff. Let us love beauty, but let it be the beauty that appeals to the eye of the heart. Let us love beauty, but let it be worthwhile, praiseworthy loveliness. Righteousness kindles our minds; people inflamed with righteousness are stimulated to speak, to shout aloud the beauty of it, to tell everyone within earshot, "It's lovely, it's splendid!" What have they seen? In what sense is an old, bent person beautiful?[24] Put a righteous old man on show: there is nothing lovable in his bodily appearance, yet everyone loves him. He is loved for that part of his being that we cannot see; or rather, he is loved for that part of him where he is seen only by our hearts. For the Lord will grant sweetness and our earth shall yield its fruit,[25] so that you are enabled to carry through by love what you found difficult when your motive was fear. Why do I say, "difficult"? Impossible rather, as long as our attitude is that we would prefer some command not to be laid upon us, impossible as long as we are not impelled to carry it out by love but constrained by fear. "Do not steal; fear hell"; and such a person would rather there were no hell to be thrown into. But when do they begin to love righteousness? Only when they would rather there were no robberies, even if hell did not exist to swallow up those who commit them. This is what it means to love righteousness.

---

23. See Mt 5:17.
24. The last three sentences translate a variant given in the best codices; the punctuation in the received text is slightly different.
25. See Ps 84:13(85:12).

7. But what is this righteousness like? Who is to describe it for us? What kind of beauty does God's wisdom have? Through it all those things that appeal to our eyes are beautiful, and to see it, to embrace it, our hearts need to be cleansed. We profess ourselves its lovers, so it sets us to rights,[26] so that we may not fail to please it. And when people berate us for anything we do to please the one we love, how lightly we take their complaints, how we despise them, how completely we discount them![27] Think of certain odious, fickle and amorous young men. When their hair and clothes are arranged by their girlfriends according to the girls' own liking they think this is fine provided that they are now pleasing to the girls they fancy, and they do not care if other people find them objectionable. Indeed they usually are unattractive to sensible people—or, rather, not usually but always—and are rebuked by persons of sounder judgment. "Your hairstyle is a disgrace," says a sober-minded man to a depraved youth. "It is unworthy of you to go about sporting those long curls." But the young man knows that his hairstyle pleases someone; he hates the man who rightly rebukes him and hangs onto the style that is attractive to perverted taste. He regards you as his enemy if you cut off that offending hair.[28] He keeps out of your way, and pays not the slightest attention to the reasonable standards that prompted the rebuke. So then, if such youths take no notice of those who administer well-judged admonitions, and prefer to remain pretty deceivers, should we pay any attention to unrighteous scoffers, people who have no eyes to see what we love, in matters where we are seeking to please the wisdom of God?

As you ponder all this, you upright of heart, *confess to the Lord on the lyre, and sing psalms to him with the ten-stringed psaltery.*

Verse 3. The song of the heart

8. *Sing him a new song.* Strip off your oldness, you know a new song. A new person, a New Covenant, a new song. People stuck in the old life have no business with this new song; only they can learn it who are new persons, renewed by grace and throwing off the old, sharers already in the New Covenant, which is the kingdom of heaven. All our love yearns toward that, and in its longing our love sings a new song. Let us sing this new song not with our tongues but with our lives. *Sing him a new song, sing skillfully to him.* Each one of us is anxious to know how to sing to God. Sing to him, yes, but not out of tune. We don't want to grate on his ears. Sing skillfully, my friend. If you have to give a performance

---

26. *Componit.*
27. Variant: " . . . the one we love, how we are considered depraved by those who rebuke us, and worthy of their contempt, and entirely discounted by them!"
28. Or, more mildly with a variant, "censure" it.

before some musical expert, and you are told, "Be sure to sing in a way that will please him," you are nervous about attempting it without any musical training, lest you displease the maestro,[29] because any shortcoming which someone ignorant of music might overlook will be criticized by the expert. Which of us, then, would volunteer to sing skillfully to God, who so shrewdly judges the singer, who so closely scrutinizes every detail, who listens with such discrimination? When will you ever be able to present him with so polished a performance that you at no point jar upon such a perfect ear?

Do not worry, for he provides you with a technique for singing. Do not go seeking lyrics, as though you could spell out in words anything that will give God pleasure. Sing to him *in jubilation*. This is what acceptable singing to God means: to sing jubilantly. But what is that? It is to grasp the fact that what is sung in the heart cannot be articulated in words. Think of people who sing at harvest time, or in the vineyard, or at any work that goes with a swing. They begin by caroling their joy in words, but after a while they seem to be so full of gladness that they find words no longer adequate to express it, so they abandon distinct syllables and words, and resort to a single cry of jubilant happiness. Jubilation is a shout of joy;[30] it indicates that the heart is bringing forth what defies speech. To whom, then, is this jubilation more fittingly offered than to God who surpasses all utterance? You cannot speak of him because he transcends our speech; and if you cannot speak of him, yet may not remain silent, what else can you do but cry out in jubilation, so that your heart may tell its joy without words, and the unbounded rush of gladness not be cramped by syllables? *Sing skillfully to him in jubilation*.

Verse 4. The fidelity of God

9. *Because the Lord's word is straight, and all his works are done in faith.* By its very straightness it is abhorrent to those who are not straight themselves. *And all his works are done in faith.* All your works should be performed in faith, because the one who lives by faith is just,[31] and faith works by choosing to love.[32] Yes, whatever you do must be done in faith, because it is by believing in God that you become a faithful person. But how can God's works be done in faith? Are we to suppose that God lives by faith? No, of course not, but we have experienced the faithfulness of God. This is not just my assertion; listen to what the apostle

---

29. Variant: ". . . will please him, then, if you want to sing with some musical competence, you are nervous lest you displease the maestro."
30. *Iubilum* in classical Latin evokes rustic songs, mountain cries, whoops of joy, shepherds' shouts.
31. See Rom 1:17.
32. See Gal 5:6.

says: *God is so faithful that he does not allow you to be tempted more fiercely than you can bear, but along with the temptation ordains the outcome, so that you may withstand it* (1 Cor 10:13). So you have heard him call God faithful there, and now listen to what he says elsewhere: *If we hold out, we shall reign with him; if we deny him, he will deny us; if we do not believe, he still remains faithful, for he cannot deny himself* (2 Tm 2:12-13). It is clear from this that God is faithful, but obviously we must distinguish our faithful God from a faithful man or woman. A faithful human being is one who believes in God who promises; our faithful God is he who delivers what he promised to his human creature. Let us keep a tight hold on our supremely faithful debtor, because we hold onto him as the supremely merciful promisor. It is not as though we had lent him anything, so as to be able to hold him as a debtor; rather do we receive from him whatever we have to offer him, and whatever good there is in us is his gift. All the good things that gladden us are from him. Who has understood the mind of the Lord, or been his counselor? Who ever forestalled him in giving, and so deserved a recompense? From him and through him and in him are all things.[33] We have given him nothing whatever, and yet we can hold him to his debt. How can he be a debtor? Because he is the promisor. We do not say to God, "Give back what we gave you," but "Give what you have promised." *Because the Lord's word is straight.* Straight in what sense? He does not deceive you, so you must not deceive him; indeed, you must not deceive yourself. But iniquity has lied to itself.[34] *The Lord's word is straight, and all his works are done in faith.*

Verse 5. Uniting mercy and judgment

10. *He loves judgment and mercy.* Practice these yourself, since God does. Look carefully at these two, mercy and judgment. This present time is the season for mercy, but the season for judgment will come later. Why do we say that this is the season for mercy? Because at this present time God calls those who have turned away from him, and forgives their sins when they return; he is patient with sinners until they are converted, and when they are converted at last he forgets everything in their past and promises them a future, encouraging the sluggish, comforting the troubled, guiding the eager and helping the embattled. He deserts no one who struggles and calls out to him; he bestows on us the wherewithal to offer him sacrifice; and he himself gives us the means of winning his favor. Let us not allow this time of mercy to pass away, my brothers and sisters, let it not pass us by. Judgment is coming. Then there will be repentance,

---

33. See Rom 11:34-36.
34. See Ps 26(27):12.

certainly, but a repentance that is sterile. *Groaning in anguish of spirit, the wicked will ruefully say within themselves*—these are the very words of scripture, from the Book of Wisdom—*what good has our pride done us, or what benefit has come to us from our vaunted wealth? All these things have passed away like a shadow* (Wis 5:3.8.9). Let us admit even now that all things are passing away like a shadow. Let us say now, while we can say it with profit, "They are passing away," so that we may not be reduced to saying uselessly later, *They have passed away*. This present time is the season of mercy, but then will be the season for judgment.

11. Make no mistake, brothers and sisters: in God these two realities cannot be separated. We might think that they are mutually exclusive, so that a person who is merciful is not allowing judgment its rights, while someone who insists on judgment is forgetting mercy. But God is almighty, and he neither loses sight of judgment when exercising mercy, nor abandons mercy when passing judgment. He looks mercifully on his image, taking our frailty into account, and our mistakes and our blindness; he calls us, and when we turn back to him he forgives our sins. But he does not forgive those who refuse to turn back. Is he merciful to the unjust? He has lost sight of judgment, has he? Is he not right to judge between the converted and the unconverted? Or does it seem just to you that the converted and the unconverted should receive the same treatment, that one who confesses and one who lies, the humble and the proud, should all be welcomed without distinction? Even as he exercises mercy God has a place for judgment.

But within the judgment itself he will find room for mercy too, for he will deal gently with those at least to whom he can say, *I was hungry, and you fed me* (Mt 25:35). We know it, because in one of the apostolic letters we are told, *Merciless judgment will be passed on anyone who has not shown mercy* (Jas 2:13); and the Lord says, *Blessed are the merciful, for they shall obtain mercy* (Mt 5:7). Even in his judgment, then, there will be mercy as well, yet not at the expense of judgment. Mercy will be shown, if not to all and sundry, at least to anyone who has first shown mercy, and the mercy shown to such a person will itself be just, because discriminating. It is certainly a mercy that our sins are forgiven, and a mercy that we should be granted eternal life; but notice the judgment that enters into it: *Forgive, and you will be forgiven; give, and gifts will be given to you* (Lk 6:37-38). Unquestionably the promise that *gifts will be given to you* and *you will be forgiven* is a mark of mercy; but if there were no place in it for judgment, the Lord would not have said, *The same measure that you measure out will be measured in turn to you* (Mt 7:2).

Against favoritism, a cautionary tale

12. Well now, you have heard how God exercises both mercy and judgment; so exercise both mercy and judgment yourself. Do you imagine that while these qualities belong to God, they are no business of humans? Not at all. If they were no concern of ours, the Lord would not have said to the Pharisees, *You have neglected the weightier matters of the law: mercy and judgment* (Mt 23:23). They are your business, then. Do not imagine either that, while you have a duty to exercise mercy, judgment is no affair of yours. Suppose it happens that you have to hear a case between two people, one rich and the other poor, and it turns out that the poor party has a weak case, while the case of the rich is sound. Now, if you are not well schooled in the kingdom of God, you may think you are acting virtuously if out of would-be kindness to the poor person you play down and conceal his wrongdoing, and try to vindicate him, and make his case appear better than it is. Then if you are criticized for giving an unfair judgment, you pretend that you were motivated by mercy, and reply, "Yes, I know, but he was poor, and deserved mercy." How did you hang onto mercy, if you let judgment slip? "But," you object, "how could I hold onto judgment without letting mercy go? Ought I to have decided the case against the poor defendant who had no means of making restitution, or, if he had, would have had nothing left to live on after restitution had been made?" Your God tells you, *You shall not show partiality to a poor person in giving judgment* (Lv 19:15). It is easy to say that we should not be prejudiced in a rich person's favor. Everyone can see the point of that; would that everyone acted on it! But where someone can go wrong who thinks to please God is in giving unfair preference to a poor litigant, and then saying to God, "Look, I showed favor to a poor man." You should have held tight to both, mercy and judgment. To begin with, what kind of mercy have you really shown to the poor person, by making yourself an accomplice in his dishonesty? You spared his purse but struck a blow to his heart. The poor man remained dishonest, and all the more so for seeing that you, a just man, seemed to approve of his dishonesty. He left your presence unjustly assisted, and remained in God's presence justly condemned. What kind of mercy have you dealt to him, by conniving at his injustice? You are to be judged more cruel than merciful. "What should I have done, then?" you reply. You should have given judgment on the merits of the case, and convicted the poor person, and then sought to mollify the rich man. There is a right place for judging, and a different place for making an appeal for clemency. If the rich litigant had watched you holding fast to justice, and giving no preference to a dishonest poor man, but justly finding him guilty as his crime deserved, would not that rich claimant have been inclined to mercy at your petition, as he had been rendered happy at your judgment?

Conclusion

Many verses of the psalm still remain, brothers and sisters, but we must take into account the mental and physical stamina of an audience comprising a wide variety of persons; for even though we are refreshed by the same wheat, we all taste it differently. And to drive away any weary aversion, let this be enough.[35]

---

35. Variant: " . . . we must take mental and physical stamina into account and provide refreshing variety for each hearer, for the same wheat yields many different flavors. So to drive away any aversion. . . ."

Exposition 3 of Psalm 32

*Second Sermon, preached on a Wednesday at the shrine
of Saint Cyprian*[1]

Introduction: hard work needed

1. Proclaiming the word of truth is hard work, and so is listening to it. But we can face the labor with cheerfulness, my brothers and sisters, if we keep in mind the Lord's sentence and our human condition, because from the very dawn of our race human beings heard, not from any other human who might have deceived them, nor from the devil who had seduced them, but from truth itself, issuing from the mouth of God, *In the sweat of your face you shall eat your bread* (Gn 3:19). Accordingly, if God's word is our bread, let us sweat away at listening to it, rather than die of fasting from it. A few verses from the early part of this psalm were dealt with at the solemn vigil we celebrated recently.[2] Let us now turn our attention to the rest.

The account to be rendered

2. The remaining part of the psalm we have just sung begins like this: *The earth is full of the mercy of the Lord. By the word of the Lord the heavens were established.* Prior to this it had urged us, *Sing skillfully to him in your triumphant joy* (that is, sing without confining yourselves to words), *because the Lord's word is straight, and all his works are done in faith.* He promises nothing that he does not deliver; he has made himself a faithful debtor, so you must be a greedy creditor. After stating that *all his works are done in faith*, the psalm told us why this is so: *he loves mercy and judgment.* Anyone who loves mercy deals mercifully. Is anyone who deals mercifully capable of promising and then not giving what was promised, if he could have given it anyway, even had there been no promise? He who loves mercy must therefore deliver what he promises; and because he also loves judgment, he must demand back what he gave. This is clear from what the master said to a servant: *you should have invested my money,*

---

1. The *mensa Cypriani* at the *Ager Sexti*, on the site of Cyprian's martyrdom; see section 9; not the same basilica as the one where the preceding sermon was preached.
2. Compare Exposition 2, 5.

so that on my return I could have reclaimed it with interest (Lk 19:23). I am reminding you of this parable so that we may better understand what we have just heard, for the Lord says in another part of the gospel, *I do not judge anyone; the word that I have spoken will itself judge them on the last day* (Jn 8:15; 12:48). If any of us is unwilling to hear the word, hoping that if we do not hear it there will be nothing to be demanded of us, let us dismiss that as an empty excuse. Exactly the same demand will be made, because when the gift was offered we refused to receive it. It is one thing to be unable to receive, quite another to refuse; the former does excuse us because we are constrained by necessity, the latter is willful guilt. So when the psalm says that *all God's works are done in faith; he loves mercy and judgment*, accept his mercy and fear his judgment, lest when he comes to settle his accounts with us, he may find us worthless and fit only to be discarded.[3] He demands an account; once the account is rendered he rewards us with eternity.

Well then, brothers and sisters, accept his mercy; let us all accept it. No one among us must go to sleep when he ought to be accepting it, lest we be rudely awakened by the summons to account. God shouts to us, "Receive mercy!" as though he were calling to us in time of famine, "Have some wheat!" If you heard that during a famine, your own need would spur you on to run as fast as you could, rushing hither and thither, looking for the place where you could get what was promised by that invitation, "Have some!" And once you had found it, would you hold back? Would you hesitate?

In just the same way the invitation is made to us now: "Here's mercy for you take it!" For God loves mercy and judgment. When you have received it, make good use of it, so that you may have a profitable account to render when the time comes for God to judge—God who in this time of famine has paid you his mercy on deposit.

Verses 5-6. God has caused his mercy to abound everywhere

3. Do not ask me, "Where can I get it? Where must I go?" Recall the verse you have sung: *The earth is full of the mercy of the Lord.* Is there anywhere where the gospel is not preached nowadays? Where is the word of the Lord silent? Where is salvation not at work? You must simply want to receive; the barns are full. This plenitude and rich abundance have not waited for you to arrive; they themselves sought you out while you were asleep. Scripture does not say, "Let the nations arise, and gather in one place." These things have been proclaimed to the

---

3. Or, possibly, "may send us away empty," as in Lk 1:53.

Gentiles wherever they were, so that a prophecy might be fulfilled: *They will worship him from their own homes, every one of them* (Zep 2:11).

4. *The earth is full of the mercy of the Lord.* What of the heavens? I will tell you about the heavens. They have no need of mercy, because there is no misery.[4] On earth human misery abounds, and the Lord's mercy abounds even more; the earth is full of the misery of humankind, and the earth is even fuller of the mercy of the Lord. Does that mean that in heaven, where there is no misery, and they do not need mercy, they do not need the Lord? By no means. All things need the Lord, whether they are miserable or happy. Without him a miserable person cannot be lifted from wretchedness, and without him a happy one cannot be kept on the right course. In case you might wonder about the heavens when you hear, *the earth is full of the mercy of the Lord*, the psalm tells you that the heavens too need the Lord: *by the word of the Lord the heavens were established.* They did not provide a solid foundation for themselves, nor did they endow themselves with their stability. *By the word of the Lord the heavens were established, and all their strength by the breath of his mouth.* It is not as though they had some resources of their own, and received supplementary strength from the Lord. No, *from the breath of his mouth* comes not a part, but *all their strength*.

5. Notice, brothers and sisters, that the work of the Son and the work of the Spirit are one. This point is not to be passed over carelessly, because there are people who wickedly separate them or grossly confuse them. Both attitudes are wrong. Some confuse them by failing to make the proper distinction between creature and Creator, and although the Spirit of God is the Creator, they rank him among creatures. Or perhaps they recognize this distinction but confuse the Persons; may they be confused themselves, and converted. Listen instead to the truth, that there is one work common to Son and Holy Spirit. The Son of God is, without doubt, the Word, and the breath of his mouth is the Holy Spirit. *By the word of the Lord the heavens were established.* But what does being established mean? Surely to have firm, stable strength. So it continues, *And all their strength by the breath of his mouth.* The psalm could just as well have said, "By the breath of his mouth the heavens were established, and all their strength by his word"; for *all their strength* is the same thing as *were established.* This, then, is the work of both Son and Holy Spirit. Without the Father? No, of course not, for who else is it who works through his Word and his Spirit, but the Father, whose Word, whose Spirit, they are? This Trinity is the one God. Anyone who knows how to worship worships this one God, and anyone who is converted possesses this one God in every place. He is not sought by those who turn away, but he calls those who have turned away, that he may fill them once they have turned back to him.

---

4. *Misericordia . . . miseria*, a favorite association with Augustine.

6. I shall not attempt to speculate about the highest heavens, brothers and sisters, for they are unknowable to us as we struggle along on earth, and inquire about them after our fashion, by human guesswork. I am leaving those lofty heavens out of consideration, not asking how they tower above one another, or how many there are, or how they differ from each other, or who are the inhabitants who fill them, or how they are ordered, or how one single hymn that never falls silent is sung in unison there by all, in praise of God. It is too much for us to find out all this; but let us make every effort to find our way there, for that is our homeland, though we may have forgotten it on our long pilgrimage. Our own voice laments in another psalm, *Alas, how long-drawn-out is my wayfaring!* (Ps 119(120):5). It is difficult, if not impossible, for us to teach anything about those heavens, and for you to understand. If anyone else's intelligence has outstripped mine, let him or her enjoy that further region it has gained, and pray for me so that I may follow. But meanwhile, leaving those loftier heavens out of consideration, I have plenty of other heavens which I may attempt to discuss, the heavens closest to us, the heavens which are God's holy apostles, preachers of the word of truth. Through these heavens we were plentifully watered, so that the Church's harvest might spring up throughout the world. For the time being the crop and the weeds drink in the rain together, but they are not destined to share the barn.

7. The psalm has told us that *the earth is full of the mercy of the Lord*, and so you might wish to ask, "How was it filled with his mercy?" First of all the "heavens" were sent[5] to spray the Lord's mercy over the earth, the earth in its entirety. Consider what is said elsewhere of these "heavens": *The heavens proclaim God's glory, and the firmament tells of his handiwork* ("heavens" and "firmament" mean the same thing). *Day speaks the message to succeeding day, and night imparts knowledge to night.* Their preaching never stops, never falls silent. But where did they preach, how far did they penetrate? *There is no speech, no language, in which their voices are not heard.* This refers to the time when they spoke in one single place in the languages of all peoples.[6] By so speaking in the tongues of all they fulfilled the prophecy, *there is no speech, no language, in which their voices are not heard.* But the question I am asking now is this: this voice of theirs which spoke in all languages, how far did it penetrate, what did it fill? The psalm goes on to answer: *Their sound went forth throughout the world, their words to the ends of the earth* (Ps 18:2-5(19:1-4)). Whose words? The words of the heavens, of course, who proclaim the glory of God. So then, since their sound has gone forth throughout the world, and their words to the ends of the earth, let him who sent them out tell us what they preached to us. He does tell

---

5. The apostles.
6. See Acts 2:4.

us, he tells us faithfully, because even before they existed, he whose works are all done in faith foretold what was to happen. He rose from the dead, offered his limbs to the disciples to be handled, and after they had recognized him he said, *It was necessary for Christ to suffer, and to rise from the dead on the third day, and for repentance and forgiveness of sins to be preached in his name*. From where, and to where? *Throughout all nations, beginning from Jerusalem* (Lk 24:46-47). What more generous mercy can we hope for from the Lord, brothers and sisters, than that our sins be forgiven? Since the forgiveness of sins is the mighty mercy of the Lord, and he himself foretold that this forgiveness of sins was to be preached throughout all nations, *the earth is full of the mercy of the Lord*. Full of what? The Lord's mercy. Why? Because God is forgiving sins everywhere, having sent us the heavens to pour out his rain all over the earth.

Sheep among wolves

8. But how did it come about that they went so confidently, weak people as they were, to be made into "heavens"? How else, but because *by the word of the Lord the heavens were established*? Whence could sheep among wolves have derived such great courage, except from *the breath of his mouth* which gave them *all their strength*? For the Lord warned them, *Lo, I am sending you like sheep into the midst of wolves* (Mt 10:3). Yes, most merciful Lord, this is what you do, so that the earth may be full of your mercy. If you are so merciful that you must fill the earth with mercy, look whom you are sending, and where you are sending them. Where, I ask, are you sending them, and whom are you sending? Sheep into the middle of a pack of wolves! If even one wolf were released amid innumerable sheep, which of them could put up a fight? What comfort would there be for them, unless perhaps the hope that the wolf would be quickly gorged? It would devour everything in sight. And do you send your vulnerable disciples out among savages? "Yes," the Lord replies, "I do send them, because they turn into heavens which can soak the earth with rain." But how do weak humans become heavens? You forget: *all their strength comes from the breath of his mouth*. "The wolves will seize you and hand you over, and deliver you to the authorities for the sake of my name. Arm yourselves now." With your own strength? Perish the thought. *Do not wonder what you are to say; it is not you who are speaking, but the Spirit of your Father who speaks in you* (Mt 10:19-20), because *all their strength comes from the breath of his mouth*.

9. This is indeed what happened. The apostles were sent out, and they suffered persecution. Does it cost us today such suffering to hear their message, as it cost them to sow it? By no means. Does that mean, brothers and sisters, that our labor will be fruitless? No again. I can see how densely you are packed together here, and you see how I am sweating over this sermon. If we endure, we

shall also reign with him.[7] That was how things turned out for them. The consequence of those sheep being sent out among wolves is that we celebrate the
memorials of the martyrs. This place here, where the body of a blessed martyr[8]
received the death-blow, was full of wolves then. One captive sheep conquered
all those wolves, and one slain sheep filled the place with sheep. The savage sea
was heaving then with the towering waves of persecutors, but God's heaven
made its way to the thirsty earth.[9] Through their sufferings they broke through
the enemy's ranks, so that now the name of Christ has been glorified; he has
taken possession even of the territory of those same powers, and walked over the
heads of those swelling breakers.

And since these things have happened, what is their effect on people who do
not yet believe, but watch our assemblies, our celebrations and our regular festivals, and the praise we now offer openly and publicly to our God? Do you not
think they are chagrined, do they not rage? But this is only the fulfillment of the
prophecy made about them: *The sinner will be enraged at the sight.* What if he is
enraged? O sheep, do not fear this wolf. You have no need now to be afraid of
their threats and their howling. The sinner is enraged, yes, but what does the
psalm say next? *He will gnash his teeth and pine away* (Ps 111(112):10).

Verses 7-9. Fear God, and fear nothing else

10. The salty sea water remains, but it no longer dares to attack Christians. It
keeps up a secret growling within itself, for its brackishness is shut up inside a
mortal skin. Accordingly our psalm goes on to say, *He gathers the waters of the
sea together as though into a bottle.*[10] When the sea raged in earlier days its
waves crashed where they would, but now this bitter force is confined within
human hearts. He who made the waves, he who was victorious over them, he
who once assigned to the sea its boundaries,[11] has caused its waves to turn back
and break. He has gathered the waters of the sea together as into a bottle, and now
a mortal skin conceals bitter thoughts; for the unbelievers fear for their own
skins, and hold in what they dare not speak outwardly. It is still the same bitterness; they hate as ever, they loathe us as much as ever. But since they no longer
rail against us openly as once they did, but now only in secret, what else can I say
of them but what the psalm said, *They will gnash their teeth and pine away?*

---

7. See 2 Tm 2:12.
8. Saint Cyprian.
9. Or perhaps "God's heaven took refuge in the thirsty desert," referring to preachers going into
hiding.
10. A bottle made of skin, naturally.
11. See Prv 8:29.

Let the Church go boldly ahead, then, let it march on. The road is laid down, and fortified by our Commander-in-Chief. Let us be brisk and energetic in the ways of good works, for this is how we walk. If by any chance painful trials arise from unexpected quarters (unexpected, since the waters of the sea are now bottled up) let us understand that this is arranged for us by the Lord as discipline, to rid us of any complacency about temporal things, and guide us toward his kingdom by our steady desire. This desire is fostered in us by the troubles that batter us on every side, to render us tuneful in the Lord's ears, like long trumpets. This too is mentioned in the psalms, that we should praise God on ductile trumpets.[12] A ductile trumpet is made by hammering the metal out thin, and so too a Christian heart is stretched toward God by the blows of affliction.

11. Even in our own day, when the water of the sea has been bottled up, we must keep in mind, brothers and sisters, that God does not lack the means to chastise us when we need it. That is why the next verse says, *He shuts up the depths in his treasure-houses.* By his treasure-houses it means the hidden recesses of God. He knows the hearts of us all, and knows what to bring out at the appropriate time, and where to bring it from. He knows how much power to grant the wicked against the good, so that while the wicked incur condemnation, the good are educated. He who shuts up the deeps in his treasure-houses well knows how to bring these things about. And so may the next petition be realized: *Let every region of the earth fear the Lord.* There is no room for any proud, cocksure person to be complacent, saying, "The water of the sea is safely confined now; it is even bottled! Who can touch me? Who dare hurt me?" Do you not realize that God has shut up those depths in his treasury; do you not see that your Father can bring out from there whatever is needed to whip you? He keeps the treasures of the depths in store to discipline you with, so that he may make you fit for the treasures of heaven. Turn back to reverent fear, you who were wandering off into carelessness. Let the earth leap for joy, and tremble with fear. Leap for joy? Why? Because the earth is full of the mercy of the Lord. But tremble with fear? Why? Because God bottled up the waters of the sea in such a way that the deeps remained stored in his treasure-houses. The earth obeys the twofold command given elsewhere: *serve the Lord in reverence, and rejoice before him with awe* (Ps 2:11).

12. *Let every region of the earth fear the Lord, but let it be by him that they are thrown into turmoil, all the world's inhabitants.* Let them not fear anyone else instead of him, but *let it be by him that they are thrown into turmoil, all the world's inhabitants.* Is there a wild beast on the rampage? Fear only God. Is the serpent sneaking in? Fear only God. Does someone hate you? Fear only God. Is

---

12. See Ps 97(98):6.

the devil attacking you? Fear only God. The whole of creation is subject to him whom you are commanded to fear, *for he himself spoke, and they were made, he gave the order, and they were created*. This is how our psalm continues; for it had said just now, *Let it be by him that they are thrown into turmoil, all the world's inhabitants*, and just in case people might shrink from other things and be afraid of them, turning away from the fear of God and revering some creature instead of him, worshiping what was made and neglecting him who made it, the psalm warns us against this mistake. It confirms us in the fear of God, as though saying to us, "Why are you inclined to fear anything that comes from sky or earth or sea? *He himself spoke, and they were made; he gave the order, and they were created*. He who spoke and brought them into being, he at whose order they were created, issues his command now, and throws them into commotion, issues it again, and they are quieted." Human malice may certainly entertain the desire to do harm, because that desire is something that belongs to it,[13] but it does not have the power to realize its design unless God gives it. *There is no power except from God* (Rom 13:1); this is the apostle's authoritative teaching. He did not say, "There is no desire except from God," for there is an evil desire that is not from God; but what he means is that this evil desire cannot harm anyone if God does not allow it. *There is no power, except from God*, he says. The God-Man, standing before a man, said the same: *You would have no power over me, had it not been given you from above* (Jn 19:11). Pilate was judging; Christ was teaching. Even as he was being judged, Christ was teaching, so that he might later judge those whom he had taught. *You would have no power over me*, he said, *had it not been given you from above*. What did he mean? Are we to think that it is human beings only who have no power, unless they have received it from above? What about the devil? Would he have dared to take so much as one tiny lamb from the holy man Job, without having first said to God, *Stretch out your hand* (Jb 2:5), that is, "Grant me the power"? The devil wanted something, but God did not permit it; when God did permit it, then the devil had power. And that proves that the power belonged not to him but to the One who gave permission. Job knew this; he was well instructed. As I often remind you, his response was not, "The Lord gave, and the devil has taken away," but *The Lord gave, and the Lord has taken away; this has happened as the Lord willed* (Jb 1:21). Not, you notice, "as the devil willed."

My dear brothers and sisters, you are having a hard job eating this salutary bread which is so good for you; but make sure of this: fear no one at all except the Lord. Scripture tells you that you must be afraid of no one else. But let every

---

13. Variant: " . . . issues it again, and human malice is quieted, and with it human desire. A human being may entertain the desire to do harm, because that desire is something that belongs to him. . . ."

region of the earth fear the Lord who has stored up the deeps in his treasuries. Let it be by him that they are thrown into turmoil, all the world's inhabitants, *for he himself spoke, and they were made; he gave the order, and they were created.*

Verse 10. Human plans

13. The day of evil rulers has passed, and our kings are good now. They too have found faith, and now they carry on their foreheads the sign of Christ's cross, a sign more precious than any jewel in their crowns. The rulers who savagely persecuted have been overthrown. But whose achievement was that? Yours, maybe, and that is why you are so pleased with yourself? No, *the Lord frustrates the plans of the nations; he rebukes the thoughts of the peoples and rejects the designs of rulers.* Time was when they said, "Let us rid the world of Christians. The Christian name will disappear if we pursue this policy: kill them in such-and-such a fashion, torture them thus and thus, penalize them in determined ways." That is what their edicts enjoined, and in the face of all this the Church grew stronger. God *rebukes the thoughts of the peoples and rejects the designs of rulers.*

Verse 11. Divine plans

14. *But the Lord's plan abides for ever, the thoughts of his heart endure from age to age.* In this verse there is a repetition of the same thought: where the first phrase had *plan*, the second has *thoughts of his heart*; and where the first said, *abides for ever*, the second says, *endure from age to age*. The repetition strengthens the statement. But when the psalm speaks of *the thoughts of his heart* you must not imagine, brothers and sisters, that God sits down to think what he ought to do, or seeks advice as to whether he should take a certain course of action or not. These slow procedures are yours, men and women; but his word runs, and runs very swiftly. How could there be any pause for thought in that Word, the one single Word that embraces everything? But the psalm speaks of God's thoughts so that you may understand, and may dare to lift your heart after your human fashion to words which match your own feeble experience, because the reality itself is too great for you. *The thoughts of his heart endure from age to age.* What are these thoughts he has in his heart? What is this plan of the Lord that abides for ever? What is the plan against which the nations raged, and the peoples devised vain schemes?[14] The Lord rebukes the thoughts of the peoples, and rejects the designs of rulers. In what sense, then, does the Lord's plan abide

14. See Ps 2:1.

for ever? Surely in that he knew us and predestined us from eternity. Who can interfere with God's predestination?[15] Before the world came into being he saw us, made us, corrected us, sent to us, redeemed us.[16] This is his plan, the plan that abides for ever, this is the thought of his heart that endures from age to age. In earlier days the nations raged openly like a tempestuous sea; now let them pine away in their chagrin, gathered together and confined as though in a bottle. Of old they gave free expression to their impudence; now they are restricted to cruel, bitter thoughts. When will they ever be able to defeat what he is thinking, his thought that abides for ever?

Verse 12. Happiness in possessing God, and being his possession

15. But still, what is he thinking? *Happy that nation.* . . . Anyone would perk up on hearing that! We all set store by happiness; that is why wanting to be bad, while wanting not to be miserable, is a contradictory attitude. Since misery is the inseparable companion of malice, those people are perverted who not only want to be bad and not miserable (which is impossible), but even want to be bad as a way of escaping misery. What do I mean by saying that they want to be bad in order to avoid being miserable? Give the matter a little thought. All the people who act wrongly want to be happy; they always want that. Suppose someone commits a theft. You ask why. Because he was hungry; he was driven by necessity. So in order to escape from unhappiness he was bad; and yet for that very reason he was all the more unhappy because he was bad.[17] Whatever people do, good or bad, their motive is always to get rid of their misery and win happiness; invariably they want to be happy. People who lead good lives and people who lead bad lives, they all want to be happy; but what they all want does not come the way of all. They all want happiness, but the only ones who will get it are those who want to be just. It may even happen that someone wants to be happy in order to do wrong. And where do people look for happiness? To money, silver and gold, estates, farms, houses, slaves, worldly pomp, the prestige that will swiftly slip away and be lost. They want to be happy by possessing things. Think carefully, then, what you need to possess in order to be happy. When you attain to happiness you will certainly be in a better state than when you are miserable. But

---

15. See note at Exposition 1 of Psalm 30, 16.

16. See Eph 1:4.

17. Saint Thomas Aquinas (c.1225-1274) would have respectfully disagreed. In discussing whether it is always sinful to take another's property he says, "In cases of need, everything is common property, so it is not sinful then to take someone else's property, because the necessity has made it common. . . . If the need is manifest and urgently demands a remedy . . . it is lawful for a person to relieve his need by taking what belongs to another . . . and this, properly speaking, is neither theft nor robbery" (*Summa Theologiae* IIa IIae, 66,7).

it is impossible for anything inferior to yourself to put you into a better state. You are a human being, and anything you crave for, thinking to be happier by possessing it, is inferior to yourself. Gold, silver, anything bodily that you look at—all these are inferior to you. You are better, you are nobler. Now it is obvious that, since you want to be happy, what you want is to be better than you are now when you are miserable, because clearly being happy is better than being miserable. So you want to be better than you are; and to this end you seek, determinedly seek, things worse than yourself! Whatever you seek on earth is inferior to you. It is the same with anything a person wishes for a friend. We may say in all sincerity to our friend, "We hope you will improve your fortunes; we really hope to see you doing better, and we shall be overjoyed if things turn out more favorably for you." What we want for a friend, we want for ourselves. Take my advice, then; it is sound advice. You want to be better; I know it, we all know it, and we all want the same for ourselves. All right, then, seek what is better than yourself, so that you may thereby become better than you are.

16. Contemplate the sky and the earth. All the material things in them are attractive to you, but do not be seduced into wanting to be happy by means of them. What you are seeking is within your soul.[18] You want to be happy: very well then, seek in your own soul what is better than yourself. There are two dimensions to you, soul and body, and since that which we call soul is the better of the two, the body has the potential to become better by means of that better part, in being subject to the soul. It is possible, therefore, for your body to become better through your soul, so that when your soul has been justified, your body may be immortal later on. By receiving illumination from the soul, the body deserves incorruption; so the restoration of your lower part comes about through the better part of you. If, then, your body's good is your soul, which is better than your body, it follows that when you are looking for what is good for you, you must look for what is better even than your own soul. But what is your soul? You must be careful here, because if you despise your soul, and consider it something base and worthless, you may seek things more worthless still to make it happy. In your soul is the image of God; the human spirit is capable of receiving it. It did receive it, but by stooping to sin it defaced[19] the image. He who had originally formed it came himself to reform it, for all things were created through the Word, and through the Word the image was stamped upon us. The Word himself came, so that we might hear from the apostle, *Be reformed by the renewal of your minds* (Rom 12:2).

---

18. *In animo*, which might more usually be translated "in (your) mind." But "soul" has been preferred in this passage because Augustine is clearly talking about the whole spiritual dimension of human beings, not the intellect in a narrower sense.

19. Variant: "disgraced."

All you need to ask, then, is: What is better than your soul? What can be, except your God? You will find nothing else better than your soul, because once your nature has been made perfect, it will be equal to that of the angels. And there is nothing higher than that, except the Creator. Raise yourself up to him, do not despair, do not say, "That is far beyond me." Much further beyond you is it to get your hands on the gold you may be coveting. Perhaps you want gold, and can't get it, but when you want God, you will have him, because even before you began to want him he came to you, and when you had deliberately turned away from him he called you, and when you had turned back to him he struck terror into you, and when in your terror you confessed[20] he comforted you. He who poured all your gifts upon you, who brought you into existence, who bestows on you his sun and his rain in common with all your neighbors even if they are wicked, who gives you crops, springs of water, life, health, and immense consolations, he is keeping for you something which he will give to no one else but you. What is this that he is keeping for you? Himself. Ask for something else, if you can think of anything better. God is reserving himself for you. Why look longingly at sky and earth, you greedy wretch? He who made the sky and the earth is better than they, and you will see him, you will possess him in himself. Why do you wish that country estate belonged to you, so that as you pass by you say, "It's a lucky fellow who owns that"? What a lot of passers-by say the same, and having said it go their way; they can shake their heads and sigh, but can they gain possession of it? Greed is speaking; iniquity is sounding off. But you are not allowed to covet your neighbor's property.[21] It is a happy person to whom that country estate belongs, to whom that house belongs, to whom that field belongs, is it? Check your sinful craving, and listen to the truth: *Happy the nation whose. . . .* Whose what? You already know what I am going to say. Desire it then, desire it for your own, and then at last you will be happy. By means of this alone you will be happy, by means of what is better than yourselves you will be better. But this, I tell you, is God, God who is better than you, God who made you. *Happy that nation whose God is the Lord.* Love this and possess this. You will have it whenever you want it, and you will have it free.

17. *Happy that nation whose God is the Lord.* Their God, our God? But is there anyone of whom he is not God? No one; but obviously he is not God of everyone in the same way. He is more truly ours, ours because we live on him as on our bread. May he be our inheritance and our possession. Or perhaps we are making a rash claim in representing God as our possession? After all, he is the Lord, he is the Creator! No, this is not rashness, it is the longing of love, the sweetness of hope. Let the soul say in complete confidence, "You are my God,"

---

20. Variant: "were contrite."
21. See Dt 5:21.

for he says to our soul, *I am your salvation* (Ps 34(35):3). Let the soul say it, then, say it unabashed. We shall not outrage God by saying it; rather we shall outrage him if we do not say it.

Were you aspiring to own some trees, to make you happy? Then listen to what scripture has to say about wisdom: *She is a tree of life to those who possess her.* It calls wisdom our possession. But to make sure you do not take the statement that it is your possession to mean that wisdom is something inferior to yourself, scripture continues, *And she is safe to lean on, like the Lord*[22] (Prv 3:18). So you see, your Lord has made himself like a staff for you. We can put our weight on him, for he will not buckle. Speak to him with full assurance, then, for he is your possession. The words scripture uses are: *to all who possess her*; it brushes aside your hesitation and fills you with confidence. Say it with complete assurance, love with assurance, hope with assurance. Let those psalm-words be yours too: *the Lord is my allotted inheritance* (Ps 15(16):5).

18. Our happiness, then, will consist in possessing God. How should we understand this? We shall possess him, yes; but will he not also possess us? Certainly he will, because if not, why does Isaiah say, *Take possession of us, Lord* (Is 26:13, LXX)? God both possesses and is possessed, and all this is for our benefit; for although we possess him in order that we may be happy, the converse is not true: he does not possess us in order that he may be happy. He possesses us, and he is possessed by us, to no end other than our happiness. We possess him, and he possesses us, because we pay cult to him and he cultivates us.[23] We pay cult to him as the Lord God, and he cultivates us as his soil. That we pay cult to him goes without saying; but what evidence have we that he culti-vates us? His own words prove it: *I am the vine; you are the branches. My Father is the vine-dresser* (Jn 15:5,1). Notice that in the present passage we are instructed on both points; both sides of the truth are put before us. It has already said that we possess God: *Happy that nation whose God is the Lord.* Think of other instances of ownership. One might inquire, "Whose farm is this?" "His." "And whose is that one?" "His." "And that other one?" "His." Now let us speak similarly of God, and ask whom he belongs to. When we ask about who owns farms, or broad estates of great beauty, we are usually told that there is a certain senator called So-and-So, and they belong to him; and we say, "Lucky fellow!" And if we ask in the same way, "To whom does this God belong?" the answer is that there is a certain happy nation to whom he belongs, for he is the Lord their God. But the way in which that senator owns his farm is not the same as the way

---

22. Variant: "like a house."
23. Here and in the following lines Augustine plays on the different meanings of *colo*: to till, tend, cultivate (land, etc.); to care for, and hence (in the case of temples and the gods) to worship, honor, reverence.

we own God, because the senator is not also owned by his farm. But while God does belong to this nation, we have to work hard in order to belong to him. God and this nation belong to each other reciprocally. You have heard already that we possess God: *Happy that nation whose God is the Lord*; now listen to the corresponding truth: *the people the Lord has chosen as his inheritance.* This nation is blessed in its possession, and this inheritance is blessed in its Possessor, this *people whom the Lord has chosen as his inheritance.*

Verses 13-15. God's knowledge of individual humans and their actions

19. *The Lord looked down from heaven, and saw all the children of men.* You must take the word "all" to mean all the members of the nation who hold the inheritance, or who themselves constitute the inheritance of the Lord. His inheritance consists of all these people. Upon all of them the Lord looked down from heaven, and he who saw them was none other than he who said, *When you were under the fig tree, I saw you* (Jn 1:48), for the Lord "saw" Nathanael in the sense that he had mercy on him. Often when we are begging for mercy we say to someone, "Look at me!" And what would you say of someone who despises you? "He doesn't even spare me a glance." So there is a way of looking proper to someone who takes pity that is different from that of someone who intends to punish. The latter kind is a severe attention to a person's sins, and a psalmist who did not want his sins scrutinized like that prayed, *Turn your face away from my sins* (Ps 50:11(51:9)). He wants them overlooked, not looked at,[24] so he says, *Turn your face away from my sins.* When God has turned his face away from your sins, will he not be able all the better to see you? Surely yes, because the psalmist says elsewhere, *Do not turn your face away from me* (Ps 26(27):9). May he avert his eyes from your sins, but not from you; may he see you, and have mercy on you, and come to your help. *The Lord looked down from heaven, and saw all the children of men*, all those who are one with the Son of Man.

20. *From his own prepared dwelling*, the dwelling he has fashioned for himself, he saw us. From the apostles he saw us, from the preachers of truth, from the angels he sent to us. All these are his house, all of them are his dwelling, because all of them are the heavens that tell out the glory of God.[25] *He saw all the children of men; from his own prepared dwelling he looked on all the inhabitants of the earth.* They are all his; they are that happy nation to whom the Lord God belongs, for they are distributed throughout all lands, not confined to one region.[26] *He looked on all the inhabitants of the earth.*

---

24. *Quod vult ignosci, non vult agnosci.*
25. See Ps 18(19):1.
26. A point Augustine often likes to make against the Donatists.

21. *He fashioned all their hearts individually.* With the hand of his grace, with the hand of his mercy, he fashioned hearts; he molded our hearts, fashioned them individually, giving a different heart to each of us, yet without prejudice to our unity. In the body all the members are individually formed, and all have their separate functions, yet they all thrive within the unity of the body. The hand does what the eye has no power to do; the ear is capable of something impossible to both eye and hand; yet all of them work in harmony. Hand and eye and ear do different jobs, but there is no conflict between them; and similarly within the Body of Christ there are individual persons, like members all enjoying their particular gifts, because he who chose this people to be his inheritance fashioned their hearts one by one. *Are all of them apostles? Are all prophets? Are all teachers? Do all have healing gifts? Do all speak in tongues? Do all interpret them? To one is given wise utterance through the Spirit, to another knowledgeable speech according to the same Spirit, to another faith, to another gifts of healing* (1 Cor 12:29-30, 8-9). Why is this? Because he shaped each heart individually. As there are varied functions among our members, but one single state of good health, so among all the members of Christ there are varied gifts, but one single charity. *He has fashioned their hearts individually.*

22. *He has understood all their actions.* Why does it say, *He has understood*? It means that he sees in secret, he sees what is hidden within. In another psalm you find the prayer, *understand my cry* (Ps 5:2(1)). It is not as though words were needed to reach God's ears. Now the vision of something secret is called understanding. By putting it like this the psalmist has made it clearer than he would have done by saying, "He sees all their actions," because then you might have thought God sees their actions in the way you see the actions of someone else. One human being sees the actions of another by observing that person's bodily movements, but God sees within the heart. And because he sees inwardly, the psalm says, *He has understood all their actions.* Suppose two people give alms to the poor: one is seeking a heavenly reward in doing so, the other seeks human approval. You see the same action in both cases, but God understands the two as different, for he understands what is within and appraises what is within; he sees their purposes, he sees their intentions. *He has understood all their actions.*

Verse 16. The inadequacy of human resources

23. *A king will not be saved by his extensive power.* All of us should be looking to the Lord, all of us should be grounded in God. Let God be your life, let God be your strength, let God be your constancy, let him be the focus of your most earnest entreaty, let him be the object of your praise, let him be the end in which you find rest, let him be your helper when you are tackling hard work. Listen to the truth: *a king will not be saved by his extensive power, nor will even a giant be saved by his immense prowess.* A giant represents proud persons who

pit themselves against God, as though they were something in themselves or of themselves. But such persons will not find salvation, however mighty they are.

Verses 17-19. Only God saves

24. But what if someone has a big, strong horse, powerful and swift? Can he not quickly deliver his owner if danger threatens? Let the owner make no mistake, but listen to the next verse: *a horse cannot be relied on for salvation.* Have you understood what I have just said? Do not let your horse promise you safety; if he does, he will be lying. If God wills it, you will be freed from peril; if God does not will it, you will have all the further to fall and the horse will fall with you. (Do not be misled into thinking that when the psalm said, *A horse cannot be relied on for salvation*, it meant that a just man cannot be relied on.[27] It did not say *aequus*, which is related to equity, but *equus*, the four-footed animal. The Greek text makes this clear.) It is bad animals that are being shown up here, that is, people who seek opportunities to deceive, although scripture warns that *a lie in the mouth kills the soul* (Wis 1:11), and *you will destroy all those who speak a lie* (Ps 5:7(6)). What, then, does the psalm mean by *a horse cannot be relied on for salvation*? Your horse is lying to you if he promises to save you. But does a horse ever speak to anyone, making such a promise? No, but when you see a fine, mettlesome horse, capable of magnificent speed, all these qualities seem to promise you that you will be safe on him. But they are fallacious, unless God is looking after you, because *a horse cannot be relied on for salvation.*

You can also take *horse* in a figurative sense, to mean any worldly distinction, or any public position to which you proudly mount. The higher you climb, the more you think yourself not only grander but even safer. But you are wrong. You do not know how you will be unseated, and the higher you were riding, the more shattering will be your downfall. *A horse cannot be relied on for salvation, nor will anyone be saved by his own strength, however great.* How will we be saved, then? Not by our strength, nor by our own power, nor by the office we hold, nor by our high reputation, nor by a horse. How, then? Where am I to turn? Where can I find the means to be saved? You have no need to look for long, or to look afar. *Lo, the Lord's eyes are upon those who revere him.* These are the same people upon whom he looked from his heavenly dwelling. *Lo, the Lord's eyes are upon those who revere him and trust in his mercy*, not in their own merits or their virtue or their strength or their horses, but in his mercy.

---

27. Augustine is making it clear to listeners who may not quite have caught the drift that the word is *equus*, horse, not *aequus*, a fair or just man.

25. *To deliver their souls from death.* He promises us eternal life, but what are we promised while still wayfarers? Does he abandon us now? Look at the next phrase: *and sustain them amid famine.* This present life is the season of famine, but the life to come will be the season of full satisfaction. If he does not desert us now, in this corruptible state where we are hungry, how will he not satisfy us once we have been rendered immortal? But as long as the time of famine lasts, we must endure it, hold out, persevere until the very end. Let us leap over every obstacle and get on with our race, for the way is straightforward and we need to be careful what we carry. Those who are still spectators in the amphitheatre may be crazy with excitement, and they are seated, but in the sun; as for us, even if we are standing up, we are in the shade, and we are looking at much more profitable and more beautiful spectacles. Let us keep our eyes on beautiful things, and let ourselves be watched by One who is beautiful. Let us gaze with the eyes of our minds at what is conveyed by the various senses of the divine scriptures, and rejoice at the sight. But who is the spectator who watches us?[28] *Lo, the Lord's eyes are upon those who revere him and trust in his mercy, to deliver their souls from death, and sustain them amid famine.*

Verses 20-21. Endurance and reward

26. Since then we have to endure as long as the famine lasts, we need to be refreshed along the road, or we may flag. What terms are imposed on us, what undertaking must we give? *Our soul will wait patiently for the Lord.* With serenity it will await him who mercifully promises, who mercifully and faithfully fulfills his promises. What are we to do until that fulfillment? *Our soul will wait patiently for the Lord.* But what if endurance even in this patient expectation is more than we can manage? That is not to be thought of: we shall most certainly endure, *because he is our helper and protector.* God stands by you in the fight, shades you from the heat, and never deserts you. So endure, stand fast. *Whoever perseveres to the end will be saved* (Mt 24:13).

27. And when you have endured all the way, when you have been patient, when you have persevered to the end, what will your prize be? What reward do you expect for holding out? Why did you keep going so long through such great hardships? Because *in him our heart will rejoice; we have hoped[29] in his holy name.* Hope here, that you may rejoice there; hunger and thirst here, that there you may eat at his table.

---

28. The text as translated here recalls the imagery of Heb 12:1-2, and makes good sense. But instead of *spectemus, spectaculo, spectator* many codices have *exspectemus, exspectaculo, exspectator,* which would yield the following meaning: "Let us await beautiful things . . . and rejoice in what we await. But who is awaiting us?"

29. Variant: "will hope."

Verse 22. Conclusion: pray for the Donatists

28. The psalmist has given us all this exhortation; he has filled us with the joy of hope; he has pointed out to us what we should love, in whom we should trust, on whom we should rest our confidence. After all this he concludes with a brief and salutary prayer: *may your mercy, Lord, be upon us.* And how do we deserve it? *As we have hoped in you.*

I have gone on too long for some of you, I know; but for others among you I have brought my sermon to an end too soon; this also I know. The weak must forgive the stronger, and the stronger pray for the weak. Let us all be members of the one body, invigorated by our Head; in him is our hope, in him our strength. Let us never hesitate to demand mercy from the Lord our God; he likes nothing better than to have this demand made on him. He will not find the demand a nuisance, or be put into a tight corner by it, like someone who does not have what you are asking for, or has only a little of it, and is unwilling to give you any for fear of running short. Would you like an illustration of how God dispenses mercy to you? Dispense charity yourself; let us see if you run short of it while you are dispensing it. Well then, if there can be such lavish generosity in God's image, how much must there be in the Most High himself?

29. Finally, brothers and sisters, I exhort you above all to practice this charity not only among yourselves but also toward people outside, whether they are still pagans who do not yet believe in Christ, or people divided from us who confess the Head along with us but are separated from the body. Let us grieve over them, my brothers and sisters, grieve over them as our brethren. Whether they like it or not, our brothers and sisters they are. They will cease to be so only if they cease to say, *Our Father.* A prophet said of certain people, *To those who say to you, "You are no brethren of ours," you are to say, "You are our brethren"* (Is 66:5, LXX). Look around you and ask of whom that could be said. Of the pagans? No, for according to the usage of scripture and ecclesiastical custom we do not call the pagans our brothers and sisters. Perhaps the Jews, then, who have not believed in Christ? No. If you read the apostle you will see that when he speaks of "brethren" without further qualification he always means us to understand Christians. So referring to marriage, he says, *A brother or sister is under no compulsion in this respect* (1 Cor 7:15), and by "brother or sister" he means a Christian man or woman. Again he asks, *But you, why are you sitting in judgment on your brother? Or what right have you to scorn your brother?* (Rom 14:10). And in another place he tells them, *You deal unjustly and defraud even your own brethren!"* (1 Cor 6:8).

It follows that those who say to us, "You are no brethren of ours,"[30] are making us out to be pagans. That is why they want to rebaptize us, alleging that

---

30. The Donatists.

we do not have what they are conferring. Their error in denying that we are their brothers and sisters springs from this. But why did the prophet command us, *You for your part are to say to them, "You are our brethren,"* unless because we do acknowledge what they have, acknowledge it by not repeating it?[31] So they, by not recognizing our baptism, deny that we are their brethren, but we, by not repeating theirs but recognizing it as ours, say to them, *You are our brethren*. Let them ask, if they will, "Why are you seeking us? Why do you want us?" and let us reply, *You are our brethren*. Let them say, "Get away, we are not interested in you." Maybe not, but we are very interested in you. We confess one Christ, and we ought to be in one body under one Head. They continue to object, "Why pursue me, then, if I am lost?" What a stupid thing to ask, what a crazy question! Why pursue you if you are lost? Why else would I be pursuing you, except because you are lost? "If I am lost, then," says the Donatist, "how can I be your brother?" Because I want to hear it said to me, *Your brother was dead, but has come back to life; he was lost but is found* (Lk 15:32).

I entreat you, brothers and sisters, through that tenderhearted charity, through Christ our Lord with whose milk we are nourished, on whose bread we grow strong, I entreat you to pray for them. This is the time when it behooves us to lavish great charity upon them, and unstinting mercy as we pray to God on their behalf. Let us ask him at long last to grant them sober judgment, so that they may come to their senses and consider their position, and realize that they have no argument whatever to allege against the truth, for nothing is left to them except the disease of animosity, which is all the more crippling for thinking itself the stronger. For them, for these sick people who can only think carnally, for these who are materially-minded and carnal yet who for all that are our brothers and sisters, who celebrate the same sacraments not with us, yet the same, who reply with the same "Amen" one single "Amen" yet not with us: for all these I entreat you to pour out your prayers to God from the bottom of your loving hearts. We took some measures for their salvation at the council,[32] but there is not enough time for me to tell you about that in detail today. I urge you, therefore, to assemble tomorrow at the Basilica of the Tricliae. Come with even greater eagerness, and make sure that our brothers and sisters who are not present today hear about it from you, so that numbers may be greater too!

---

31. Donatists who converted to Catholicism were not rebaptized.
32. Perhaps the Council of Carthage in 411. But it has also been suggested that this sermon was preached earlier, in September, 403, and is referring here to the Council held in August of that year.

Index of Scripture

(prepared by Michael Dolan)

(The numbers after the scriptural reference refer to the section of the psalm)

Old Testament

Genesis

1:3	7, 19
1:4-5	7, 19
2:17	II, 29, 15; II, 29, 17
2:24	10, 10; 18, 10
3:4	II, 29, 17
3:5	7, 5; II, 29, 17
3:14	7, 4
3:19	7, 4; 10, 7; II, 30, 7; III, 32, 1
15:6	II, 31, 2
22:16-18	III, 30, 9

Exodus

3:14	1, 6; 9, 11
8:19	8, 7

Leviticus

19:15	II, 32, 12

Deuteronomy

13:3	5, 4; 6, 1
25:4	8, 12

2 Samuel

12:12	18, 6
18:33	3, 1

1 Kings

19:10,18	II, 25, 5

Job

1:9-11	II, 29, 7
1:21	II, 29, 7; III, 32, 12; IV, 30, 12; II, 32, 3; II, 32, 5
2:5	III, 32, 12
2:9	II, 29, 7
2:10	II, 29, 7
7:1	II, 29, 8

Psalms

2:1	7, 6
2:2	28, 6
2:7-8	II, 21, 30
2:8	5, 1; 7, 6; 27, 9; III, 30, 8; III, 30, 14
2:11	III, 32, 11
3:4(3)	7, 18
3:6	3, 1
3:7	6, 1
3:9(8)	II, 31, 18
4:7	7, 11
4:7(6)	8, 10
5:2(1)	III, 32, 22
5:5(3)	6, 7; II, 26, 8
5:7(6)	III, 32, 24
6:3(2)	7, 10
6:5(4)	7, 8
7:13(12)	9, 8
7:15-17(14-16)	5, 10
8:5(4)	5, 8
9:17(16)	7, 17
9:20-21(19-20)	9, 29
10:3(11:2)	8, 9
11:5(12:4)	8, 13
11:9(12:8)	III, 30, 11
13:5(14:4)	IV, 30, 4
15(16):5	5, 1; III, 32, 17
15(16):5.6	1, 4
15(16):7	1, 2

Proverbs

Ecclesiastes

Song of Songs

Wisdom

Sirach

Isaiah

Index

(prepared by Joseph Sprug)

The first number in the Index is the psalm number.
More than one "Exposition" is cited by the number in parentheses, for example (2)
The number after the colon is a paragraph number.

431